KING ARTHUR

By the same author:

Classic Landforms of the Sussex Coast
(1982; second edition 1996)

The Wilmington Giant: The Quest for a Lost Myth (1983)

The Stonehenge People: An Exploration of Life in Neolithic Britain,
4700–2000 BC (1987)

The Knossos Labyrinth: A New View of the 'Palace of Minos' at
Knossos (1989)

Minoans: Life in Bronze Age Crete (1990)

Book of British Dates: A Comprehensive Dictionary of British Dates
from Prehistoric Times to the Present Day (1991)

Neolithic Britain: New Stone Age Sites of England, Scotland and Wales
(1992)

The Making of Stonehenge (1993)

World History: A Chronological Dictionary of Dates
(1994; second edition 1995)

The Cerne Giant (1996)

Knossos, Temple of the Goddess (1997)

Atlantis Destroyed (1998)

Ancient British Hill Figures (1999)

KING ARTHUR

The truth behind the legend

Rodney Castleden

illustrated by the author

London and New York

First published 2000
by Routledge
11 New Fetter Lane, London EC4P 4EE

Simultaneously published in the USA and Canada
by Routledge
29 West 35th Street, New York, NY 10001

Reprinted 2001

Routledge is an imprint of the Taylor & Francis Group

© 2000 Rodney Castleden

The right of Rodney Castleden to be identified as the Author of this Work
has been asserted by him in accordance with the Copyright,
Designs and Patents Act 1988

Typeset in Stempel Garamond by
Keystroke, Jacaranda Lodge, Wolverhampton
Printed and bound in Great Britain by
TJ International Ltd, Padstow, Cornwall

All rights reserved. No part of this book may be reprinted or
reproduced or utilised in any form or by any electronic, mechanical,
or other means, now known or hereafter invented, including photocopying
and recording, or in any information storage or retrieval system,
without permission in writing from the publishers.

British Library Cataloguing in Publication Data
A catalogue record for this book is available from the British Library

Library of Congress Cataloging in Publication Data
Castleden, Rodney.
King Arthur : the truth behind the legend / Rodney Castleden.
p.   cm.
Includes bibliographical references (p.   ) and index.
1. Arthur, King. 2. Great Britain—Antiquities, Celtic.
3. Britons—Kings and rulers—Folklore. 4. Great Britain—History—
To 1066. 5. Camelot (Legendary place) I. Title.
DA152.5.A7C37   1999
942.01′4—dc21   99–29051
CIP

ISBN 0–415–19575–6

For Aubrey Burl

Year 72 (516): Battle of Badon, in which Arthur carried the cross of our lord Jesus Christ on his shoulders for three days and three nights, and the British were victors.

Year 93 (537): Strife of Camlann, in which Arthur and Medraut fell.

Easter Annals (probably contemporary, certainly before 800)

As an historical figure [Arthur] should be laid to rest once more as an unwarranted and retrospective intrusion on the fifth century. Not only did Arthur himself not exist but the age which led to his invention was no less fictional.

Nicholas Higham (1994)

This is no time for dry as dust historical reservations. Dig, dig, dig, Dr Wainwright.

Daily Telegraph (1998)

CONTENTS

— *Contents* —

FIGURES

— *Figures* —

PLATES

—◆•◆•—

xi

PREFACE AND
ACKNOWLEDGEMENTS

———◆———

It was in 1984 that I received a picture postcard from Cornwall, signed 'King Arthur' below the command 'WRITE ABOUT ME NEXT'. Just that. Something made me doubt its authenticity; it was partly the lack of sixth-century orthography that aroused my suspicions, partly that I did not see the King using a biro, still less a second-class Queen Elizabeth stamp. This bowshot from the past nevertheless found its target and some years afterwards I floated the idea to Routledge of a modest treatment of the Arthur theme, a re-examination of the archaeological evidence for Arthur as a Cornish king, prompted mainly by Charles Thomas's convincing re-interpretation of Tintagel as a royal stronghold.

I am grateful to my editors at Routledge past and present, Andrew Wheatcroft and Vicky Peters, for their enthusiasm for this project. Andrew Wheatcroft argued that reviewing the 'matter of Britain' in its awesome entirety would not only make my hypothesis more persuasive, and make a better book, but that the time was right to take a comprehensive look at the Arthurian problem. By coincidence, in the 1970s, it was Andrew who had been the editor of John Morris's *The Age of Arthur*, a ground-breaking work then and still powerfully convincing, still the standard work on the subject, and he saw me as the right person to attempt to replace it. Whether I have lived up to that expectation I cannot say: not just through self-doubt, but because I have lived so close to the data and the whole complex of interweaving controversies that I can no longer judge whether someone coming new to the issues will be able easily to understand what is at stake.

There is a curious stand-off by scholars with regard to sixth-century Britain. The Arthurian legend is so powerful and magnificent, with a dynamic of its own, that it actually deters many of them from looking at the period at all. Studies of Roman and sub-Roman Britain tend to peter out into generalities around the middle of the fifth century; studies of Anglo-Saxon England deal with the fifth and sixth centuries as a kind of thinly documented preamble. Only a few brave spirits like Ken Dark tackle the Celtic Britain of AD 450–600 with any determination to get at the truth in the way that historians attack later centuries. If he lived at all, Arthur lived during that period. The pursuit of Arthur as an historical figure necessarily involves re-constructing that lost century and a half of British history, which was and is as real as any other century and a half of history. The stakes are therefore high. I thank

Andrew and Vicky most warmly for encouraging me to make the project more ambitious than I originally intended. Reconstructing what was going on in Britain as a whole was an exercise of incalculable value, and led me to conclusions more exciting than I could ever have imagined.

I also thank Brian McGregor and his staff at the Ashmolean Library in Oxford, and John and Celia Clarke for their generous hospitality during my Oxford reading weeks. It was entirely fortuitous that my friend Diana Cooke acquired a cottage on a mountain side in Wales a short woodland walk from a stream called Gamlan; staying at her cottage and exploring the area round it made me radically reconsider my ideas about the nature of Arthur's last battle. Arthur Koestler wrote of the Library Angels who guide us to the sources we need for our research; Diana has been a Fieldwork Angel, and I am grateful to her not only for her hospitality but for guiding me unwittingly to one of the key Arthurian locations.

The project has, for me, been a long labyrinthine journey through nascent dark age archaeology, Arthurian folklore, early and late medieval literature, and the quagmire of earlier theories about the nature of Arthur and the alleged events of his alleged life. It led me back to familiar and much-loved places like South Cadbury and Tintagel, and also to places I never suspected of an Arthurian connection. I little expected to find the grave of Arthur at all, let alone find it beneath the site of an eighteenth-century rectory extension.

I hope the reading of the story of my quest may be as enjoyable as the writing of it.

CHAPTER ONE

'WHO THIS ARTHUR WAS'

—◆·—

For over a thousand years, the story of Arthur's life and death has been the principal myth of the island of Britain. The circumstances of his rise to power from obscure origins, the saga of his career as a king and war-leader of the Celts against the Saxons, the establishment of a long and secure peace, the disintegration of his court, the descent into civil war and finally his death as a result of treachery on the field of battle – these elements have been retold and rewoven continually in new ways to carry new messages for new ages, until they are sometimes transformed virtually beyond recognition. The recycling continues from Geoffrey of Monmouth in the twelfth century through Malory in the fifteenth and Tennyson in the nineteenth, to John Arden, Monty Python and John Boorman's *Excalibur* film in the twentieth century. Each century, each sub-culture, re-creates its own Arthur, sometimes further from, sometimes closer to, the collection of folk stories told in the middle ages.

The Arthurian saga is nevertheless much more than a hotchpotch of tales made up by medieval minstrels, and it is essential to try to separate the Arthur of the romances – the Arthur of Geoffrey, Malory and the medieval troubadours – from the historical Arthur – the dark age warrior on whom all the rest of the superstructure was built.

We need to strip away the later anachronisms, the ornaments and grace-notes, the bits of medieval infilling, if we are to reconstruct the biography of the historical Arthur. This requires enormous care. The material that appears in the medieval stories though not in the sixth- or seventh-century documents might at first sight look like a later invention, yet we cannot ignore it as some may derive from oral traditions maintained in Cornwall, Wales or Brittany, or even written accounts copied in the intervening centuries and later lost. Some scholars have taken everything out, argued everything away, leaving just two brief mentions in the *Easter Annals*:[1]

516: Battle of Badon, in which Arthur carried the cross of our lord Jesus Christ on his shoulders for three days and three nights, and the British were victors.
537: Strife of Camlann, in which Arthur and Medraut perished [or fell].

These two listings are the bottom line, our irreducible minimum. Within these few words we have the nearest thing to proof of Arthur's existence and prominence in the early sixth century: we also have evidence of his celebrity as a warrior and war-leader.

I

They nevertheless do not mention his kingship as such, and some have argued on the strength of this that Arthur cannot have been a king, but that, as we shall see, is going too far. The Ages of Reason and Science have thrown up many attacks on Arthur's historical reality, attacks that have been understandable reactions to the excesses of medieval credulity. The addition of magical elements – Merlin, the Grail stories, the sword in the stone, the Lady of the Lake – was the last straw. The magic goaded rational historians into rejecting Arthur altogether as a historical figure, and even led some to treat him as a re-processed ancient Celtic deity.[2]

But evidence *does* exist to show that Arthur was a real person, and the purpose of this book is to explore that evidence and see how the historical Arthur fitted into the realities of the sixth century. Archaeology is very unlikely ever to be able to prove or disprove his existence, simply because it follows different paths, but it can supply the social, economic, cultural and political setting for the living people of his day. Once we see Arthur as real flesh, bone and blood, his contemporaries as real people with whom he had real personal, social and political relationships, and sixth-century Britain as a real landscape with its own geography, its own towns and villages, fields and farms, its own ports, strongholds, networks of roads and trade routes, its own multiplicity of kingdoms – then we shall see the dynamics of dark age society at work. We shall see how Arthur's career was created by the troubled and changing times in which he lived; we shall see how the careers of other military leaders were shaped in rather similar ways. Arthur was, as we shall see, very much a child of his time.

Traditions, whether local or regional, are notoriously difficult to evaluate. Some are no more than old wives' tales invented to explain a peculiar landform or an uncomprehended megalith, tales that have been accorded a certain dignity through repetition and familiarity. But other traditions have turned out to be true. The story of Troy, as told in Homer, was for a long time thought to be pure poetic fiction; then the work of Frank Calvert and Heinrich Schliemann proved that Troy had really existed. At a more local level, there was a Cornish tradition that a ninth-century church lay buried at Perranzabuloe; sands shifted by a storm in 1835 revealed that a tiny ancient church had indeed been buried there. Another, more fanciful, West Country story held that druids once dispensed wine out of a gold cup at the Cheesewring; in 1837, a bronze age gold beaker was found inside the Rillaton Barrow just 400m away.[3] Quite how the knowledge was acquired, retained and transmitted in that instance must be a matter for speculation, but the local lore turned out to contain some truth.

There were other war-leaders besides Arthur. He had his forerunners in the fifth century, and there were others after him in the sixth and seventh centuries who also made defiant and heroic stands against the westward advance of the Saxons. There were war-leaders among the Saxons too, and the names of several have come down to us in the *Anglo-Saxon Chronicle*. Yet there was something particular, something special, about Arthur that caused his memory to be cherished and honoured far above that of any other warrior. What was it that made Arthur so special?

The once and future king

One distinctive feature of the Celtic culture was that, though victory was earnestly sought and fulsomely praised, it was the great defeats that were remembered longest and most yearningly. Something of this survives in modern Britain, which is after all still part-Celtic. When we hear of the heroic bravery witnessed at Dunkirk we have to remind ourselves that what is being described is a massive British retreat in the face of enemy attack, not a victory at all. Yet Dunkirk has acquired the flavour of something that was in some mysterious way greater than victory. Long, long before, the British dwelt nostalgically on Arthur's great defeat, gloated over the hero's death at Camlann. As Leslie Rouse has said, 'It was the hero of the *losing* side, king Arthur, who imposed himself on the imagination.' It is not uncommon for conquerors to succumb to the spirit of the conquered. Jung commented on what he called the indianization of immigrants of various racial origins arriving in the New World; American college initiation ceremonies derive from Indian rites of passage, while the white leaders of American religious sects have a tendency to turn into Indian shamans. In a similar way, the Roman Empire succumbed to a mystery religion originating among an obscure and oppressed subject people.[4] It is perhaps not so out of the ordinary for the English to have adopted Arthur. In the centuries that followed his death, Arthur became a symbol representing the glory of Britain as it once was, and might yet have been had it not been destroyed by the Saxon invader.

The idea of Arthur then became a seminal influence in the evolving idea of British nationhood. In the dark ages and early middle ages, the Celts saw in Arthur the lost leader who had given them the sweetness of victory and peace, if only for four decades or so. He became the perfect symbol of a kingdom and a culture lost when they were disinherited by the Saxons. Vain hope that kingdom and culture might one day be restored was embodied in a strange belief that Arthur had somehow escaped death at Camlann, never really died at all, but lay sleeping in a cave or under a hill waiting for the day when he would wake and drive the enemy, whoever it might be, from Britain's shores. Arthur was now more than a king: he was a god.

The image of this dark age warrior-king hung over the aristocracy of the middle ages like a faded, tattered, war-torn battle standard hanging in a royal chapel, redolent of past greatness and signifying exemplary virtues that could never be matched by the living. Medieval kings of England sought to be worthy of his memory, to identify themselves subliminally with Arthur, by both image and lineage, but it was an anachronistic Arthur they tried to imitate, a figure substantially re-written and taking the stage as a thinly disguised medieval king. They were imitating an ideal king who in his turn was imitating them. The idea of Arthur became a force in medieval British politics. Henry II wanted to prove that Arthur was dead in order to remove any hopes the Celts may have entertained that he would rise again to do battle against the Plantagenets. There are conflicting views about it, but it was probably for this reason that in 1190 Henry II arranged for Arthur's coffin to be 'discovered' at Glastonbury and exhumed. We know that when Henry II visited Dyfed in 1179 and met the bard who told him where Arthur's grave was, he was also told of the tradition that Arthur would ride once more.[5] If Arthur's bones had been found, there was little chance of Arthur riding into battle again.

The story virtually repeated itself 100 years later, when Edward I was subduing the Welsh. To make it clear that Arthur would not be returning to help them, in 1278 the king went to Glastonbury and had the bones removed from their casket and put on public display, with the ostensible motive of reburying them in a place of great honour right in the centre of the abbey church. In 1283 Edward I was presented at Aberconwy with a collection of relics that included the regalia of the ancient British kings; amongst this was a crown alleged to be Arthur's, by which Edward was plainly signalling in typical medieval language his succession to Arthur's throne. In case anybody missed the point, the English chroniclers decoded it: 'and so the glory of the Welsh, though against their will, was transferred to the English'.[6] Edward III went a step further in identifying himself as Arthur's successor when he contemplated re-establishing the Round Table as an order of chivalry. In the end, in 1348, he founded instead the Order of the Garter in imitation of Arthur's order of Round Table knights.

Arthur had come to be seen as the model for kingship. But for accidents of destiny, two royal princes named Arthur might have become kings of England: one was forestalled by murder (by King John), the other, Henry VIII's elder brother, by fatal illness. Arthur's virtues were without limit. He was a renowned warrior and a just leader, a sponsor of youth and defender of the Celtic realm, he was a righter of wrongs, an enforcer of the law and the ultimate authority in time of danger. He was, in short, the best and greatest of kings, and it was natural that, right through to the time of Victoria and Albert, he was seen as the ultimate model for the British monarchy.

The idea of Arthur has not just fired the imagination of kings and princes, but of ordinary people too. In 1220, an abbot used Arthur as a desperate measure to get his monks' attention. 'Seeing that many were asleep [in the Chapter House], some even snoring, he cried out: Hark, brethren! I will tell you of something new and great. There was a mighty king whose name was Arthur!' This electrified everyone in the room. 'Had they not come to a sad pass, when they would not stay awake to hear of holy things but were agog at the mention of Arthur?'

That power to excite is still there. In 1113 men knocked each other about in Bodmin, drawing blood in their disagreement as to whether Arthur was dead or not. Now, they don't, but the interest is still strong. Part of that interest lies in Arthur's association with mystery and magic. In the legend, magic was used by Merlin to enable Uther to father Arthur on Ygraine in Tintagel Castle. There was mystery surrounding his death too. The Welsh tradition poses 'a grave for Arthur' as one of the great puzzles; there was the myth of his 'sleep' and eventual return. Malory famously described him as *rex quondam rexque futurus*, 'the once and future king'. The fifteenth-century poet Lydgate described him as 'a king y-crowned in Fairye'.[7] There was the Holy Grail saga, probably added on relatively late, but which gave Arthur's kingdom and reign a special yearning spirituality that appealed to the medieval mind.

It may well be Arthur's strange position midway between king and demi-god, between Christianity and paganism, between history and myth, that appeals to so many people now. How far these Merlinesque elements were part of the dark age reality we shall later explore, but one thing is certainly true, and it is that the myth, magic and mystery elements have become an integral part of the Arthurian myth. The brief bright gleam from Excalibur sent glancing across one-and-a-half millennia of British history still influences the way we think about Britain as a land, and Britain as a nation.

Doubts about Arthur's existence

It was very largely because Arthur's name was later surrounded by so much mystique, and because it became so richly symbolic, that many historians refused to believe he ever existed. The magical conception, the strange manner of his accession, the mysterious disappearance after Camlann: all made it look as if Arthur was a fictitious character, a figment of the medieval minstrels' imagination. The settings of some of the stories – the Dolorous Tower, the Red City – strongly suggest a fictional world, a world of rich romantic fantasy, a world not to believe in.

Attempts have been made, most notably and most successfully by John Morris, to strip away the magical and fanciful elements that look like later accretions and reconstruct the reality of dark age Britain. This is perhaps the best way to begin: to look at the documentary evidence for the period AD 450–550, the century in which Arthur must have lived (if he lived at all), and build an historian's eye view of events. We need at least temporarily to forget the glinting twilights and special effects of Boorman's wonderful *Excalibur* and see the dark age setting as a period of real history. As such, it becomes a legitimate field of academic study and falls subject to the normal discipline of an historian's scrutiny. The documents will be reviewed in Chapter 2, to see how far they prove, support or corroborate the existence of a king called Arthur. Then, in Chapter 3, the archaeological evidence from a range of British sites will be considered, some of it independently corroborating the documentary evidence, some adding entirely new detail and fleshing out the picture. From these two strands, historical and archaeological, the setting for Arthur's alleged career should emerge.

We can, using recognized, conventional academic procedures, test whether Arthur existed. We may be able to go further and assemble elements of his biography. Who and what was he? What did he really achieve? Where did he operate? Did Camelot and the knights exist too?

Arthur began to re-emerge from the misty land of legend in the late eighteenth century, with the writings of Sharon Turner. Joseph Ritson's 1825 *Life of King Arthur*, completed in about 1803 but not published until twenty-two years after his death, was in some ways the seminal work. While maintaining a rigorous scepticism about the reliability of the sources in detail, Ritson could see that it was 'manifest from authentick history' that Arthur was a real person who had been a brave warrior and probably a dark age chieftain or sub-king. In the 1930s, R.G. Collingwood saw him as holding the late Roman military office of *Comes Britanniarum*, Count of the Britons, employing cavalry to defeat Saxon foot-soldiers. The cavalry idea has outlived the rest of Collingwood's theory, much of which relied perhaps too heavily on the assumptions that the list of battles in Nennius is genuine and that their names are traceable to identifiable locations. The sites that could be identified are widely scattered, therefore Arthur must have been very mobile. While Kenneth Jackson rejected much of Collingwood's theory, he too looked for likely locations for the battles in Nennius' list, confirming a wide geographical distribution. Jackson thought Arthur was probably, though not certainly, real. If he existed, Arthur was a 'supreme British commander of genius' active mainly in southern Britain.[8]

Reports on Glastonbury and South Cadbury Castle lent support to the idea of Arthur as a real historical figure,[9] a line of thought that culminated in John Morris's important 1973 work, *The Age of Arthur*, which confirmed Arthur's royal – indeed imperial – status. Since this high water mark, the tide of belief in Arthur has begun to ebb away again. In history as in politics, there is a periodic pendulum swing, first one way, in favour of the historical Arthur, and then the inevitable other, against him. The post-1973 anti-Arthur writers include D. N. Dumville (1977) and Peter Salway (1981). David Dumville crushingly criticized the use of Welsh sources as historical evidence, and the scholarly pursuit of the historical Arthur seemed to come once more to a halt, with Leslie Alcock retreating into agnosticism and Philip Rahtz waving Arthur aside as 'this non-subject'.[10] Nick Higham is even more dismissive:

> As an historical figure [Arthur] should be laid to rest once more as an unwarranted and retrospective intrusion on the fifth century. Not only did Arthur himself not exist but the age which led to his invention was no less fictional.[11]

Perhaps the most unrelenting opponent of the historical Arthur is Oliver Padel.[12] His arguments and assertions will be considered at appropriate points during this book. It may usefully be said here that the powerful overall effect of his 1994 article relies heavily on the accumulation of sceptical though poorly founded remarks. He says, for example, of the reference to Arthur in the sixth-century poem *The Gododdin* that the line might have been added in the ninth century; there is no reason to suppose that it was, and we would not normally resort to this method of argument in studies of later centuries (or earlier, for that matter). For a second example we may take Padel's citation of a tenth-century poem *The Prophecy of Britain*, which does not mention Arthur. Clearly this will not suffice as proof that Arthur never lived. Today's newspaper may omit to mention the Queen, but it would be a rash reader who inferred from this that the United Kingdom had become a republic.

Padel's approach to Arthur – presupposing that all references to him must be unhistorical, late, anachronistic intrusions – is closer to conspiracy theory than to history. His method is to press the mythic persona of Arthur to the fore, asserting that this was the earlier Arthur and that pseudo-historical details such as battles and dates were added later. Padel draws interesting parallels with the Irish folk-hero Fionn, but the quasi-historical details added to Fionn's story are entirely inconsistent; he is alleged to have fought the Vikings, yet died in 283.[13] It is very much against Padel's line of reasoning that Arthur, conversely, was alleged to have fought his major campaign between 516 and his defeat at Camlann in 537, which was exactly the right time for him to have waged a successful campaign against the Saxons.

A serious flaw in Padel's scenario is that his Arthur is a legendary sixth-century folk hero, an icon to whom pseudo-historical matter is attracted in the seventh and eighth centuries.[14] One problem with this is the speed with which fiction is supposed to have become fact; another is the fact that the alleged 'Welsh historicizing' of Arthur is both consistent with known historical events and, as later chapters in this book will show, believable in the context of both history and archaeology.[15] A further and, I believe, fatal flaw in Padel's argument is that in his 1994 paper he takes the line that he has demolished the whole concept of an historical Arthur, then with startling inconsistency produces a candidate for the historical Arthur, one Lucius Artorius Castus, a Roman centurion of the third century who led two legions from Britain against the Armoricans. Having offered this candidate for an historical Arthur, he recants at once and says it is not necessary to propose an historical figure after all. This vacillation on the final page of his paper seriously weakens his argument.[16]

The reasons for doubting Arthur's existence are not hard to find. The available dates seem inconsistent with each other, stretching Arthur's activities across an incredible span of 70 or 80 years. Nennius, otherwise apparently reliable, overstretches credulity by telling us Arthur killed 960 men in a single battle: that must be legend, not history. The powerful brew of magic, miracle and myth already mentioned invites, indeed virtually commands, scepticism. It is not surprising that some have seen Arthur as a hero of romance, a pure myth. On top of that, there is the documentary evidence, or lack of it. Arthur is *not* mentioned by the principal British sixth-century historian, a monk who wrote vociferously and outspokenly about kings and the nature of kingship about a decade after Arthur's death. Gildas named kings and listed their shortcomings and vices, so his silence about Arthur is certainly hard to explain,[17] if in fact he really was silent; it may be that when we come to examine the text of Gildas more closely we will be able to detect indirect allusions to Arthur. Arthur was not mentioned in the *Anglo-Saxon Chronicle*; nor was he mentioned by Bede.

Some have suggested that Arthur was a late transformation of a pre-Roman Celtic god. Others have proposed that he was a phantom figure, no more than an invented name to whom the military exploits of Ambrosius Aurelianus were mistakenly transferred.[18] Still others have proposed that he was an unimportant sub-king of whom all we really know is that he died in a squabble with another Briton; but if that is so, he is a poor peg on which to hang a legend. Uncertainty about the true nature of Arthur – whether he was a king, whether he was Welsh, Cornish or Scottish, whether he was a phantom, even whether he was a god or a man – has surfaced repeatedly during the last thousand years. The situation was well expressed three hundred years ago, in 1694: 'In short, who this Arthur was, and whether any such ever Reign'd in Britain, has been doubted heretofore, and is by some to this very day.' That is still true.

In view of this uncertainty, we must look long and hard at the evidence and try to settle at the very least the key question. Did Arthur exist? If he did, whole strings of further questions present themselves. If he existed, for instance, when and in what form did he exist, where was his kingdom, and what was the nature of his achievement?

CHAPTER TWO

THE DOCUMENTS

—◆•◆—

Very little narrative history of any kind was written in the fifth or sixth centuries in Western Europe. The 'darkness' of the dark ages is a product of this simple fact. There are nevertheless several primary sources, documents that were written at that time, which enable us to assemble an historical context for Arthur (see Chapter 4). A small number of them actually tell of Arthur and his actions. The major sources for Arthur's time are the works of Nennius and Gildas, giving a view from the native British side, and the *Anglo-Saxon Chronicle*, giving a view from the side of the Germanic colonists. We often look back at the Anglo-Saxons with the benefit of hindsight and think of Athelstan, Alfred and Edward the Confessor, but the early Germanic colonists were interlopers, intruding upon a culture that had been a long time evolving, including a recent creative interaction with the Roman civilization. The Saxons had only an imperfect understanding of the British and Roman cultures. There is an Anglo-Saxon poem about the ruins of a Roman city, generally thought to be Bath, in which a Saxon gazes uncomprehendingly at the havoc committed by his own ancestors; he stares awe-stricken at the ravaged buildings, 'masonry shattered by fate, buildings raised of old by giants'. This is atmospheric, filling the listener with wonder, but it is the response of an ignorant barbarian excited by ruins, shadows, giants and ghosts. By contrast, the courts of the British kings were civilized and decorous places where courtiers sipped Mediterranean wines out of fine imported glasses, places where education and the dual heritage of both British and Roman pasts was valued.

First, we shall glance at the minor sources, which supply crucial details.

Constantius' *Life of Germanus*

The *Life of Germanus*, written not long after his death in about 448 by Constantius, presbyter of Lyons who lived from about 410 to about 480,[1] gives us some vivid glimpses of Britain in 429 and 445, the years when the saint visited Britain. Most saints' *Lives* were written so much later and were consequently filled with so much stock hagiography that they cannot be treated as history in the modern sense at all. The *Life of Germanus* is different in that it was written almost immediately after the events it describes; a note of realism can be heard on occasion, too, in that Germanus is not always successful.

The *Life of Germanus* is invaluable in telling us about Vortigern, a mysterious but powerful king who ruled Powys from 420 onwards.[2]

> He had three sons, whose names are Vortimer, who fought against the barbarians [non-Christian Saxons] as I have described; the second, Cateyrn; the third, Pascent, who ruled over the two countries called Builth and Gwerthrynion after his father's death, by permission of Ambrosius, who was the great king among all the kings of the British nation. A fourth son was Faustus, who was born to him by his daughter. St Germanus baptized him, brought him up and educated him. This is his genealogy. Ffernfeal, who now rules in the countries of Builth and Gwerthrynion, is son of Tewdwr. Theodore is king of the country of Builth, the son of Pascent, son of Gwyddgant, son of Moriud, son of Eldat, son of Elaeth, son of Paul, son of Meuric, son of Briacat, son of Pascent, son of Vortigern the Thin, son of Vitalis, son of Vitalinus, son of Gliou. Enough has been said of Vortigern and his family.

The sharpness of detail here is breathtaking. It is a snapshot of the early and middle fifth century in Britain and its 'great tyrant' Vortigern. He has nevertheless put in too many generations between his own time and Vortigern's; ten generations back in time from 470 would put Vortigern in the second century when he obviously belongs to the fifth. Though very much an outsider and a bishop, Germanus was a soldier and also a great scholar with an unusually large library, and he gained a clear impression that Vortigern was more or less in overall control in Southern Britain. The date of Germanus' first visit, 429, is confirmed by a well-informed contemporary, Prosper of Aquitaine. During this visit he took part in the fighting against a joint attack by 'Saxons and Picts'. As well as being a bishop, Germanus was a soldier, and he offered his services as a *dux praelii* of the British army, in other words to take a command.

> His light troops thoroughly explored the country through which the enemy's advance was expected. Choosing a valley set among high hills, he drew up his army in ambush. As the enemy approached, he ordered the whole company to respond with a great shout when he cried out. The bishops cried out three times 'Alleluia'.[3] The whole army replied with a single voice and the great cry rebounded, shut in by the surrounding hills. The enemy column was terrified. The very frame of heaven and the rocks around seemed to threaten them. They fled in all directions.[4]

Germanus' biographer Constantius knew Lupus personally and clearly heard this vivid description from Lupus himself. There is no reason to suppose that this confrontation was anything but a real event. The landscape described sounds very like Wales, and there are very early traditions about St Germanus in and near the Vale of Llangollen, which could easily be the location. It may seem a long way west for Hengist's Saxon army to have ventured. Nevertheless, as we shall see, very long distances were travelled by both individuals and armies in these centuries.

Helped by a later document about the warrior saint in the Nennius collection (see below), Morris suggests that Germanus was fighting on behalf of the lowland Cornovii people based in the Severn valley and headquartered at Viroconium (Wroxeter), in their attempt to recover the hill country to the west that had been colonized by outsiders. Possibly these were Irish as well as Pictish and Saxon; perhaps Germanus and Lupus were mistaken, and the intruders were Irish rather than Pictish. A British force sent out from Wroxeter, Vortigern's stronghold, broke this evolving alliance and the Cornovii's enemies were overthrown and ejected. Out of this, Morris proposes, the powerful kingdom of Powys was forged.[5]

We can see, through the eyes of Germanus, the sharp hatred of the poor for the rich in Britain in the fifth century. But his main mission, his reason for coming to Britain, was to stop the spread of the Pelagian heresy. Pelagius, who lived in the 420s and 430s, was opposed to Augustine's doctrine of original sin and believed in the redemptive power of God's grace. The teachings of Pelagius appealed to Christians who wanted to establish a direct relationship with God. We can see in this approach an embryonic Protestantism, so it is perhaps not surprising that it found strong adherents in Britain.[6]

But Germanus' mission was to put a stop to this decentralizing movement and try to establish a feeling of kinship with the European mainstream of religious thought. To this latter end, he made an incredible melodramatic gesture at St Albans, where he opened the shrine of St Alban, apparently already at this time the centre of a 'national' cult, and inserted relics belonging to a number of foreign saints. In this daring and to some minds sacrilegious act, Germanus tried to show that European saints were just as worthy of veneration in Britain as British saints. Nevertheless, since Constantius does not claim any triumph on the ecclesiastical front, it is fair to assume that Germanus failed in his mission and that the British church remained Pelagian – and that presumably is why he had to return to Britain in 445.[7] On the second visit, we are told that he managed to unseat two heretical bishops, and this again shows no great degree of success. On his second visit he condemned Vortigern.

It is the detail, the unwitting illumination of the way of life and the thought processes of fifth-century Britain, that is important. And the glimpse we get of the mighty Vortigern and his dynasty is invaluable.

Writings on stones

Another, less obvious source of historical information, is the small body of carved inscriptions on standing stones. Each inscription tells us something more than just who is buried there; the style of the lettering, the language, vocabulary, emphasis: all say something about the nature of the culture.

The Llanerfyl Stone in Montgomeryshire has an inscription in Latin, Romanized in style but nevertheless post-Roman in date.[8] It reads as follows:

HIC. [IN]	Here [in]
TVMVLO IΛ	the tomb lies
CIT. ROSTE	Rustica

ECE. FILIA. PA	daughter of
TERNINI.	Paterninus.
ANI XIII. IN	Aged 13. In
PA [CE]	peace.

The uncertain spelling of the Roman name Rustica shows that this is a Romanized British family, probably of the first half of the fifth century, when Germanus was in Britain and Vortigern was king in Powys. Stating the girl's age was a pagan practice, so the inscription probably pre-dates the introduction of Christianity. Stating her filiation was a pagan tribal formula, which shows that a native tribal tradition had been absorbed.

Some sixth- and seventh-century stones from southern Scotland, Wales and Cornwall have the lettering vertical, miss out the usual HIC IACIT and use FILIUS instead. For instance:

CONETOCI FILI TEGERNOMALI	(Cornwall)
Conetocus, son of Tegernomalus	
(CON)TIGERNI FILI TIGERNI	(Lundy)
(Con)tigernus, son of Tigernus	
QVENATAVCIC DIHVI FILIUS	(Guival, Cornwall)
Here [is the grave] of Quenataucus, the son of Dinuus.[9]	

The Vortipor Stone at Castell Dwyran commemorates a dark age king: MEMORIA VOTEPORIGIS PROTICTORIS, 'the memorial of Vortipor the Protector' (see Figure 2.1). This corroborates and supplements Gildas's reference to 'Vortipor, the usurper of Demetia'. Usurpers and tyrants often preferred to represent themselves as the protectors of their people: they still do.[10]

The Llangadwaladr Stone on Anglesey commemorates a king of Gwynedd who died in about 620, almost a century after Arthur:

CatamaNus	Cadfan
rexsapIeNtisi	king, wisest,
mus OpINatIsIm	most renowned
us OmnIumreg	of all
um	kings

Its lettering suggests a date around 620, and this fits with what is known from the Welsh Annals, that Cadfan's father died in 616 and his son Cadwallon was killed in 633 by Oswald of Northumbria. To an extent, then, memorial inscriptions can corroborate documentary evidence; documents can be altered, especially during copying, but stone inscriptions are virtually unalterable – and therefore reliable evidence.

Two cross shafts at Llantwit Major carry the name of St Samson, a contemporary of Arthur. One reads, 'In the name of the most high God. Begins the cross of the saviour, which Samson the abbot prepared for his own soul and for the soul of Ithel the king and for Arthfael and for Tecan.' The other says simply, 'Samson put up this cross of Christ for his soul.'[11]

Figure 2.1 The Vortipor Stone

Some stones mention 'sacerdotes,' which is often translated 'bishops'. The slab at Kirkmadrine in Wigtownshire is dedicated to 'the holy and eminent bishops Ides, Viventius and Mavorius', which tells us that there was an organized church with bishops in south-west Scotland in the fifth century. Similarly, there are stones at Aberdaron in Caernarvonshire which read:

VERACIVS PBR HIC IACIT
Here lies Veracius, priest.
SENACVS PRSB HIC IACIT CUM MULTITUDINEM FRATRUM
Here lies Senacus, priest, with a host of the brethren.

So there was at least one monastic community in Gwynedd in the fifth–sixth centuries. Other stones in Gwynedd use the titles *medicus* and *magistratus*, which were Roman functionaries, so they hint at continuity with the past as well as a settled and ordered civil existence. Occasionally an inscription allows us to catch sight of a personal relationship, even of love; the Llantrisant Stone from Anglesey reads, 'A most holy woman lies here, who was the very loving wife of Bivatigirnus, servant of God, bishop.'[12]

There is one later inscription which throws light on our period, the Pillar of Eliseg. As read and translated by Edward Lhuyd in 1696, the Pillar inscription gives us a useful royal genealogy and a little of the dark age history of Powys:

Concenn son of Cattell, Cattell son of Brohcmail, Brohcmail son of Eliseg, Eliseg son of Guoillauc. Concenn, who is therefore great-grandson of Eliseg, erected this stone to his great-grandfather Eliseg. Eliseg annexed the inheritance of Powys throughout 9 years from the power of the English.

The inscription also tells us that 'Britu moreover was the son of Vortigern whom Germanus blessed', which seems to tell us the name of King Vortigern's successor.

Of the 'Arthnou Stone' from Tintagel we shall hear later.

Genealogies

On the face of it, a genealogy should be very useful to the historian. A dynastic history, or better still a collection of the dynastic histories of neighbouring kingdoms, can provide a skeleton of a region's political history. It can also act as a means of testing the chronologies, especially useful when those preserved by British and Saxon annalists turn out to be very different from one another; a genealogy or set of genealogies could help to reconcile the two histories.

The native peoples of the British Isles were unlike those of mainland Europe, in that many of them preserved long pedigrees of their royal families. Some of the incoming Saxon peoples seem to have brought an oral tradition with them, but it faded because it was not valued sufficiently by succeeding generations.[13] Irish pedigrees were more developed, complete and ancient than any in Europe. From them, an astonishing 20,000 named Irish people are known, from the period before AD 900. The Welsh and English chronicles seem to derive both their form and the substance of their earliest entries from the Irish annals. For instance, the *Welsh Annals* for the fifth and sixth centuries have 18 out of their 22 earliest entries copied straight from *Irish Annals*. If the Welsh genealogies were written down later than the Irish, it would seem both appropriate and advisable to correct the *Welsh Annals* entries where they differ from the Irish. There are nevertheless problems with this. Morris seeks to adjust the date of the plague from 547 (Welsh text) to 551 (Irish text),[14] assuming that the two events were synchronous, but it is possible that the plague, which spread to Britain from the European mainland, was transmitted to Ireland later: the two events may not have occurred in the same year. The adjustments we need to make to the chronicles are by no means straightforward.

A major problem with the genealogies is that we have few ways of checking their accuracy. Some scholars take the view that, since the descent of kings was essential to the cohesion and stability of dark age society (in both Celtic and Saxon territories), it had to be remembered accurately. Genealogies were recited at public occasions as a way of ensuring that the bards had remembered them correctly. On the other hand, we know that there were changes of regime by usurpation, and on public occasions such as those just mentioned the usurpers would have been exposed if the genealogies were accurate. A usurper would certainly have caused his bards to make up a respectable genealogy for him, much as a new life peer has a coat of arms concocted for him out of nowhere, as it were, by the College of Arms. The fabricated genealogy would inevitably incorporate great names from the past and indicate the legitimacy of the present ruler by asserting his kinship with his predecessors. If two previously separate Anglo-Saxon kingdoms were joined, the pedigrees of their royal families were often falsified to make them dovetail; there was a pragmatic political need to create a sense of the new state's unity, stability and endurance.[15]

It is difficult to see how these two conflicting needs were reconciled, but it is the case that as soon as genealogies came to be written down, inconsistencies emerged;

the early manuscripts can be compared. Because of these inconsistencies, it is difficult to put much faith in the oral traditions on which they are based. Another problem is that there were phases, such as Offa's time, when genealogies were fashionable and therefore compiled to order for many prominent families: they were inevitably often elegant fictions, with strings of heroic noble figures from the remote past.

Even so, historical information for the Arthurian period is in short supply, and we must glean what we can from fifth- and sixth-century genealogies. Fortunately, many of them are likely to be *partly* true. Certainly they are worthy of perusal. In constructing a time-line from a genealogy, it is traditional to attribute thirty years to a generation on average,[16] but it will still leave us with a fairly unreliable framework, one in need of corroboration from other sources.

Before the *Easter Annals* began there may have been some regulation of historical dates from king lists. It seems likely that now-lost king lists lie behind some of the surviving annals and chronicles.[17] There is a Northumbrian king list which runs back from 737 to 633, the period of overlap and agreement with Bede's account, and on back from there to 547, when the dynasty was founded by Ida.

But even king lists are not always reliable. The regnal list for Wessex in the 'A' manuscript of the *Anglo-Saxon Chronicle* does not agree with the dates given in the main body of the *Anglo-Saxon Chronicle*. At many points a shift of exactly ten years occurs, and that is easy to explain as a scribal error, but there is a big error in Ceawlin's case. The *Anglo-Saxon Chronicle* has him succeeding in 560, being deposed in 591 and driven out in 592, giving him a reign of 31 or 32 years, whereas the king list gives him only 17 years. Divergences of this kind may be beyond unravelling, but I suspect that sometimes a recurring name was sometimes overlooked by a copyist. Let us suppose there were, for argument's sake, not one but *two* Ceawlins, father and son; one may have ruled for 17 years, the other for 15, making 32 years in all.

Sometimes it appears that the opposite has happened: a name has been written down twice by mistake. In Genealogy XII we find the sequence 'Kyngar-Peder-Arthur-Peder-Arthur-Nennue'.[18] It is possible that there were two Arthurs and two Peders, but more likely that a scribe has made a mistake, possibly when his eye was caught by a name that started a distracting line of thought, as Arthur's always has, and wrote down the pair of names twice. In the pedigree of the kings of Powys, constructed from Genealogies XXII, XXVI, XXX and XXXI, we seem to have a continuous sequence from around 220 to Elisse, who reigned from 700 to 750; in this pedigree the names Cadell, Elisse, Cyngen and Brocmail each appear twice, but not in a repeating sequence, so in this case it is more likely that there really were two princes of each name.

Similar problems occur with Maelgwn, king of Gwynedd. Genealogies make him the grandson of Cunedda, yet Nennius' *Historia Brittonum* has Cunedda migrating to Gwynedd '146 years before Maelgwn ruled', which is really too long a gap for only two generations (both Cunedda and his son would have needed to father offspring at the age of 75 which, though possible, is relatively unlikely). On balance, two generations have probably been missed out of a king list; this is supported indirectly by a reference elsewhere in *Historia Brittonum* to Cunedda as the *atavus* or 'ancestor' of Maelgwn.[19] Alternatively, we may believe that the grandfather–grandson relationship was correctly identified but the '146 years' was a mistake.

Here is an example of a South Welsh royal pedigree, taken from the *Book of Llandaff*:[20]

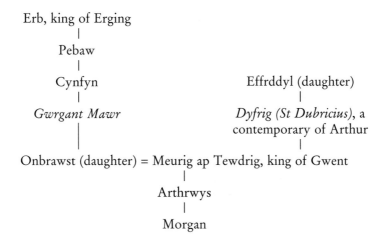

```
Erb, king of Erging
        |
      Pebaw
        |
     Cynfyn                      Effrddyl (daughter)
        |                                |
   Gwrgant Mawr               Dyfrig (St Dubricius), a
        |                       contemporary of Arthur
        |                                |
Onbrawst (daughter) = Meurig ap Tewdrig, king of Gwent
                             |
                         Arthrwys
                             |
                          Morgan
```

A 31-generation-long Demetian pedigree, too long to quote in full here, relates a prince named Arthur back to the Emperor Constantine the Great.[21] This Arthur lived in the late sixth century, and was probably born in about 550, around the time of King Arthur's death. The generations immediately before and after this 'Pembrokeshire' Arthur are given as follows;

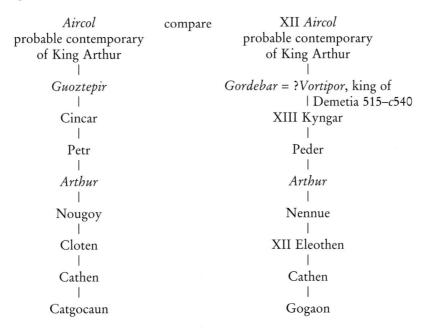

```
     Aircol          compare      XII Aircol
probable contemporary          probable contemporary
   of King Arthur                 of King Arthur
        |                                |
    Guoztepir              Gordebar = ?Vortipor, king of
        |                           | Demetia 515–c540
     Cincar                    XIII Kyngar
        |                                |
      Petr                         Peder
        |                                |
     Arthur                       Arthur
        |                                |
     Nougoy                       Nennue
        |                                |
      Cloten                   XII Eleothen
        |                                |
     Cathen                       Cathen
        |                                |
   Catgocaun                      Gogaon
```

Genealogy X does not have anyone called Arthur in it,[22] but it is nevertheless of great interest because it is a rare Cornish pedigree, and therefore supplies a Dumnonian context for Arthur.[23] The ancestral figures in Genealogy X are Erbin and his son Gereint, and it must be significant that another genealogy (XI) *ends* with these two names. The Arthurian period has to fall somewhere in this sequence, and Gereint and his son Cado are both named in early sources as close and important associates of Arthur in Dumnonia; in fact, they are named as rulers *who ruled with Arthur*, a significant concept that we will return to later.

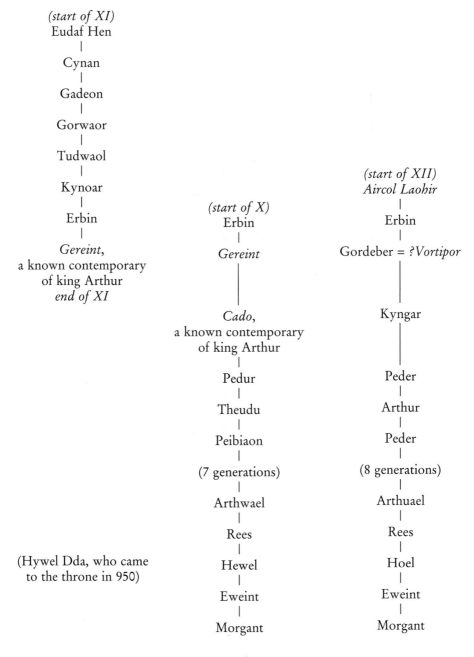

(start of XI)
Eudaf Hen
|
Cynan
|
Gadeon
|
Gorwaor
|
Tudwaol
|
Kynoar
|
Erbin
|
Gereint,
a known contemporary
of king Arthur
end of XI

(Hywel Dda, who came
to the throne in 950)

(start of X)
Erbin
|
Gereint
|
Cado,
a known contemporary
of king Arthur
|
Pedur
|
Theudu
|
Peibiaon
|
(7 generations)
|
Arthwael
|
Rees
|
Hewel
|
Eweint
|
Morgant

(start of XII)
Aircol Laohir
|
Erbin
|
Gordeber = *?Vortipor*
|
Kyngar
|
Peder
|
Arthur
|
Peder
|
(8 generations)
|
Arthuael
|
Rees
|
Hoel
|
Eweint
|
Morgant

Other early medieval manuscripts fill in further details. The Penarth Manuscript enables us to flesh out a family tree for Geraint as follows:[24]

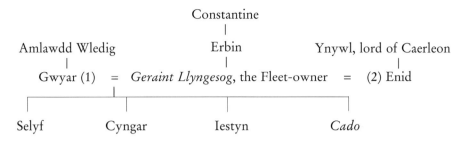

Erbin held lands in south-east Wales and Dumnonia. Geraint held lands in Dumnonia and Brittany. When too old to govern all his territories, Erbin resigned his kingdom in Dumnonia to his son.

If we allow the standard average of thirty years to a generation and count back from Hywel Dda, we can arrive at approximate birth dates for some of the key people in the story. According to this reckoning, Arthur, son of Peder, was born in about 570 and Cado was born in about 510, too young to fight at Badon, but not too young to fight at Arthur's side at Camlann; Cado's father Geraint was born in about 480, which makes him almost exactly contemporary with Arthur. The dates extrapolated from the pedigrees therefore corroborate the other written sources and strengthen the credibility of the pedigrees as documents: Arthur's military career, which I infer from the annal entries for Badon and Camlann lasted from close to 493 until 537, spanned the lives of King Geraint and his son Cado.

Nennius' *Historical Miscellany*

The surviving copy of this important collection of documents is in the British Library.[25] It has no title, no date, no author even, but from the handwriting style it must have been copied in about 1120 from earlier texts. The 'originals' of the documents as they stand were written no earlier than the late tenth century, as the death of a Welsh prince in 957 is recorded. The *Easter Annals* were probably taken from the Easter Table at St David's, so it may be that all the other documents in the collection were compiled by monks there too. There is a sharpness of focus in the Dyfed genealogies that suggests local knowledge, so it seems likely that it was the scriptorium at St David's which produced the documents in 960–70.

They were nevertheless drawn from still older sources. Although the monk Nennius wrote the *Historia Brittonum* in 830 he certainly drew information from much older sources, some of which originated in the sixth century. It is true that it is tainted with mythic elements, such as the repeated overnight disappearance of the building materials for Vortigern's castle in Snowdonia and the discovery of the two dragons. Padel (1994) argues that Nennius shows Arthur already with a dual nature, mythic and quasi-historical. Padel argues that the fictional Arthur came first and that pseudo-historical elements accreted round this fiction later. The internal consistency of a great deal of the quasi-historical material will, I believe, support the view that the historical Arthur came first; clearly this difference in view is more than academic. Nennius, in any case, contains some invaluable material, a series of snapshots of sixth- and seventh-century documents: a list of *The Wonders of the Island of Mona* (Anglesey), a note on *British and Irish Origins*, *The Tale of Emrys* (Ambrosius), the *Life of Germanus*, *The Campaigns of Arthur*, *The Northern History*, *The Genealogies of Britain*.

The Genealogies must have been collected from an Anglo-Saxon source, probably in Mercia in the eighth century,[26] while *The Northern History* must have come from a Northumbrian original. Possibly the *Welsh Annals* entries also came from material written in a scriptorium in Northumbria or Rheged in 600–625, incorporated into a subsequently lost *Northern History* some time between 750 and 775, probably in Bernicia.[27] These different originals were copied by a Welsh scribe: Anglo-Saxon names are frequently given a Welsh spelling: Osguid is written instead of Oswy, for instance. Well-known battles are called by British rather than English names. *Nechtanes Mere* is called by its evocative British name, *Gueith Lin Garan* – the Strife at Crane Lake. The details about Arthur's campaigns may have come from a battle-listing poem, originally in the British language and later paraphrased in Latin. This poem may have been composed in Arthur's lifetime by his own bard for triumphant recitation at royal feasts and celebrations, or it may have been written as part of an elegy or celebratory funeral epic shortly after his death.

In the decades following Arthur's death, the bard Taliesin wrote at least two battle-listing poems. *Rheged arise* lists six of Urien's battles;

> There was a battle at the ford of Alclud,
> a battle for supremacy,
> the battle of Cellawr Brewyn,
> long celebrated,
> battle in Prysg Cadleu, battle in Aber,
> fighting with harsh war-cry,
> the great battle of Cludwein,
> the one at Pencoed.

The Battles of Gwallawg lists ten battles: two by the sea, one in the land of Troon, one near Gwydauk and Mabon, and the battles of Cymrwy Canon, Arddunion, Aeron Eiddined, Coed Baidd, Gwenster and Rhos Eira. Taliesin gives only the smallest detail about each encounter, probably for the sake of metre. It is likely that this was a standard formula in widespread use, and that Arthur's bard wrote a very similar poem to celebrate a selection of Arthur's greatest battles.

Some of the original material for the *Historia Brittonum* must have come from a purely British source, such as the details about King Urien of Rheged (Cumbria), the bards Taliesin and Aneirin, and about the war-leader Arthur. The detail about the court of King Urien strongly suggests that Carlisle, Urien's capital, was the source of some of the information, and Chadwick has convincingly argued that it was one of Urien's sons who wrote it down.[28] The earliest surviving version of the *Historia Brittonum*, the Chartres text dating from around 900, says that a son of Urien (not named) was responsible for the 'Book of Germanus' that followed. There are four independent sources that state that a book on St Germanus existed in Britain in about 800; not much more than a century separates the son of Urien who wrote the *Life of Germanus* in around 620–640 and the summary of the story in the *Historia Brittonum*, written between 750 and 800, so there was probably a continuous tradition for which Urien's son was responsible. This would certainly explain the grandeur of Urien's image, and perhaps the emphasis on his death resulting from treachery.

We are not told the name of the clerical son of Urien who wrote the *Life of Germanus*, but we do know the name of a son of Urien's who was in holy orders – Rhun. Possibly it was Rhun who wrote the *Life of Germanus*. Rhun is said by Nennius to have baptized Edwin king of the Anglians in Northumbria. The *Welsh Annals* similarly insist on this point: '626: Edwin is baptized. And Rhun son of Urien baptized him.' Bede tells a different story. He has Paulinus officiating at Edwin's baptism. There are many reasons why there are inconsistencies between sources. Some are straightforward mistakes. But there was also a political motive for Bede's revisionism. Writing when he did, Bede may have wanted to show the first Christian Anglian king as sponsored by the Roman church, not by the Celtic church. A power struggle between the two churches had been going on since Augustine's arrival at the end of the sixth century, and Bede would have had a bias and a strong motive for reducing the role of the British priesthood and exaggerating that of the Roman. It seems likely therefore that it was Rhun who baptized Edwin and, moreover, that it was Rhun who actually wrote the account of the baptism ceremony, first-hand, in 627.

The way later events in the north of England and Scotland were recorded shows an intimate knowledge of the names of Pictish and Scottish people and places, so it looks as if historical material went on being recorded and saved at Carlisle until around 685.[29]

Since the annals in the Nennius collection cover a span of 533 years, they must have come from a Great Cycle Easter Table. A Great Cycle is 532 years long, so the annals covered one complete cycle plus one year of the next. The years are not given conventional 'AD' dates. Each year is marked *an'* (*annus*). Presumably the AD dates stood to the left of the *an'* column and it is regrettable that the copyist left them out, but the situation is saved by the mention of an event datable from other chronologies: 'Easter changed by Pope Leo'. This enables us to fix Year 1 as 445 (or 447 according to some computations). This calibration works for all the events mentioned that are known or inferred from other sources, to within one or two years, so we can be confident with the chronology. It is also likely that events were added to the list as they happened from around 450 onwards,[30] so the entries are an exactly contemporary record of the events they describe.

All this is very significant, as the crucial documentary links between us and the historical Arthur are the two references to Arthur in this sequence. The first comes in Year 72, which is AD 516:

Bellum badonis in quo arthur portavit crucem domini nostri jesu christi tribus diebus & tribus noctibus in humeros suos & brittones victores fuerunt.
[Battle of Badon in which Arthur carried the cross of our lord Jesus Christ on his shoulders for three days and three nights, and the Britons were victors.]

The second reference comes in Year 93, or AD 537:

> *Gueith camlann in qua arthur & medraut corruerunt.*
> [Strife of Camlann, in which Arthur and Medraut perished.]

Those who challenge the historical existence of Arthur suggest that the fictitious characters of Arthur and Modred were added later by a copyist, embedded in an otherwise 'straight' history. This seems perverse. None of the other people mentioned in Nennius are treated in this way, so it is more natural to believe that Arthur and Modred existed, that they both fell in a battle called Camlann and that this happened within a couple of years of 537. Equally, there is no reason at all to doubt that the Battle of Badon took place, especially since the sixth-century British historian Gildas mentioned it as well and emphasized that it happened round about the time when he was born, which would have been towards the beginning of the sixth century.[31] The only thing that might cast doubt on the entry is the superhuman feat of carrying the cross of Jesus (or a replica, for that matter) into battle, and this has led some to assume that the entry as a whole was interpolated later, when the myth-making about Arthur had begun.[32] Perhaps only the cross reference was added afterwards and the original entry read 'Battle of Badon in which Arthur and the Britons were victors:' as we shall see later it is possible that the reference to the cross was part of the original, but that it was mistranslated.

The description of Camlann as a 'strife' may suggest the choice of a poetic word for an event that had, by some later stage, become the stuff of legend. 'The strife of Camlann' sounds like a phrase lifted from a battle-listing poem, which might be more fiction than fact. But other battles are referred to as strifes too. The Battle of Chester is referred to as 'gueith cair legion': the battle in which Cadwallon of Gwynedd and Penda of Mercia killed Edwin of Northumbria is called 'gueith meicen'. There is no doubt that these strifes happened. 'Gueith' was evidently a natural alternative word for a British scribe to use for a battle.

Another objection that has been made to the Badon entry is that it is rather long and complicated, with the implication that it has been filled out by some tenth-century editor after the Arthurian legend had gained currency. There are nevertheless other long entries, such as that for the Battle of Meicen in 633, which is exactly the same length as the Badon entry. The entry length is simply an indication that the annalist was aware of the relative importance of the events he was recording. The momentous slaying of the great king of Northumbria in 633 justified a long entry. The landmark battle of Badon over a century earlier similarly justified a long entry, and was seen in that way at the time, not just by the annalist but by the historian Gildas too. The *Welsh Annals* have long, Camlann-like entries for the years 613, 626, 629, 630, 644, 645, 682, 689, 722, 760 and very long for 814. Length of entry cannot be offered as evidence of forgery.[33]

The cross borne by Arthur on his shoulders may have resulted from a mis-translation. The Old Welsh word for shoulder, *scuid*, is very similar to the Old Welsh word for shield, *scuit*. It is possible that in earlier versions of the annals the word was *scuit* and that it was miscopied by a later scribe. Copyists regularly read whole phrases from the documents they were copying and muttered them over to themselves as they wrote: it was easy to make mistakes, especially when words both looked and sounded similar. So the original description may have read, 'Arthur carried the cross of our lord Jesus Christ on his shield.' The image of the cross could easily have been painted onto the shield, or designed into the shield's metalwork, or embroidered into a fabric covering for the shield. It may be significant that high-ranking officers in the late Roman army frequently carried portraits of emperors on their shields. It would be quite logical for a Christian British commander-in-chief educated in the late Roman tradition to carry an emblem of Christ: after all, he recognized no earthly overlord.[34]

Poetry

Although no document has reached us direct from the sixth century – everything we have seems either to have been transmitted orally for a time before being written down or to have been re-copied in the interim – some of the poetry we find in twelfth- and thirteenth-century manuscripts clearly has its roots in the sixth century. Although both fiction and history may be coloured by the passage of time, it is usually possible to detect the anachronisms that creep in.

Many of the stories were preserved in Wales, simply because other parts of the Celtic fringe were overrun by the Saxons relatively early and the Welsh kingdoms retained their independence longer. The fact that often the subject matter is not Welsh is an indication that the Welsh bards were acting as a bank for the British culture. The stories about Celliwig in Cornwall, for instance, are more likely to have been generated in Cornwall before that area fell to the Saxons than to have been invented later in Wales. The Cunedda connection may help to explain the survival of so much northern British history; the court bards of Gwynedd would have a strong interest in exploring the northern origins and early history of the dynasty of king Maelgwn.[35]

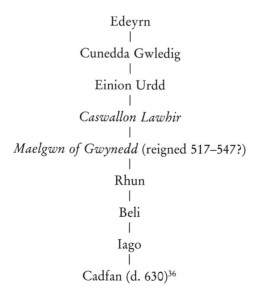

Edeyrn
|
Cunedda Gwledig
|
Einion Urdd
|
Caswallon Lawhir
|
Maelgwn of Gwynedd (reigned 517–547?)
|
Rhun
|
Beli
|
Iago
|
Cadfan (d. 630)[36]

To make it easier to remember, material was often grouped into threes: this is the origin of the often cryptic Triads, some of which certainly go back to the sixth century. *The Triad of Arthur and His Warriors* has its origins in Arthur's time: 'Arthur the chief lord at Kelliwic in Cornwall, and bishop Bedwin the chief bishop, and Caradaure Vreichvras the chief elder.'

Fragments of sixth-century bardic writing have certainly survived, although it may be difficult to be certain about specific pieces. Taliesin, Llywarch Hen, Aneirin and Myrddin were all bards and all lived in the sixth century, even though there is no manuscript of their compositions earlier than the twelfth century. Dickinson was sure they must have been written down in between, perhaps in the ninth century, and then those intervening copies lost,[37] but there is no reason why oral tradition should not sustain a poem or a Triad for six centuries as well as for three.

Twelve poems by Taliesin are now reckoned to be authentic productions of the dark age bard. Eight are conventional praise poems for Urien as a 'successful battle prince', 'generous patron of bards', 'protector of Rheged' and 'ruler of Catraeth'. Seven end with Taliesin's signature tune, an identical formula expressing the wish to praise Urien until death. In one poem, Urien has 'overcome the land of Brynaich, but after having been a hero he lies on a hearse'. This is interesting in showing that the (allegedly) conquered land was in the last quarter of the sixth century still being called by its British name, Brynaich, rather than its Anglian name, Bernicia, at least by the Britons.[38]

In *Rheged arise*, Taliesin says to Urien, 'I have watched over you even though I am not one of yours', and the praise poem *To Cynan Garwyn* implies that he may have come originally from Powys, serving Cynan, king of Powys, before moving to Rheged. Taliesin was loyal to the British cause above all else and when he saw Urien's power beginning to wane at the close of the sixth century he shifted his efforts to the support of Gwallawg, king of Elmet: there are two poems in praise of Gwallawg, *The Battles of Gwallawg* and *Gwallawg is other*. Urien was nevertheless still alive and nettled at this shift of loyalty and it was probably then that Taliesin wrote *The Conciliation of Urien* by way of apology.

Several important themes emerge from Taliesin's poems. One is that the kingdoms of the north were allied in a loose confederation against the Anglo-Saxon menace, sometimes under one king, sometimes under another, and Urien is portrayed as one of these commanders-in-chief. Another is the in-fighting among the British and the wide geographical range of sixth-century military expeditions; Cynan of Powys is described as waging war on Brycheiniog, the Wye valley, Gwent, Dyfed, Gwynedd and Dumnonia, and Urien as 'ranging himself' against Powys. There are also insights into the motives for warfare. *The Battle of Wensleydale* mentions that Urien is king of the rustlers, farmer leader, suggesting that acquiring livestock was a prime motive for fighting. Acquiring wealth was essential in order to make the show of gift-giving that was the hallmark of great kingship. In *You are the best*, Urien is Christendom's most generous man; 'a myriad gifts you give to the world. As you hoard, you scatter.' In *Gwallawg is other*, Taliesin tells us, 'Hoarding kings are to be pitied . . . they cannot take their riches to the grave: they cannot boast about their lives.' A further recurring theme is the importance of horses in British warfare. *The Spoils of Taliesin* say, 'fine are fast cavalrymen' and 'fine is the rush of a champion and his horse'. Taliesin was unable to go on an expedition with Urien, but wished that he could have gone 'on a frisky horse' to be 'with the foragers'. The sound of battle was dominated by the horses: 'From the stamping of the horses a furious din.' Horses ranked among the most highly prized gifts; Taliesin claimed that Cynan gave him a hundred steeds with silver trappings.

The situation is nevertheless complicated by the repeated later recopying of sixth-century poems, and new compositions in the same style on the same subject matter. Often it is like watching twentieth-century Westerns, very few of which portray events which took place in the nineteenth century. Several so-called Taliesin poems have to be rejected because they contain contaminating later material or are written in a mystical prophetic style, like the *Battle of Godeu*. Medieval copyists tended to expand and develop early material that was too terse or cryptic for medieval taste. The nature of the problem is most transparently seen in a poem about Gwallawg ap Lleenawg in the *Black Book of Camarthen*, where a medieval monk has written an additional stanza in the margin.

It is impossible to doubt that the *Geraint* poem, an elegy for those who fell at the Battle of Llongborth, is anything other than a genuine sixth-century poem, written perhaps within days or weeks of one of Arthur's battles. *The Verses of the Graves* are also likely to be late sixth century. The bard alludes in a list of memorable horses to 'the steed of Arthur', which confirms what we read in the *Geraint* poem, that British princes were dependent on their horses for military success. There are frequent references to Arthur, for instance on one of his expeditions:

And when we went with Arthur, a splendid labour,
but for seven, none returned from Caer Vedwyd.[39]

The Gododdin is a series of elegies about a disastrous expedition of the bodyguard of Mynyddog Mwynfawr, king of Din Eidyn, against the Anglians at Catraeth. It is preserved in a single manuscript called the *Book of Aneirin*. The title is the original one: we are told simply, 'This is *The Gododdin*. Aneirin composed it.' The subject matter and detail favour its genuineness as a sixth-century poem, actually by Aneirin. Sir Ifor Williams devoted thirty years of exacting analytical work to the 103 stanzas of the poem, so his belief that *The Gododdin* is a genuine product of the sixth century should be followed. Nennius dated Aneirin to the second half of the sixth century. The warriors included not just Gododdin, i.e. men of the Votadini tribe, but hand-picked men from all over Britain – Elmet, Clyde, Gwynedd and Dumnonia – which tells us that communications among the British kingdoms must have been effective, and that they were ready to assist one another against the Anglo-Saxons. The Gododdin king feasted them for a year at Din Eidyn before sending them to fight the 'Lloegrwys' (men of England) or the 'Dewr a Brynaich' (men of Deira and Byrnaich). Aneirin comments grimly, 'They paid for that feast of mead with their lives.' The British attack on Catterick was probably pre-emptive, an attempt to annihilate the embryonic Anglian community while it was still relatively small and powerless; the crushing defeat would have been all the more traumatic because it was unexpected. Few of the heroes escaped alive.[40]

One line in *The Gododdin* mentions Arthur in passing. A warrior is praised for his fighting, 'though he was no Arthur'. Oliver Padel, who denies the historicity of

Arthur, says that the line may have been added in the ninth century, but there is no reason whatever to suppose that it was added in this way.[41] Indeed, its very casualness and incompleteness suggest that it was a genuine near-contemporary reference to Arthur.

The *Anglo-Saxon Chronicle*

The great value of the *Anglo-Saxon Chronicle* is that it gives a parallel narrative of events in fifth- and sixth-century Britain that is completely independent of the Celtic sources. Obviously there is always a danger that Celtic sources will have inflated and exaggerated the achievements of a Celtic leader, and it is healthy historiographically to have an account of the period written by people without that bias. The *Chronicle* gives an outline history of the Anglo-Saxon settlement of Kent, a sketchy report of the conquest of Sussex, and a more detailed history of the colonization of Wessex. Even from this brief description it is obvious that there are gaps; there is no record of the roughly contemporary settlement of Lincolnshire and East Anglia, and very little on the Thames valley, which is only mentioned where the dynasty of Wessex is involved.

A basic text of the *Chronicle* was compiled before 891, probably at Alfred's instigation, possibly under his supervision. When this was completed, copies were circulated to various cathedrals and abbeys, where the basic text was developed independently, with monks adding entries continually until as late as about 1100.[42] The divergence of these late editions need not concern us, but even 891 may seem far too late for the *Chronicle* to be at all reliable for the events of the sixth century. In fact, copying errors apparent in the 891 manuscript show that it must have been preceded by at least two earlier documents. Probably the records were written down from the year 635, when the West Saxon king Cynegils was baptized, Birinus' mission in Wessex was firmly and securely established and the Easter Tables constructed at Dorchester-on-Thames provided a natural framework on which to peg reports of major contemporary events. From the start, dates were given in years AD, which removes one area of uncertainty. From there it would have been a short step for a Dorchester monk to begin extrapolating the Table backwards and compose an outline history of the Wessex dynasty. This would also explain why the Wessex record is the most complete.

Later, the West Saxon annals were combined with other material, some written, but probably mostly oral, for the period before the conversion to Christianity to create the *Chronicle* itself. As in the British record, a key ingredient in the source material was probably battle poetry; this can be inferred from what is known generally of Germanic societies at the time and from later Old English verse, which is based in the same tradition. There are also some poetic phrases included: for instance in 473 we are told, 'the Britons *fled* from the English *as from fire*'. Entries like these sound as if they have been lifted from poems.

The backward computation of dates from 635 means that we cannot take the earlier dates as precisely correct: they must in many cases be estimates. It is noticeable that there are entries for the years 540, 544, 547, 552, 556, 560, 565 and 568, though not for any dates in between, and all but 547 and 565 are leap years, years highlighted in the Easter Table. These were clearly seen as convenient slots for entering major events and cannot be taken to be perfectly accurate.

The *Chronicle* for the crucial period when corroboration is needed is therefore, as it stands, artificial and untrustworthy. An awareness of this limitation can nevertheless help in reconciling Gildas's remark that there were some decades of peace following the Battle of Badon (whenever that happened) with the unceasing series of battles given in the *Chronicle*. The later chronicler seems to have distributed battle dates through a sequence of leap years with an eye to the balanced and artistic appearance of the document, whereas the battles themselves may have been clustered, for instance in the period before Badon, as Gildas says.

A second distortion is the propaganda element. The *Chronicle* emphasizes the fire and slaughter inflicted by the English, emphasizes the English victories. Reverses and humiliating defeats are not mentioned. Arthur himself is never mentioned, partly because he is successful, the instrument of major defeats the Saxons want forgotten, partly because very few British leaders are mentioned at all. In the *Chronicle*, the Britons tend to be undifferentiated, lumped anonymously together, the common fate of 'foreigners' everywhere.

A third, minor, problem is that it is not clear when the Anglo-Saxons began their year. It may have been the 25 March following our 1 January date for the New Year, or it may have been 24 September, the Caesarian indiction date. More commonly, Christmas was the major calendar landmark, and the New Year was probably deemed to begin on 25 or 26 December. Because of these uncertainties, an exact equation of English and British dates is not possible: a year either way has to be allowed.

A fourth problem, one which is receding with modern scholarship, is that antiquated and incorrect translations have been in widespread use. These have changed the thrust of some of the entries significantly. Davis in 1905, for example, translated what should have read, 'Then they committed every atrocity' as 'Then did they all wonder.' In 1939 Sir Charles Oman translated what should have been 'Wherever there was tillage the earth bore no corn for the land was ruined by such deeds' as 'The earth bears no corn: you might as well have tilled the sea.'

Nevertheless, forewarned is forearmed and, in spite of all the shortcomings and disappointments, the *Anglo-Saxon Chronicle* gives us an Anglo-Saxon view, very much a view from south-east England, of Britain at the time of Arthur.

Gildas's *Book of Complaint*

The main importance of the British monk and scholar Gildas the Wise lies in the fact that he lived and wrote in the sixth century, at the time of Arthur, and wrote at length about the condition of Britain at that time. Gildas opened his book with a surprisingly lyrical description of Britain's watery beauty, which evidently made a strong impression on him. 'This land of such dear souls, this dear, dear land ... decked with lucid fountains, abundant brooks wandering over snow white sands, transparent rivers that glide with gentle murmur, lakes which pour forth cool torrents of refreshing water.' Gildas's book, *Liber querulus de excidio et conquestu Britannia* ('Book of

Complaint on the Ruin and Conquest of Britain'), was written in about 540 with a retrospect back not just to the Battle of Badon but beyond, into what were for Gildas the less certain events of the fifth century.

This articulate eyewitness account of the time of Arthur is invaluable but also frustrating. It is emotionally highly charged, with a great deal of invective directed at one British ruler after another: Gildas was dissatisfied with all of them. Probably with conscious understatement, Gildas called his thunderous accusations *admonitiuncula*, 'just a little word of warning'. His text is also compiled largely from biblical quotations, making the book more sermon than history.

A third problem is that it is written in an obscure Latin style that creates many ambiguities and is susceptible to more than one interpretation. It is also possible that a parallel version containing significant variations existed, but was subsequently destroyed. There is disagreement among scholars as to whether (in the surviving text) Gildas claimed to have been born in the same year as the Battle of Badon, between 43 and 44 years before the time when he was writing, or meant something else by his remarks about the passage of time. It looks as if Bede, writing about 190 years later, was using an alternative copy of Gildas which was worded differently and said something else again. Bede's paraphrase of the key passage is as follows; 'until the year that Mount Badon was besieged, where they gave the same enemy a great defeat, and which was about the forty-fourth year of their coming into Britain'.[43] It is very unlikely that Bede completely mistranslated the version of Gildas that has survived: we must assume that there was another version, putting the date of Badon 43 years after the Saxon colonization. This is not especially helpful, in that the *Anglo-Saxon Chronicle* gives several dates for the colonization. If Aelle king of the south Saxons was bretwalda at the time of Badon, it may be that it was the coming of the south Saxons that was referred to; the *Chronicle* gives 477 as the date for this, which in turn yields a date of 520 for Badon, not far from the 516 or 518 derived from British records.

In spite of these problems, we lean heavily on Gildas as a witness for the period from Badon to Camlann and after. However defective, he is one of the very few sixth-century witnesses who wrote down what he saw and heard. Bede discovered this too when he came to write his history in 731. Bede tried to strip away some of the ambiguities and the rhetoric. The oldest surviving text we have of Gildas dates from the eleventh century, but we can be sure that it was copied faithfully between the eighth and eleventh centuries, because the paraphrases embedded in Bede are, with the exception of the '43 years' passage, essentially the same as the content of the eleventh-century text. There is no reason to believe that there was any significant alteration to Gildas's text between the sixth and eighth centuries, and no detectable motive for any such alteration.

Sometimes Gildas's reliability is called into question, because he made mistakes about events in the period of the Roman occupation. He ascribed the Antonine and Hadrianic Roman walls, both second-century, to Magnus Maximus in the fourth. But even if Gildas is unreliable on the period 100 years before his own birth, what he said about events in his own lifetime and immediately before it must be at least approximately true. What he described would have needed to be recognizable to his contemporaries and elders or his homily would have been meaningless. So, when he says that in the years since Badon Britain had been free from external attack, though not civil strife, he must have been telling no less than the truth. Other evidence, both documentary and archaeological, as we shall see later, tells us that Britain post-Badon was not a united Celtic kingdom: it was – it remained – several separate kingdoms, although to say that it was 'partitioned' is misleading as it implies earlier unity.[44]

There is also, following the same line of logic, every reason to believe him when he tells us that a British leader called Ambrosius initiated a more successful period for the British in their struggle against the Saxons in the run-up to Badon. Gildas is tantalizingly sparing with names and details, yet he homes in on the Battle of Badon as a landmark battle. By the 540s Badon was seen as a watershed engagement, a battle that decisively marked the end of one phase of history and introduced another, much as Trafalgar and Waterloo hung over British historians of the mid-nineteenth century and the D-Day landings stuck in the minds of war veterans of the late twentieth century. Three or four decades on, the battle had acquired a special mystique.

It is disappointing that Arthur is not mentioned in connection with Badon, or with the period of exemplary government that followed it – or in any connection at all. It is a great puzzle, rather like Aristotle's total silence about his pupil, Alexander. Many suggestions have been made to explain Gildas's silence. One medieval tradition is that Gildas had a brother who betrayed Arthur and was executed for his treachery. Whether Gildas hated Arthur's memory for causing his brother's death or was an admirer of Arthur and therefore embarrassed by his brother's disgrace, it would be understandable for Gildas to remain silent about the king. Presumably Gildas did not wholly disapprove of Arthur, or he would have included some reference to him in the list of kings he despised; if he wholly approved, why not hold him up as an exemplar for the new generation of kings? Alternatively, if Arthur was no longer king at the time Gildas was writing, as is likely, Gildas may have seen him as no longer relevant to the sermon. It may be that Gildas's feelings about Arthur were mixed. He may have admired the man (who seems to have been a blood relation or a friend) and been wholly satisfied with the results of his policies and strategies as a ruler, yet been uneasy about some aspect of Arthur's behaviour. There are references to Arthur's mildly anti-clerical behaviour in the *Life of Carantoc*, in which he uses an altar as a table, and the general thrust of the *Lives* of the saints, showing Welsh monks as un-friendly towards Arthur,[45] suggests that Arthur antagonized them, possibly by requisitioning church property to maintain his troops. If that is so, it would explain why Gildas's feelings about the king were confused. His invective against the kings living around 540–50 implies opposition to some policy or strategy of Maelgwn's which he saw as shared by Maelgwn's contemporary rulers. Gildas infuriatingly does not say straight out what this was, but since he refers to the kings as usurpers he may have been thinking of them as guilty of seizing church lands.[46] It begins to look as if this fault was shared by many dark age kings, and was by no means a particular fault of Arthur's.

An alternative explanation for the silence is that there was simply no need for Gildas to remind his readers that Arthur had been the victor of Badon nor that Arthur had been the great king who ruled after Badon, any more than Victorian readers needed to be told that it was the Duke of Wellington who had been the victor at Waterloo or that it was a monarch by the name of Queen Victoria who currently sat on the British throne: everybody knew that. He was ready enough to tell his readers that Arthur's predecessor as commander-in-chief, Ambrosius Aurelianus, was 'modest, strong and faithful', but this may have been necessary because Ambrosius belonged to the previous generation: none of Gildas's readers could have known him.

Dickinson found a simple explanation; Gildas, and for that matter Bede and the *Anglo-Saxon Chronicle* too, did not mention Arthur because he was not the British commander-in-chief.[47] Dickinson sees Ambrosius as commander-in-chief of the British forces, with Arthur as Gwledig or Imperator. This explanation fails on two fronts. Nennius makes it clear that Arthur was commander-in-chief, *dux bellorum*, and that it was his successes on the field of battle that made his reputation. In addition, if Arthur had been a mere figurehead, a kind of presidential head of state, it would be rather more likely that Gildas would have something to say about him. Dickinson argues that Arthur was active in the west, and that therefore the Saxons (active in the east) did not really know about him, which is just about credible, but it would mean that the young Gildas, who probably lived in Dorset, would have been very aware of him. Dickinson thought it particularly odd that Bede found no place for Arthur as a Christian champion,[48] but that in turn may be explained easily by Bede's use of Gildas as a source; Gildas mentions Ambrosius and not Arthur – and it is the same in Bede.

Another construction that could be put on Gildas's silence is that Arthur did not exist, and those who are predisposed to doubt Arthur's existence can and do use Gildas as a 'negative witness'. But if that line of argument is applied as it then should be to other major historical figures, we find ourselves in a strange predicament, with one figure after another disappearing into oblivion. To take an example, neither Gildas nor Bede refers to St Patrick – and no fifth-century writer mentions Patrick at all.[49] Are we as a result to deny the existence of St Patrick?

It may be that Gildas *did* mention Arthur, indirectly, in the passage he wrote about Cuneglasus. He described Cuneglasus as having, when young, been *The Bear's* charioteer: '*aurigaque currus receptaculi Ursi*'. The identity of *The Bear* is not immediately obvious, nor is the name's significance, until we realize that Gildas played games with words and in other passages gave kings animal nicknames that were puns on their personal names. Gildas called a king whose real name was Conan, Cynan or Kynan 'Caninus', *The Dog*. *The Bear* translated into Welsh is *Arth*, which is close to Arthur's personal name. Given the time when Gildas was writing, about 540, it is quite possible that a contemporary King Cuneglasus might, as a young prince twenty years earlier, have served as an officer in Arthur's army and might even have had the privileged position of driving Arthur's chariot.[50] Of all the various possibilities, I find this the most persuasive. A recently revised interpretation by Alcock and Jackson in 1982 translates the passage as 'the driver of the chariot of the Bear's Stronghold', and interprets this as a Latinization of the place-name Dineirth, probably Bryn Euryn at Dineirth in north-east Wales. According to this idea, Cuneglasus was no more than 'a chariot driver at Dineirth', which on the whole seems less likely.[51]

Gildas gave vent to some violent prejudices, but even in these he tells us something very definite and real about Arthurian Britain. 'Kings Britain has, but usurpers; judges has she, but ungodly. Priests Britain has, but foolish ones.' The way he denounces all those about him is reminiscent of the behaviour of St Samson (see Chapter 4); what we see is a sixth-century type, the scourging prelate, inveighing fearlessly and recklessly against wrong-doing wherever he sees it, storming sarcastically against kings, queens, judges and priests, apparently with impunity. The narrative of St Samson's *Life* nevertheless shows that some contemporaries found this kind of abrasive self-righteousness too strong to take, and asked Samson to move elsewhere. These were the early days of the Celtic church, and both Gildas and Samson displayed the coarseness of the pioneering spirit.

Gildas gives us a glimpse of the uneasy frictive relationship between priest and king, a welcome shaft or two of steel-grey light in an otherwise misty landscape. But he does leave several major issues unresolved. He does not, for instance, give us the names of any of the Saxon leaders, which would enable us to check and corroborate the version of events given in the *Anglo-Saxon Chronicle*, nor even the name of the *superbus tyrannus* of the British. He does not make it clear whether Badon was Ambrosius' victory or Arthur's, nor does he say whether it was Saxons or Britons who were under siege at Badon.

He *does* tell us about Arthur's predecessor as *dux bellorum*, though, the great Ambrosius Aurelianus.

> When the cruel plunderers [the Saxons attacking the British in around 460 or 470] had gone back to their settlements, God gave strength to the survivors [i.e. the British]. Wretched people flocked to them from all directions, as eagerly as bees to the beehive when a storm threatens, begging burdening heaven with unnumbered prayers that they should not be destroyed. Their leader was Ambrosius Aurelianus, a gentleman who, perhaps alone of the Romanized Britons, had survived the shock of this great storm [the Saxon invasion]; certainly his parents, who may have worn the purple, were slain in it. Under him our people regained their strength and challenged the victors to battle.

After this the British began to win battles, not always, Gildas admits, but they were eventually rewarded with the overwhelming victory of Badon.

In his diatribe against the evils he saw around him, Gildas sounds like an old campaigner from the Second World War regretting the ending of compulsory National Service and the softness and decadence of Britain in the 1960s and 1970s, perceived as the fruits of the peace. Gildas tells us that it was the victor of Badon who maintained orderly government for an entire generation, and that recently, that is not long before 540, power had passed into the hands of regional warlords whose violence overrode law and convention and corrupted the church. Under the victor of Badon,

> kings, public and private persons, priests and churchmen, kept to their own stations. But they died; and an age succeeded them that is ignorant of the storm and has experience only of the calm of the present. All the controls of truth and justice have been shaken and overthrown, leaving no trace, not even a memory, among the orders I have mentioned: with the exception of a few, a very few.[52]

Gildas describes Celtic Britain divided into several separate kingdoms (see Figure 2.2) under local kings or 'tyrants' who ruled by *force majeure*; the picture he describes coincides with what we hear from the fifth-century Byzantine historian Zosimus and

Figure 2.2 Gildas's kings. The dashed line is the eastern boundary of the late Roman province of Britannia Prima.

the sixth-century historian Procopius about the political structure that emerged after the Roman withdrawal. The kingdoms Gildas knew and wrote about were in Wales and the West Country, so it is almost certain that he lived in that part of Britain. But if he lived in Dorset, then part of the kingdom of Dumnonia, how was he able to criticize a Dumnonian king and escape punishment? If the king of Dumnonia at the time when Gildas was writing was Constantine, the same Constantine who dressed as an abbot in order to get into a church and cold-bloodedly murder two young aristocrats, it may seem unlikely that he would have tolerated Gildas's accusations.[53] But maybe the rulers of Arthurian Britain were used to the outspoken style of the Christian brothers: possibly they shrugged it off as of no consequence. Morris suggested that Constantine had been deposed by the time Gildas wrote, in which case the king would have been in no position to retaliate, though it is not clear on what evidence Morris's suggestion is based. It is more likely that Gildas was not writing a 'book' in the modern sense at all, but simply a circular letter that he believed would be read by a few like-minded friends. Some of his asides reinforce this idea, and it would help to explain the silence regarding Arthur, whose nature was too well known to his correspondents for Gildas even to need to mention him.

Gildas tells us of British kings and queens who were Arthur's contemporaries and near-contemporaries, but often elliptically. We hear of 'Constantine, tyrant whelp of the filthy lioness of Dumnonia', perhaps intending that the kingdom of Dumnonia is to be considered a filthy lioness, perhaps meaning that he disapproved more specifically of King Constantine's mother. Ironically, in spite of the vehemence of the language, it is often not entirely clear (now) what Gildas means. Constantine was

Arthur's successor. Gildas with similar lack of inhibition condemns Maelgwn the great king of Gwynedd; Cuneglasus, Maelgwn's cousin and probably king of Powys; Aurelius Caninus, probably an otherwise unknown king called Cynan ruling in the Gloucester region; and Vortipor king of Dyfed.[54]

He also implies that there was an important Saxon power base in the north of England. He describes the Saxons as coming *south* into a region where there were British cities: presumably the Midlands.[55] But, given that Gildas was viewing the situation from Dorset,[56] the northern power base of the Saxons may not have been very far north, and could have been as far south as Lincolnshire. This would fit in well with other evidence that the Saxons were established early on in the Lindsey district of Lincolnshire. It is also known that there were the British cities of Cirencester and Gloucester in Calchvynnydd, the kingdom that lay in the lower Severn valley, between Dumnonian Dorset and the Midlands.

Geoffrey of Monmouth

Geoffrey of Monmouth wrote his *History of the Kings of Britain* at Monmouth Priory, probably in 1138.[57] Geoffrey's review of British history was outstandingly popular throughout the middle ages from the moment of its publication onwards, and it had a strong influence on medieval romances. He made Arthur a king with a higher profile than any other king in British history. In modern times, Geoffrey's popularity has suffered a reverse: he has frequently been dismissed and outspokenly derided as a bad historian, or indeed accused of being no historian at all.

There are many reasons for modern historians taking this hostile view. Geoffrey locates Arthur's courts at Caerleon, London and Winchester; although Caerleon was firmly in British-held territory, London and Winchester have been seen as being in the English zone; the pre-eminence Geoffrey gave to these cities was an anachronistic importation from later centuries. Geoffrey featured Tintagel as the castle of Gorlois, the place where Arthur was conceived and, by implication, born and raised. In the 1930s, the Ralegh Radford interpretation of the remains on Tintagel Island as those of a dark age monastic site seemed to exclude the site's use as a royal power base; this view persisted for half a century.[58] If Radford was right, then Geoffrey of Monmouth had to be wrong.

Geoffrey's claim that he was drawing on 'a certain very ancient book' as his source has been treated with scepticism; many have dismissed it as a cloak for un-substantiated romancing. That charge seems to carry more weight because it was even levelled by some of Geoffrey's contemporaries. In 1190 William of Newburgh condemned him out of hand because 'it is quite clear that everything this man wrote about Arthur . . . was made up, partly by himself, partly by others'.[59]

Geoffrey was good at adding circumstantial detail to make pseudo-historical events seem real. For instance, his description of a battle between Arthur and Lucius Tiberius is purely fictional and yet finely detailed – the hallmark of the incorrigible liar.

Geoffrey brings Stonehenge into his story as a dark age burial place – he makes it the last resting place of Ambrosius and Uther – but the archaeology of the site shows clearly that Stonehenge was not used for burial as such[60] and the area round Stonehenge was only used for high status burial in the bronze age, not the dark ages.

There are obvious chronological errors, such as having Arthur marching over the Alps and attacking Rome, which may have resulted from mixing Arthur up with Magnus Maximus, who marched on Rome in 387, or making Arthur a contemporary of King Urien of Rheged, when Urien lived two generations later. Worse still, Arthur is described as if he was a medieval king. Geoffrey shows us an aristocratic court which is really more like a court of the twelfth century than the sixth. There are hints at courtly love in the way he describes the role of women in ensuring the good behaviour of knights, and hints at medieval heraldry too.

Geoffrey's view of Arthur was both the basis and the stimulus for a flurry of romances and fantasies which ranged further and further from the historical Arthur. Small wonder that modern historians have shown such impatience with Geoffrey and been keen to dissociate themselves from him as a source.

Yet, in spite of this seemingly unanswerable battery of faults and flaws, I believe that Geoffrey of Monmouth's account of Arthur should be taken seriously. He may have told no less than the truth when he claimed to have taken his material from an old book. That book may have been the 'pseudo-Geoffrey' discovered in the 1950s by Jacob Hammer, or more likely a source that was subsequently destroyed, like many others.[61] Geoffrey was very insistent that his contemporaries, the historians Caradoc of Llancarfan, William of Malmesbury and Henry of Huntingdon, should leave the kings of the Britons alone: *he* had the source book and *they* did not! Given the large allocation of space in Geoffrey's book to Gallic warfare, Geoffrey's source probably came from Brittany, as he said, and it is possible that it was brought from Brittany by the scholarly Walter of Oxford, to whom Geoffrey freely acknowledged he owed a great debt for procuring the material for him.

Both during his lifetime and repeatedly since, Geoffrey has been accused of lying about the 'ancient book' given to him by Walter. If Geoffrey told a lie about the book, it was a dangerously risky lie. Geoffrey's *History* was published in 1138, when Walter was still alive: indeed, he lived on for another thirteen years, during which time the book was much talked about. As far as I know, Walter of Oxford never refuted Geoffrey's version of events, so we should assume that in this at least Geoffrey was telling the truth. Geoffrey was so vilified, that Walter presumably would have had every motive to expose the fraud. A manuscript exists in the Vatican Library, a 1474 copy of a *Prophecy of Merlin* written by John of Cornwall in the tenth century, so there is proof that at least one source on the subject in a British language was available to Geoffrey, and there is no reason why we should doubt that others, perhaps now lost, also existed.[62]

It should not be assumed that Geoffrey or indeed any other twelfth-century scholar had no access to sources. Some of his sources were the same ones we now have, such as Nennius which we know Geoffrey used; others were different, such as the 'lost' texts mentioned earlier, or oral traditions that have disappeared between Geoffrey's time and our own. It is certain that sources were available and being transmitted effectively from the sixth century to Geoffrey's day. The romance of Tristan, for instance, was based on some real sixth-century events and was incorporated in the original of Beroul's poem. Geoffrey himself is very clear and straightforward on the issue. He said he could not find any written account of the kings before or after Arthur, 'although their deeds be as pleasantly rehearsed from memory by word of mouth in the traditions of many people, as though they had been written down'. As Dickinson sensibly observed a hundred years ago,

> no manuscript has reached us from Arthur's time, but there were those who could compose, remember and recite the leader's deeds. What was crystallized in metre was easily remembered and handed down with fair accuracy. Oral tradition is not to be ignored.[63]

The transmission of information in the Celtic world was mainly oral, so we have to accept that the history of the sixth century will be likely to survive to later centuries mainly in the form of recited ballads, songs, funeral panegyrics, elegies and triads, in other words, in poetic and musical forms that were relatively easily committed to memory. The memorizing was done by highly trained bards and when the material was eventually written down, in the seventh, eighth, ninth or even later centuries, much of it will have arrived in little-altered condition. A lot of this written recording was done in South Wales, where independent British kingdoms still survived. Geoffrey himself set a high value on the material he acquired in this way, as did his slightly later Icelandic counterpart, Snorri Sturluson (1179–1241). In his preface to *Heimskringla*, a prose history of the early Norwegian kings, Snorri shows how aware scholars of his time were of both the value and the danger of using this kind of evidence:

> In this book I have transcribed traditions of those chiefs who ruled in the northern lands . . . as I have heard them from men of knowledge, and also certain of their genealogies as they have been taught to me. Some of this is found in the ancestral pedigrees in which kings and other men of noble lineage have traced their kindred; some, however, is derived from old poems or narrative verse composed for entertainment. And although we do not know the truth of these, yet we know this much, that men of knowledge in past times have held them to be true.[64]

The Stonehenge theme, often dismissed as legendary, may be explained by a genuine association between Ambrosius and the ancient monument. If Ambrosius's power base was near Amesbury, as the place-name (Ambres-byrig) suggests, that base could have been the adjacent hillfort of Vespasian's Camp, which stands within sight of Stonehenge (see Plate 2.1).

The figure of Merlin may as he stands be a fiction, but he was developed in part from the personality and exploits of one or more of the sixth-century saints or pagan magi who were Arthur's contemporaries. We know from accounts of other kings of Arthur's day in Britain, Brittany and Ireland that it was common for them to adopt a holy man, pagan or Christian, according to royal taste. It is also clear that Geoffrey was not the first to write about Merlin. He drew on a thoroughgoing ninth-century British saga tradition and probably some semi-historical material too relating to the bard Myrddin. The distinguishing feature of Geoffrey's account is that he changed the name – from Myrddin to Merlin.

Plate 2.1 Stonehenge

Merlin comes across as a magical, semi-pagan figure, while Arthur is a Christian hero. This we perhaps take for granted now, after reading the Arthurian literature that, often at several removes, is based on Geoffrey, but it stands in distinct contrast to other eleventh- and twelfth-century portraits of Arthur, which show him as a perverse, lustful anti-hero. The eleventh-century *Life of Illtud* is a conventional genre piece in which Illtud is made to visit Arthur's magnificent court, where the king functions as no more than a foil to the saint's Christian virtues: Arthur is shown as grasping, tyrannical and childishly greedy.[65] Geoffrey's image is in this respect much closer to the Arthur we glimpse in *sixth*-century sources, and that suggests that he had access to material based on a reliable sixth-century tradition.

Large numbers of the personal names and place-names in Geoffrey's history are real, even if they are often distorted out of recognition: this suggests that we may be seeing the end of a long, possibly mainly oral, tradition. Arthur, he tells us, was crowned by Dubricius, Archbishop of Caerleon. As we know from the independent evidence of the genealogies, Dubricius was a contemporary of Arthur's, and Caerleon was on the same evidence a likely location for him. Piran (Piramus in Geoffrey's text) and Samson, Archbishop of Dol, are mentioned as Arthur's contemporaries, as indeed we know they were. Although Samson was probably not driven out of York, he was certainly driven out of other places. Piran is described by Geoffrey as Arthur's 'own chaplain', and it is worth remembering, in the context of later chapters when we will attempt to follow Arthur to his den, that Piran was not only based in Cornwall, but had his hermit's cell on the Camel estuary.

Geoffrey has been proved right by archaeology in some unlikely and unguessable details.[66] For instance, he connected Vortigern and his son Pacentius with Ireland,[67] and this seems to be supported by ogham stones at Ballybank and Knockaboy which have Vortigern's name carved on them.[68] The remarkable and intrinsically unbelievable story of Merlin bringing Stonehenge from Ireland seemed entirely fanciful until the discovery in the twentieth century that the bluestones at Stonehenge had in fact been transported from south-west Wales. This story was clearly not an invention of Geoffrey's but based on a mainly oral tradition of great antiquity: what he described was a version of what really happened in 2100 BC.[69]

There are countless other significant and telling details too. Geoffrey said the Venedoti decapitated a whole Roman legion in London and threw the heads into a stream called Nantgallum, or Galabroc in the Saxon tongue. When the Saxon tongue prevailed, Galabroc became *Wallbrook*. In the 1860s a large number of skulls were found in the bed of the Wallbrook, providing apparent confirmation of Geoffrey's story of massacre and mass decapitation.

Nor are the seemingly anachronistic Roman names Geoffrey uses an anachronism. We know now from the study of inscriptions that it was relatively common for British families in the post-Roman period to use Latinized names sometimes, so names such as Lucius, Urbgennius, Richerius and Borellus were relatively normal for Celts in sixth-century Britain.

It has been generally assumed that Geoffrey invented the Cornish setting for Arthur, that folkloric associations between various Cornish locations and Arthur's name grew up in the middle ages following the publication of Geoffrey's enormously popular book. There is nevertheless strong evidence that Geoffrey did not invent the Cornish setting, that instead the people of Cornwall held a strong oral tradition of a Cornish Arthur well before Geoffrey wrote his book in 1135. A book by Herman of Laon, written soon after 1145 describes a fund-raising tour in northern France straight after the fire at Laon in 1112.[70] In the following Lent, when the funds ran out and the rebuilding work was still unfinished, nine Laon canons set off again to 'Danaxaveria',[71] the English West Country, where they were told they were in 'terra Arturi', the land of Arthur. They had Arthur's Oven and Chair pointed out to them. The Oven has been identified as the King's Oven on Dartmoor, an ancient tin-smelting furnace at SX: 674812, which could easily have been on the canons' route from Exeter to Bodmin. In Bodmin itself there was a fracas when one of the French party ridiculed the locally held belief that Arthur was still alive. Some have suggested that Herman made up the story after the publication of Geoffrey's book, but obscure local dignitaries are named accurately and they are consistent with the 1113 date; this indicates that real events are being related, and that they were recorded when they occurred, well before Geoffrey's book was written.[72] This is the first documented post-sixth-century reference to real enthusiasm for Arthur, and the earliest reference to any special region claiming to be Arthur's kingdom. On that level alone, the story must have a claim to our attention.[73]

Finally, the status of Tintagel in the sixth century is under review. The Ralegh Radford view of the Island as a monastery has to be set aside because of the extraordinary range of imported pottery found there. It is thought now that it makes better sense to interpret Tintagel as a high-status secular or ceremonial site, and this means that Geoffrey was not necessarily wrong after all to portray it as a royal stronghold.

We are left with an intriguing problem. Much of what we read in Geoffrey's book is unreliable and unacceptable as it stands, but there are some extraordinarily vivid historical fragments visibly embedded in the fiction. He gives the date of the Battle of Camlann, for instance, as 542, which is accurate within 3–5 years of the date we find in the Easter Tables, 537 or 539. Geoffrey was determined to turn what he had into a good story, so some parts of the narrative have to be rejected. In the end, none of it can be accepted unless it is corroborated.[74] Sometimes discovering how and why Geoffrey's version is wrong can open new doors of understanding and interpretation. For example, Geoffrey's assertion that Arthur was Uther's son is probably unfounded. Geoffrey used Nennius as a source and Nennius described Arthur as *mab uter, id est filius horribilis*. It has been convincingly argued that here the Welsh phrase *mab uter* means 'marvellous son', just as helpfully translated in the Latin phrase that immediately follows; Geoffrey jumped to the conclusion that *uter* was Uther, making Arthur 'son of Uther'.[75]

Geoffrey and, in the same way, the whole raft of medieval romances that followed stand under suspicion. They cannot be used unsupported as evidence for anything. It is only when used in conjunction with independent lines of evidence from other sources entirely that they may shed significant light. Each line of evidence, whether documentary or archaeological, is in itself partial, incomplete. Each is a thin beam from a spotlight: but if several spotlights shine from different directions, even if dimly, they can reveal the figure at the centre of the sixth-century stage – and reveal him in the round.

CHAPTER THREE

THE ARCHAEOLOGY

Background problems

In the *Laws of Hywel Dda* there are inventories of the objects to be seen in a typical free household in Celtic Britain. The lists include boilers, blankets, bolsters, coulters, fuel axes, broad axes, augers, gimlets, fire-dogs, sickles, baking griddles, trivets, pans and sieves. Archaeologists have turned up scarcely a fraction of these at any site, illustrating the first major problem in dark age archaeology: that what survives in the archaeological record is only a small part of what actually existed.

Disentangling the chronology of the fifth- and sixth-century sites we are interested in is made harder by the lack of new coins in this period. The Romans issued coins which were in circulation in Britain, but these began to go out of use after about 430. The Saxons were to issue coins of their own in the seventh century; but in the two hundred years in between no new coins were issued. This inevitably leads to imprecision in dating Arthurian period sites.

A third problem is that the map of dark age Britain is far from complete. Some sites have been identified because of name survival. *Badon* has been recognized as Bath.[1] *Cat Coil Celidon* must be in Caledonia, and the Southern Uplands have been suggested. *Linnuis* has been identified as Lindsey (Lincolnshire.) *Dunatt* is easily recognized in the virtually unchanged Dunadd. Some sites identified by name have also been verified by archaeology. The Dunatt mentioned in the *Irish Annals* is easily identifiable as a natural rocky stronghold on the Crinan isthmus in Argyll. The Mote of Mark was occupied at the right time to be associated with a living Tristan. There is also the well-known association of the South Cadbury hillfort with Camelot – a tradition mentioned by Leland – and it has been confirmed by Leslie Alcock's excavation that the hillfort was indeed re-occupied during the Arthurian period. At the same time, a great many sites mentioned in the annals or romances are very difficult to identify.

The pattern of British and Saxon burials suggests that, in the fifth century at least, Britons heavily outnumbered Saxons. At the time of Ambrosius and Arthur, the patterns of settlements, ports, roads and strongholds in Britain must still have been predominantly British. Nevertheless, when early fifth-century settlement sites in the upper Thames Basin are mapped and compared with those for the late fifth century, change was clearly under way; in the earlier phase there were concentrations near the major river confluences at Abingdon and Dorchester-on-Thames, whereas later settlement spread up the Thames and its tributaries to give a diffused pattern across the whole region. This may reflect the spread of Saxon colonization through the Upper Thames Basin, or, more likely, the displacement (flight?) of the British westwards as the Saxon threat from the east strengthened.[2]

Few dark age farmsteads have been identified and excavated. The humble site at Gwithian in Cornwall is nevertheless probably representative. The people there ate their food from very practically designed and stoutly made round platters which were 15–30cm in diameter with flat bases and low vertical sides to stop the food falling off:[3] this sensible design was suitable for almost any meal. When working the land, they methodically manured it with domestic waste from the middens round their settlement, using a land management practice known to have been in use in the iron age.[4] In fact it is likely that throughout the west, where the impact of Rome was slight, the 'iron age' way of life continued more or less unchanged through the Roman occupation and on into the post-Roman period.

Another example, at Holyhead on Anglesey, shows a similar farmstead that was rebuilt at intervals. Of the eight houses found there, probably only two were standing at any one time; three gave radiocarbon dates in the sixth century and were associated with the cultivation of the surrounding fields. They were 9 or 10 metres in diameter with south-east-facing entrances. The stone walls were probably low, with conical thatched roofs supported on post-rings.[5]

Limited archaeological excavation may be supplemented to an extent by place-name evidence. *Tre-* place-names in Cornwall, for instance, are thought to have been coined as early as the sixth century, so it is possible, at least in western Dumnonia, to map the rural settlement pattern, which was fairly dense but extremely dispersed, with settlements spaced 600–1000 metres apart along the valley sides. High ground was avoided.[6]

The towns of the Roman occupation limped on. One of the commonplaces of histories of this period is the standard description of Roman towns abandoned and gradually crumbling to pieces. It has often been flatly stated that town life broke down in Britain;[7] but evidence concerning population in the dark ages is extremely difficult to interpret. It may be, as Arnold says,[8] that there was a marked reduction in numbers of people during the period 300–500 because of emigration, epidemics, falls in fertility rates, increases in mortality rates – but it is pure speculation. In the crucial period that we are interested in the evidence fails us. The collapse hypothesis rests too heavily on mentions of pestilence in Gildas and plagues in the annals, and on a shortage of positive evidence for post-Roman activity generally. Because the dark age settlement pattern is not fully known, attempting estimates of population totals or densities is fruitless. In consequence, we cannot assume that population totals declined; we cannot assume cultural decline or collapse either. There is also a widely held belief that climate deteriorated during the dark ages, presumably because of a residual belief in environmental determinism, but there is no evidence that agriculture stopped, and it would in any case take a substantial climatic change to marginalize agriculture in southern Britain. Changes there most certainly were, but they were changes in society, not environment.[9] It may be that the standard picture of empty and disintegrating towns sprang initially from Gildas, who wrote, 'Neither to this day are the cities of our country inhabited as before but being forsaken and overthrown still lie desolate.'

But in this, as doubtless in other matters, Gildas exaggerated. Although many Roman buildings fell into ruins, people went on living among them, if in smaller numbers. Isca (Exeter) in Dumnonia, Moridunum (Carmarthen), Venta (Caerwent), Magnis (Kenchester) and Viroconium (Wroxeter) in Wales and the Welsh Borders – all had some continuing existence as settlements. It is clear from the *Anglo-Saxon Chronicle* that the Saxons saw the cities as British power centres, mentioning kings of Gloucester, Cirencester and Bath. St Albans, a Roman cantonal capital with grandiose buildings, was being maintained by an active city council as late as 460, several decades after the Roman withdrawal. Some towns, such as Wroxeter, were substantially repaired and rebuilt. In the north of England, Isurium (Aldborough), Luguualium (Carlisle), Cataractonium (Catterick) and Coriosopitum (Corbridge) appear to have been the only Roman settlements in the Celtic upland areas to see any activity. In the lowlands there were the Roman cantonal capitals of Corinium (Cirencester), Durnovaria (Dorchester) and Lindinis (Ilchester). Some British elites of the post-Roman period went on governing their lands from these old imperial centres and held their courts in them. Carlisle, for instance, was the stronghold-city of King Urien of Rheged (Cumbria), just as Wroxeter was the capital of King Vortigern of Powys (Central Wales and the West Midlands) (see Figure 3.1).

But this must not be pressed too far. Many of the old native hillforts dating from before the iron age were also in use, and some of these were of greater importance in the armed struggle against the Saxons than the crumbling walled towns on the lowlands. Dorchester seems to have been abandoned for a substantial period between the fifth and twelfth centuries; two ditches dug right across the town site show that it was given over to agriculture. Nevertheless, some of the Roman buildings must have continued in use for a time, and perhaps right through the sixth century.[10] In the east, Canterbury too was in use for a time in the post-Roman period. A unique Visigoth gold coin minted in 480 shows that there was some sort of post-Roman settlement, but then there is a complete absence of any finds until the Anglo-Saxon houses that were raised at the end of the sixth century, apparently associated with St Augustine's revival of the city by rebuilding or restoring its Roman churches.[11] Lincoln's stone buildings continued to be used until 350, but went out of use before the end of the fourth century. The City of Lincoln seems to have been deserted by the time the large Anglo-Saxon cremation cemeteries were begun, in the surrounding countryside, in the early fifth century.[12] Lincoln was not occupied by the Saxons until probably as late as the ninth century: nothing has been found between a Roman coin from about 400 and Saxon pottery of the tenth century.

In some areas – Cornwall, for instance – no Roman towns had been established at all. There were no baths, theatres or villas with mosaic floors, and it must be remembered that in those areas the iron age lifestyle and organizational structure had continued more or less without interruption.[13] It must have been relatively easy in the fifth and sixth centuries for the Dumnonian chiefs to organize resistance to the Anglo-Saxon invasion as they had little adjustment to make. Iron age Dumnonia issued no coinage, and no royal or dynastic names survived from the iron age. These

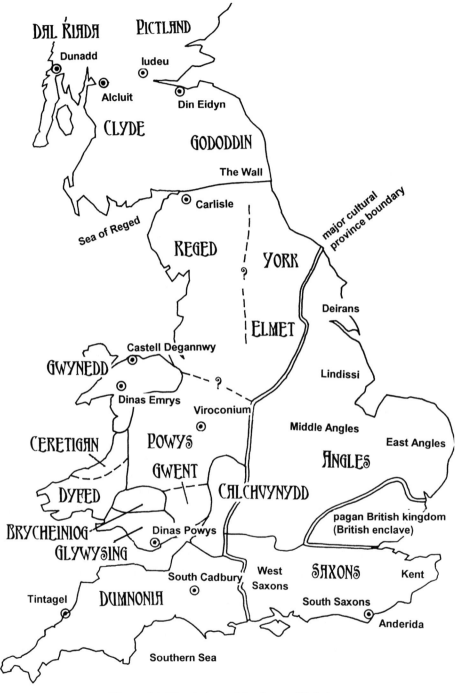

Figure 3.1 The dark age kingdoms of Britain
Source: After Dark (1994)

factors suggest that in the iron age Dumnonia was politically decentralized, with power dispersed among petty kings and chiefs: possibly there was no supreme monarch of Dumnonia at all, and this power structure, or lack of it, may have continued into the middle of the fifth century.[14]

Finds of fifth- and sixth-century pottery, some of it from the Mediterranean, can tell us which sites were high status. The distribution of these finds can tell us something of the political boundaries. In England, the distribution of findspots of Mediterranean ware coincides with the extent of the dark age kingdom of Dumnonia: Cornwall, Devon, Somerset and Dorset.

A fourth problem that besets archaeological studies is the wide variation in approach, with Roman specialists applying one set of methods to the pre-fifth-century period and Anglo-Saxon specialists applying a different set to the sixth and seventh centuries. The disparity makes the study of the 'interregnum' doubly difficult.

A fifth is that it is not certain whether sixth-century British kingdoms were unifocal or polyfocal. Was there, for example, a great king of Dumnonia with a stronghold and capital at Exeter, or was Dumnonia ruled by petty kings based in a score of minor centres, or was there an itinerant elite moving periodically, perhaps even seasonally, round a circuit of several major centres?[15]

Strongholds of the North

Dunadd

Among the high-status sites are many that were established long centuries before. The old sites had maybe acquired a special mystique through long use, as well as in many cases offering natural defence.

The fortress of Dunadd is a low rocky crag that presides like a disintegrating pyramid over the old trade route across the Crinan isthmus in Argyll. It stands for many another dark age fortress in that it was fortified earlier, in the iron age, then re-occupied after the Romans departed. When the Kintyre peninsula was colonized by Irish settlers in the fifth century and became part of the British kingdom of Dal Riada, the ruling dynasty made this little drystone-walled citadel, just 30 metres long, its capital and it continued in use for 300 years.

Though the citadel itself is small, natural terraces on the slopes around it were enclosed by loops of additional walling still a metre high, to make a series of 'baileys'. A narrow entrance passage was presumably closed by a wooden gate.[16] This type of nuclear fort can be seen elsewhere in Scotland too. Dunadd has been excavated, though not with any great care. Imported pottery found on the site shows its high status. Crucibles, moulds and stone sketch-pads were also found, showing that metal-work was forged: there was also a large range of iron objects, including tools, ornaments and spearheads.[17] The survival of the name 'Dunatt' from the contemporary *Irish Annals* almost unchanged to the present day makes it absolutely certain that this is the place referred to in the dark age documents.

Alcluith

The chief stronghold of the next kingdom to the east, Clyde, was also perched on a rock, Dumbarton Rock, or *Alcluith* (Alclud) as it was known in the dark ages. Alcluith meant 'Clyde Rock', while the later name of the adjacent settlement, Dumbarton, is derived from *Dun Breatann*, meaning 'Fort of the Britons'. Bede called it *civitas Brettonum munitissima usque hodie*, 'a town of the Britons, strongly defended right down to the present day [731]'. There is also a mention of the site in the seventh-century *Life of Columba*, which refers to 'King Roderc [= Rhydderch] son of Tothal who reigned in Alclut'. The natural defences of this site are formidable. It is surrounded by near-vertical rock walls that drop on three sides into the Clyde estuary.

So far the site has yielded very little of its past as a dark age fortress other than a scatter of imported pottery and evidence of metalworking there in the sixth century.[18] Quite how the site was used is unclear, because the rock's summit is restricted in area, much of it too craggy to be habitable. It is clear, however, from other sites that dark age fortresses were often less than a tenth of the size of their iron age forerunners, little more than massively defended royal households. Alcluith is likely to have been the principal royal stronghold of the kingdom of Clyde. A small-scale excavation in 1974–5 revealed a timber-reinforced rampart defending the landward side, but no surviving sign of any buildings in the interior.

Din Eidyn

Din Eidyn, now Edinburgh's Castle Rock, was the principal stronghold of the Gododdin, the kingdom that occupied the eastern half of the Scottish Lowlands and much of the Southern Uplands. The people of this kingdom were called Votadini by Ptolemy in the second century, but the name had been transmuted into Gododdin by the sixth century, when they were immortalized in the heroic poem, written around 600, which refers for the very first time to Din Eidyn, ancient Edinburgh.

So far the only traces of the dark age stronghold that have been found are some midden deposits that included a fire-steel and a double-sided bone comb,[19] but it was from Edinburgh's steep-sided volcanic plug that the Gododdin warriors set out on their long march south to attack the new Anglian kingdom of Deira, as described in the poem by the British bard Aneirin. Once again, the site is a relatively low but very steep-sided rocky crag with a small area for habitation on the summit.

Craig Phadrig

North of the Gododdin and the Clyde, the two halves of southern Scotland, lay the huge mountainous expanse of Pictland, which consisted of the entire Scottish Highland region. Some scholars have assumed it must have been divided into two, a northern and a southern Pictland, but there is little evidence for this. Bede's remark about King Bridei sugests that he was ruler of all the Picts. In one version of the Pictish king list, a king called Galam Cennaleth appears to reign with Bridei, though only for one year; this may be the Cennaleth, king of the Picts, whose death is recorded in the *Irish Annals* for 580. This may indicate a brief reign rather than two kings ruling two separate kingdoms, just as in an outline English chronology the entries for the years 1553 and 1936 might make it appear that there were three monarchs reigning at a time, when in fact they simply followed one another in rapid succession.

An alternative is that Bridei was Pictish overking and that Cennaleth was a sub-king.[20] It may be significant that Bridei kept both the regulus or sub-king of Orkney and some Orcadian hostages at his court, implying that his power was not unchallenged and that far-off Orkney had a tendency to go its own independent way.

It is often suggested that King Bridei's seat of power was Craig Phadrig, not far from Inverness; Craig Phadrig is an iron age vitrified fort that may well have been re-used in the sixth century. Asomnan describes St Columba as 'climbing the exhausting way up to king Bridei'.[21]

Carlisle

We know from late sixth-century amd seventh-century documentary sources that Carlisle was the capital of Rheged, the headquarters of King Urien. Its situation in relation to Cumbria, the Eden valley and the routes north, north-west and east made it an obvious location for an important administrative and political centre, yet so far no traces of the dark age British settlement there have been recognized.[22]

Strongholds of Wales and the Welsh Borders

Castell Degannwy

In Gwynedd, the mountain kingdom of North Wales, the tribal leadership probably survived unbroken through the Roman occupation, emerging intact when the Romans left.[23] This may account in part for the strength of their dark age kingdom, which had a long history. Colin Burgess has proposed that the major iron age tribal territories of Wales and the West Country (the Ordovices, Cornovii, Dobunni, Silures, Demetii, Dumnonii and Durotriges) were based on bronze age chiefdoms. Since the dark age kingdoms of Gwynedd, Powys, Calchvynnydd, Glevissig, Demetia and Dumnonia closely match the iron age territories, it looks as if the dark age kingdoms of Arthur's time may have existed for up to 2000 years.[24]

Castell Degannwy, Gwynedd's great fortress headquarters on a rocky twin-peaked hilltop overlooking the Conwy estuary, is a refortified iron age stronghold. The medieval castle embraced both peaks, but the dark age stronghold only occupied the larger, with its level summit area measuring 70 metres by 50 metres. The gentler slope on the east side was defended by a drystone wall which was exposed in two of the 1961–6 trenches at the northern end and in the centre of the eastern side, though the wall itself has not been dated. Between the two hills is a saddle and it may be that a bond settlement subordinate to Maelgwn's court was built there, but no traces of any buildings have been found.[25] Excavation produced sixth-century pottery, showing that the tradition that this was the seat of Maelgwn of Gwynedd may contain some truth. In fact its location close to the eastern frontier of Gwynedd suggests a frontier fort, and it may well be that the main residence of the ruling dynasty of Gwynedd was at Aberffraw on the west coast of Anglesey. Gildas's description of Maelgwn as 'dragon of the island' suggests that the king was based on Anglesey.

Coins of Valens (364–78) show that Castel Degannwy was occupied in the late Roman period, and it may have been occupied continuously from the Roman through into the post-Roman period. Pottery evidence strongly suggests that the citadel was in use in the fifth century as well as the fourth and sixth.[26] Class B imported wares from the Black Sea have been found here, marking this as another high-status post-Roman site, a likely royal stronghold.[27]

A substantial British town is thought to have been situated in the low-lying area between the hills of Degannwy, Bryn Maelgwn and Bodysgallen.[28]

Dinas Emrys

Craggier still is the hilltop of Dinas Emrys, 'the fort of Ambrosius'. The legendary confrontation between Vortigern and Ambrosius is said to have taken place here.[29] Excavations in 1954–6 by H. N. Savory uncovered part of a Class E cooking pot, an amulet with alpha–omega and chi–rho signs on it, parts of B amphorae and evidence of metal-working, therefore it was probably a prosperous and powerful Christian chief's stronghold in the late fifth and sixth centuries. The hilltop was about 150 metres by 100 metres and defended by a weak drystone wall. There is an eastern entrance defended by two outworks consisting of lengths of walling filling gaps in the crags. The walling cannot be certainly tied to the sixth century: it may be third or fourth.[30]

It is hard to believe, in spite of the name, that Ambrosius Aurelianus had any connection with this place.[31] Nennius seems to be referring to this same Ambrosius when he uses the title *Gwledig Emrys*. *Gwledig* means 'prince' in Welsh and *Emrys* is the Welsh form of Ambrosius. Although this might seem to associate Ambrosius with Wales, and therefore conceivably with Dinas Emrys, the Britons living in the West Country, the Severn valley, the Midlands and the north of England also spoke a language very close to Old Welsh. The fact that the form *Emrys* survives now only in Wales does not mean that someone called Emrys (or Ambros) in the sixth century was Welsh.[32]

Dinas Powys

In South Wales was the kingdom of Glevissig (later Glamorgan). Its principal fortress was Dinas Powys, just 5 km southwest of Cardiff. This sixth- and seventh-century site was discovered by chance during the excavation of an eleventh-century castle. In the late fifth century, the northern end of a steep craggy hill was cut off by a low bank 3 metres wide and just over a metre high with an external rock-cut ditch: this barrier enclosed an area 60 metres long by 30 metres wide. Inside were several carefully built hearths, especially in the north-east corner where iron-smelting and metal-working went on. The crag was evidently the fortified court of a powerful chief. Although no remains of buildings were recovered, two pairs of drainage gullies cut into the rock survived, and it is thought these mark the outlines of two buildings with bowed sides and rounded ends; the larger, probably the chief's hall, was about 10 metres long and 5 metres wide.

The eleventh-century rampart used some fresh rock but also large amounts of weathered rock and rubbish from the sixth and seventh centuries, showing that rock was taken from the ruins of the dark age castle. The dark age buildings probably had thick drystone walls and thatched roofs, but in terms of size the Dinas Powys buildings must have been fairly unimpressive compared with the hall at Castle Dore or, indeed, with earlier Roman villas. The iron-smelting furnaces were tiny, only 20cm across compared with the 1-metre diameter Roman furnaces, the crucibles no bigger than teacups, and there were only small quantities of slag, ore and cinders, so metal-working was on a very small scale. Conceivably the industry existed to ensure a supply of spear and arrow heads in an emergency and to repair the weapons of the chief's bodyguard.

Glass was imported to Dinas Powys, millefiori glass from Alexandria, probably with the intention of recycling old trinkets to make jewellery inlays. The craftsmen who made jewellery like the pennanular enamelled brooch found at Dinas Powys were probably itinerant.[33] The Dinas Powys chief and his retinue were great pork eaters. They ate bread and maybe cakes as well, as the round sandstone slabs used as baking griddles have been found. The small amount of evidence from the fortress suggests a domain where both stock-rearing and the cultivation of cereals went on.

The overall picture emerging from Dinas Powys is of a compact but well-defended homestead inhabited by a powerful chief and his retinue. It contrasts with the medium-sized and larger iron age hillforts of southern Britain which were probably designed to house a whole clan or tribe. This dark age 'shrinkage' was quite normal. For instance, the dark age enclosure at Garn Boduan was only 0.1 hectare, yet set within an 11-hectare iron age fort. Clearly the dark age strategy was very different from the iron age; defence was scaled down to the chief and his warrior elite, while the tribe as a whole went undefended.[34]

Viroconium

Between Glevissig and Gwynedd lay the huge and powerful kingdom of Powys, whose principal centre was Viroconium. The still visible and still impressive walls of Viroconium stand in farmland outside the village of Wroxeter near Shrewsbury. An ancient brick wall that dominates the site is the south wall of a huge aisled basilica that in 150 functioned as an exercise hall for the public bath-house. The visible ruins represent only a small part of the Roman town, much of which awaits excavation beneath the surrounding fields. On the opposite side of Watling Street, which ran right through Viroconium, is a long line of column bases, originally the eastern colonnade of the forum. When Vortigern made it his capital, much of the Roman town was still standing, and the location in the Severn's lowland valley next to the Welsh heartland was strategically important.

The excavation by Philip Barker in the 1960s provides evidence of Viroconium during the post-Roman period. Immediately after Roman control collapsed, Viroconium was substantially rebuilt, timber buildings replacing stone. Nor were these timber structures primitive in conception: they were big elaborate buildings of classical design, with symmetrical facades, colonnades and often a second storey. Then there was a second stage of rebuilding, still in the first half of the fifth century. This, probably the work of Vortigern, was even more grandiose in design. New buildings were raised and a new system of water mains and drains was installed; long stretches of Roman road were dug and relaid. The great Roman leisure complex was replaced by an industrial and trading centre, and the street passing to the north of the bath complex was transformed into a covered market or shopping arcade with workshops; at its western end, where it joined Watling Street, a big gatehouse with a guard-room was built; towards the eastern end were large storage barns beside substantial factories containing hearths and furnaces. The central focus of Vortigern's Viroconium was a massive winged building raised on the site of the Roman basilica; it was a pseudo-classical building with a clutch of ancillary buildings and outhouses, and it seems likely that this was Vortigern's palace.[35] Unfortunately there is nothing to be seen of the palace of Vortigern today; the site has been 'restored' back to its Roman state. Vortigern's palace stood on the levelled basilica site between the tourist kiosk and the imposing fragment of Roman wall known for centuries as 'the Old Work' (see Plate 3.1).

The archaeological evidence of revitalization at Viroconium is out of line with what we have been led to expect in Britain in the wake of the Romans' departure, and nothing quite like it has been found at any other Roman town in Britain. The implication is that some new, powerful, wealthy and well-organized authority took

Plate 3.1 'The Old Work' at Wroxeter, the ruins of Roman Viroconium. Behind this still-imposing wall stood Vortigern's post-Roman palace.

over, clearly not Celtic peasant villagers nor yet Saxon colonists. The writings of Bede, Nennius and the *Anglo-Saxon Chronicle* and the geographical location all favour the tyrant or overking Vortigern. Bones and other organic material found among the debris produced a mean radiocarbon date of 420; the date too favours Vortigern.

Excavations in 1979 uncovered the skeleton of a man buried on the site of a building that stood beside the market street. His grave had been dug through a soil layer that covered the rubble of the town after it had been abandoned. The skeleton has been radiocarbon dated, and from this, allowing for an interval for the soil formation, it is possible to estimate that Viroconium fell out of intensive use in about 520. By this time, the Arthurian period proper, Vortigern's dynasty was no longer in power. During the 1967 dig, a tombstone was discovered just outside the town with the inscription *Cunorix macus Maquicoline*, meaning 'King Cuno son of Maquicoline.' The name element *Cun* is often found in the Cunedda family, the ruling dynasty in the kingdom of Gwynedd, so it seems that in about 480, the date of the tombstone, Viroconium was occupied by the North Welsh.

The archaeological evidence suggests that, at its end, Viroconium was not burnt, destroyed or overrun by enemies. Instead it seems to have been taken down and moved away. The most likely explanation is that its low-lying site and two miles of perimeter walls made it difficult to defend. The ancient hillfort up on the Wrekin just to the south-east of Viroconium was an obvious alternative, so the occupants (or at least the elite) retreated up onto this higher ground. Since in 520 the Saxons were still held at bay far to the east, the only reason for this retreat can have been internal strife among the British war-bands. Even so, the process of dismantling and removal implies a strong, well-organized leadership in Powys in 520, just as a century earlier.[36]

Gloucester

To the south, in the lower Severn valley, lay the territory that before the Roman occupation had been the lands of the Dobunni: in the dark ages this territory seems to have been called Calchvynydd, and Gloucester was one of its principal centres. Gloucester was a *colonia* or provincial capital in the days of the Roman occupation, along with York, London, Lincoln and Cirencester. The Romans probably gave Gloucester the formal name *Colonia Nervia Glevensis* and called it Glevum for short, a name based on a pre-existing Celtic name. The post-Roman name was Cair Gloui. Like its peers, Gloucester probably had a palatial complex at its centre. The archaeological evidence from Gloucester suggests a change in the fifth century from the typical late Roman pattern to a polyfocal settlement including religious, market and elite residential functions.[37] These persisted through to the ninth century, when it became an Anglo-Saxon town. Certainly there is a certain amount of evidence that Gloucester was occupied by Britons during the dark ages,[38] in spite of the wholesale erosion of the levels dating from the fifth to eighth century.[39] During the Arthurian period the main street to the north was re-routed, passing through the ruins of the Roman baths palaestra.

Gleawcaester was listed as one of three British towns taken by the Saxons in 577 as a result of their victory at the Battle of Dyrham, and there must have been enough people in these towns for the Saxons to see the towns as worth taking, and for the taking to be worth boasting about. The running-down of the town during the fifth and sixth centuries, mentioned by McWhirr,[40] cannot have been too extreme. There is positive evidence that at least some empty Roman buildings were re-occupied, such as a Roman stone building with brightly painted walls and fine mosaic floors that was certainly in use in Arthur's time,[41] and on through the Saxon period. The road beside it remained in use throughout, too.[42] A few pieces of Bii amphorae imported from the Eastern Mediterranean suggest that there was an elite group in Gloucester, and that accords with the *Anglo-Saxon Chronicle* mention of a king of Gloucester called Coinmail. Coinmail's kingdom presumably extended into surrounding farmland, but how far is not certain. There are no fifth- or sixth-century Saxon cemeteries within 15 km of Gloucester and only one within 20 km, suggesting that British Gloucester commanded a territory of roughly that radius.[43] This reinforces the idea that the British petty kingdom of Gloucester coincided with the Roman *territorium*, which is thought to have been about the same size.

Gloucester was almost certainly occupied by Britons when the Saxons took it over. The latter evidently heard its name, Gleva or Gloui, from the Britons living there, incorporating it into their new name for the place, Gleawa-ceastor.[44]

Cirencester

Nor was Cirencester largely abandoned by the sixth century, as has been recently stated.[45] Doubtless fewer people were living there than in the Roman period, and many buildings were allowed to fall into disrepair. A certain amount of debris from this process of disintegration littered the town, but the courtyards or farmyards of the farming families who went on living there were swept clear, and footways were swept through the debris to enable people to move easily about the town.[46] The Forum was kept clear until the very end, which is often assumed to have come around 430;[47] but the sheer lack of coins, pottery and other datable material makes the end impossible to date, and Cirencester could have gone on functioning for another century, with the forum used for meetings or just kept clear out of residual civic pride.

The roadside ditch beside Ermin Street became filled with dark organic material derived from weeds and dead leaves, and this layer seems to indicate the final cessation of town life. The two bodies found not properly buried in the same sediment may be taken as evidence of civil order breaking down, in line with the received idea of Britain descending into chaos and mayhem after the Roman legions left,[48] or of an epidemic as McWhirr suggests,[49] but they could equally be seen as evidence of a violent Saxon take-over of the city in the aftermath of the Battle of Dyrham in 577.

The Roman amphitheatre just outside the town walls was converted into a fortlet; the north-east entrance was blocked and a big dark age timber building of uncertain shape raised inside. Possibly the population of Cirencester was not large enough to defend the long loop of city wall and the small fort was created as an emergency refuge, rather like an air raid shelter, for the urban population. Alternatively, it may have been created as a shelter specifically for Cirencester's king and his household during the run-up to Dyrham.[50]

Dark age Dumnonia

In west Dumnonia, that is to say in present-day Cornwall, it is possible to identify the dark age power centres with some confidence. There is in many instances a reassuring convergence of tradition, folklore, documentary evidence, place-name evidence and archaeology. There was tendency generally for pre-Roman sites to be re-used, which is probably more than just an economical way of recycling old earthworks; archaeologists tend towards the ideas that in the dark age west there was a reversion to the old pre-Roman ways, that in many areas the iron age society was scarcely touched by Rome, except perhaps to introduce a few luxury goods and some new ideas like Christianity to the native elites.[51] The general lack of Roman impact on Cornwall and the continuity of the regional name (iron age *Dumnonii* = dark age *Dumnonia*) suggest that the local tribal leadership and traditions were also continuous,[52] as they were in Gwynedd and Glamorgan, and possibly one or two of the other Welsh kingdoms.

In Somerset, iron age hillforts and hilltops perhaps previously unoccupied were occupied in the first and second centuries (e.g. South Cadbury Castle, Cadbury Congresbury and Glastonbury Tor), presumably as refuges against the Roman occupation. Cadbury was the scene of a massacre in 61. When the Romans eventually relinquished control in Britain and the new threat was from the Saxons, it was natural for the native population to look again to the old forts for their defence and as rallying points for retaliation. Probably over large areas of Dumnonia socio-economic control lay in the hands of Celtic kings and sub-kings through the iron age, the Roman occupation and on into the dark ages without interruption.

South Cadbury Castle

South Cadbury Castle is an imposing fortress occupying the summit plateau of a free-standing hill that prowls like a sentry beside the Ridgeway. Today the ancient fortifications are largely hidden by trees, but the four earth ramparts are still impressive (see Figure 3.2). The hill has a long history. People lived there from the middle neolithic (3500 BC) onwards. In common with many other 'iron age' hillforts, work on this one began in the late bronze age. The earliest date for the defensive works is 1040 BC. From then on, the fortifications were progressively developed and Cadbury became a very important Durotrigian central place in the late iron age, a focus of metal-working, trade and administration.

During the Roman occupation, the British were forcibly removed after a revolt in AD 61 and the site returned to agriculture.[53] In the post-Roman period around 500 South Cadbury was reoccupied and refortified by the British: this was during the Badon campaign to stop the Saxon advance westwards. There is a well-documented eleventh-century re-occupation of South Cadbury when moneyers from Ilchester on the low ground to the west took up residence in the hillfort in the face of a Danish invasion threat. It seems possible that something similar happened in the late fifth and early sixth centuries, when the Saxon advance will have prompted those living in undefended settlements to secure a refuge.[54] Ambrosius lived at the right time to organize the refortification of Cadbury in around 470, and it is likely that it would

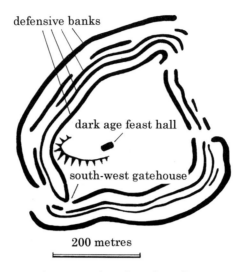

defensive banks

dark age feast hall

south-west gatehouse

200 metres

Figure 3.2 Plan of South Cadbury

have taken more than the resources of the local sub-king to organize something as large in scale.[55]

Cadbury may seem remote from the action at the time when the dark age rampart was raised, but the Saxons were already in the Oxford area, 120 km from Cadbury, 4 or 5 days' march or just 2 days' ride away.[56] When the refortification took place the late iron age earthworks were still very imposing, yet a completely new wall was built on top of the innermost rampart. Vertical timbers probably rose above the level of the solid walkway to support a plank or wattle breastwork. Horizontal timbers tied the vertical posts into the wall. Dressed stones from Roman buildings, perhaps in nearby Ilchester, were robbed to make the wall's core and drystone outer facing.[57]

After this work was completed, the major status of Ilchester probably transferred more or less automatically to the newly refurbished fortress. Nevertheless, Ilchester seems still to have been occupied in 500, when the name *civitas Durotrigum Lendeniensis* was mentioned: unless of course the name too had been transferred to South Cadbury.

Leslie Alcock's major 1967–70 excavations showed that in the Arthurian period an elaborate new south-west gate was built of timber on the site of the iron age entrance (see Figure 3.3). The size of the four gateposts implies that a substantial structure stood at this entrance, probably two or three storeys high to carry the rampart walkway over the entrance and provide a useful fighting platform. At ground level, the posthole arrangement shows that there was probably a double outer gate consisting of two doors each a metre wide, and a similar double inner gate. The design of the gate was almost certainly derived from Roman models, some of which may still have been standing only a few decades before Cadbury was refortified, so those who built the gates may actually have seen a Roman equivalent elsewhere.[58] It is tempting to think that whoever designed the Cadbury gate had seen the gates of Nanstallon, which were built to a ground plan based on six posts, but since Nanstallon seems to

Figure 3.3 Reconstruction of the Arthurian south-west gate
Source: After Alcock 1972 and Radford and Swanton 1975

have been abandoned by the Romans fairly early, before the end of the first century, it is unlikely that its wooden gates were still standing 400 years later – and there is no archaeological evidence that they were rebuilt.[59]

Inside the huge enclosure only a small area near the centre was excavated. Within that the plan of a substantial dark age aisled hall 19 metres long and 10 metres wide was recovered (see Figure 3.4). The 3- or 4-metre gaps between the posts were possibly filled with wattle and daub, and the presumed pitched roof was possibly thatched. The hall was divided into two rooms by a wooden screen two-thirds of the way along. A lens of ash in the middle of the larger room shows where the hearth was. Pottery fragments in the larger room were of the Bii amphorae (roughly 40cm high), while the pottery fragments in the smaller room were of the slightly smaller Bi amphorae.[60] What this means is not clear, but it suggests that the two rooms had significantly different uses: perhaps the smaller room was a service area or buttery. Its dominating position on the highest point at the centre of the enclosure reinforces the

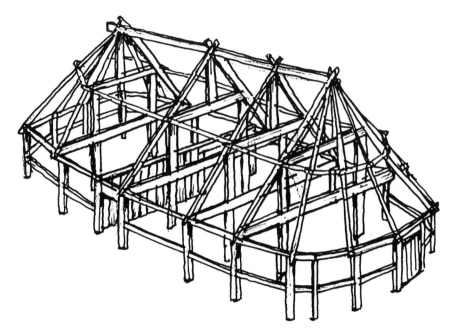

Figure 3.4 The Arthurian feast-hall at South Cadbury: a reconstruction of the timber frame
Source: Based on Alcock 1972

feeling that this hall must have been the principal building in the Arthurian period. Substantial though it is, the hall is only three-quarters the size of the great hall at Castle Dore yet, as Alcock says,[61] we can reasonably assume that it is the feast-hall of an Arthurian king.

The wall-line of the hall encloses thirty-six pieces of imported pottery. The presence of A-ware shows the hall was in use before 525; a ring pendant shows it was in use in 550 or so; the absence of continental E-ware shows that it went out of use before 600. So we know the hall was in use from the time of Badon to the time of Camlann, and possibly on to Dyrham. The concentrations of pottery show the location of the feasting that we know from documentary evidence British dark age warriors went in for: they were 'reared on wine'. We also know from documentary evidence that they drank from fine glass vessels, and the remains of these have been found round the hall at Cadbury and other sites. The glass vessels were imported complete, not made from smashed glass (cullet) as previously thought.

The two roundhouses that overlap the dark age hall may be iron age or early dark age in date: we know that a dark age roundhouse was built at Cadbury Congresbury. Maybe the round houses represent the Ambrosian phase, the rectangular hall the Arthurian: the question is unresolved.

Later, in 570, the roadway was re-surfaced, coinciding with renewed military activity on the 'Eastern Front'. This archaeological trace is evidence of the British resistance to a renewed Saxon thrust westwards, the Dyrham campaign.

Where Cadbury differs from most of the other dark age sites discussed is in the colossal area of the site. The area enclosed by the dark age wall is 7.3 hectares, at least five times bigger than most other dark age forts. It is not enough to explain this as Arthurian-period engineers simply following the pre-existing iron age defences; at other sites, such as Cadbury-Congresbury, old enclosures were subdivided and at South Cadbury it would have been relatively easy to confine the refortification to the (higher) northern half of the enclosure. For what reason would a dark age military commander have needed to defend such a large area, unless he wanted to provide a refuge for the war-bands from a very large hinterland?

The strategic position of South Cadbury makes this mustering very likely. It was centrally placed between Bristol and English Channels, and centrally within eastern Dumnonia. It was not too close to the 'war zone' with the Saxons, and this made it a relatively safe rallying-point in the period 500–570. It was also adjacent to the Ridgeway and the Andover–Lindinis Roman road and just 5 kilometres from the major Roman nodal centre of Lindinis: it would have been possible to get cavalry relatively quickly from here to any part of southern Britain. The complicated history of South Cadbury shows it to have been a centre of Celtic resistance to invaders at least three times – in the rebellion against Rome in 61, in the Badon campaign against the Saxons in 500–520 and in the Dyrham campaign in the years around 570.

Cadbury-Congresbury

The low hilltop of Cadbury-Congresbury at the northern end of the Mendips was one of several in east Dumnonia that was reoccupied in the first and second centuries during the Roman occupation, as is shown by the presence of Romano-British pottery, and then again after the Romans left. The fort stands on a defensible plateau of around 5 hectares and is enclosed by an earthwork raised in the iron age. In the dark ages some time between 400 and 600, the fort was divided in two. It was common at this time as we have seen to require smaller forts, presumably to shelter the local war-band and its leader rather than an entire population. Another change in this post-Roman period was the increasing use of local handmade pottery together with wares imported from the Mediterranean. This marks the site as another of the elite group of forts frequented by users of fine imported pottery.[62]

There was a large dark age roundhouse 11 metres in diameter, with a three-post screen set across its entrance, possibly for privacy or security, possibly as a wind-break. The house was kept scrupulously clean, which has led some to assume it was used for ritual, but it may simply be that the occupants had very good servants to clean up after them; there was a lot of pottery and glass just outside the door.[63]

To judge from the spacing of hillforts in Somerset, Cadbury-Congresbury's territory was about 8 kilometres across, a territory that would have offered diverse economic activities and a wide range of land uses: summer grazing, fowling and fishing down on the Levels, some high quality arable land, wooded hill slopes for timber and upland pastures.[64] But Cadbury-Congresbury is a paradigm for British dark age archaeology: only part of the picture is known. Only 5 per cent of the area of the hillfort has been excavated, which means that 95 per cent of it is unknown. Interpretation is not clear-cut either. It can be seen as having religious (whether Christian or pagan) as well as secular (whether elite or communal) elements; the site could have been generated and sustained entirely by the local community, the people living in the notional 'territory' just described, or by a colonial group or by members of some 'national' Dumnonian elite force. There are alternative ways of viewing the site too. It might be seen in dynamic, systems theory, terms, as one of a series of replacement centres following the collapse of the Roman central administration and the decline of Rome-run central places such as the towns and villas. It might be seen as an expression of the Celtic re-emergence, of the re-assertion of some elements of the pre-Roman system and a return to an earlier form of socio-political organization. It is probably most fruitful to think on these lines, and see the dark age centres of the west as signs of a regenerating chiefdom system, expressing an earlier, and perhaps very ancient pattern of segmentary societies.[65]

Glastonbury Tor

Glastonbury Tor was another hilltop of Cadbury-Congresbury type, in use in the Romano-British period and continuing into the post-Roman period.[66] Although from some angles the Tor looks like a pinnacle, there is a fairly flat area 30 metres by 15 metres on the summit and a gentle access ramp up from the west: the very steep slopes to east, north and south offer excellent defence. There is a shoulder or terrace 100 metres by 30 metres to the west and numerous smaller terraces on the other slopes. The conventional explanation for these terraces is that they result from agriculture, but they could, bearing in mind the occupation terraces on the eastern slope of Tintagel Island, just as easily have been made for settlement.

Professor Philip Rahtz excavated much of the Tor's summit and part of the western shoulder in 1964–6. Remains from the Arthurian period were found on the eastern and southern edges of the summit; on the summit itself and the shoulder they appear to have been destroyed by Saxon rock-quarrying and levelling for the building of a medieval church. The Arthurian remains were found covered and preserved by the products of erosion and weathering on the summit.

Two graves on the north side of the summit contained the remains of children, their heads to the south, generally a pagan orientation. The main approach was almost certainly from the west up a series of broad rock-cut steps which led to a series of platforms or terraces cut out of the bedrock. On these stood post-built wooden build-ings, though so little remained of them that it was impossible to work out their shapes. The rock surface was coated with enormous quantities of dark age dirt, including the remains of food which had evidently been carried to the Tor already butchered into joints of beef, pork and mutton. There was also a great deal of charcoal. More difficult to explain are the hundreds of ammonite fossils. Although these occur naturally in the bedrock here, they have evidently been collected together for some reason, and it is difficult to think of any practical purpose for the collection.

In the east was a hollow sharply defined on its eastern edge by the remains of a fence. Among the debris here were bits of Roman tile (for unknown use), a bone needle, several iron ferrules suitable for iron-shodding the pointed ends of stakes, and an iron lamp-holder. This holder would have been embedded in a stone or wooden wall: the exposed ring would have held a lamp. This provides positive proof of the existence of an inhabited building. A peculiar rectangular cairn 4 metres long also occupied the eastern terrace; it was oriented north–south, like the graves, and it looked very like a tomb, but was found to contain nothing at all. An alternative is that it was an altar; given the 'pagan' orientation of both graves and cairn, it would seem natural to assume that it was an altar for some form of pagan worship. Perhaps the ammonites were connected with this.

The south terrace, cut about a metre below the Tor's summit, has been naturally weathered away along its southern edge, where it was probably bounded by a wooden fence or palisade. Some of the postholes on this terrace were large, so a substantial building must have stood there. There were two hearths and the fragments of crucibles suggest that metal-working went on.

Amongst many other small finds, the dozen pieces of imported sixth-century Mediterranean amphorae must rank among the most significant, showing that the occupants of the Tor were members of the Dumnonian elite. Until 1972 a Mound marked the western extremity of the Glastonbury peninsula. Beside the River Brue, it would in dark age winters have risen out of sheets of flood water, an ideal place for landing imports of Mediterranean amphorae that were sent along the coast from Tintagel; a few fragments of these were found on the Mound.[67] On the Tor, a small cast bronze head was found, probably a mounting for a cauldron or the head of a staff: it is of great interest because it clearly shows the shape of a British warrior's helmet in the sixth century: hemispherical with a strengthening furrow across the brow and ear-flaps (see Figure 3.5). It was found close to the crucibles and hearths, so it may well have been made on the Tor.[68]

Glastonbury Tor would have been inconvenient to live on permanently, because it is cramped, exposed, windswept and a long way from water. Presumably this was the eyrie-fortress of the local sub-king, who took refuge here when danger threatened, quaffing Mediterranean wine and eating choice joints of meat carried up to him from the surrounding pasturage. It is assumed that the area was Christian by the sixth century, but little is known of the work of Christian missionaries here, and the area is deficient in Christian finds. The north–south burials and the unparalleled 'altar' strongly imply that this hilltop was a pocket of dark age paganism.

Maybe this was the refuge of Melwas, chief or sub-king of the Aestivo Regio, 'the Summer Land', the king whom Arthur besieged in his stronghold at Glastonbury, as

Figure 3.5 The dark age British warrior from Glastonbury Tor

we are led to believe by Caradoc of Llancarfan in his *Life of St Gildas*.[69] Melwas is said to have raped and abducted Guinevere, holding her captive at Glastonbury. Perhaps Arthur's wife was indeed imprisoned on the Tor by a pagan rival: the archaeology cannot contradict Caradoc. The 'island' of Glastonbury was in the dark ages defended to north, west and south by undrained marshland that was probably under a shallow sheet of water in winter. The Levels would thus have offered significant natural protection to Glastonbury. The dry-land approach from the east was a weak point, so it was defended by the Ponters Ball earthwork; this may bear comparison with the short but impressive *vallum* created at Tintagel to mark off the isthmus.

Tintagel

Tintagel was occupied in the late Roman period. In the 1956 excavation season, a hard dry object was found, apparently in the masonry of the Upper Ward; soaked in glycol by a boy in the village, the object turned out to be a Roman leather purse containing ten bronze coins dating from 270–361. The purse was presumably hidden in the ancient walling in the 360s.[70]

Tintagel was some sort of focus in the late Roman period, though it is not clear what its role was (see Figure 3.6). For a long time the existence of two Roman milestones or route markers in close proximity to Tintagel has been taken to show a Roman interest in the headland, certainly the existence of a road following the coast-line and used in the late Roman period (200–400). One, a granite pillar bearing the

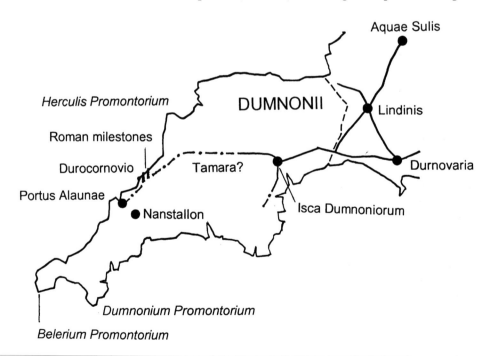

Figure 3.6 The late Roman *civitas* of the Dumnonii. The eastern boundary is uncertain; possibly the River Axe–River Parrett?

names of Gallus and Volusianus (251–3), was found at Trethevy on the modern coastal road (B3262) between Boscastle and Tintagel. The other, a large slab of slate, was found built into the lychgate stile of Tintagel churchyard in 1889. It dates to the reign of Licinius (308–24). There is no shortage of this type of stone, so it was probably obtained very close by.[71]

The distribution of parish churches and early medieval farmsteads suggests that by the eleventh century there was a well established near-coastal road route, skirting the deep coastal ravines: indeed, the road from Tintagel to Boscastle winding inland to avoid the deepest section of Rocky Valley is a classic example of this.

The *Ravenna Cosmography*, a list of itineraries compiled or copied in around 700, has a section relating to the West Country. The garbling of the names is extreme: for instance *Scadu namorum* is a corruption of *Isca Dumnoniorum* (ie Exeter). One sequence may include our Tintagel road:

Eltabo. Elconis. Nemetotacio. Tamaris. Purocoronavis. Pilais.

This has been reconstructed by Charles Thomas as follows:

Fl.[umen] Tavo. Fl. Cenio. Nemetostatio. Tamara. Durocornovio. Pilais.

In terms of modern place-names, this would mean, 'Crossing place on the River Taw, crossing place on the River Cenio, Bury Barton, crossing place on the River Tamar, Tintagel, Padstow'. (The River Taw seems to be misplaced in this itinerary, and should follow Bury Barton.) *Pilais* may be a corruption of *P[ortus] Alaunae*, the port on the estuary of the river Alan, the older name for the River Camel, so Portus Alaunae could be Padstow. The sequence of rivers and estuaries leaves Tintagel as the most likely location for the otherwise unknown Durocornovium or Durornavis, literally the Stronghold of Cornwall.[72] Roman red slip ware has been found at Tintagel, and on both east and west banks of the Camel estuary, at Padstow and St Enodoc.

There is thus a suggestion that even during the Roman occupation Tintagel was recognized as Cornwall's principal stronghold. What is surprising is that there is no pottery or other artefactual evidence of any earlier occupation of Tintagel Island. Given that, physically, the site would have been absolutely ideal for an iron age promontory, it is odd that it was not used for that purpose. Perhaps the island had some other function that precluded its military occupation at that time – an idea to return to later. In the dark ages, Tintagel Island continued to be a formidable citadel, protected on its landward side by a great rock-cut ditch. The local tradition was that the ruler who held this stronghold was King Mark, but there is no reason to believe it. The site's pre-eminence right across the Arthurian period (from 400 to 600) means we have to study it seriously within the Arthurian scheme, in spite of a whole body of literature, both academic and popular, which seeks to dissuade us from this course. Tintagel was abandoned after 600 and the Island remained unoccupied until 1230 apart from an isolated chapel built there in about 1000.[73]

The site was visited by Geoffrey of Monmouth, perhaps between 1120 and 1130 (certainly before 1138), and seen by him as an Arthurian site before the medieval castle we now see was built by Richard, Earl of Cornwall; the idea of the site as that of a castle must therefore have come to Geoffrey from some literary or oral source. Geoffrey describes 'the *town* of Tintagel, a place of great safety. There is but one entrance to it and that along a straight rock, which three men shall be able to defend against the whole power of the kingdom.' The chasm separating the Island from the mainland was evidently narrower in the middle ages than now, and there are mentions in both Leland and Carew of a bridge made of long elm logs connecting the two. Even allowing for the progressive erosion of the 'neck' it seems very unlikely that in Geoffrey's time there was an isthmus that could be walked across, but there must have been such an isthmus in earlier centuries. Geoffrey seems to have been describing the place before his own time, both in terms of its physical geography and in terms of the fortress or refuge, which had not been there for 500 years. This points to Geoffrey's use of oral tradition.[74]

When Geoffrey visited Tintagel Island there were no buildings on it at all apart from a small chapel. The small rectangular huts that covered the Island in the sixth century would not have been visible in the twelfth century. The few huts that were consolidated and built up for the tourists following the 1930s' excavations, and which are now very clear (see Plate 3.2), would not have been more than low bumps in the grass in Geoffrey's time. The destruction of a large area of turf in the central area in a fire in 1983 revealed the degraded footings of many more huts, but they had not been visible until then, even to the archaeologists. It turns out that these humble dwellings covered most of the available level ground. When standing to their full height, perhaps not much more than half a metre, and topped with a variety of roofs, some of slate,

Plate 3.2 Dark age dwellings on the east side of Tintagel Island

Plate 3.3 Tintagel Castle – high medieval version

some of skin, they would indeed have amounted to something that would have looked like the 'town' Geoffrey described. But he cannot have inferred that from what he could see at Tintagel; he can only have got it from some historical source, whether written or oral.

The castle was probably built at Tintagel in the thirteenth century as a piece of political propaganda to reinforce the Geoffrey of Monmouth version of Tintagel's connection with Arthur and to suggest the strength of Richard's own claim to the earldom, equivalent to claiming Arthur as an ancestor. Though curtain walls were built to Upper, Lower and Inner Wards and a Hall was installed in the Inner Ward, the medieval castle must always have been something of a folly, a make-believe castle (see Plate 3.3). It can never have been the thoroughgoing stronghold visualized in Thomas Hardy's drawing.[75] Richard was the brother of Henry III and created Earl of Cornwall in 1227. Between 1233 and 1236 he went to some trouble to acquire not only Tintagel Island but the manor in which it lay. The castle could therefore not have been begun until 1233 at the earliest.

Here, we are more concerned with what stood at Tintagel before 1200, before Richard's castle and before Geoffrey wrote about the site. It was obviously not a monastery, or Geoffrey would not have conjectured a castle. Only some slight bumps marking the footings of a few buildings at best would have been visible here and there, and a chapel on the top. Geoffrey has Ulfin say,

No power on earth can enable us to come to [Ygerna] where she is inside the fortress of Tintagel. The castle is built high above the sea, which surrounds it on all sides, and there is no other way in except that offered by a narrow isthmus of rock. Three armed soldiers could hold it against you, even if you stood there with the whole kingdom of Britain at your side.[76]

The 'narrow isthmus of rock' is gone, but there is still a recognizable path that is narrow enough for three soldiers to defend visible as the path leading to the entrance to the Lower Ward on the east flank of the Upper Ward (see Plate 3.4). It is currently 4 metres wide and it has been widened to accommodate the needs of tourism. Originally there was a path only about two metres wide here, between the high wall atop the crag on one side and the 5-metre deep (now only 3-metre deep) ditch on the other. It could indeed have been defended by a handful of soldiers. This creates a problem for the proposal that Geoffrey was describing not something that he saw but something that existed in the past and which he had heard about. The vallum certainly existed at the time when Geoffrey saw Tintagel, and it seems likely that this was created in the dark ages rather than later.[77]

Within this massive defensive ditch, i.e. in the Lower Ward, the remains of hearths have been found and dated by archaeo-magnetism to 450–500. Perhaps more of these existed on the narrow isthmus that once connected the Lower and Inner Wards, but they have crumbled away into the sea. The area beneath the Hall was also occupied in the fifth and sixth centuries. When part of the cliff collapsed immediately to the east of the Inner Ward's curtain wall in 1918, dark age pottery was found among the debris on the beach below.[78] Cuttings and photos of the natural exposures round the inner Ward show that in the fifth and sixth centuries there was a hollow or saddle sloping down towards the east under the site of the thirteeenth century hall.[79] This spot would have been well sheltered from north-west, west and south-west winds, a natural focus for a dark age habitation, whether the Island was used as a stronghold, refuge, royal dwelling, ceremonial or religious cult centre.

A circular granite rotary handmill of a known post-Roman type was found on the Island, showing that people ground grain there in the dark ages. The 1994 excavations uncovered large quantities of the Mediterranean pottery imported to Tintagel in the fifth and sixth centuries on site C and in an isolated excavation in the centre of the Island.[80] Large quantities of the same pottery were picked up by Ralegh Radford in the 1930s at many points, including the Iron Gate landing, north of the Chapel and the medieval walled garden.[81] The imports were finely made red-slipped bowls and dishes (Late Roman B and C in Mediterranean archaeology terms), amphorae and a grey ware with black slip; they came from Tunisia, Carthage and Asia Minor.[82] The North African dishes can be firmly dated to 525–35 in Carthage itself, and their exportation to Tintagel cannot be outside that period;[83] significantly this is the period between Badon and Camlann, the period when Arthur was in power. Some of the pottery, when broken, was recycled to make crude discs 6 cm in diameter, used as stoppers for amphorae and probably fixed with dabs of pitch. This proves that the landing of imported wares was not an isolated event but part of an ongoing trading arrangement. Some vessels from the eastern Mediterranean had Roman numerals scratched onto them, such as XXV, which suggests that they had been handled and transhipped somewhere in the western Mediterranean before reaching Tintagel.[84] One had a lading mark painted on its shoulder.

Plate 3.4 The Neck, looking from the Island, with the mainland
strong-point top centre

The people who occupied Tintagel in the dark ages were using local as well as imported pottery, simple food platters made of a serviceable hard-wearing grey fabric, very similar to the ones used at Gwithian.[85]

The archaeological evidence from Tintagel may look far from spectacular, but it does show that the place was occupied in the first half of the sixth century and that there were buildings across both the level plateau surface and down the sheltered slopes to the south and east. The imported pottery can be dated according to its fabric and style and much of it was imported no later than 535, i.e. during the reign of Arthur. Detailed excavations in the 1990s of some of the buildings on the narrow terraces on the north-east slope show what seem to be three distinct phases of occupation. In the middle of the fifth century there was a 'pioneer' phase. People occupied the Lower Terrace at Site C, lit fires there and put up simple windbreaks; they were not users of imported pottery. During the lifetime of Arthur the accommodation improved, with a proper walled and slate-roofed building as well as hearths; imported and native Dumnonian pottery were in use together (see Figure 3.7). In the later sixth century, after Arthur's death, there was further rebuilding, new hearths and, at least in this small area, even more imported pottery.[86]

What the dark age occupation of Tintagel and the importing of high-quality pottery meant is an open question. Maybe the site was a religious cult centre and the pottery was a series or even a single consignment of votive offerings. Alternatively, the site was a trading centre and goods were exchanged, but it is by no means clear what these exchange goods or materials might have been. It is legitimate to wonder why Tintagel is pointed out as a stronghold of King Mark in the Tristan cycle and why Geoffrey of Monmouth chose to make Tintagel the fortress of the Duke of Cornwall; presumably the Cornish had for centuries circulated stories that made Tintagel

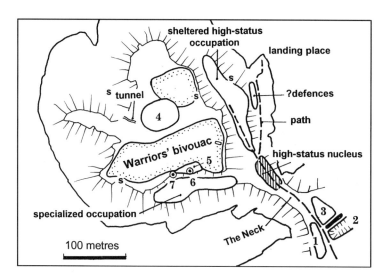

Figure 3.7 Tintagel: dark age functional zones. 1= walled strongpoint; 2 = defensive ditch; 3 = occupied forepart; 4 = caretaker settlement; 5 = ceremonial summit platform; 6 = King Arthur's Footprint; 7 = King Arthur's Seat; s = spring

the headquarters of the rulers of Cornwall. The idea that Tintagel was some sort of emporium for a hinterland seems an unlikely one, as there are far more obvious and suitable harbours, like the Camel estuary. Archaeology rules this out anyway, as there are far too few finds of the imports within the hypothetical catchment area, whether it is given a radius of 15 or 30 or more kilometres. The votive offering idea also seems unworkable, as a Europe-wide cult centre would surely have been documented by at least one Mediterranean commentator.

The most acceptable interpretation is that it was a secular citadel, defended from the sea by impressive cliffs and from the land by an ostentatious ditch and bank.[87] The windswept surface of the Island was probably uninhabitable in winter, so some seasonal or occasional use is implied. The importance of the site within Dumnonia is shown by the quantity of imported pottery: not only has more been found there than at any other site in Britain or Ireland, but more than at all the other sites put together.[88] The many small hutments emerging across the Island suggest that, on occasions, large numbers of people converged on it. This was a rallying-point for war-bands from all over Tricorium and possibly from all over Cornwall to swear fealty to a new king, engage in other ceremonies such as promotion from rank to rank, to hear discourse on important matters, possibly to vote, to be briefed before going off on campaign. It is likely that a dark age king with an entourage of 100–300 people would quickly exhaust the food supply in any one place in Cornwall, so itineration, moving on from place to place, would have been essential to the economy.

In the interior of Tintagel it is possible to guess at some of the specialized uses of space. The crag where the Upper Ward of the medieval castle was later built was an obvious strong point from which to supervise the entrance through the bank and ditch to the east. The Upper Ward has yielded dark age pottery, so we know that it was indeed occupied. Thomas suggests that the lower, rougher courses of the Upper Ward walling were standing in the sixth century,[89] and the find of the leather purse, apparently within this walling, implies that parts of it at least were actually built in the late Roman period.

The Lower Ward, which lies inside the citadel's entrance but before the narrowest neck of the isthmus, may have provided stabling for the warriors' horses. At the north-west end of the neck, on the site of the medieval hall, was the likely nucleus of the citadel, the lowest and most sheltered position and the first part of the site reached after the isthmus. The Iron Gate, a rock platform making a natural wharf with a defensive medieval (i.e. later) wall behind, is the likely dark age landing place.[90] While much of the rock platform is too high out of the water to have been used directly for loading and unloading, and the dark age sea level would have been a metre lower, there is a low shelf along the northern edge which is less than a metre above present high water mark, and this would have made an excellent wharf. A path still runs southwards up the slope from the Iron Gate platform towards the nucleus. Where the ruler's hall stood is at first sight not obvious, but it may have stood directly under Earl Richard's hall, at the upper end of the path.

Across the centre and south of the plateau were many rectangular buildings with slate footings and low turf walls held in place by rows of stakes. An arc of at least seven holes made in the rock where stakes were driven through the turves can still be seen on the southern edge of the plateau. The roofs would have been made perhaps of tarpaulins or animal hides. The exposed, windswept position of these lean-to huts suggests that they were accommodation for a war-band used to roughing it. Rough though the huts were, they were rectangular and that may mark them out as belonging to a special group. The norm for iron age and dark age housing in Cornwall seems to have been the round house so the use of a rectangular plan for the Tintagel houses suggests reservation for special use or for use by a special group of people.[91] Probably the turf walls and the skeletal timber frames were left there permanently, while the easily portable roof covers were brought in by visiting war-bands.

Another, smaller area to the north of the plateau, north of the walled garden, may have been more seasonal accommodation for the war-bands, although the presence there of what looks like the footings of a dark age hall suggests a more specialized use. Officers presumably had the accommodation on the terraces on the lee side of the Island. There were over seventy buildings in all.

The discovery of a slate plaque inscribed PATER COLIAVIFICIT ARTOGNOU on one of the eastern terraces was greeted prematurely as the proof we have been looking for (see Figure 3.8). The inscription means, 'Arthnou, father of a descendant of Coll, has had this [building] made'. Broken and recycled as a drain cover in the later sixth century, this stone appears to have been a wall plaque or name-plate for a building raised in the time of Arthur. Whether Arthnou and Arthur are one and the same person has not been established. Certainly this Arthnou was an educated nobleman who both knew and was proud of his lineage. Whatever else the plaque proves, it certainly shows that Tintagel was the focus in the early sixth century for an elite group of Britons, who included proud dynastically minded aristocrats. Whether traces of the building it came from, Arthnou's building, can be found remains to be seen.[92]

Tintagel churchyard, on the mainland cliff edge south of the Island, is also emerging as a dark age focus. The Roman and post-Roman coast road must have passed close to it. In the fourth century, Christianity had not reached Cornwall even as a minority faith except in St Ives Bay, where there are traces of Christianity from about 450. For the rest of Cornwall, the advent of Christianity was no earlier than 480–530, i.e. the lifetime of Arthur. Gildas upbraided a post-Arthurian king of Dumnonia, Constantine, for being a sinful Christian, a Christian in name only. Given the spread of Christianity into Cornwall from Wales from 480 onwards, it is

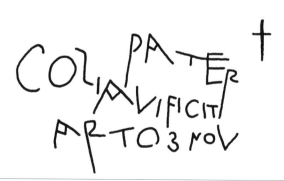

Figure 3.8 The inscription on the Arthnou Stone

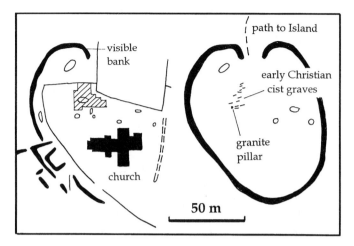

Figure 3.9 Tintagel churchyard. Left: today, showing area of 1990s' excavations (shaded). Right: reconstruction of dark age graveyard enclosure. At least three of the early slab-lined graves were aligned on the granite pillar.

reasonable to assume that whoever was the ruler at Tintagel at the time of Arthur would have been either first or second generation Christian. There is some evidence that there was a pre-Christian cist-burial cemetery on the site, as a slate box was destroyed in the field south of the churchyard in the 1950s (see Figure 3.9). There is excavated evidence of thirteen of the earliest known Christian burials, in slate-lined cist graves and unlined body-length hollows, all oriented roughly west–east.[93] At least three of the graves were aligned on an uninscribed granite pillar (see Plate 3.5), which shows a back-reference to the standing stones of the bronze age. Some of the graves had mounds raised over them, showing a kinship again with the barrow burials of earlier times. Pieces of imported Mediterranean pottery brought over from the Island were found and oak charcoal that had been burnt in about 500. The cross is scratched on some stones with the point of a knife, and the cross as a Christian symbol was not in general use in Britain until the early sixth century.

It is not known whether the sixth-century graveyard was open or enclosed, but it is likely that an open burial site with granite monolith and cist graves dating to 490–520 was enclosed with a curving, heart-shaped bank in about 550. Traces of this ancient bank survive in two sections, the modern churchyard boundary on the south-west, and a section outside the north-west corner of the churchyard. The ancient graveyard probably had its incurving entrance on the north, significantly oriented towards Tintagel Island, and it is certain that the (royal?) graveyard was intimately associated with the sixth-century use of the Island.[94] A road, still detectable as a hollow way, led north from the cemetery entrance to the Island entrance over the Great Ditch.[95]

The sixth-century soil gave seed evidence of the Tintagel environment. Oats were growing nearby, and hulled barley; there were also weeds common in arable land – fat hen, orache, corn marigold. Similar plant remains were found on the Island. There

Plate 3.5 The granite monolith

was also henbane, a poisonous plant associated with wilderness sites, so it may be that the graveyard was an oasis of overgrown scrubland amid the arable lands.[96] A tiny stone church or oratory 8 metres by 6, probably dedicated to St Petroc,[97] was built in the middle of the ancient cemetery in the tenth century, its south wall oriented towards the granite pillar. At about this time, the unique burial-less mound '1071' was raised over a carefully laid line of greenstone and quartz blocks: no-one knows what this peculiar structure was for, but it cries out to be described as 'ritual'. It looks as if unusual, archaic, backward-looking religious practices were a feature of the site right through to the tenth century.

Of the dark age burials at Tintagel, little more can be said. There were glass beads, slate pendants and some badly corroded ironwork. It may be that these few finds could indicate the status of the dead. The presence of special graves, that is to say graves with *unusual* characteristics, in Tintagel churchyard and the fact that there is a relatively small number of them suggest that this area may have been reserved as a royal burial ground and used very sparingly over a period of two or three centuries.[98]

The presence of both sixth-century amphorae and also at least one disc clipped out of an amphora to make a stopper implies that liquid, possibly wine or mead, was carried in stoppered containers across from the Island to the cemetery, perhaps for consumption in commemorative meals, on the Mediterranean model. Beyond that, little can be said except that the burial ground at Tintagel dates from the beginning of Christianity in this part of Britain and that it clearly was the burial place of a small Christian community or elite who were using Tintagel Island (see Plate 3.6) as a gathering place at the time of Arthur.

We may legitimately ask where Tintagel's territory or pagus lay and whether archaeology can define it. It is likely that the hundreds date from the dark ages (see Figure 3.10). Wivelshire formed one pagus, in south Cornwall, and Tricorshire or Triggshire another, in north Cornwall. Tricorshire seems to have survived as a complete entity until the ninth century. Trigg (Latin form *Tricurium*) is mentioned in the seventh-century *Life of Samson*. The word Trigg probably meant 'three war-bands' and therefore may indicate that within the original territory of Tricorshire there were three divisions, each contributing a war-band; in that case, the three later medieval hundreds of Trigg, Lesnewth and Stratton may conceivably represent the three dark age communities contributing war-bands to the warlords who summoned them to Tintagel. The land division would have been necessary in order to assess and levy military service, especially as the Saxons advanced.[99]

It was in about 575 that imports of luxury goods from the Mediterranean ceased. After that date supplies of pottery, glass and probably wine came from Gaul instead. It is not known how or why this change came about, but Alcock implies that as a consequence Tintagel went into decline, ceasing to be the major port to which imports were shipped.[100] Tintagel's dominance of the status hierarchy came to an end and it in effect disappeared for several centuries as far as the archaeological record is concerned. The explanation for both of these changes could lie in what was happening further to the east. The Battle of Dyrham fought in 577 was a decisive blow, with Saxons hammering on the north-eastern frontier of Dumnonia and cutting off Dumnonia's land link with the Britons in Wales. The reduction of Britain into a

Plate 3.6 View from Tintagel Island

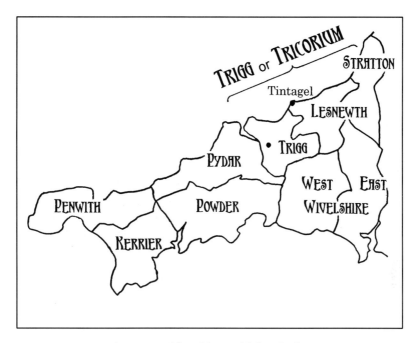

Figure 3.10 The old Cornish hundreds

number of separate and isolated 'islands' (Dumnonia, Wales and the North) seriously weakened the British cause, and may have weakened the Dumnonian high kingship. Maybe Dyrham precipitated a palace revolution in Dumnonia and the ceremonial and hierarchical role of Tintagel was removed, together with the costly high-status goods that went with the high status of the ruling elite. It must be significant that the feast hall at South Cadbury went out of use at about the same time.

Castle Dore and other sites

It was, above all else, the exotic pottery imported from the Mediterranean that marked Tintagel as a high-status site. There are seven sites in Cornwall that have the same pottery, though in much smaller quantities: these places too must have been used by the ruling elite. One of these special sites is Castle Dore, a small iron age hillfort commanding the low rounded ridge of the Fowey peninsula. It consists of a circular bank and ditch within a pear-shaped bank and ditch, each with entrances to the north-east. Castle Dore was apparently abandoned between 50 and 100, presumably evacuated when the Romans arrived in Cornwall. There is sharp disagreement as to the post-Roman history of the site, but the defences were evidently repaired: the fallen bank was strengthened with a drystone wall and the entrance was fitted with a 2-metre-wide rough cobbled roadway. A small oval porter's lodge was built within the gate of the inner enclosure on the south side.

More strikingly, the fortress was equipped with two large timber halls (see Figure 3.11). Stone-lined post-holes carried roughly squared timbers about 0.3 metres across. Hall 1 was an aisled hall of four bays, about 26 metres long and 12 metres wide. The post pattern implies a ridged roof, and the narrow side aisles suggest that lower pentise roofs may have covered them, with the main roof rising above a clerestory, Roman basilica-style. A fire burned on a huge central hearth, and there was a porch in the centre of the north wall. The side aisle was continued across the eastern end of the hall, reminiscent of the buttery passage of an Oxford college hall and possibly built for the same purpose: the discreet and efficient serving of food. There was a 7-metre square withdrawing room of some kind built onto the southern corner.

Immediately to the west of Hall 1 stood a second hall, rather smaller, of only three bays, but once again with an annexe built onto its southern end.

Two small rectangular buildings one or two metres across were built close to Hall 2. The stoutness of the posts that stood in these sockets implies that the structures were designed to carry a great weight: maybe they were tall grain silos, their floors raised well off the ground to fend off rats. Traces of other buildings have been seen elsewhere in the 1-acre enclosure at Castle Dore, but no more was excavated. Presumably there were kitchens, privies and stables somewhere in the enclosure. Unfortunately the dark age floor levels were ploughed off, but what survives looks very like a king's household as described in the ninth-century *Crith Gablach*.[101]

Dissenting voices have been raised, especially since Radford's interpretation of dark age Tintagel has collapsed. There is no positive dating evidence for a dark age origin for the two great timber halls, Quinnell and Harris argue,[102] so they may instead belong to the pre-Roman iron age. Even the imported amphorae, they argue, may be pre-Roman. The substantial halls nevertheless seem to belong more naturally to the sixth century, and they are admitted to belong to the fourth and latest phase of Castle Dore's development. There is a significant difference between the period IV structures and the earlier ones. Rahtz says that they could be Roman, but since there

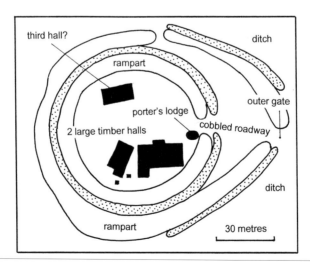

Figure 3.11 Castle Dore in the sixth century

were no Roman finds on the site it seems much more likely that they are post-Roman.[103] According to Rahtz at least five pieces of pottery are neither Roman nor iron age; the beads are most likely post-Roman. The small amount of available archaeological evidence therefore points to the final phase at Castle Dore belonging to the Arthurian period.

Local tradition has long held that Castle Dore was King Mark's palace, and the halls do seem to accord with the re-use of the round earthwork as a fortified royal household. The 'Lancien' of the early medieval *Roman de Tristan* may not have existed but if so it is hard to explain other than by coincidence the presence, close at hand, of an ancient farm called 'Lantyan'.[104] Near Castle Dore stands the famous Tristan Stone (see Figure 3.12), commemorating in sixth-century script the ill-fated son of Cunomorus, and Cunomorus was a Latin form of King Mark's name. If Mark had estates in Brittany too, as sixth-century documents attest, a Cornish base very close to a natural harbour on the south coast would have been essential.

CRVSTNVSHICIACIT CVNOWORIPILIVS

Figure 3.12 The inscription on the Drustanus Stone

On the east side of the Fowey estuary, roughly opposite Castle Dore, a defensive bank called Giant's Hedge begins, winding eastwards then south-eastwards to reach the Channel coast at West Looe (see Figure 3.13). This is thought to mark the boundary of a dark age petty kingdom and it may be that this together with the Fowey peninsula to the west of the estuary was King Mark's personal domain. When the post-Roman occupation sites of Cornwall are mapped, it can be seen that there is a much higher density of sites within the Giant's Hedge, i.e. to the south of it, than further inland. There are two further zones of higher density, one following the road from Padstow and Wadebridge to Bodmin and Liskeard, skirting the southern flank of Bodmin Moor, and the other in a broad belt following the route from Tintagel to Altarnun and Tavistock, skirting the Moor's northern flank. The distribution of inscribed stones confirms that these were major dark age routes, the Tintagel–Tavistock road continuing south-eastwards along the south-west flank of Dartmoor to reach the Channel coast at Bantham, 18 km south-east of Plymouth. Finds of fifth- and sixth-century imported pottery at Bantham imply that Bantham was a port. We have tended to assume that goods were imported straight to Tintagel, but perhaps some were imported via Bantham or Wadebridge and transferred to Tintagel by road.

Just 4 miles west of Castle Dore, at Trethurgy, is a fine example of a Cornish 'round'. This possibly late iron age, more likely dark age enclosure, with its bank, surrounding ditch and east-facing entrance is reminiscent of Castle Dore but covers only half the area. Presumably this was the household of someone of lower rank than at Castle Dore, but whoever it was they were of sufficiently high rank to possess

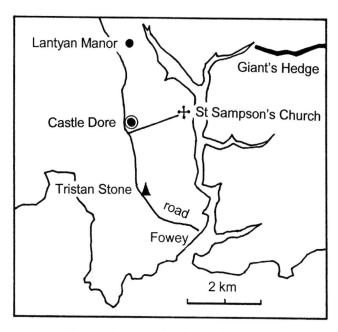

Figure 3.13 The Fowey peninsula: Castle Dore's setting

imported Mediterranean pottery. The entrance at Trethurgy was paved and defended by a wide double gate. Inside there were about six oval houses, each about 12 metres long, grouped round a stone yard.

Another site where sixth-century imported pottery was used was Chun Castle, far to the west in Penwith. Chun Castle, like Castle Dore, was an iron age fort that was reoccupied during the dark ages. Inside the two concentric walls are the remains of some round huts dating to the iron age phase, but most of these are obliterated by the footings of the rectangular huts raised in the sixth century. The fires in some of the huts were used to smelt iron and tin.[105] Two kilometres to the north-east of Chun is a sixth-century inscribed stone. Its inscription reads: 'RIALOBRAN. CUNOVAL. FIL', which means '[The grave of] Rialobran, son of Cunoval'. The names 'Rialobran' and 'Cunoval' literally mean 'Royal Raven' and 'Famous Chieftain,' and here we catch a glimpse of the style and self-image of the royal dynasty occupying Chun Castle in the Arthurian period. Two miles to the south-west of Chun Castle is another stone, the Selus Stone, thought to commemorate Selyf, the brother of Yestin (also known as St Just) and son of Geraint, a sixth-century king of Dumnonia.

Trevelgue Head on the north Cornish coast near Newquay carries a magnificent iron age cliff castle, a fortress defended on all sides by sea cliffs and six lines of ramparts and ditches. As at Tintagel, there was probably a narrow neck joining the island to the mainland and providing access at cliff-top level, but it has been eroded away leaving a deep sea-cleft which now must be crossed by a footbridge. Inside the fortress there were round huts excavated in the 1930s. One hut was 14 metres in diameter with stone walls and a central hearth. Trevelgue is a site of considerable antiquity and long continuity of use. There are two bronze age barrows in the fort, the defences were raised in the third century BC and the presence of sixth-century imported pottery shows that it was reoccupied in the dark ages as another high-status centre: almost certainly the power base of another dark age chieftain.

There are other Dumnonian sites that can be identified as power bases. At St Agnes, 12 km south-west of Newquay, there is another dark age boundary marker bank, Bolster Bank, marking off a relatively small domain 2 kilometres across. On the south Cornish coast at Trewithian, 9 km south-south-east of Truro, is the coastal iron age hillfort of Dingerein Castle. Although no sixth-century activity has been proved archaeologically, the name of the castle, Dyn Gereint, implies a local belief that it belonged to the sixth-century King Geraint, or Gerontius, of Dumnonia, who is known to have existed from documentary sources.

At St Dennis, 9 km north-west of St Austell, the parish church has been found to stand in a dark age enclosure. Close by is a farm called Domellick. And this brings us back, full circle, to Castle Dore. Here, as at Castle Dore, the ancient farm name confirms the link between the site and one of the threads in the Arthurian story. According to Geoffrey of Monmouth, it was at Damelioc that Gorlois, Duke of Cornwall, had his second castle, his first being Tintagel. While not amounting to proof, this is an interesting convergence of archaeology, place-name evidence and Geoffrey of Monmouth's version of oral tradition. There is also a suggestion here that dark age chiefs had more than one castle each: a useful idea to bear in mind when we come to consider Arthur's association with dark age fortresses.[106]

CHAPTER FOUR

ARTHUR'S BRITAIN

———·◆·———

Arthur the great, the tower of spears.
(Attributed to Taliesin, *Gorchan Maelderw*)

No cataclysm overtook Britain when the Romans abandoned it. Contrary to popular belief, fifth-century Britain without Rome was in a vital and vigorous state and to a great extent the Romans had prepared the way for their departure by allowing the native dynasties to rule as clients of Rome; this in turn allowed a continuity of culture and polity from the pre-Roman period that could be resumed later. When Diodorus described Britain in around 50 BC, before the Roman occupation, he described an already ancient and evolved way of life, with the island divided up into a multiplicity of kingdoms: 'Britain . . . is held by many kings and potentates, who for the most part live at peace among themselves.'[1] These many kings and their kingdoms and dynasties continued without too much interference during the Roman period and carried on after the Romans went away. The vigour of post-Roman Britain is amply proved by the way it resisted invasion; the Britons successfully fended off a concerted Pictish attack from the north and an Irish invasion along a wide front from Argyll to Cornwall in the west: it was only in a limited area north of Strathclyde that the Irish were able to gain any lasting, regional, toehold on the mainland of Britain.[2] Small-scale Irish infiltration nevertheless did occur; the distribution of ogham inscriptions shows that there were several areas, such as west Wales and west Dumnonia, where the Irish were able to settle (see Figure 4.1).

Nevertheless, there were changes. When the legions left, many external stimuli to the economy were removed and the emphasis shifted. Imports and exports went on, but probably on a smaller scale than before. The central organizational thrust from Rome itself had gone and there was a tendency for Britain to fragment, to fall back on pre-Roman tribal groupings, to implode, from the Roman perspective to under-develop. Societies in general became more local in orientation, economically less ambitious, with less pressure to generate surpluses for trade: there is little evidence of surplus extraction of any kind, little evidence of kingly ostentation. There appears to have been no money, which must have been a serious inhibition to trade. The settlement evidence shows a mainly agrarian peasant society based emphatically on

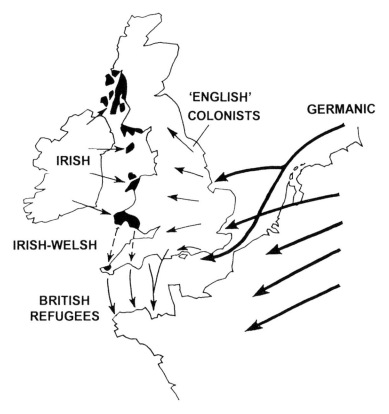

Figure 4.1 Migrations of the fifth and sixth centuries. Black areas represent Irish colonies.

family and kinship ties.[3] Yet there were exceptions. There were elites who strove to achieve more than subsistence. There were leaders who were keen to re-establish what they saw as the best in Roman values, to co-ordinate resistance to invaders; to do these things they had to construct, resurrect or exaggerate hierarchies, and find ways of displaying relative status within their society. The ostentatious use of fine pottery imported from the eastern Mediterranean or North Africa was one way in which this status could be expressed, and there will have been many other ways that are archaeologically invisible.

The landing of large quantities of expensive Mediterranean pottery and wine at Tintagel tells us that some equally valuable resource or manufactured product must have been exported, at least from Dumnonia. There is nothing on Tintagel Island itself or the immediate area that could have been exported or exchanged, so the resource was brought to Tintagel, as Charles Thomas suggests, under some system of enforced obligation, and the hierarchy of kingship would have come into play here in forcing the populace to produce, supply and transport it. There are later hints that it might have been tin. The *Life of John the Almsgiver*, an Egyptian saint, was written in about 625; it mentions a ship sailing from Britain to Alexandria with a cargo of tin.[4] It is likely that the tin trade was flourishing a century earlier, though so far no traces of tin have been found at dark age Tintagel.

The export may have been perishable, archaeologically invisible commodities, such as cloaks, dogs or horses – or even people. There is evidence that slavery and a thriving slave trade were commonplace in Arthur's time. Certainly slavery was a major feature of the Anglo-Saxon world: Bede refers to the slave trade as an aspect of commerce between Anglo-Saxon England and Europe.[5] It was also a major feature of the Roman culture that Arthur inherited, and a major aspect of the relationship between Rome and Britain. Tacitus, writing in the first century, said that one of Britain's attractions was the number of slaves to be had there.[6] It may be that the distinctive drum-shaped brochs built in the extreme north of Britain were designed and built specifically to provide protection against slave traders.[7] There is archaeological evidence of slavery in Britain in the first century. A votive hoard found in a sacred lake at Llyn Cerrig Bach in 1943 included an iron slave-gang chain complete with neck shackles. We can assume that Britons were regularly captured and abducted as slaves by the Romans until around 400, and that this practice was part of Arthur's post-Roman cultural inheritance.

Slaves were not just part of the Roman social system, but of the British and Anglo-Saxon social systems too. The social divisions in sixth-century Britain were fundamentally the same as those of the late Roman empire.[8]

ROMAN	BRITISH	ANGLO-SAXON	MODERN ENGLISH
imperator, *dux bellorum*	*amerawder*, *gwledig*, *pendragon*	*bretwalda*	overking, 'emperor', commander-in-chief
rex	*tighern*, *gwledig*	*cyning*	king
homo nobilis	*uchelwr*	*eorl*	noble
comitatus	*teulu* or *altrix*	*heord-geneatas*	king's hearth companion
ingenuus	*boneddig*	*frigman*	free-born citizen
colonus	*taeog*	*theow*	bondman, unfree
servus	*caeth*	*esne*	slave

There were slight differences, and Anglo-Saxon society was slightly different again, as we can see in the seventh-century laws of Kent and Wessex.[9] There were, for example, far more slaves in Anglo-Saxon communities than in British, but there were slaves in all of them. Presumably most were acquired by abduction, and provided a major motive for warfare.

Gildas, writing about Britain just after Arthur's death, mentions slaves: in his opinion, St David was too radical in preferring slaves to their masters. St Patrick gives evidence of the slave trade in the half-century before Arthur. In about 405 or 410 Patrick was himself abducted as a 16-year-old boy by Irish slave traders and sold to a chief called Milchu in Antrim. He managed to escape after six years of captivity and trained as a priest in Gaul before returning to convert his captors. As a slave himself,

Patrick had the strongest personal motive for preaching against slavery. In an open letter probably written between 440 and 450, he censured King Coroticus of Clyde for stealing Irish women and selling them to the Picts.[10]

> You kill [baptized captives] or sell them to a foreign people which does not know God: you commit the members of Christ as though to a brothel . . . God will judge. So then, what of Coroticus and his villains, those rebels against Christ? Where will they see themselves, they who allot poor baptized women as prizes, for the miserable temporal kingdom which will in any case pass away in a moment?[11]

Coroticus was one of the outstanding members of Clyde's ruling dynasty, and it is likely that his seizure of Irish women for resale in Pictland was prompted by economic motives, to keep his 'miserable temporal kingdom' going, rather than by wickedness. When the Romans were trying to control the north, they were probably glad to delegate the policing of the two walls to the local dynasties of Clyde and Gododdin, work that would have been handsomely rewarded. When the Romans withdrew, the two kingdoms were left with a significantly reduced income, and the slave trade may have been seen as an alternative source of income, a way of reflating a sagging economy. Slave-trading was very profitable, and the kings of Clyde were conspicuous for their wealth: probably, in Arthur's time, much of this wealth was based on the slave trade.[12] When St Columba made his famous visit to Bridei, king of the Picts, he asked Broichan, Bridei's chief magician, to set free his Irish slave girl. This shows that the flow of slaves into Pictland continued through Arthur's lifetime and beyond.[13] There is also a Pictish carving showing people sitting on chairs, and a near-naked man sitting abjectly on the ground: he, presumably, is a slave.[14] The Taliesin poems show that hostage-taking was routine, and maybe some hostages were eventually returned, but it is easy to imagine hostages becoming slaves as warfare dragged on without resolution. 'They [the warriors of Gwallawg] will take wealthy hostages from Caer Glud and Caer Garadawg and the post of the land of Penprys. O Gwallawg, kings are stung to silence and submit.'[15]

The attraction of slave trading to British dark age kings is obvious. Slaves commanded a high price and if there was a military machine in place to defend the home territory, or even launch an attack on the Saxons, it could equally be deployed in raids to acquire slaves. In the absence of coinage, the word for slave-girl, *cumal*, became the standard monetary unit in Ireland, and it was equivalent to three cows, which gives a good idea of the high value of slaves. In St Patrick's time, Irish warriors returned home from raids on Clyde, Rheged, Wales and Dumnonia enriched by slaves, and some of these warriors became so rich they were able to set themselves up as lords. Male slaves were often found as the personal servants of kings.[16] Given the cultural and economic climate of the time, it is likely that most British kings were involved in the slave trade. We cannot exclude the hero Arthur from this sordid commerce; indeed, he is likely to have been a more active slaver than most kings, partly since he commanded the military machine needed to acquire slaves, partly because he presumably needed a significant source of wealth to fund the campaigns against the Saxons.

This brings us back to the mystery of Tintagel, where we know expensive goods were unloaded in large quantities. Were they perhaps exchanged for slaves gathered in Dumnonia and further afield by Arthur and his war-bands, slaves for shipment to the Mediterranean? Was Arthur's wealth and the transient wealth of early sixth-century Dumnonia based on the abduction and sale of slave-girls and slave-boys? If so, it could be that the collapse of the British slave trade was at least partly responsible for the system collapse that led to Dumnonia's decline. We need to examine why the demand for slaves within the Roman Empire may have dropped during the latter part of Arthur's reign.

It was Justinian I (about 482–565) who was emperor of the Eastern Empire from 527. His was one of the most brilliant and successful reigns in the history of the late empire, in that under his generals Narses and Belisarius the Empire was largely restored to its ancient limits and the Eastern and Western Empires were reunited. There was an outbreak of political unrest that almost toppled him in 532, but it was vigorously and violently suppressed by Justinian's generals and he remained in power. Under Belisarius, the Persians were defeated at Dara in 530, the Vandals in North Africa were defeated twice in 534 and 535, and Sicily was conquered in 536. These major conquests flooded the Roman Empire with huge numbers of cheap slaves in the 530s. The Mediterranean demand for British slaves therefore vanished, and also the profitable trading relationship between Dumnonia and the countries of the eastern Mediterranean. Justinian's conquests seriously weakened the position of Arthur and his successor by undermining the source of their wealth, in effect devaluing the only international currency they had.[17]

St Germanus and Vortigern

St Germanus of Auxerre made two visits to Britain. On his first, in 429, which was intended to investigate the Pelagian heresy that had taken root in Britain, he found southern Britain under the rule of one man. The Romans had shortly before relaxed their formal control over the island. In 410 the Emperor Honorius had been unable to respond to British pleas for reinforcements to keep invaders at bay and the British had become in effect independent by default. Coel Hen, a northern chieftain, had been appointed *Dux Brittanorum*, and the island had begun to fragment in a series of civil wars. Yet by 429 a large area had been drawn back together into some semblance of unified control. This was achieved by Vortigern, a mysterious figure who is of interest because he in some ways foreshadowed Arthur, and who had become king of Powys in 420.

This powerful kingdom comprised the mountains of central Wales, the lower hill country of the Welsh borders to the east and a large slice of the West Midlands. The capital of this kingdom was the Roman, now post-Roman, city of Viroconium (Wroxeter), which stood more or less in the centre of the territory. Vortigern had partly rebuilt it.[18] It may be that St Germanus, a visiting bishop who nevertheless led a British army, was instrumental in restoring east central Wales to Vortigern's control in 429: his confrontation, rather than battle, with interloping Saxon and 'Pictish' (possibly Irish?) settlers was described to Germanus' biographer by Lupus, who was at Germanus' side. Vortigern certainly gave Germanus the impression that he was in overall control in southern Britain, and there are several references elsewhere to a great king who ruled the south at about this time. Gildas, writing later, referred to Vortigern as a *tyrannus superbus*, a proud tyrant, but this is likely as with some of the other names he used to have been a play on words, just as 'Caninus' was a joke, a scathing nickname for a king called Cynan; in Ireland the title *superior tyrannus* was in common use to describe an overking, and Gildas's phrase is almost certainly a reference to this.[19]

Some think Vortigern was a royal title rather than a personal name. 'Vawr-tighern' means 'overking'[20] and it may be that more than one powerful ruler held this title. It would explain how it was that when Germanus returned in about 446, seventeen years later, southern Britain was still in the hands of 'Vortigern'. Against the idea that Vortigern was a grandiose royal title is the evidence that some very humble and ordinary people were also called Vortigern; one of them, known by the Cornish variant form 'Gurthiern', was a hermit monk who came from northern Britain and eventually settled in a cell by the River Tamar.[21] Whether Vortigern was a title or a personal name, John Morris argues that it is easier to explain events if at least two kings called Vortigern existed, one of whom was also known as Vitalinus. The existence of at least one King Vortigern is confirmed by mentions in both Gildas and Nennius. In Welsh sources he appears as Gwrtheyrn Gwrthenau; although this name seems very different, the word Gwrtheyrn means 'supreme leader' in Welsh. The problem may be resolved quite simply; one or two successive charismatic leaders were known by the title Vortigern (= overking) and subsequently there was a fashion for naming children Vortigern as a personal name.

The Vortigern genealogy according to Nennius' *Historia*

Glovi (eponym of Gloucester)
   |
Guotelin (Vitalinus, also known as Vortigern [the Elder])
   |
Guital (Vitalis)
   |
Guorthigirn (Vortigern [the Younger])

The great Vortigern, if seen as one king, ruled as high king of Southern Britain from around 425 until 447. What happened to him then is unclear. There are several different lurid versions of his fate, and this in itself may support Morris's idea of there having been two or more King Vortigerns who suffered different fates. Vortigern the Elder, Vortigern Vitalinus, may have died or abdicated in 447 and been replaced by Vortigern the Younger, who Morris thinks may have been called Britu.

The closing years of Vortigern's (Vortigern the Elder's) reign were darkened by a double disaster, an overt attack from the north by the Picts and a more sinister and treacherous attack from the east by people of Germanic origin . These are sometimes conveniently lumped together as 'Saxons', as frequently they are in this book, and sometimes, with a misleading air of precision, distinguished as Saxons, Angles and

Jutes, more often generalized as 'Anglo-Saxons' or even, especially later on, as 'English'. These people from the eastern shores of the North Sea had begun arriving and colonizing eastern England in small numbers even during the Roman occupation; now they came in increasing numbers, exploiting the political fragmentation of Britain and the lack of strong military control. Vortigern unwisely took on Jutish mercenaries under their leaders Hengist and Horsa in an attempt to keep the Pictish invaders from the north at bay, while at the same time opening the door to more Jutes settling in Kent.

A third attack came from within the British community. A nobleman called Ambrosius the Elder ('Emrys' in Welsh sources) launched a rebellion against Vortigern in 430, apparently in protest against Vortigern's use of Germanic auxiliaries and the costs that this must have involved in increased taxation. But by 440 Vortigern was enlisting more mercenaries from the same source, and in the following year their numbers were large enough for them to begin demanding higher payment from Vortigern, in what is called the First Saxon Revolt.[22] Vortigern gave them the Isle of Thanet at the eastern end of Kent. The dangers of employing Hengist's and Horsa's mercenaries were now obvious, and Vortigern's son Vortimer took an army to drive the Jutes back through Kent and confine them to the Isle of Thanet, at that time still separated from the mainland by a broad stretch of open water, the Wantsum Channel.[23] Vortimer himself was killed in the fighting.

There are three independent sources for the historicity of these events, which illustrates how some rather tenuous and individually doubtful dark age material may, to within a little, be reconciled and corroborated to tell the story more fully and objectively. It is Nennius who tells us that Vortigern's son Vortimer drove the Jutes back to Thanet and was killed in the process. Celtic sources speak of three great battles, one on the Darent, one at a ford called Rithergabail (in which both Horsa and Vortimer's brother Categirn were killed), and one at Richborough in which the Jutes were defeated and Vortimer was killed. The *Anglo-Saxon Chronicle* also speaks of three battles that took place in the years 445–50. The first was the Battle of Aylesford, a river crossing on the Medway, and it was in this that Horsa died. The second was at Crayford, on the River Darent, and was a Jutish victory in which the British were pushed back from Kent into London, then the heart of an independent Celtic kingdom. The third battle was at 'Wippedsfleot', apparently the old name for the Wantsum Channel, and since this is not claimed as a victory in the *Anglo-Saxon Chronicle* it is probably the same battle as the one at Richborough in which the Jutes were roundly defeated.

Among other things, this episode shows how important natural features were in the unfolding of events. Two of these decisive battles were fought close to major fords across estuaries, the third close to a crossing to a refuge island. The importance of physical geography in the Arthurian story will emerge again and again.

While Vortigern's campaign against the Jutes was in itself successful, he lost two of his sons and his forces were depleted by plague. At the same time the Picts resumed raiding in the north of Britain and the Irish raided west Wales. It was at about the time of the Battles of Aylesford and Crayford that St Germanus made his second visit. He is said by his biographer Constantius to have joined in the fighting against 'Picts and Saxons' during his earlier visit to Britain in 429 but there is no reason to believe that he took part with Vortimer in any of the battles against Hengist and Horsa.

The Jutish army remained bottled up in Thanet for about five years before breaking out in 465.[24] There was no lull in the struggle between the Germanic incomers and the native Celts as the Saxons (in the broad sense) established their control over patches of Eastern England. The British response was to rebel against Vortigern, in about 459. As the situation became increasingly unstable and unsafe, many of the surviving members of the British nobility in Eastern England emigrated to Brittany. The Battle of Wallop may have been the decisive battle which toppled Vortigern from power. Morris suggests that it was in this battle that Ambrosius the Younger defeated and deposed Vortigern.

Ambrosius Aurelianus

The origins and status of this Ambrosius are unclear, and it is odd that he is mentioned by Gildas and Nennius but not by any other historian until the middle ages. He nevertheless undoubtedly existed and his existence is attested by a score of place-names that seem to have origins in a personal name like Ambros or Emrys, still just recognizable even after the English colonists added English endings. He seems to have been a Celtic nobleman, and it has been argued that the 'Ambros' place-names may represent the stations of units raised and led by Ambrosius and styled 'Ambrosiaci'.[25] The location of these garrisons is significant. One group surrounds and seems to protect the territory of the Dobunni (known as Calchvynnydd in the dark ages).[26] A second group of Ambrosiaci was positioned in the Lee and Stort valleys, well located to defend London, then a British enclave, against attack from the East Anglians along the Roman roads from Cambridge and Colchester. It is nevertheless unclear how Amberley in West Sussex, so close to the South Saxon heartland, could have functioned as such a base.

The Latinized form of his name could have been accorded by a chronicler, or adopted by Emrys himself as a mark of formal respectability, something other British noblemen also did: it does not prove, as some have suggested, that he was a member of a Roman family who stayed on after the Roman troops left. Ambrosius Aurelianus is the only person of the villa-owning class of rural landowners mentioned by Gildas. It is interesting that Gildas makes no attempt to locate his military activities, and it may be that he did not fully understand how and where this man who lived a century before him fitted into the sub-Roman scheme of things.[27] The reference in Gildas to Ambrosius' parents as 'Roman' and 'wearing the purple' may have been no more than figurative; he was probably trying to establish in his reader's mind the family's patrician, Romanized political leanings, which we know were shared by other dark age princely families.[28] Ambrosius represents a class of post-Roman or sub-Roman aristocrats who clung to an older order of things and disapproved of Vortigern's reckless politicking with the untrustworthy Germanic colonists. It seems likely that the two Ambrosiuses, Elder and Younger, were father and son and formed a focus for dissent among the Britons over the way in which Vortigern was leading the confederation to disaster.

There is nevertheless another view of Ambrosius. In the late biography of St Germanus contained in Nennius' *Miscellany*, as opposed to the earlier and more reliable biography written by Constantius (410–80), Ambrosius is described as 'the great king among all the kings of the British nation'. This may mean simply that Ambrosius' reputation grew steadily after his death and that he was in effect promoted by history, rather as Arthur was to be a little later. It may alternatively be an accurate reflection of Ambrosius' status during his lifetime. Maybe this document is telling us that he was *dux bellorum* or commander-in-chief – there is really no equivalent modern term – a kind of overking. A *dux* was able to muster and lead into battle not only his own people or *gens* but warriors from other clans as well. If so, it will reflect in several significant ways on the likely rank or status of Arthur himself when we come to consider it later. It has been suggested that the term 'Aurelianus' was more a title than a name. Cynan of Powys was later also called Aurelianus or Aurelius. This may have been another title of the *dux bellorum*.

Myres proposes that Ambrosius owned land at Amesbury, which was spelt *Ambresbyrig* in a charter dated 880[29] and may therefore derive its name directly from Ambrosius himself; 'Amesbury' would therefore be a very rare survival of a post-Roman estate name. If Ambrosius held Salisbury Plain or at any rate this part of it, he would in effect have controlled the north-eastern corner of the iron age Durotriges tribal territory that seems to have survived into the dark ages as a British territory. The Battle of Wallop, in which Ambrosius is thought to have deposed Vortigern, was fought within 12 km of Amesbury, and therefore in the marches of this territory. Whether the Durotriges territory remained an independent territory as Dark believes or formed part of a greater Dumnonia is not known.[30] This greater Dumnonia would have comprised Cornwall, Devon, Dorset and most of Somerset. In favour of the greater Dumnonia is the distribution of early sixth-century imported Mediterranean pottery, which is found throughout the enlarged kingdom, but not beyond its boundaries: in other words, not north-east of the Wansdyke. The Wansdyke lies only 12 km north-east of Amesbury. If Ambrosius was the landowner at Amesbury, he occupied a key position to defend the Celtic West Country and would have been keenly aware of the danger of any penetration further west or south by the Saxon invaders. He also stood to lose more than any other landowner by any such incursion.

Where Ambrosius' stronghold was is not known. The obvious candidate in the Amesbury area is the iron age hillfort known as Vespasian's Camp, 2 km east of Stonehenge. This spacious fortress would have made an excellent rallying point for the forces Ambrosius gathered; it would also help to make sense of the association Geoffrey of Monmouth made between Ambrosius and Stonehenge.

Wherever Ambrosius the Younger was based, we are told that from about 460 he organized a national (i.e. island-wide) resistance of the British citizenry to the Anglo-Saxon invasion. In 461 Hilary became pope. At about the same time a chieftain from Southern Scotland, from a kingdom called Manaw Gododdin, was evidently invited to North Wales to help the Britons expel Irish settlers; Cunedda and his Gododdin followers founded or re-founded the north Welsh kingdom of Gwynedd as a British kingdom. Meanwhile, to the south and south-west of Gwynedd the Irish were allowed to establish themselves in Demetia (Dyfed).

Ambrosius' campaign against the Anglo-Saxons prospered. The *Anglo-Saxon Chronicle* is silent about this period, suggesting that the British were in the ascendancy: there is no boast of Saxon victory until 473.[31] The British monk Gildas enthused about Ambrosius: 'though brave on foot, he was braver still on horseback'.

This implies a preference for cavalry action, which his successor Arthur would also exhibit. 'The Britons fled to him like swarms of bees who fear a coming storm. They fought the war with Ambrosius as their leader.'

In the 470s, three new warriors appeared on the British scene to change the situation. Hengist was still the Jutish leader, but by 473 his son Aesc had emerged as a major warrior and general, his father's right-hand man; in that year the Jutes succeeded in pushing the British army right out of Kent, completing and consolidating the break-out from Thanet launched eight years earlier. A second major event was the birth of another, even more important, young warrior, Arthur, who was born around the year 475 and was later to serve as lieutenant to Ambrosius.[32] A third major event was the arrival on the coast of Sussex, from 477 onwards, of a new group of Saxon settlers under another young leader, not yet a king, called Aelle. With the British army under Ambrosius forced back out of Kent by the Jutes, the South Saxons were able to establish a small but powerful bridgehead on the Sussex coastal plain and eastern South Downs. They were to a great extent insulated from events in the rest of Britain by a broad east–west clay zone of forest and marsh, crossed only by three (probably deteriorating) north–south Roman roads. Ambrosius could have entered the new Saxon heartland from south Hampshire using the South Downs Way had he wished, but it may be that the infiltration appeared too localized, too small in scale, too insignificant to be worth attacking. It may have been thought that the Britons based in and round the old Roman fort of Anderida (Pevensey) could deal with the invaders. If so, the threat from the newcomers was seriously underestimated, and Ambrosius repeated the mistake his predecessor Vortigern had made with the Jutes.

Aelle, the leader of the South Saxons, is a fascinating and instructive figure in that his career closely paralleled Arthur's. They were near-contemporaries, with Arthur born just as Aelle's military career was beginning, in the mid-470s: Arthur was perhaps twenty years Aelle's junior. Indeed, it is likely, as we shall see later, that they met, perhaps repeatedly, in battle and came to occupy similar ranks as supreme commanders in their opposing armies. When doubt is cast on the historical existence of Arthur on the grounds that too little is known about him, we should remind ourselves that very little is known about Aelle, yet no-one has seriously questioned *his* historical existence.

Nothing, for instance, is known about Aelle's ancestry or antecedents. There is no reliable genealogy of the South Saxon royal family and the relationship between Aelle and the rulers whose names appear in Sussex charters recording land grants only 200 years later is unclear. His sons according to the *Anglo-Saxon Chronicle* were called Cymen, Wlencing and Cissa, but these names may well have been invented by the chronicler to fill a gap in his information and in an attempt to post-rationalize place-names such as Cissbury, Chichester (Cissa's Ceaster?) and Lancing. In support of this fabrication hypothesis is the fact that none of the three names for Aelle's sons appears in a genealogy for a later king, sub-king or duke mentioned in a seventh-century charter. Incredibly little is known about Aelle, yet he successfully founded the colony of South Saxons and became, as Bede tells us, overking of all the Saxons, the first bretwalda or overking of Saxon 'England'.[33] This must also have happened as a result of Aelle's personal seniority among the Saxon kings or his reputation as a military commander, as it is clear from the chronicles that the tiny kingdom of Sussex never conquered Kent, East Anglia and the middle Thames.[34]

This is very reminiscent of the scanty knowledge we have of Arthur's antecedents, family or successors. We know little except that for a brief time he emerged as the key figure in a great military and political struggle.

Christian missionaries

Another thread in the story of Arthur is Christianity, and it was in about 480 that St Illtud, bred in the steady manners of a pre-war civilization,[35] founded his monastic school at Llantwit in Glamorgan, next to a ruined Roman villa and discreetly hidden in a side valley 2 km back from the coast. It was quite common to hide settlements in this way; Llys Bradwen in Gwynedd is a later example of a secular settlement carefully secreted on a hillside. The pattern of establishing a monastic community close to a villa site can also be seen elsewhere, for example at Cadbury-Congresbury, and it has been suggested that the founder of the religious community in each case was the post-Roman aristocrat who had inherited the Roman estate. Certainly many of the fifth- and sixth-century saints came from princely families and Illtud was said in the sixth century to have been Arthur's cousin, though he must have been some twenty years older than the king. He was ordained by Dubricius in the time when Merchiaun Vesanus (Merchiaun 'the Wild') was king of Glevissig (Glamorgan).[36] Many of the boys who passed through Illtud's school were, like himself, from aristocratic families, educated from the age of 5 and then sent out into the world at 16 or 17 to be enlightened influences as scholars and missionaries in a disturbed and unstable world. Illtud's achievement was considerable, in turning out men of the calibre and importance of Samson, Paul Aurelian, Gildas, Leonorus, David and possibly Maelgwn, king of Gwynedd. Early accounts stress Illtud's gentle understanding of his pupils; we know of his efforts to make the 15-year-old Paul Aurelian reconsider his decision to seek a hermit's life, to make him examine deeply his motives for wanting to do this, yet ultimately allowing the boy to make the decision. He is known to have been alive in 525, when Leonorus was 15, but dead by 547, when Samson left Britain.[37]

The motives and methods of these men can be traced in early documents that rest on contemporary originals. Lest it should be imagined that St Samson was a fictional character invented by chroniclers, his existence is documented independently, as he is recorded as attending a church council in Paris in 557; Gregory of Tours dated the events that led Samson back to Brittany to the closing weeks of 560. He died shortly after this, apparently of old age. Samson was born in about 490, and was therefore around fifteen years younger than Arthur. The oldest surviving *Life of Samson* dates from about 600, but rests on a contemporary original written by Samson's cousin Enoch, who probably wrote down what he knew before the saint died and is known to have gone to the trouble of interviewing Samson's mother for details of his childhood. Enoch's nephew also travelled to Britain to collect extra information.

Sources such as these early *Lives* give us a remarkably clear picture of the aristocratic society into which Arthur was born, and more importantly how that society looked to people who were alive at that time. Samson's father was a Demetian

(SW Wales) landowner and also an *altrix*, a companion of the king, who was then probably Agricola. The idea that Samson should attend Illtud's school came from 'a learned master who lived in the far north', probably Maucennus, Abbot of Whithorn, who is known to have visited Demetia at the right time. We shall hear more of Whithorn, in some ways a similar institution to Llantwit, later. Samson was not tearful at the school gates, but immediately set to work learning his letters. By the age of 15 he was already very learned and was ordained priest and deacon at an unusually young age by Bishop Dubricius. This aroused the jealousy of Illtud's nephews, who feared that he might succeed as the school's head when Illtud retired and so deprive them of their inheritance. Perhaps because of this ill feeling, perhaps – less likely, as events turned out – to be nearer his ailing parents, Samson gained a transfer to another of Illtud's monasteries, newly set up by Piro on Caldey Island, where his great scholarship and austerity – he fasted immoderately – astonished the Caldey monks.

In winter a message came that his father was seriously ill. At first he did not want to go, but Piro insisted that he had 'to care for the passing of souls', so he journeyed home. On the way, Samson encountered a desperate, distraught old woman waving a three-pronged spear and shrieking horribly. It turned out that she was the only member of her family left: she could not leave the wood where her husband had died. In her distress she knocked a man down. Samson, unsympathetically to modern eyes and sensibilities, called on God to prevent her from doing any more harm and she fell down dead. It is a glimpse of the harsher side of sixth-century Britain. Many people, crazed by suffering and hardship, must have been left like this in their declining years, frightened and frightening, to starve in makeshift woodland shelters once they could no longer earn a living. We might feel, fifteen centuries on, that Christianity after all was supposed to be the leavening that made the Celtic British different from the Germanic incomers. Bishop Dubricius took the same view, and when he visited Caldey in Lent he conducted a thorough enquiry into Samson's fatal curse, which had disturbed many who heard about it. Whatever doubts Dubricius may have harboured about Samson's behaviour, he acquitted him and confirmed his appointment as steward of the Caldey monastery.

Samson did not stay at Caldey. He hungered for hardship, 'longed for the desert', and was really more suited to the hermetic life than the monastic. He travelled to Ireland, returned briefly to Caldey, left it for an abandoned fort on the River Severn, then went to live in a cave at Stackpole. He was, like many another religious, guided by visions, and he was directed by his voices to cross to the monastery of Landocco founded by Docco at St Kew in Cornwall, where he was not made welcome. This is the earliest monastery that we know of in Cornwall, already well established, already old when Samson arrived: Docco, a nickname of Cyngar, was born in about 410, when the Romans were still in Britain.[38] The abbot at Landocco, Iuniavus, told Samson plainly, 'Your request to stay with us is not convenient, for you are better than us; you might condemn us, and we might properly feel condemned by your superior merit. You had better go on to Europe.' Samson was stupefied, made his way across Cornwall to 'the Southern Sea', and sailed to Brittany to become bishop of the kingdom of Jonas of Dumnonie, based at Dol.

But before he left St Kew there was a revealing encounter with a crowd of non-Christians. This happened in the district or sub-kingdom of Tricurium, later called

Trigg, in North Cornwall. He came upon the crowd, subjects of a Count Gwedian, celebrating pagan rites at a standing stone. Samson dispersed the crowd and carved a cross on the stone with his pocket knife, an *ad hoc* example of the Christianization of pagan monoliths which was very common in Brittany.³⁹ When St Petroc landed in Tricurium, he found Samson living, not surprisingly, alone in a cell beside the Camel estuary. After some dispute, Petroc forced him to leave. Samson crossed the Cornish peninsula to Castle Dore, the power centre of one of the south Cornish sub-kings, Mark Cunomorus. He may have built a chapel there; certainly a chapel dedicated to him was raised within a few years.

The Petroc who evicted Samson was another early sixth-century Christian. He was a Cornishman, the son of Clemens, another Cornish sub-king; on his father's death he shared the kingdom with his brother Gwynlliw, then left to teach in Ireland. Later he returned with his disciples Credanus, Medanus and Dachanus, landing on the shore of the Camel estuary, in Harbour Cove north of Padstow, where he was received by Bishop Wethenoc and where he evicted Samson from his oratory; Wethenoc made Samson's oratory over to Petroc. Petroc then went on a seven-year odyssey that took him to Rome, Jerusalem, Arabia, Persia and India, returning to Cornwall after the death of King Theodoric. When Wethenoc returned to Padstow, Petroc withdrew for diplomatic reasons, setting up his own oratory at Little Petherick, 5 km south of Padstow, with Petrus and Dator, establishing a rule for eighty monks, each living in a separate wooden cell. Petroc baptized Constantine, Arthur's successor. It is a sign of Petroc's status that a powerful and pious citizen called Kynan erected an oratory in his honour at Boconion, 2 km north of Bodmin. After many years in the Padstow (Petroxstowe) area he moved with Dator alone to Bodmin, which he took over from the hermit Wronus (or Guron); Wronus was obliged to move a day's journey south to Gorran. Intolerance, quarrels and forced evictions seem to have been a routine part of the lives of these early saints. A few years after this move to Bodmin, Petroc made what was probably a routine visit to Padstow and Petherick and died during the journey at Treravel.⁴⁰

Mark Cunomorus wanted another of Illtud's pupils, Paul Aurelian, to be bishop of his own small kingdom: Mark was *not* king of all Dumnonia. The bishop Wethenoc whom Petroc met on the Camel estuary was similarly not bishop of all Dumnonia, the sort of figure we might expect to see enthroned at Exeter, but bishop of the local sub-kingdom, probably of Tricurium.⁴¹ By the seventh century, the political structure of Britain had stabilized to some extent and the ecclesiastical structure began to crystallize round it, so that by then the greater abbots functioned as bishops of large kingdoms – Gwynedd, Powys, Cardigan, Demetia. But in the sixth century there was, in this as in all matters, strife, dispute, change and confusion.

Paul Aurelian was the subject of another *Life*, by Wrmonoc. Once again the *Life* that has survived may be late, ninth century in this case, but contains spellings showing that much of it must have been copied from a sixth-century original. The biography of Paul gives us a rare glimpse of King Mark and is worth studying for that reason. Paul was the son of a Cornish landowner who served as a military companion (i.e. a knight or count) to a sub-king in Glevissig (Glamorgan). Paul was sent to Illtud's school in Glevissig and when he left he hankered for 'the desert wilderness' and settled with a few disciples on a deserted site on his father's lands in Dumnonia. He was summoned to the court of 'King Mark, also called Quonomorius' who ruled over 'different peoples who spoke four languages'.[42] He ruled from a palace called Villa Banhedos or Castle Dore. Paul refused and, like Samson before him, migrated to Brittany.

But this is to move ahead of the story. Paul Aurelian's snub to King Mark may have taken place between 540 and 550, since Mark himself died in 560. The world that Arthur was born into was a predominantly pagan one, but the work of men like St Illtud and his pupils saw to it that as he grew up he was surrounded by increasing numbers of influential, well-educated and well-travelled Christians, although many of them were isolated, quirky, sententious and given to following inner voices at short notice – behaving, significantly and revealingly, in much the same way that the Merlin of the later romances behaved. Arthur, given his dates, was very likely a convert to Christianity, though the son of pagan parents. The kings of Dumnonia were probably nominally Christian from around 500 onwards.[43]

The journey that St Samson made from south Wales to north Cornwall was repeated by a steady flow of missionaries. A common route seems to have been due south from the religious community on Caldey Island, past Lundy to make landfall on the north Cornish coast at the port of Tintagel.[44] Not all of the missionaries making the crossing were from Illtud's school. St Madryn was said to be a Welsh princess who left her country for Cornwall in about 500. She settled at Talkarn, meaning 'rock cell' or 'rock chapel', a secluded and peaceful valley near Boscastle. Madryn lived the life of a hermit until her death, healing people with prayer and the water from a sacred spring. A church, St Merthiana's Church, was built beside the spring and she is said to have been buried beneath its chancel. Madryn's activities were very closely confined to this area, as is borne out by the fact that there are only two churches that could have been dedicated to her, the one at Boscastle and the other at nearby Tintagel, where she is at best half-remembered as St Materiana. But it seems more likely that 'Materiana' is a corruption of the word 'Martyrium', a name used by sixth-century Britons who were familiar with Latin, and given by them to a handful of sacred Celtic sites in the sixth century: compare the survival in the Welsh place-name 'Merthyr'. Possibly a martyrium was a pagan place of worship where a sixth-century saint boldly bore witness to his faith by dedicating the site to Christianity, an idea to bear in mind when we come to consider the role of the churchyard as a sacred place in the history of Tintagel.[45]

The Saxons

By 485, Ambrosius was fighting against the Angles, people of Germanic origin who now occupied East Anglia and Lindsey and were spreading westwards. In Sussex, Aelle became king of the South Saxons. Three years later, Hengist, the first Jutish king of Kent, died and was succeeded by Aesc. Three years later still, Aelle consolidated his position by laying siege to the British fortress of Anderida (Pevensey Castle) and killing every one of the Britons sheltering inside it (see Plate 4.1). There now seemed nothing to stop the Germanic domination of Kent and Sussex. What happened to the ordinary Britons in these now-counties, then-kingdoms, is not known. It can only be guessed that some were killed or driven out and some were kept as slaves and servants,

Plate 4.1 Pevensey, East Sussex. The ruined shell of the Roman fort of Anderida,
where the Britons were massacred by Aelle.

but probably many of the ordinary people survived. Although the later Saxon kings
of Kent were known as *Oiscingas*, 'the descendants of Aesc', the people of Kent were
calling themselves *Kentings*, a word that preserved the old pre-Jutish, pre-Roman
name of the Cantii, suggesting that substantial numbers of Cantii survived the change
of regime.

With this solid foothold in Kent and Sussex, the incomers were ready to expand
westwards. In 495, according to the *Anglo-Saxon Chronicle*, a new wave of Saxon
settlers led by Cerdic landed in Hampshire and began to settle the Hampshire Basin.
The genealogy of the West Saxon royal house may be given as follows (see facing
page).

In the much later *Tale of Geraint*, a highly charged battle poem describing the
exploits of two Dumnonian kings, we hear of the Battle of Llongborth in which King
Geraint fought against the Saxons and was defeated and according to one reading
killed.

Before Geraint, the enemy's scourge,
I saw white horses, tensed, red.
After the war-cry, bitter the grave.

In Llongborth, I saw the clash of swords,
Men in terror, bloody heads,
Before Geraint the Great, his father's son.

In Llongborth, I saw spurs
And men who did not flinch from spears,
Who drank their wine from glass that glinted.

In Llongborth I saw Arthur [or Arthur's]
Heroes who cut with steel,
The emperor, ruler of our labour.

In Llongborth, Geraint was slain,
Heroes of the land of Dyfnant,
And before they were slain they slew.

That, at any rate, is the reading by John Morris, in which Geraint is described as falling in the battle.[46]

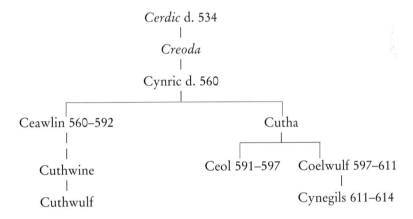

Cerdic d. 534
|
Creoda
|
Cynric d. 560
|
Ceawlin 560–592   Cutha
|
|
Cuthwine   Ceol 591–597   Coelwulf 597–611
|
Cuthwulf   Cynegils 611–614

The *Anglo-Saxon Chronicle* tells us baldly that in 501 there was a battle at Portsmouth Harbour in which an important British prince was killed. 'In this year Port and his sons Breda and Maegla came to Britain at a place called Portsmouth, and slew a young Welshman, a very noble man.' This has been taken by Morris as a rare instance of the two independent traditions describing the same event. 'Llongborth' is not obviously the same place-name as Portsmouth, but it means 'port of the warships', which describes the Portsmouth Harbour of those days, and of subsequent centuries, very well. A naval station where a Dumnonian prince fell is likely to be the westernmost Saxon shore fort, Portchester, at the head of Portsmouth Harbour; this is a likely location of the battle of Portsmouth/Llongborth.[47] The *Tale* tells us that Arthur was there too, as Geraint's commander-in-chief, and shared in Geraint's defeat with the 'men of Devon'.[48] King Geraint was succeeded by Cato or Cado[49] and both Geraint and Cato, whether father and son, uncle and nephew, or brothers, are remembered in later traditions as close associates of Arthur in war and peace. Geraint held lands on the south Cornish coast, while Cato's lands lay on the north Devon coast.

There is nevertheless another reading of the *Tale of Geraint*.[50] One verse reads literally:

> In Llongborth, I saw to Arthur
> heroes – accustomed to slay with steel –
> the emperor, the leader of toil.

This has the sense, 'In Llongborth I saw heroes who were the vassals of Arthur, the emperor and ruler of all our labours, heroes accustomed to slaying with their swords.' Another verse which is usually taken to mean that Geraint was killed in the battle has an almost exactly similar form, but with the *y* ('to') missing in the first line (in both Black Book and Red Book versions):

> In Llongborth were slain [to?] Geraint
> heroes from the region of Dyfnaint;
> and before they were slain they slew.

If the missing *y* was omitted in error by an early copyist, as is quite likely, the verse was originally intended to mean, 'In Llongborth heroes from the region of Dumnonia who were Geraint's vassals were slain; but before they were slain they slew.' The use of 'heroes' rather than 'hero' reinforces the idea that it was not Geraint himself but his followers who were killed. The poem therefore does not necessarily admit that Geraint was killed at Llongborth, and there is reason to believe that Geraint survived. The *Life of Teilo* tells how St Teilo sent a stone coffin from Brittany across to Cornwall for Geraint many years later, when Geraint was dying of wounds inflicted in a much later battle.[51] If Geraint did not die at Llongborth, there is no compelling reason to equate the battle with the Battle of Portsmouth in which a noble Welshman was killed. This means that we have, after all, no positive connection between the Saxon and Celtic versions of events, and no firm date or location for Llongborth. The question remains open.

One interesting feature of the *Tale of Geraint* is the emphasis on his association with horses, sustained through eight verses; Arthur and his followers were renowned for their cavalry exploits at the expense of Saxon infantry.

> Swiftly there ran under Geraint's thigh
> long-shanked [horses fed on] grass of wheat,
> roans [with the] onrush of speckled eagles.

In 508, thought to be the year of Ambrosius the Younger's death by sword or poison, the Saxons defeated the British at Cerdic's Ford (Charford), killing the local sub-king Natan-leod and thousands of Celtic warriors. Yet it was only in 519 that the *Chronicle* says that Cerdic and Cynric became kings of the West Saxons.[52] There are other problems with this episode. Cerdic and Cynric are described as *ealdormen*, not kings or sub-kings, and this implies that they were appointees, or officials, which is odd if they were leaders of an autonomous band of invaders from mainland Europe. Cerdic is, moreover, not a Germanic but a British name.

The reality, the historical existence, of Cerdic is not in doubt. Three places were named after him – Cerdicesford, Cerdicesleaga and Cerdicesbeorg – and presumably they embody authentic memories of an early leader.[53] One alternative explanation to consider is that Cerdic was not an invader but the head of a British or partly-British noble land-owning family with estates at the western end of the Saxon Shore. Cerdic's family may have been entrusted in the last days of sub-Roman administration in southern Britain with the defence of this stretch of the Saxon Shore, perhaps from Hurst Castle Spit to Chichester Harbour; as an appointed official, he might be referred to as an ealdorman. When, as time passed, it became obvious that no central control was going to be re-asserted, Cerdic may have gone further, taking a slice of the hinterland and making himself king, even though this would have involved stifling pockets of resistance from uncooperative British sub-kings, such as the mysterious Natan-Leod. In support of this interpretation is the lack of Germanic archaeological evidence in south Hampshire west of the Meon valley, and the presence of a group of British place-names – Micheldever, Andover, Candover.[54]

Another alternative is that Cerdic and Cynric and their followers had not come from Germany and were not local either, but had been sent along the coast as an advance party by Aelle of the South Saxons. This would explain why they were described as appointees; they were acting, initially at any rate, under South Saxon orders. Their origin in Sussex could also explain the acquisition of Celtic names: Cerdic was a name picked up, perhaps as a nickname, perhaps even as a joke, from the British population in Sussex. This adoption of British names was not unique, either; Caedbaed, Anglo-Saxon king of Lindsey at about the time of Arthur's last battle, had a British name. The date of Cerdic's arrival in Hampshire, 495, also fits in so well with the consolidation and securing of Aelle's kingdom, marked by the fall of the British fort of Anderida in 491, that we might suspect a planned connection between the two events. The mastermind, the bretwalda-to-be, Aelle, was behind both.

In 512, according to the *Anglo-Saxon Chronicle*, Aesc, king of the Jutes in Kent, died and was succeeded by Octha. Aesc (or Oesc) may be the 'Osc Bigknife' who according to Welsh sources 'fought with Arthur at the time of Badon'. The dates are close enough for this to be possible, and no scholar has so far succeeded in tying the two chronologies, English and British, convincingly together.[55]

In 516, came the great Battle of Badon (see Figure 4.2), in which the British were victorious over the Saxons. Ambrosius the Younger was by now dead and the command had passed to Arthur. Gildas, writing not long after the event, does not say who the commander was at Badon. Much has been made of this by opponents of the historical Arthur. Oliver Padel argues that Gildas implies Ambrosius was still in command. The passage in question reads, 'Wretched people fled to them from all directions . . . their leader was Ambrosius Aurelianus . . . This lasted right up till the year of the siege of Mount Badon.' Modern editions invariably separate the sentence about Badon from the preceding sentence, but the oldest surviving copy of Gildas, a tenth-century manuscript, has no paragraph division here.[56] Padel argues from this that Ambrosius was still commander in 516, but the passage implies a series of battles between the mention of Ambrosius' leadership and Badon, so it is possible for the leadership to have changed hands and for the successor to have commanded at Badon. Other documents, such as the *Welsh Annals*, specifically identify Arthur as

Figure 4.2 Badon, in the war zone between established British defended sites
and the westernmost Saxon settlements

commander at Badon, so it is more natural and consistent to suppose that Arthur had
succeeded as commander by 516.[57]

So decisive was Badon that it held the Saxons back for several decades, and it is
largely to his exploits during this single action that Arthur owes his reputation as a
great warrior.[58] There has been much discussion about the site of the battle, and many
candidates have been offered. Gildas was close enough to Badon – according to one
reading he claimed to have been born in the same year as the battle, but this is disputed
– to have correct details about it. Yet the name 'Mons Badonicus' must be a
Latinization of the real place-name, which may subsequently have been anglicized to
an extent that it is no longer easy to identify.

The village of Badbury is one place-name that seems to have the right resonance.
The village is adjacent to an escarpment south-east of Swindon carrying a hillfort,
which was once called Badbury although it has for several centuries now been known
as Liddington Castle. The fort commands an important junction of dark age road
routes; it stands beside the Ridgeway where it is crossed by the Roman road
from Cirencester (Coriniva) to the north-west to Silchester (Calleva) to the south-
east. It also looks down on the place just 6 km to the north-west where the
Cirencester–Silchester road is joined by a north–south Roman road to Marlborough
(Cunetio) and Winchester (Venta). The Liddington Castle area was therefore a major
sub-Roman communications centre.

A second candidate for the battle site is Baydon, a village 3 miles to the south-east
of Liddington Castle, also on the Roman road to Silchester. It is likely that most
battles took place on or near major roads, as these would have been the obvious

medium for moving large numbers of troops from one region to another, whether on foot or horse. Baydon is at the highest point reached by the road. Set high between deep valleys to north and south, it does justice to Gildas' use of the word *mons*. There is nevertheless no sign of any earthwork at Baydon, which makes it an unlikely site for a siege lasting a number of days.

Myres argues that Gildas may have been referring to this general area. 'Mons Badonicus' may have meant less 'Mount Badon' than 'the hill country of Badon', in which case he could have meant the whole area from Baydon westwards to the escarpment.[59] One can imagine large numbers of warriors converging on the defended earthworks of Liddington Castle, with skirmishing breaking out across an area of several square kilometres as war-bands from both sides met and clashed, the hillfort itself making an obvious refuge and a focus for a siege.

It has nevertheless been very convincingly argued that Bath was Badon (see Figure 4.3), and there are unmistakable early references to Bath, specifically mentioning its hot and cold springs, in which the place-name is spelt *Badon*. The location makes sense in terms of general situation. For instance, when we look at a map of findspots of sixth-century Mediterranean ware imported into Dumnonia, we can see that Bath is located just off the eastern edge of that distribution (see Figure 4.4). When findspots of early Anglo-Saxon pottery are mapped, Bath is located just off the western edge of that distribution. It is, in effect, in the no-man's-land or buffer zone between two

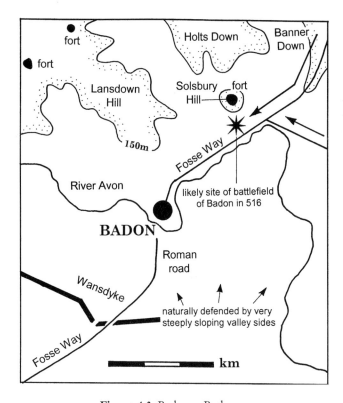

Figure 4.3 Badon = Bath

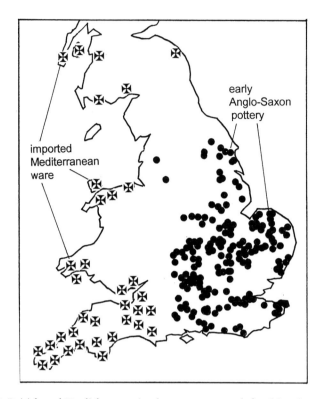

Figure 4.4 British and English zones in about 500–20, as defined by the pottery. The imported Mediterranean pottery indicates high-status British sites. Notice how Dumnonia stands out as a privileged kingdom.
Source: Mainly after Burkitt and Burkitt 1990

sixth-century cultural provinces and must for some time have been on or very close to the political frontier, however defined, separating Celt from Saxon.[60]

Another location has been suggested, at Baden Hill east of Thornbury. Although it too is in the likely conflict zone and its name has the right sort of sound, its claim is not as strong as that of Bath.

All in all, Bath makes excellent sense as a location for a decisive frontier battle in the year 516, Liddington and Baydon less so because there were well-established Anglo-Saxon settlements close at hand to the east, north, south, north-west and south-west: that area was already a lost cause.

Tellingly, the spellings Bathe, Baderan and Badan were the same as far as thirteenth-century scribes in England and Wales were concerned. Even Nennius seems to be using the spelling 'Badon' to mean 'Bath'. In *The Wonders of Britain* he refers to 'the hot lake' 'in quo balnea sunt Badonis', 'the hot lake where the baths of Badon are'. Nennius mentions that Badon is in the country of the Hwicce; Osric of the Hwicce granted land to Bath Abbey in 675, so Badon/Bath was in the hands of the Hwicce in the years up to 650 and it had hot baths. There really cannot be much doubt that when Nennius referred to the Battle of Badon he knew what he meant by the name Badon, nor can there be any real doubt that he meant Bath.

In the seventeenth century one of the hills round Bath was known by two names – Lansdown Hill and Mons Badonica.[61] The Latinized form is suspicious, of course, because it implies that an antiquarian had looked at Gildas and maybe Nennius too, and worked out that this was the right place to be Mount Badon; I am doubtful whether this is a piece of locally preserved folk memory of the great battle. The idea that Bath was Badon is certainly not a new discovery; as early as 1848 Todd noted that 'no doubt can exist of Badon being Bath'.

The Roman and post-Roman city of Bath lay beside the River Avon, at the bottom of a steep-sided 200-metre-deep valley. On the north side there are three major hills, Lansdown Hill to the north-west, Holts Down to the north and Banner Down to the north-east. Any of these could have been the focus of an encampment and therefore a siege. Lansdown Hill seems to lend itself to that use rather more favourably: its level surface carries two ancient enclosures surrounded by earthworks – but the small outlying hill, Solsbury, to the east, is more promising still. It carries the remains of a hillfort and stands commandingly directly above the line of the Roman road. Fosse Way comes from the north-east, and descends the spur of Banner Down to pass between Solsbury Hill and the Avon just 3 km before reaching the centre of Bath.

The British were evidently expecting to be attacked from the north-east, to judge from the orientation of the Wansdyke, the massive sixth-century earthwork thrown up on the crest of the south valley side. It blocked off Fosse Way as it came south out of Bath. The Wansdyke, still in places up to 4 metres high from ditch bottom to bank top,[62] also expresses a clear determination to stop the invaders at Bath. If ever archaeology shouted 'they shall not pass!' it was here in dark age Bath. The large-scale managerial and organizational skills required to create the Wansdyke reinforce the argument for overkingship in dark age Britain: someone must have been co-ordinating the project.

The place may have had strategic value, or it may simply have been an existing defined boundary, the River Avon. It may alternatively be that Bath was still regarded by the British as an important ancient central place, a part of their heritage with which they were not prepared to part. Bath had, after all, been a major rural sanctuary, a sacred spring in a marsh, long before the Romans came to turn it into a city. The Wansdyke shows that the British had decided to stop the Saxons penetrating any further south-west than Bath. Approaching Bath from the north-east, Fosse Way passes beneath the small hillfort of Solsbury Hill. We can imagine a Saxon army appearing over the north-eastern horizon and approaching Bath down the long ramp of Banner Down, ready to seize Bath, and being ambushed by British warriors sallying from Solsbury Hill. Before they could go on, the Saxons had to stop, surround the fort and wipe out resistance.

The *Welsh Annals* refer to the 'Battle of Badon, in which Arthur carried the cross of Our Lord Jesus Christ three days and three nights on his shoulders and the Britons were victorious.' As we have already seen, what is meant is probably that Arthur carried a painted cross on his shield, which was mistranslated as shoulder by a scribe. The siege may literally have lasted for three days, or the number three may be dismissed as recurring so often in story-telling that it may be simply code for 'a long time'.

What is certain is that Badon was a decisive battle. Gildas, remembering it as a turning-point in the fortunes of the British, wrote

> victory went now to our countrymen [the British], now to their enemies [the Saxons]. . . . This lasted right up to the year of the siege of Badon Hill, which was pretty well the last defeat of the villains, and certainly not the least.[63]

A change came over Britain as a result of this hammering of the Saxons. It was a *de facto* division of the island. The Angles, Saxons and Jutes remained confined to the east, while the British in the west and north were left to develop without hindrance. It was in the aftermath of Badon, in 519, that Cerdic and Cynric became 'kings' of the West Saxons. Perhaps having their western border fixed for them made them turn back to the areas of Hampshire and Wiltshire they had turned into Saxon lands, and made them consolidate their achievements.

The medieval vision of a Britain joined into a single nation under Arthur's kingship was probably never achieved in reality; from both archaeology and documents, the signs are that the multiplicity of old British kingdoms continued to exist. Arthur's status in the south may have been such that he enjoyed overlordship of all the West Country; what his political powers may have been in the rest of Celtic Britain must be left for later discussion.

In the year before Badon, 515, Vortipor became king of Demetia (Dyfed). His gravestone can still be seen at Castell Dwyran: it reads, 'Memoria Vorteporigis Protictoris,' although Gildas had a low opinion of this Vortipor the Protector, accusing him of murder and incest. Gildas supplies us with the names of Vortipor and of other kings of the post-Badon phase, such as the great Maglocunus (Maelgwn) king of Gwynedd from 517 until about 550, and Cuneglasus (Cynlas) who became king of Powys in 520.

As well as the kingdoms of Dumnonia, Dyfed, Gwynedd and Powys, there were the kingdoms of Glevissig (Glamorgan), Brycheiniog (Brecon), Gwent, Calchvynydd, Rheged, York, Deira, Byrnaich, Elmet, and in Scotland Dal Riada, Clyde, Gododdin and Pictland. It is hard to imagine any overall unity emerging from such a complex British polity, and it is revealing that Gildas commented, 'external wars have stopped, but not civil wars'. In fact, that *is* the tradition that underlies the medieval Arthurian romances – the half-memory of ongoing disputes and abductions, of treachery, revenge and usurpations – and it probably represents the historical reality.

This Arthurian period, the period when Arthur as commander-in-chief held back the Saxons but ultimately failed to create unity among the British, lasted for twenty-one years. In 537, at the Battle of Camlann, Arthur was mortally wounded. The nature and location of this last battle of Arthur will be discussed in detail later, but one important fact about it is that it is not mentioned in the *Anglo-Saxon Chronicle*. We might have expected the Saxons to have gloated over the death of their archenemy. The fact that they did not strongly suggests that they had no hand in it, that Camlann was a battle among the warring factions of the British. This is also implied by the tradition that Arthur was killed by his kinsman Modred. Whether this is true or not, the brief archive mention of the battle tells us that in the 'strife of Camlann' both

'Arthur and Modred perished'. The entry is ambiguous. Arthur and Modred could have been on the same side, which is on the whole more likely. But these are matters to return to later.

The repercussions of Arthur's death are not clear. There seems to have been little movement from the Saxon side, and that would be consistent with the British stifling news of his death. There were migrations of Saxons from England back to the European mainland between 530 and 550, with significant numbers of families resettling in Normandy, Artois and Flanders and even 're-invading' what are now the Netherlands and Denmark,[64] which implies that many Saxons in south-eastern England did not at that stage regard expansion into the Celtic west as a realistic prospect.

It was not until about 560 that the numbing effect of Badon wore off.[65] By then Cerdic had been dead twenty-six years. He had been succeeded by Cynric, possibly his grandson, who had fought against the Britons at Salisbury in 552 and Barbury in 556. In 560, Cynric too died and was succeeded by his son Ceawlin, who was to become the second man to hold the prestigious title bretwalda, or overking, of the English.

The world moved on. Old kings died and were succeeded. Saints came and went, driven by their visionary inner voices. The Anglo-Saxons began to encroach and consolidate their gains. In the far north the old British kingdom of Byrnaich was formally taken over by the Germanic colonists and the new name of Bernicia came into use – in 547 according to Bede.[66] And there were plagues. Around the year 540, Eliffer became king of York, Morcant became king of Clyde and Gabran became king of Dal Riada. In 543 an epidemic of bubonic plague broke out in Europe, spreading from country to country over the next four or five years, reaching Britain in 547.

The plague of 547 is said to have taken, amongst its many victims, King Maglocunus or Maelgwn of Gwynedd, the great-grandson of Cunedda from Manaw Gododdin, grandson of Enniaun Girt, and who had held the kingdom of Gwynedd since 517.[67] Maelgwn had at that time succeeded his father Caswallon Law Hir as king of Gwynedd.[68] There is no doubting the historical reality of Maelgwn; he is mentioned on an inscription made in about 540 at Penmachno, in which he appears as MAGLO MAGISTRATUS – 'King Maelgwn'. Nennius tells us, in his *Kings of the Bernicians* of his high status – 'King Maelgwn the Great was reigning among the British, in Gwynedd' – and of his descent from Cunedda.[69] Of the five kings Gildas singled out for vituperation, it was Maelgwn who was dealt with most harshly.

> What of you, dragon of the island [Anglesey?], you who have removed many of these tyrants from their country and even this life? You are last in my list, but first in evil, mightier than many both in power and malice, more profuse in giving, more extravagant in sin, strong in arms but stronger still in what destroys a soul, *Maglocunus*. Why wallow like a fool in the ancient ink of your crimes like a man drunk on wine pressed from the vine of the Sodomites? The king of all kings has made you higher than almost all the generals [*ducibus*] of Britain.

Gildas accuses Maelgwn as a young man of killing his uncle the king, but then praises him for reforming his ways. 'Where you had been a raven, you became a dove.' Then he reviles him for sliding back into evil, 'like a sick hound returning to its vomit'. His first marriage was illegal, then he compounded the crime by taking the wife of his brother's son, then killing his nephew and his own wife. Gildas was shocked at the idea that Maelgwn could behave in this way when he had been educated by Illtud. Evidently not all of Illtud's pupils turned out well. Geoffrey of Monmouth's *British Succession* is a muddle, in that he has Arthur succeeded by Constantine, then Aurelius Conanus, then Vortiporus, then Malgo. Vortiporus is evidently the Vortipor who was king of Demetia. Malgo must be Maelgwn, king of Gwynedd. But aside from these confusions, Geoffrey significantly describes 'Malgo' as handsome, generous and courageous, but homosexual: and therein may lie the real root of Gildas' hatred and condemnation.[70]

The great Maelgwn, dead of the plague, was succeeded by his son Rhun as king of Gwynedd. It was at about this time that the voyages of St Brendan took place.

In 550 St David was born and Drustanus, the legendary Tristan, died. Tristan was the son of King Mark Cunomorus of Dumnonia. Presumably either King Mark or Drustanus lived at Castle Dore; the memorial stone to Drustanus was raised a short distance south of Castle Dore. The still-legible inscription cut in two vertical lines on the Tristan Stone reads DRUSTANUS HIC IACIT / CUNOMORI FILIUS: 'Here lies Drustanus, son of Cunomorus'. If Drustanus was Mark's son and not his nephew, then he eloped with his stepmother; here we may be seeing the harder dark age reality behind the medieval romance version of the Tristan and Iseult story. Possibly the historical events were considered too improper for the courtly romance versions.

Just as Drustanus is the Latin form of Tristan, Cunomorus is the Latinized form of the British name Cynfawr, who is known to have been a Dumnonian king, the predecessor and probably the father of the Constantine who was denounced by Gildas. It may have been Constantine who raised the memorial to Drustanus, his brother, when an old man and Drustanus had been long dead: perhaps he had to wait for their father Cunomorus to die before the memorial could be erected.

The association of Mark Cunomorus and presumably his son and successor Constantine with Castle Dore is almost irresistible. The earliest surviving version of the Tristan and Iseult romance is Beroul's Anglo-Norman poem. Beroul places King Mark's 'lofty palace' at Lancien. This name survives in Lantyan Manor ('Lantien' in 1086) just 2 km north of the earthworks of Castle Dore itself. Beroul has Iseult going by a paved road to the monastery of St Samson, to which she gave a gold-embroidered robe, later converted into a chasuble and still in use in Beroul's time – or the time when his source was writing. The monastery of St Samson could be the church of St Sampson 2 km east of Castle Dore, and very likely founded by Samson himself. He died at Dol in Brittany in 565. There is a road from Castle Dore to St Sampson's in Golant, possibly the 'paved road' along which Iseult herself passed. There is enough circumstantial evidence in Castle Dore, the Tristan Stone, St Sampson's Church and Lantyan, to show that the stories about Tristan, Iseult and Mark were strongly associated with this area, the Fowey peninsula, from the time when they were first drafted.

The Giant's Hedge, a north-facing defensive earthwork and estate boundary of probable dark age date on the east side of the Fowey ria, may represent the limits of King Mark's royal estate. Mark no doubt used his commanding position here to control the southern harbours that linked Cornwall with Brittany, where he apparently also held lands. The *tyrannus* whom St Samson helped in the struggle against the Breton prince Judal was called Conomorus, and he may have been the same king.

The Saxons meanwhile were stirring, gradually consolidating their holdings in the east. In 552 Cynric and the West Saxons took Salisbury from the British. Three years later, in the year when Aethelbert became king of Kent, Buckinghamshire fell to the Saxons. In the next year, 556, Cynric, aided by his son Ceawlin, fought against the British in a battle at Beran Byrg; Barbury Castle was an iron age hillfort near Swindon, 30 miles north of Salisbury, that had recently been re-fortified by the British. The *Anglo-Saxon Chronicle* does not say that Cynric and Ceawlin won this battle and he is not said to have advanced any further north.[71] Even so, by this stage the Saxons were occupying most of the chalklands outside Dorset. Four years later, in 560, Cynric died and command of the West Saxons passed to Ceawlin who, like his father, had a British and not a Saxon name and he seems to have spent his first few years in power in internal reorganization and re-grouping and in developing relationships with Saxons to the north of his own kingdom; there was no attack on the British for eight years. He was preparing for the great thrust to the west.[72] He fought in 568 in alliance with Cutha or Cuthwulf, who seems to have been the leader of the Eslingas in what is now Cambridgeshire.

Aethelbert had reached out westwards across the Medway, apparently to try to capture London for Kent. London had been an autonomous British enclave, but it was falling under English control as the Anglo-Saxon settlers increasingly dominated the areas immediately to the north, south and west. London was in effect surrounded. The purpose of Ceawlin's strategy in forming an alliance with Cutha now becomes clear; the two Saxon forces could close, pincer-like, on Aethelbert, defeat him and force him back. It was wholly successful and the result of the Battle of Wibbandun (Wimbledon) was that from then on the Saxons were in complete control of the London region. Curiously, though, the city itself remained a British settlement. There is no trace of a sixth-century Saxon burial ground, for instance, and only a hint that a few individual Saxons visitors perhaps from Croydon or Mitcham, were admitted. The London Basin was English territory, yet there were no English actually living in London itself yet.

The South Midlands seem to have attracted the Saxons' attention next. In 571 Cutha routed the British near Bedford, opening the way to a massive expansion westward; he was able to sweep through the Vale of Aylesbury to Abingdon, where a colony of English had, until now, been surrounded by British-held territory and living virtually under siege conditions. After the relief of Abingdon, Cutha went on to consolidate Saxon control of the middle Thames by taking Eynsham, 60 km north-west of Abingdon, and Benson, 60 km to the south-east. No more is heard of Cutha after he marched on Oxford and it is assumed by some that he died there and was buried at Cutteslowe just north of Oxford, but (see below) it seems more likely that it was a later Cutha who was buried there. The earlier Cutha was succeeded by Cuthwine, who maintained Cutha's alliances with the West Saxons and the Abingdon English.[73] Even in Arthur's time there had been Saxons in the Oxford area. There is archaeological evidence of the Saxon infiltration at Dorchester-on-Thames, where nearly 200 British Christian burials date from the period 420–50, and remains of a Saxon house built between 500 and 550 show that Saxons colonized there between 450 and 500.[74]

Now the Saxons held a virtually unbroken swathe of territory from sea to sea, slanting across Britain from the Solent to the Humber. From this front they were able to strike westwards once more and, in 577, they attacked near Bath. Arthur had stopped them at Badon in 516. Now they were back and instead of a crushing and reverberant defeat they gained a decisive victory.

Arthur's achievement had been the containment of the Saxons in the east. Now, after a pause of sixty years, they were on the loose again and threatening Dumnonia's eastern frontier. At Dyrham, just 8 km north of Badon, the Saxon allies under Ceawlin and his son Cuthwine killed Coinmail, Farinmail and Condidan, the British kings who ruled the lower Severn valley, then sacked the cities of Gloucester, Cirencester and Bath. The major territory of Calchvynydd, the ancient lands of the Dobunni before the Romans arrived, fell to the Saxon sword. The land link between Wales and the West Country was now broken. This territory also yielded one of the greatest concentrations in southern Britain of dark age metalwork, military (buckles and belt-fittings) and civilian (brooches). Ceawlin was therefore doing something even more significant than avenging Badon: he was striking at an industrial power centre that he probably saw as a major threat to the security of the Saxons living in the Thames valley.[75]

Cirencester, for two or three decades surrounded by Saxon villages, its Roman amphitheatre pathetically turned into a mini-fortress by its besieged British inhabitants,[76] was now taken over by the Saxons. Archaeology tells us that by 600 at least one Saxon warrior had been buried in the city; other finds also speak of a Saxon settlement. As yet there is no sign that the Saxons settled the newly conquered territory for the next thirty years and it may be that there was no formal government of the territory by the allies. The British kings and sub-kings had been killed, so there was no leadership to rally the British. Doubtless Britons went on living there, even in the cities, though Gloucester had a population of only 300 families altogether in 650. Bath may also have continued to house Britons after the Saxons took over the city, but the British no longer had control; Myres has proposed that the western Wansdyke immediately south of Bath was built in the run-up to Dyrham rather than earlier, with a view to stopping the Saxons penetrating into Dumnonia at the end of the sixth century rather than the beginning.[77]

On the strength of the success of this campaign, Ceawlin was appointed bretwalda just as, in recognition of *his* success in the Badon campaign over 60 years earlier, Arthur had been appointed British *dux bellorum*.

It was at about this time that, according to Welsh sources, a new Arthur emerged, in answer to a prayer of St Cadoc for a strong king for Glevissig (Glamorgan).[78] His name was Mouric. His father was Theodoric, son of Budic, and his mother was Teitfallt or Theodora, the sister of King Urien of Rheged (Cumbria and Lancashire). In characteristic Celtic style, as Theodoric grew old he abdicated in his son's favour and retired to Tintern to lead the life of a monk, having only briefly regained his throne after years in exile. Mouric, Cadoc's choice for the throne of Glevissig, was faced in 577 with the difficult task of defending a land of small lordships against predatory neighbours – the kings of Brycheiniog (Brecon) immediately to the north and the armies of Gwynedd still further to the north.[79] Mouric was attacked by the Saxons from the east as well, and Theodoric, bidden by an angel to leave his hermit's cell, decided to go to his son's aid. Theodoric was mortally wounded in the battle at Tintern Ford (Brockweir-on-Wye), where the Saxons were halted, and Mouric pursued them as they retreated eastwards.

The Welsh and Irish texts fill a gap in the *Anglo-Saxon Chronicle*, where we are told of the Saxon breakthrough at Dyrham in 577 and in general terms of an expansion phase; then we hear of Ceawlin's battle against the British at Fethanlea in 584, from which he 'went home in anger' and presumably in defeat. The expansion across the Severn and the encounter with Theodoric and Mouric in the Wye valley happened (according to the Welsh texts) in the early 580s. Fethanlea is the old name of a field at Stoke Lyne, near Banbury. The *Anglo-Saxon Chronicle* records that Ceawlin's son, Cuthwine, was killed in the Battle of Fethanlea, and the carefully worded 'went home in anger' thinly disguises the bitter disappointment of a campaign that ended in failure.

Ceawlin must have journeyed southwards from Stoke Lyne, if he was returning to his home territory after the battle. It would have been quite natural for him to take his son's body a safe distance from the field of battle before attempting a burial. Cutteslowe, about 10 miles south along the Roman road, seems a natural geographical location for this ceremony, and the place-name seems to contain the nickname of Ceawlin's dead son: he was known not only as Cuthwine, but as Cutha. The 'hoga de Cudeslowe' described in the early middle ages was clearly the burial mound of Cutha. Unfortunately it was ordered to be demolished in 1261, as it had become a haunt of robbers.[80]

Following the major setback of Fethanlea, Ceawlin appears to have lost credibility as bretwalda, or at the very least been open to challenge from ambitious co-warriors, and in 592 he was driven out of his kingdom by a rival named Ceol; this happened after a great slaughter at Wodnesbeorg (now called Adam's Grave) overlooking the Vale of Pewsey. Ceol ruled the West Saxons from then until 597.

The Battle of Fethanlea seems to have been a paler reflection of Badon, in that it was a major setback for the Saxons, delaying their westward advance for another thirty years.[81] No battle against the 'Welsh' was recorded by the Saxons until 614.[82] If it was indeed Mouric who brought about that defeat, as is likely, he earns his title of 'the second Arthur'.

Ceawlin's power crumbled, and Mouric's kingdom grew strong. At first he was the sub-king of eastern Glevissig only, but after his victory or victories over Ceawlin his power increased. He married the daughter of the king of Gower (West Glamorgan) and inherited her father's kingdom. Later the ruling dynasty in South Gwent died out and Mouric's son became king of Gwent, evidently as a client of his father. So, while Mouric ruled there, the Saxons were unable to penetrate into South Wales.

They were, nevertheless, able to overrun Dorset. By 614, they were fighting the Dumnonians near Axminster on what is now the Devon–Dorset border, and Arthur's achievement in holding them back was already receding into folk memory. Certainly, the Saxons did not record it: they had no interest in remembering the humiliation of defeats and setbacks, only the progress of their colonial expansion.

What, meanwhile, had been happening in the north? The Scottish Highlands were the lands of the Picts, who had their own kings. The eastern half of the Scottish Lowlands and Southern Uplands was the land of the Gododdin, the kingdom of the Votadini, who had their fortress at Din Eidyn (Edinburgh). The western half of the Scottish Lowlands and Southern Uplands formed the British kingdom of Clyde, which had its capital at the stronghold of Alcluith at Dumbarton. In Arthur's time, around 500, Dyfnwal, son of Ceretic, was king of Clyde and, although memories of him are faint, he is spoken of with awe by later chroniclers.

Some believe Arthur fought one of his battles along Hadrian's Wall, where his enemies cannot have been Saxons or Angles, who had not at that early stage penetrated so far north. If Arthur did fight battles along Hadrian's Wall, they are likely to have been after the Badon campaign, and to have been battles for supremacy within the complicated networks of alliances and rivalries among the British kingdoms.[83] Dyfnwal's name is mentioned honourably, as if he acquitted himself with distinction in whatever conflicts flared up. Significantly, an independent tradition in Lothian (in Gododdin territory) mentions that a Dyfnwal was king there too, so it is possible that Dyfnwal allied himself with Arthur in the suppression of some of the Gododdin and was rewarded by Arthur with custody of an entire territory, Gododdin as well as Clyde. Some genealogies also show Dyfnwal succeeding Germanianus as ruler of the South Votadini, which supports this interpretation.[84]

The northern frontier underwent a major reorganization. It was at about this time that Cunedda of the Votadini was sent from Gododdin to eject the Irish settlers in North Wales; it is possible that Cunedda was suspected of being behind the trouble in the north and that as a commander of doubtful loyalty he was removed from his power base and given a specific task in Gwynedd to help resolve the northern problem. Cunedda was not the only one to be moved south. Caw, who was Gildas's father, was moved to Powys at the same time. People were moving surprisingly long distances, and it is well to remember that a network of serviceable long-distance roads existed. The Roman roads were still there, if indifferently maintained, and so were the long-distance trackways that had followed the crests of escarpments since long before the Romans came. The Britons spoke a common language, Brittonic, at this time, which enabled travellers of every kind, whether soldiers, kings or minstrels, to make themselves understood anywhere from Cornwall to Clyde: ballads, rumours, news, orders and military commands were easily transmitted. The people of the Welsh kingdoms and the Men of the North all described themselves as *Cymry*, 'fellow countrymen' or 'comrades', showing the feeling of kinship that existed among the Britons; the Welsh Britons nevertheless recognized the Britons of Clyde, Gododdin, Rheged and York as somewhat different from themselves, calling them *Gwyr y Gogledd*, 'Men of the North'.[85]

At around the same time, strife in Northern Ireland led to a migration of Irish across to Kintyre. The people of the tiny Irish kingdom of Dal Riada were dominated by their powerful neighbours, the kingdoms of Tir Eogain and Airgalla, and their king, Fergus, moved with his entourage, a total of only 150 people, to a place of safety, the long peninsula to the west of Arran and the Firth of Clyde. This happened in 503. Probably Fergus had been preceded by earlier Irish settlers, but the transfer of the royal household to the Scottish mainland constituted a significant shift in the power balance in Scotland. There was no immediate conflict between Dal Riada and Clyde, but plenty between Dal Riada and the Picts, whose lands had been taken from them. The kings of Clyde could not have tolerated a hostile power on a peninsula that commanded their seaway, and it is likely that Fergus's move was negotiated with Dyfnwal: probably overt aggression towards the Picts was a *condition* of Dyfnwal's agreement. It cannot be known whether this in turn was ratified, sanctioned or even planned by Arthur. The emplacement of allies hostile to the Picts would have strengthened the northern frontier, and could have been seen as part of a grand strategy for stabilizing the north.[86] One of the Dalriadic kings, Aedan mac Gabrain, had friendly relations with Britons in the south, and there was Welsh blood in the Dalriadic royal dynasty, but this alliance with the Welsh broke down under Aedan's successors and for a time the Dalriadic threat replaced the Pictish.[87]

South of Hadrian's Wall – '*The* Wall' as it was known in those times – what had been a large single kingdom under Coel Hen in the early fifth century was split into two halves, York to the east, Rheged to the west of the Pennines. The kingdom of Rheged had strongholds at Cair Ligualid (Carlisle) and Lancaster, and in the 530s – after Camlann – this large kingdom fell into two, North Rheged (Cumbria) and South Rheged (Lancashire). There was disintegration east of the Pennines too. Eleutherius of the Great Army ruled York, Keidyaw seems to have controlled the whole line of the Wall, later dividing his inheritance among his sons; Pabo Pillar of Britain ruled much of the Pennines, also dividing his lands among his sons including Dunawt, who acquired the area round Dent and seems, from a poem of Llywarch Hen's, to have been an enemy of Urien, and Samuel, who took the South Pennines to make a small kingdom called Elmet.

By the 540s, the enlarged kingdom of Dyfnwal had also fallen apart. Dyfnwal himself was dead and his grandson was king of Clyde. The Gododdin rebelled, re-establishing their autonomy. Two Gododdin kings, Morcant Bulc, heir of Germanianus, and Caten, a descendant of Leudonus, formed an alliance, overran the Clyde and expelled Dyfnwal's dynasty.

But Morcant's counter-conquest was short-lived. By around 560, Dyfnwal's heir, Rhydderch Hael, had regained the Clyde throne with the aid of several allies, Mordaf, Nud and Clytno. Another link between north and south now emerges. Elidyr, a king of South Rheged and son-in-law of Maelgwn of Gwynedd, tried to take Gwynedd from Rhun, the son of Maelgwn by his concubine Gwalltwen. This may have happened around 560.[88] Elidyr landed near Caernarvon, but was killed on the beach. It seems he was not supported by the York or Pennine kings: instead it was Rhydderch and other northern allies who sailed to Gwynedd to avenge him. There was a strong motive of self-interest here, because Rhun's half-brother Bridei had become king of the Picts in 554, mounting an expedition to Argyll in an attempt to rid the Scottish mainland of the Dalriadic Irish.[89] Bridei, king of the Picts, was not only Maelgwn's son but cousin of Egferth, king of the Bernicians. A kinship alliance of this kind between Gwynedd and Pictland was a serious threat to the security of the British kingdoms of Clyde and Rheged. The raid on Gwynedd was unsuccessful, and Rhydderch had to withdraw.

Rhun's response was to gather an army and march it north, probably via York: a march of legendary length, both in distance and duration. His army was away from home for a very long time and is recorded to have met no resistance. Rhun marched through South Rheged on his way. Elidyr's son and successor, the boy king Llywarch Hen, was in no position to resist and had not the temperament either; it was probably wiser in any case to allow Rhun's great army to pass through unopposed. Llywarch Hen was left alone, and eventually died, an elderly exile writing poetry in Powys, long after the English had overrun his kingdom.[90] Rhun went on deep into the Gododdin, all the way to the Forth, still unopposed, and after this impressive parade of military strength returned to Gwynedd.

It was a triumph. Yet it also illustrated, just as Arthur's career did thirty years earlier, how the British could organize brilliant and spectacular military *coups de théâtre* and yet fail to hold together the polity of a large kingdom. To judge from Gildas, the British *disliked* kings. They evidently felt no need to unite behind a powerful monarch or submit to central control. They simply did not see, even as late as 560, how dangerous the growing Anglo-Saxon colonies in the east and south-east were. While the soldier's loyalty was always to his lord – a local war-band loyalty – petty rivalries among the war-band leaders, the kings and sub-kings, would be likely to erupt quickly, easily and repeatedly into civil war.

The northern poems express the *Zeitgeist* well: the highest ethic involved the devoted loyalty of faithful warriors to their lord and his personal destiny. The idea of sacrificing or compromising that loyalty by serving an overlord ran against this sentiment. Long-term loyalty to a bretwalda, *dux bellorum* or overking would have been alien to the rank-and-file soldier.[91] The effect was that although British resistance to the advance of the Saxons in the sixth and seventh centuries may have been intermittently highly successful, in the long term it was doomed, in the same way that resistance to the Roman invasion had been in the first century, as contemporary Roman commentators had recognized.

In 560, the great Rhun was king of Gwynedd, Cadell Deyrnllwg, son of Pasgen, son of Rhydwf, great-grandson of Vortigern[92] was king of Powys, Peredur Steel Arm, son of Eleutherius of the Great Army was king of York, Gwallawg was king of Elmet, Owain was king of Rheged and he had killed Ida ruler of the Anglian kingdom of Bernicia the previous year, Rhydderch was king of Clyde and Conall was king of Dal Riada. It was a few years later, around 570, that Urien, son of Cynfach, succeeded to the throne of Northern Rheged. This Urien was named 'King of the Golden North' by the great bard Taliesin; it was the dark age custom for bards to flatter the kings who were their employers. Taliesin frequently sang this refrain about his patron:

> And until I perish in old age
> In my death's sore need
> I shall not be happy
> If I praise not Urien.

Urien held court at Cair Ligualid (Carlisle) and had a son called Owain who succeeded him in about 590. Urien led a coalition of northern British kings, including Rhydderch of Clyde and Gwallawg of Elmet,[93] in a campaign against the Angles under their king Hussa, who were encroaching from Bernicia[94] to the east: Urien thus became an unofficial northern *dux bellorum*, like Arthur some seventy years earlier.

His neighbour to the north was Mynyddawg Mwynfawr, king of Gododdin, who like his predecessors was based at Din Eidyn, while his neighbour to the north-west was Rhydderch Hael, king of Clyde, who fought with Urien against Theodoric of Bernicia, leader of the Angles in the north.

In 573, the great Battle of Arderydd (Arthuret) was fought at Longtown. The battle was remembered in the Triads as one of Three Futile Battles of the Island of Britain: 'the action of Arderydd, which was brought about by the cause of the lark's nest'.[95] This may seem impenetrably cryptic but it can be explained relatively easily. The lowland Scots word for lark is *laverock*, and there is an ancient castle site on the north shore of the Solway Firth that is called Caerlaverock, literally 'the fortress of the lark' or more loosely and poetically 'the lark's nest'. The battle was therefore remembered as being fought for possession of the Scottish shore of the Solway Firth.[96]

The Longtown river crossing near the mouth of the Esk at the head of the Solway Firth was an important strategic point physically; it was also the crossing place of the Roman road from Rheged into Clyde. The place was dominated by the stronghold of King Gwenddolau, son of Ceidio, one of the leading combatants who died in the battle in and round his own fortress. Gwenddolau had a bard, like all the other kings, but his bard was called Myrddin, which makes us look more closely at him. Myrddin too took part in the battle and, when he saw his lord killed, he went mad and became a hermit in the Wood of Celidon, which Tolstoy believes was up on Hart Fell, midway between Carlisle and Dumbarton.[97] There is a traditional account preserved in the Welsh Myrddin poetry, and it is corroborated by an eleventh-century archive mention:

> The Battle of Arderydd between the sons of Elifer and Gwenddolau the son of Ceidio; in which battle Gwenddolau fell; Merlin became mad.[98]

Elifer is Eleutherius of York, so the battle according to this briefest of accounts was a conflict between the heirs of the kingdom of Rheged and those of the kingdom of York – a conflict among Britons. The *Black Book of Carmarthen* contains a verse which, from its form and tone, may be an authentic sixth-century elegy:

> I saw Gwenddolau in the track of kings,
> Collecting booty from every border,
> Now indeed he lies under the red earth,
> The chief of the kings of the North of greatest generosity.

It may be an unadapted elegy for Gwenddolau, in which case it was most likely written by Myrddin, his bard. Were these the words of Myrddin himself, written in the aftermath of the Battle of Arderydd?

There may have been a religious conflict involved as well as or instead of a struggle over political supremacy in the north. If Rhydderch of Clyde was involved in the battle on his frontier with Rheged – the chronicles and poems do not say whether he was there or not – it may have been a fight between Christianity and paganism. In the late sixth century most British kings seem to have been publicly Christian, although from a comment of Gildas some were practising paganism in private.

Rhydderch was more actively Christian than most, supporting the mission of the much-loved St Kentigern. He was also noted in early chronicles as a hammer of the heathen Angles of Bernicia, against whom he fought from 572 to 579 in a great northern alliance with Urien.[99] Like Arthur and his sword Excalibur, Rhydderch had Dyrnwyn, the special sword that, when unsheathed, flamed like fire.[100] Urien, by contrast, was remembered as a pagan king. The *Red Book of Hergest* contains a *Lamentation for Urien's Death*. It is set in Urien's deserted, overgrown fortress and the bard enters bearing the king's bloody severed head. This is a direct reference to a pagan Celtic ceremony. The head of a dead prince was cut off and taken home for burial: the practice continued in pagan Ireland until at least 600. These clues suggest that a religious war between Clyde and Rheged is possible, and a religious war is often a bitter and memorable one.

Another reason why the Battle of Arderydd was remembered in later centuries is that, like Camlann, it was a battle of exceptional ferocity. In the Welsh Triads there is a mention of the 'war-bands of Gwenddolau son of Ceidiaw at Arderydd, who continued the battle for a fortnight and a month after their lord was slain'. The reason for the battle may have been religious or territorial, but it was not a battle between the British on one side and the Angles or Saxons on the other. In this way, too, it was like Arthur's final battle, a ferocious and long-remembered struggle between quarrelling British lords and their war-bands. The sixth century closed as it began, with heroic British warlords performing acts of mythic valour against one another and their bards weaving powerful poetry round them while, almost unnoticed, the colonies of Angles and Saxons crept gradually westwards like an incoming tide.

While out on a campaign, Urien was assassinated at the instigation of his ally Morcant, out of jealousy for Urien's all-surpassing generalship, 'because in him above all the kings was the greatest skill in the renewing of battle'.[101] It was in 590 that Morcant commissioned Dyfnwal ap Mynyddawg and Llovan Llawddino of Din Eidyn to murder Urien. The bard Taliesin sang nostalgically of the great dead king.[102]

> Sovereign supreme, ruler all highest,
> The strangers' refuge, strong champion in battle.
> This the English know when they tell tales.
> Death was theirs, rage and grief are theirs,
> Burnt are their houses, bare are their bodies.

Fine words, implying that the warriors of Rheged had defeated the Saxons. But death was not theirs, not theirs at all. At Arderydd, the British were destroying one another, not the English.

CHAPTER FIVE

ARTHUR
The man, the king and the kingdom

———— • ◆ • ————

This is that Arthur of whom the trifling Welsh talk so much nonsense today. He clearly deserves not to be dreamed of in silly fairy tales, but to be remembered in true histories, as one who long sustained his dying country and gave the shattered minds of his fellow citizens an edge for war.

(William of Malmesbury, *Deeds of the Kings of Britain*, 1128–30)

The man

As we have seen in earlier chapters, the dates given in the *Welsh Annals* for the two key events in Arthur's military career, the dates for the battles of Badon and Camlann, can be accepted as correct to within a year or two. Some scholars have argued strenuously for moving them as much as a couple of decades forwards or backwards in time, but accepting the annal dates of 516 for Badon and 537 for Camlann creates far fewer inconsistencies and mismatches than any of the alternatives, which in itself suggests that they are fundamentally correct.[1] For Camlann, Nennius and Bede give the date as 537, the *Welsh Annals* 539 and Geoffrey, apparently drawing on Cornish and Breton sources as well as Welsh, 542: they are all fairly close together. Henry of Huntingdon drew mainly on Anglo-Saxon sources for his *Historia Anglorum* (about 1129), but added an account of Arthur, making him active in 527–30, which is consistent with the other sources. Morris's argument for an early date for Badon, in 495, is based on a clear line of reasoning: that Gildas wrote his *Ruin of Britain* while Maelgwn was alive, that Maelgwn died in the plague year of 547, and that Gildas says Badon happened forty-three years before the time when he was writing.

One problem here is that Gildas's original meaning is not clear. Bede quotes from Gildas, but evidently read a copy of the work that was significantly different in thrust from the version that survives today. He interpreted the '43 years' quite differently, counting them from the Saxons' first settlement in Britain, with Badon coming at the end. Bede believed that the Saxon colonization began in the mid-fifth century, so he assumed a date around 500 for Badon, but if Gildas had in mind some rather later benchmark event in the Saxon colonization, such as the arrival of the South Saxons, the date for Badon would have to shift to a significantly later time. In fact, if we add forty-three years to the date given by the *Anglo-Saxon Chronicle* for Aelle's arrival in Sussex, 477, it brings Badon to the year 520, very close to the 516/518 of the *Welsh Annals*. Another alternative is that the involved Latin of Gildas's surviving account was intended to convey that the battle took place forty-three years after the British counterstroke that began the war; that would suggest one of Ambrosius Aurelianus' major victories, which could have occurred in 470–75, allowing a date for Badon in 513–18. The date for Badon given indirectly in Gildas therefore need not be as early as 500.

It is also worth considering the possibility that Gildas may not have been writing in 540 but ten years or so later. We know from Gildas's long diatribe against Maelgwn that Maelgwn was still alive when he wrote. Maelgwn is said to have died of the plague; he may nevertheless have died not in the first but a later plague year: plague was enduring and recurring. The Yellow Plague of Rhos which struck in 547 was followed in 555 by the Great Plague, an epidemic lasting seven years. It would be very easy for a chronicler mistakenly to associate Maelgwn's death with the earlier instead of the later outbreak of plague. On top of this, Gildas's Latin is unclear and ambiguous. Even so, with the later date for Badon, in 516, and Gildas writing forty-three years afterwards, he would have been writing in 559, when we know he was alive, and there were still three more plague years after that in which Maelgwn might have died. There is not enough evidence for overturning the plain and clear entries for the two battles in the annals.

If Arthur was not only an active soldier from 516 to 537 but had major successes in that period, he is likely to have been born in 475, give or take a year or two. That would have made him 41 at Badon, a mature and accomplished commander, and 62 at Camlann, physically reaching the end of his fighting life and probably thirsting for retirement. If we hypothesize a birth date for Arthur in 475, it gives credible ages for him at the two points of his military career known from the annals.

Of his lineage, nothing is known for certain. Pedigrees of the Clyde and South Welsh dynasties have survived, and these give some reference points to events elsewhere, for example in the kingdoms of York, Gododdin and Dumnonia, but there is very little direct evidence of Dumnonian dynasties. One Dumnonian pedigree or regnal list that has survived lists two known associates and underkings of Arthur (see facing page).

The fact that no Dumnonian pedigree for Arthur has survived does not preclude Arthur from being a Dumnonian. Pedigrees are missing for several other key historic figures from this period and the pedigrees that do exist are not by any means entirely reliable. As we saw earlier, no more is known of Aelle, first king of the South Saxons and first bretwalda of the English, yet historians are ready to accept him without a pedigree.

Geoffrey of Monmouth relates that Arthur's mother was Ygerne or Ygraine. Rachel Bromwich has assembled a family tree for a woman called Eigr, who is assumed to be the same woman. Eigr had a sister Reiengulid, who had a son, Illtud, which is how Illtud comes to be Arthur's cousin. Eigr's mother was Gwenn, daughter of Cunedda Wledig: Gwenn's husband, Arthur's maternal grandfather, was Amlawdd Wledig. This traditionary Welsh view makes Arthur the great-grandson of Cunedda.

surviving Dumnonian pedigree:

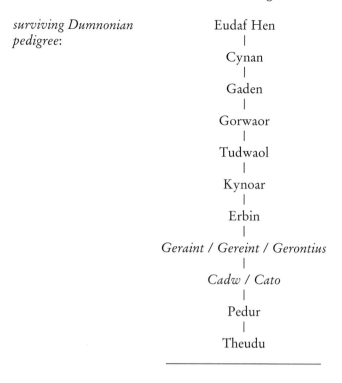

Eudaf Hen
|
Cynan
|
Gaden
|
Gorwaor
|
Tudwaol
|
Kynoar
|
Erbin
|
Geraint / Gereint / Gerontius
|
Cadw / Cato
|
Pedur
|
Theudu

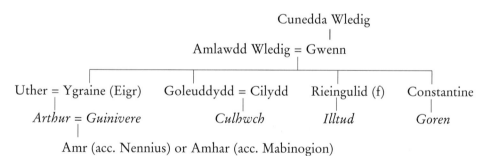

Cunedda Wledig
|
Amlawdd Wledig = Gwenn

Uther = Ygraine (Eigr)   Goleuddydd = Cilydd   Rieingulid (f)   Constantine
Arthur = *Guinivere*   *Culhwch*   *Illtud*   *Goren*
|
Amr (acc. Nennius) or Amhar (acc. Mabinogion)

Geoffrey of Monmouth, presumably drawing on non-Welsh sources (possibly Breton or Cornish), offers Arthur's paternal descent:

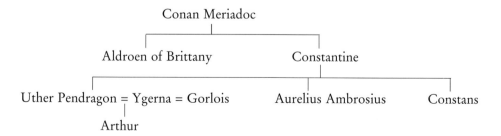

Conan Meriadoc
|
Aldroen of Brittany   Constantine

Uther Pendragon = Ygerna = Gorlois   Aurelius Ambrosius   Constans
|
Arthur

The lack of firm authenticated pedigree might be taken to suggest a humble parentage for Arthur, in line with the romance tradition of Arthur as an innocent unschooled squire without ambition who accedes to the throne by reason of his unconscious strength or divine destiny, as represented by the sword in the stone story. Alternatively, it could be seen as evidence of Arthur as a usurper: Gildas was scathing about the usurpers who occupied many of the thrones of Britain. But this would be reading too much into the absence of evidence in a period when there is relatively little evidence anyway. There were many kings in Britain in those days and we know very little about most of them, so the absence of pedigree should not lead us to assume that Arthur was of low birth or won his throne by military strength alone. It would be safer to assume that, like other kings, he inherited his title and his domain, though he may initially have inherited and worked from a relatively small power base. Inheritance was normally via family lineage. Gildas complained that Maelgwn had removed the king, his uncle, to make himself king, and a fragment in the *Historia Brittonum* notes that Maelgwn reigned because his great-great-great-grandfather had reigned 146 years earlier. There is also plenty of other evidence of sons regularly succeeding fathers in the sixth and seventh centuries.

Many modern writers have confidently written that Arthur was definitely *not* a king. Leslie Alcock for instance was prepared to declare: 'Arthur was not a king ... and founded no dynasty.'[2] Geoffrey Ashe in a similar spirit declared that Arthur was not a king but a general.[3] This assertion might be based on the absence of any royal pedigree including him, but it is more usually based on a specific passage in Nennius.

> *Tunc Arthur pugnabat contra illos in illis diebus cum regibus Brittonum, sed ipse dux erat bellorum.*
> Then Arthur fought against them in those days with the British kings, but he himself was leader of battles.[4]

This has been interpreted to mean that when the British armies took to the field of battle they were led by their kings, and that a lower-ranking Arthur (a 'duke' not a king) co-ordinated the fighting rather as a modern professional general might be commissioned to take on the role of commander-in-chief in a particular campaign. But this is to read a later, high medieval interpretation of the rank of 'duke' back into a dark age setting. It seems clear that Arthur, as one among scores of British kings, might take his place on the battlefield without his kingship specifically being mentioned or drawn attention to; it is understood rather than stated and overtaken entirely by the remark that he was giving orders to the other kings. In a very real sense, the Nennius passage is telling us that on the battlefield at any rate Arthur held a *higher* rank than the other kings. He was not only a king but a leader of kings. In *Culhwch and Olwen*, which was finally written down in around 1100 but contains dark age material, Arthur is described as 'Chief of the Kings of Britain'. It must be significant that Nennius mentions in passing that Ambrosius Aurelianus was a king, a fact which is otherwise glossed over, taken for granted by contemporaries; if Ambrosius was a king, information we are given almost incidentally, then his successor must certainly have been one too.

While Nennius calls Arthur *dux bellorum*, the Welsh and Cornish poets called him *amerawder*, which is a late pidgin-Latin version of *imperator*, or emperor; he appears unambiguously as *Yr Amherawdyr Arthur*, 'the Emperor Arthur'.[5] In the Geraint poem, which is admitted by most scholars to be very early, Arthur is described unequivocally as 'The Emperor, the ruler of our toil'. It is clear from this that Arthur's role as commander-in-chief on the battlefield automatically made him overking. There was a road system left behind by the Romans, maybe in increasing disrepair but still ridable none the less; there was also a common language, Brittonic, which meant that travellers could make themselves understood anywhere from Cornwall to southern Scotland.[6] To judge from Bede's description of the Pictish king Bridei as 'rex potentissimus', the Picts too were familiar with the concept of an overking and had one of their own.[7] If we can believe the medieval genealogies, there was a precedent for a Dumnonian king becoming overking. Coel Godhebog was prince of 'Cornwall', son of Tegvan ap Dehevraint, also prince of Cornwall, and took upon himself the kingdom of Britain in 272, holding it for twenty-eight years.[8] Arthur's role has been clear to some people for a long time. The following, for instance, was written as long ago as 1851:

> If we strip the Arthur of romance of the idea of absolute monarchy, we shall find a warrior, elected by many kings as independent as himself to be their common leader in war. He was a British Gwledig elected in emergency to be their leader, dominator or emperor of all the kings of Britain; but in his own right was only king of a small principality. Such in fact were all the British kings . . . Cadwaladr was nominally king of the whole country from Cumberland to Cornwall, but in his own right only king of Gwynedd.[9]

The title 'gwledig' was given only to certain kings, and was the Brittonic equivalent of *dux bellorum*. Before Arthur, Cunedda, Ambrosius and Amlawdd were gwledigs; after Arthur, Maelgwn and Urien were accorded the title.

When and how the dark age kings obtained their power is unclear, but inheritance was certainly a major factor, as is implicit in the genealogies. Sons inherited thrones from fathers. In some cases it may be that ascent to power was by military might rather than birthright: Gildas accuses several kings of being usurpers, although it is unclear what he means by this. The titles of some kings leaves the question wide open. Gwallawg, for instance, was described as 'the ordained magistrate of Elmet', which could mean that he was destined, born to rule, or that he was a usurper whose position had been later legalized by way of some ceremony. Either way, positive achievements were always instrumental in strengthening their position. With Arthur it was clearly the Falklands factor writ large. Actions such as organizing and building the Wansdyke or Cadbury 11 (the refortification) would have strengthened the authority and extended the power of whichever king was the organizer.

If Arthur was a king, was he crowned? Possibly. Geoffrey of Monmouth reports that after Uther's death Britons gathered 'from their various provinces in the town of Silchester and suggested to Dubricius, the Archbishop of the City of the Legions, that as their king he should crown Arthur, the son of Uther'.[10] The Saxons were going to take advantage of the loss of leadership, impetus and morale on the British side caused by Uther's death and launch a massive attack.

Dubricius lamented the sad state of his country. He called the other bishops to him and bestowed the crown of the kingdom upon Arthur. Once he had been invested with the royal insignia, he observed the normal custom of giving gifts freely to everyone.

What Geoffrey describes is an accession by entirely normal process, inheritance from father to son. Arthur's father Uther was king: now Arthur becomes king. The only peculiarity is the haste: it was important to have a new leader as quickly as possibly, given the threat from the enemy.

How realistic is this scenario? The role Geoffrey assigns to Dubricius is interesting, in that Dubricius was not only a genuine historical figure, but alive at the right time to do the things Geoffrey's story requires of him. Historically, that is, using evidence other than Geoffrey, Dubricius was a great Christian figure of the Arthurian period. He was the *only* bishop to be attached to a city, to have a see in the modern sense: most bishops were creatures of their kings, very much personal appointments.[11] Nowadays, and in Geoffrey's time, bishops are invariably linked with a specific city and diocese. That Geoffrey gets this particular peculiarity of dark age Britain right suggests that he had access to a genuine tradition.

Dubricius had the status not just of a bishop of Caerleon but of principal bishop of southern Britain. He was the patron of Samson and Illtud and he consecrated Samson as bishop of the Severn Sea. He was actively ordaining priests and consecrating bishops in the period 500–20, and was clearly the dominant churchman at the right moment for one of two types of coronation. These facts all point to Geoffrey being in receipt of an accurately transmitted oral tradition.

What Geoffrey had in mind was a simple elevation of Prince Arthur to king of Britain, but the political geography was more complex than that, with sub-kings of minor territories, kings of major territories and (I am proposing here) an overking of a larger territory still. Evidence for the existence of sub-kings comes from the *Life of Germanus*. During his second visit to Britain in 454, Germanus healed the child of a man named Elafius, who was described as *regionis illius primus*, the leading man or chief of that region.[12] Arthur presumably became a *primus*, sub-king or king first, then overking later. Dubricius could have been involved in a formal coronation of Arthur as a sub-king or king at the age of 20 *and* a formal induction ceremony as an overking ten or twenty years later, presumably as part of the military campaign that culminated in the victory at Badon. In fact, there is a hint of something like this in Geoffrey's account; Arthur is elected king/leader (perhaps something like *dux patriae*, a title Gildas uses to describe leaders of regions) at 15: then follows a career consisting of campaigning in Britain, the establishment of a peace, then a 'Gallic' campaign. After twenty-two years there is a coronation at Caerleon as a preamble to the final campaigns.

Arthur's personality is more elusive than his historical reality. Much of what we see in our mind's eye as Arthur's personality is a literary persona, a product of the medieval romances and later literary and cinematic treatments which cannot tell us much about the historical figure. The Welsh poem *Brut ab Arthur* tells us, 'God has not made since Adam was, a man more perfect than Arthur.' Eulogies of this kind are nevertheless not very helpful to the would-be biographer. We may be able to infer some of his personal qualities, his concerns, his political agenda from the observations of Gildas about the nature of Arthur's Britain. Gildas looked back to the 520s and 530s as a time when things were run as they ought to be run. If Arthur was overking at that time, the *Zeitgeist* should bear the stamp of his personality. If so, Arthur favoured orderliness in government, and was therefore, we may tentatively assume, orderly in behaviour himself; he set a high value on control and respected truth and justice. He also sought to maintain all ranks of society in their stations.

In all these respects, Arthur sounds like the very best kind of Roman patrician, and it seems to be true that the elite of the post-Roman British aristocracy consciously liked to see themselves in just that way. The fact that Arthur's contemporary, the king of Demetia whom Gildas praised as 'a good king', went by a Latin name as well as a Celtic one – Agricola as well as Aircol – shows how much some British aristocrats valued their precious Roman legacy. Agricola's father's personal name was forgotten by the compilers of the Demetian royal pedigree, and he appears simply as '*The Tribune*'. A memorial stone near Chesterholm, dating from Arthur's lifetime, is inscribed 'Brigomaglos, who is also Briocus, lies [here]'.[13] Arthur is likely to have been one of these Rome-orientated, past-orientated Celtic kings who tried hard to maintain Roman standards of law and order and probably used old-fashioned Latin at least for formal pronouncements as a mark of status. Arthur's predecessor Ambrosius was also Rome-orientated. He was described elliptically by Gildas as being of the imperial family, but Gildas uses the word *nimirum*, which means 'may have' and is heavily ironic in tone, so when Gildas says that Ambrosius's parents '*may* have worn the purple' he was probably trying to tell us facetiously that they were more Roman than the Romans.[14]

This 'Romanization' of the Britons is seen in the north as well. It has been suggested that the native Gododdin tribe was trained by the Romans to police the eastern half of the northern frontier, The Wall, and that this Romanization was marked by the adoption of a Latin name for the tribe, Votadini; during the Arthurian period, the older name was re-adopted. In Clyde too there was Romanization among the aristocracy. King Coroticus' grandfather was called Cinhil, probably a British form of *Quintilius*, son of Cluim, probably a form of *Clemens*, both Roman names.[15]

There is, however, a parallel tradition that holds that Arthur had a streak of cruelty evident even in his boyhood.[16] Indeed, it is hard to see how a successful career in dark age soldiering and leadership could be other than marked by single-minded determination and ruthlessness. On the other hand, it may be that Arthur's ferocity and viciousness were exaggerated by bards at the courts of Arthur's rivals, such as Maelgwn of Gwynedd. The many scurrilous stories told against Arthur in later centuries may have their origin in these rival courts where, we can imagine, the oppressive greatness of Arthur may well have been resented and lampooned.

We need not take too seriously the rapacious, church-goading Arthur who appears occasionally in the *Lives* of the saints. Kings are routinely portrayed as evil pagans in these narratives. By comparison with many, Arthur is shown as merely unruly and unpredictable, and open to persuasion: a fairly mild character.[17]

Tradition holds that Arthur acceded to his throne, wherever that throne was, at a very young age. Geoffrey embodies that tradition. 'Arthur was a young man only fifteen years old at the time of his accession.'[18] Geoffrey tells us of his personal qualities as remembered and probably coloured up across six centuries, of his out-standing courage and generosity, his inborn goodness and grace, his open-handedness and bravery, his keenness to redistribute the wealth of the Saxons to his own supporters. The description is reminiscent of that of Alexander, and the similarity is probably not accidental. Arthur does seem to have won the support, loyalty and then love of his followers by way of a personal cult akin to Alexander's, if smaller in scale and less extreme. Alexander, we may remember, was both lovable and ruthless.

Arthur needed the loyalty not only of his war-band but of the leaders of other war-bands if he was to be successful in stemming the encroachment of the Saxons.[19] The later and highly elaborated, highly romanticized tales of the Round Table knights must really be set aside in reconstructing the historical Arthur, but it is nevertheless likely that they represent a genuine, if highly coloured, tradition based on a sixth-century reality. Arthur may well have developed a kind of brotherhood with his allies, co-kings and client-kings, a bonding that was essential to a successful concerted effort. He must have known that each war-band could ultimately be trusted only to be loyal to its king or chief, and that he, Arthur, needed to be able in the heat of the battle, *in extremis*, to depend utterly on the loyalty of his 'brother' kings.

The great scholar, Illtud of Llantwit, was said to have been Arthur's cousin. He lived to see the period of Arthur's post-Badon greatness and may have outlived Arthur.[20] The great historian of the period, Gildas, was evidently a friend of Arthur. It was he who mediated between Arthur and Melwas at Glastonbury and negotiated the release of Guinevere.

Only two of Arthur's brother kings are known for certain by name, and neither of them corresponds with a medieval Round Table knight: Geraint and Cato of Dumnonia. These two kings are named in the sixth-century elegy on the Battle of Llongborth and the sixth-century *Life of St Carantoc*.[21] There must have been scores of other kings who served, fought for, befriended and feasted with Arthur, but those two are the only 'Round Table knights' who are a matter of contemporary record.

Britain was rich in kings. So too was Ireland, and a more complete record of them and their dynasties has survived. There were several major Irish kings – of Leinster, Munster, Connacht, Ui Neill and Ulaid – with many petty kings and sub-kings beneath them. Above them, on a third level, there was a high king of Ireland with supremacy over all. When Arthur was born, Aillel Molt was high king, but he was killed by an alliance of Irish kings in the Battle of Ocha in 482, when Arthur was still a boy. The high kingship fell immediately to King Loegaire's son Lugid, but Muirchetach mac Erca, Arthur's contemporary, succeeded to the position in 503 and held it very conspicuously for the next thirty years. Mac Erca dominated Irish political and military affairs for those three decades in much the same way that Arthur is thought to have dominated in Britain.

Who were Arthur's co-kings in Britain? Who were his peers and equals, the people he would have looked to as potential friends and allies? In what is now Scotland, the Irish king Fergus of Dal Riada took the rather surprising step of establishing his residence in what had been Pictish territory on the Argyll peninsula. This happened in 503. Not far away to the east, on the Clyde, King Ceretic of Alcluith (the same King Coroticus whom St Patrick claimed to have turned into a fox) had recently died: he was succeeded in 500 by his son Dyfnwal, who would have been roughly Arthur's age.

To the south, in what is now Cumbria and Lancashire, lay the huge kingdom of Rheged, ruled by King Merchiaun. He too would have been of Arthur's generation. East of the Pennines, and including much of present-day Northumberland, Durham and Yorkshire, was the huge kingdom of York; this was the legacy of Coel Hen, Coel the Ancient, or Old King Cole as he would later be known, and now, in Arthur's day, was ruled by his descendant, King Gurgust Lethum.

In southern Britain there were more native British kingdoms, including some that were about to be swallowed up by Saxon encroachment. We hear of a King Natan-Leod who ruled over an inland part of Hampshire at the turn of the sixth century and was defeated and killed by Cerdic, leader and later king of the West Saxons. Powys was ruled by King Ewein Whitetooth, who was later murdered by the king of Gwynedd, the notorious Maelgwn, and succeeded by his (Ewein's) son Cynlas. Cynlas was nicknamed, possibly privately by Gildas, 'Cuneglasus',[22] which probably meant Pale Dog in Brittonic.[23] The king of Glevissig (Glamorgan) was Merchiaun Vesanus, Merchiaun the Wild, the descriptive nickname possibly being a necessary addition to make sure he was not confused with the king of Rheged, who was also called Merchiaun. Mark Cunomorus, the Dumnonian king, was a son of Merchiaun the Wild, a son exiled to Dumnonia.[24]

The king of Demetia was Aircol Laohir, or Agricola, one of only two kings Gildas fleetingly praised. Aircol was mentioned as an exemplary warrior-hero by Taliesin. Cynan Garwyn of Powys was described in battle in Dyfed, Aircol's own kingdom, as 'like Aircol himself on the rampage'.[25] Aircol was succeeded in 515 by his son Gordebar or Vortipor the Protector. In Dumnonia there were several kings: Geraint, Cato, Mark Cunomorus, Conan, Caradoc Vreichvras and Theodoric. From Theodoric's name, which is pure Gothic, and his evident ownership of ships, John Morris infers that he was (perhaps one of many) expelled from Gaul in 507 by Arthur's brilliant contemporary, King Clovis of the Franks.[26] Theodoric may have put his redundant fleet at the service of the kings of Dumnonia and Demetia in return for a gift of estates in West Cornwall, where he settled and later died in a hunting accident.[27]

These are the names of the kings we know lived and reigned during Arthur's lifetime, and there must have been many more whose names have been forgotten. We can nevertheless see from this review that Britain, like Ireland, was a mosaic of petty kingdoms or sub-kingdoms nested within a framework of larger kingdoms (see Figure 5.1). By the early sixth century there were clearly great kings who controlled, or at any rate nominally controlled, territories of the order of 10,000 square kilometres. They varied in size from around 6,000 km^2 in area (like the Gododdin and Gwynedd) up to very large territories three times that size (York). Powys and Clyde were close to the average at around 12,000 km^2.

Given the large size of these kingdoms, their rulers could only have maintained control with the co-operation of their sub-kings or client-kings, each of which had the delegated tasks of maintaining law, order and loyalty within their district and levying war service for the defence of the kingdom's interests. The relationship between king and sub-king was therefore all-important, far more important than

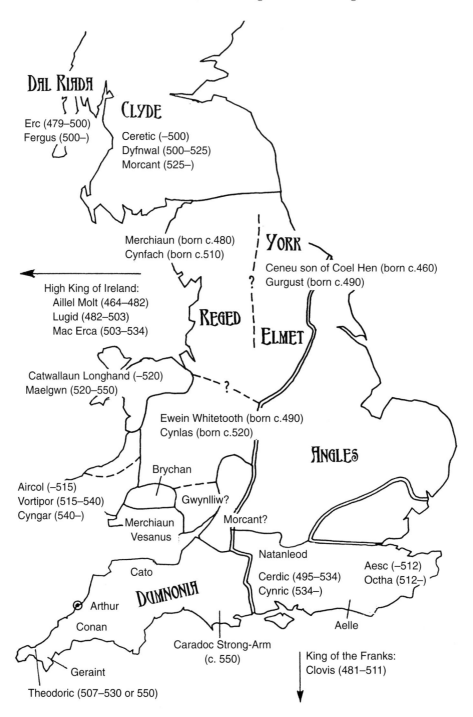

Figure 5.1 The kings of Britain at the time of Arthur. Dates are necessarily approximate, but all based on regnal lists or near-contemporary annals.

natural wealth or any other geographical advantages that the kingdom might possess. The documents tell us that Maelgwn asserted that relationship with aggression, menace, violence and cruelty, extracting obedience through fear. The way in which Arthur is remembered suggests that, if he was indeed the king of one of these kingdoms, he sustained the relationship by entirely different means, inspiring loyalty and creating an emotional bond that was closer to the bond between siblings.

To what extent the pattern of political organization in Britain followed that seen in Ireland is unclear. In both islands there were small sub-kingdoms only 100–200 km² in area nested within major kingdoms that were a hundred times larger. In Ireland there was a high king over all. Was there such a figure in Britain? Pictland in the fifth and sixth centuries remained a separate entity throughout, a large highland kingdom with its own king headquartered at Inverness. There is the possibility, though, that the southern kingdoms of Britain, faced with a common Anglo-Saxon threat on their eastern margins, would have seen the great benefit of overall co-ordination by a *dux*, a leader, a chief among kings. The tradition that Geoffrey picked up and developed certainly incorporated the belief that Arthur was the king of all Britain, and the slightly earlier king list gives us documentary evidence that this belief was an enduring one.[28]

Nevertheless, a high king of Southern Britain may not have been part of the sixth-century reality. As we have already seen, Geoffrey cannot be used as evidence without corroboration. Nor can we assume that because it was in the interests of the kings of Dumnonia, Powys, Glevissig, Gwent, Gwynedd, Rheged and York to co-ordinate and integrate their efforts against Saxon incursion that they actually did so. The British tragedy is that for the most part they underestimated the seriousness of the Saxon threat.

Gildas gives us a contemporary and critical view of a situation in which political fragmentation and power struggles among the British elites were visibly weakening and endangering the British cause. Having said that, it can also be said that if an overall British commander existed in the period 500–40, then there was an obvious arena within which he could have operated to great effect. However ill-defined and interdigitated it may have been, there was an 'Eastern Front' where the Saxons had to be held at bay (see Figure 5.2). By the time Gildas was writing, this front had crept westwards to a line snaking across the island from Whitby on the North Sea coast to Christchurch Harbour on the English Channel. If Arthur had a key role a generation earlier in holding that front it would seem probable that he co-ordinated the war-bands of at least those Celtic kingdoms with eastern frontiers threatened by Saxons, York, Rheged, Powys, Calchvynnydd and Dumnonia, as well as those of the lost kingdom of Logres, by Gildas's time already swallowed up in the Middle Anglian East Midlands and an emblem of the Celtic lands lost to the invader.

'The most powerful leader of the Britons'

Nennius tells us 'Arthur fought alongside the British kings, but he himself was *dux bellorum.' Dux bellorum.* The battle leader. Among the kings of Britain, Arthur was chosen to co-ordinate and lead the war host into battle. On first reading, the Nennius

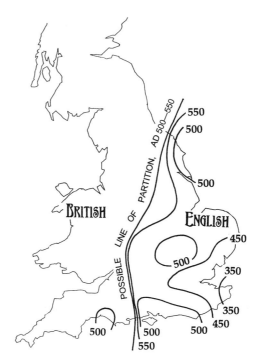

Figure 5.2 The war zone. Isolines show the earliest dates of datable Saxon finds.

statement may sound like a simple description of what Arthur did: that he led in battle, perhaps because he was the most skilful or reckless of the warriors, or simply the luckiest. But the phrase *dux bellorum* means more than that. It is not a description but an appointment or a title, and there were other dark age warrior-kings who held the position, whether under this or some other name.

An independent tradition in Brittany supports Geoffrey of Monmouth's account of a great campaign in dark age Gaul. Geoffrey has Arthur campaigning in Gaul, and the French tradition has a great war-leader, a king of the Britons (not Bretons) called Riothamus leading an army through Gaul in 468–70. Riothamus reached Burgundy and was betrayed there by a deputy ruler who conspired with the enemy. Riothamus disappeared after a final battle, and there is no record of his death. Geoffrey Ashe suggests that Arthur was Riothamus, and that Geoffrey of Monmouth drew on the Breton tradition.[29] This seems unlikely, not least because the Riothamus campaign of 468–70 was too early to be associated with Arthur, who was probably not even born until five years after the final defeat of Riothamus.[30] Riothamus may nevertheless have been a leader of Britons in exile in France. Large numbers of high-born Celts left Britain in 459, fearing ethnic cleansing as the Saxon colonists took over in the east, so there was certainly a British community in exile living in Brittany and Normandy and who could have been led into battle in Gaul by their leader. 'Riothamus' means 'supreme king', so it was a title rather than a personal name, and shows that a Celtic *dux bellorum*, who was not Arthur, was active in Gaul between 465 and 470.

It is clear from Gildas's description of Ambrosius Aurelianus that he had a similar 'ducal' role in Britain at about the same time, co-ordinating opposition to Vortigern the Younger in 459 and then organizing military resistance to the Saxons from 460 until 480 or later.

Vortigern the Elder and Vortigern the Younger evidently had a similar position as co-ordinators or overall commanders of armies. St Germanus was under the impression when he visited Britain in 429 and 445 that 'Vortigern' was in control of southern Britain. This suggests that in the early fifth century at least there was a high king of Southern Britain. It is also clear from the *Anglo-Saxon Chronicle* that the Saxons had their own equivalent of a 'battle leader', the bretwalda. The first of these bretwaldas was Aelle, who was appointed perhaps in the late 490s (after the fall of Anderida and the successful initial expansion west into Hampshire). Maybe Arthur's appointment as *dux* was a response to Aelle's as bretwalda. But, given the earlier precedents of Vortigern and Ambrosius, it looks more likely either that the Saxons were imitating an appointment that was a regular Celtic tradition of long standing or that the *dux bellorum* was part of a common North European heritage.

The difference between a *dux bellorum* and an overking is not clear, and it may be that the two concepts were elided into a single role. In the unstable conditions that prevailed, it would have been impossible to be a king without being a warlord, and to hold office as an overking would have involved being a *dux bellorum*. This idea is in a real sense continued in the early medieval list of the kings of Britain.[31] It begins with Aeneas, passes through Brutus and a host of other presumably mythical British kings before arriving at Kynwelyn (Cunobelin), a genuine British ruler of the eastern kingdom at the time of Christ, and even the date is correctly noted in the list. The kings of the Roman period include real figures such as Carausius and Allectus, which raises confidence in the list's increasing accuracy, then for the fifth and sixth centuries we have:

GORTHEYRN. GWETHUYR VENDIGEIT. EMRYS WLEDIC. UTHERPENDRIC. ARTHUR. CONSTANTINUS. AURELIUS. IUOR. MAELGON GOYNED.

This, translated and expanded, becomes:

Vortigern the Elder (of Powys): Vortigern the Younger (of Powys); Ambrosius the Overking (of Dumnonia); Uther Pendragon (?of Dumnonia); Arthur; Constantine (of Dumnonia); Aurelius (?the Aurelius Caninus of Gildas = ?Cynan ?of Calchvynnydd); Ivor (?of?); Maelgwn of Gwynedd.

Here, Maelgwn is being acknowledged as king of Gwynedd but in some sense also inflated into a king of Britain too. The only way this could happen is by the mechanism already suggested, that a pre-eminently powerful king was accorded high king status which allowed him to make some decisions over the heads of other British kings. The Welsh Laws confirm that this was the case once Maelgwn became high king: 'And his word was paramount over all, and his law paramount, and he not bound to observe their law.'[32] The king list also confirms the parallels we have been seeing between the documented careers of Vortigern the Elder, Vortigern the Younger, Ambrosius and Arthur. It is interesting that the supremacy moves sluggishly from kingdom to kingdom. Vortigern the Younger inherited his father's political and military strength and so the high kingship remained in Powys, then it passed from Powys. By 480, archaeology tells us, Vortigern's dynasty was no longer in power at Wroxeter: Powys may already have been taken over by Gwynedd. The ducal power had also shifted – though not to Gwynedd direct. First, it passed to Dumnonia for a brief period of glory. Then it seems to have gone (on the evidence of this late king list only) to Calchvynnydd, and finally to Gwynedd. The fact that Ambrosius and Constantine were both associated with Dumnonia suggests that Uther and Arthur too were Dumnonian kings. The overkingship seems to have circulated among the kings of Wales, the Welsh border country and the West Country, the region that in the late Roman period was Britannia Prima, a coherent and identifiable fourth-century administrative province. There are hints here that Britannia Prima continued as the loosest of confederations into the fifth and sixth centuries. The kings Gildas vilified were also the kings of this bloc.

History nevertheless does not suggest that three *duces* came between Arthur and Maelgwn. If Arthur fell in 537, Maelgwn must have become overking more or less straight away. We can detect in all this a post-Roman tradition of *duces bellorum* or overkings, who were (in later centuries at least) called 'kings of Britain'. It may be that they were accorded that honour at the time, although there is no evidence at all from documents or inscriptions that this was the case. The *Life of Cadoc* comes closest to it: Arthur himself is specifically described as *dux Britannorum fortissimus*, the most powerful (or illustrious) leader of the Britons. Overkingship of Britannia Prima might pass from father to son, but it was not on the whole an hereditary office, rather, won on reputation for political and military mastery.

The titles 'Wledic' and 'Pendragon' were British versions of the *dux bellorum*. 'Uther Pendragon' may therefore have been the *dux bellorum* called Uther. If Uther is really *uter*, meaning wonderful or terrible, the phrase Uther Pendragon may instead mean 'The Wonderful Head Dragon', who in turn may have been called Arthur. The kinglist should then read 'Emrys Wledic (= Ambrosius, supreme leader of the country)' followed by 'Uter Pendragon Arthur (= The Wonderful Head Dragon, Arthur)'; this would conform to the sequence of events we have already built up from various sources, with Arthur as Ambrosius' direct, immediate successor.

There is archaeological evidence that Hadrian's Wall was re-manned in the dark ages, probably co-organized by the Carvettii tribe who had the western half of the wall and the Brigantes tribe who had the eastern half. This implies collaboration between the neighbouring kingdoms of Rheged (the Carvettii) and York (the Brigantes), since neither had control over the whole Wall. This is just the sort of situation where the overriding power of a *dux* or overking would have assisted, if indeed the power of the overking of Britannia Prima extended that far north.[33]

Arthur's prowess as a warrior and leader of warriors was undoubtedly what led to his appointment or acclamation as *dux bellorum*. And that prowess was reflected in the honour in which his name was held in the two or three generations that followed his death.[34] His name was preserved in many local associations, with natural rock formations and even stars named after him: Arthur's Oven and Arthur's Quoit,

Arthur's Hall and Arthur's Seat, Arthur's Stone, Arthur's Table and Arthur's Tor. Just as with Charlemagne or Roland, the places are often incorrectly associated, but the important thing is that they record the importance that people attached to the hero. The memory of dates or locations might be suspect, but the memory of the hero himself was real enough.

The name Arthur was very rare before 500, yet after 550, i.e. after Arthur achieved fame, there were several princes of that name: then again after about 650 there were none again for a long time.[35] It is as if *our* Arthur, Arthur the king, made a powerful impression on his contemporaries and the two or three succeeding generations, but then entered the world of legend. Oliver Padel has argued that the areas where these Arthurs appeared were areas colonized by Irish settlers, unaffected by the 'British' taboo on using the names of gods for ordinary mortals.[36] But this is forced, and the evidence can equally easily be turned round and made to support the view that Arthur was not a god's name at all but the name of a much-admired warrior-prince.

We know from Welsh genealogies of an Arthur, son of King Peter in South Wales (Demetia) in the early seventh century.[37] His descendants migrated to the south coast of Ireland where they were known as the Deisi, and an eighth-century Irish genealogy traces these now-Irish back to 'Artur mac Petuir'. So, this Arthur, born perhaps a hundred years after our Arthur, is verified by two independent genealogies, one made and preserved in Wales, the other created later and independently in Ireland.

The *Life of Columba* mentions a prince of Dal Riada named Arthur: Arturius son of Aedan mac Gabrain of Dal Riada.[38] Aedan reigned from 574 and was probably born in about 525. Aedan's son Arturius, the Latin form of Arthur, was probably born in about 550. According to the *Life of Columba*, King Aedan was unsure which of his sons, Arthur, Eochaid Find or Domingart, would succeed him. Columba prophesied that

> none of these three shall be king, for they shall fall in battle, slain by their enemies; if you have any younger sons let them come to me, and the one the Lord has chosen will at once rush into my lap.

It was Eochaid Buide who ran straight to him. Arthur and Eochaid Find were not long afterwards killed in the battle of the Miathi in about 575–80:[39] Domingart was defeated and killed in battle in 'Saxonia'. Their father lived on until 606.

A third Arthur is known, Arthur son of Bicor Brito, who in the year 626 killed Morgan, son of Fiachna, Dal nAraide, with a rock.[40] A fourth Arthur seems to be referred to in the pedigree of the dynasty of York, in the cryptic entry, 'Gorgi a pheredur ac arthur penuchel'.[41] An Arthur is here associated with Peredur Steel-Arm and his co-ruler and brother Gwrgi, sons of King Eliffer of the Great Army, the king of York. Peredur was king of York from about 560 until 580, when he was killed in the Battle of Caer Greu.

So, several kings were naming their sons after Arthur in the middle and late sixth century: Aedan king of Dal Riada, his son Conang, Peter king of Demetia, Bicor the Briton, Coscrach king of Leinster. This can only have been as a mark of tribute to the great Arthur who, the annals tell us, fell at Camlann in 537. Supporting this, we have the brief mention, almost an aside, about Arthur in the poem *The Gododdin*, written in 610 by a bard probably serving the king who ruled from Din Eidyn. Even in dark age Edinburgh they knew of Arthur, of his greatness as a warrior; the bard, Aneirin, had heard of Geraint too. Aneirin laments the loss of a war-band who died fighting the Angles at the Battle of Cattraeth (Catterick). He says of one of them that he fought ferociously: 'He glutted black ravens on the wall of the fort, even though he was not Arthur.' No more is said than that, but it is enough to show that Arthur's valour as a soldier was already a by-word; certainly his was a name deemed fit for dark age princes.

Another possible early occurrence of Arthur's name, admittedly in garbled form, was noted in the nineteenth century.[42] This is a mention of an Iardurus or Iarddur ab Diwrig, though nothing further is known about him. The name Diwrig may be a lead, in that Dyfrig, essentially the same name, was St Dubricius, a known contemporary of Arthur's, and it would seem quite possible for someone who knew and admired Arthur to name his son after the king. Bishops, even saintly ones, were regularly married in the dark ages, and so also might have sons and daughters.

As a young man, Arthur emerges from the Welsh Triads, admittedly a later and therefore suspect source, as an impulsive adventurer, a feuding irregular. One Triad, *The Three Very Famous Prisoners of the Island of Britain* lists three forgotten celebrities, then adds:

> and there was one who was more famous than all three: he was three nights in the prison of Kaer Oeth and Anoeth, and three nights in the prison of Wenn Pendragon, and three nights in the magic prison beneath the flagstone of Echymeint. This famous prisoner was Arthur. And the same youth released him from each of these three prisons, Goreu vab Custennin, his cousin.[43]

Another triad, *The Three Stout Swineherds*, strongly implies that Arthur and his youthful followers were little better than pig-rustlers.[44] But above all, Arthur was remembered as a fearful and spectacularly effective killer on the battlefield, a Red Ravager. A third Triad reads, 'The Three Red Ravagers of the Island of Britain: Rhun, son of Beli, Lleu Skilful Hand, and Morgant the Wealthy. But there was one who was a Red Ravager greater than all three: Arthur was his name.'

Arthur's power base

Those who agree on the historical existence of King Arthur disagree about his power base. Those who can agree on his history cannot agree on his geography. There has, inevitably, been competition for Arthur, with the Scots claiming him for Scotland, the English claiming him for pre-Saxon 'England', and most vehemently of all the Welsh claiming him as a Welshman. Arthurian place-names and legends are spread across a huge area, but there is a noticeable clustering within a zone stretching from Cornwall and Somerset through Wales and Cumbria into southern Scotland. This is the zone where the contemporaries and descendants of Arthur and his allies managed to retain their Celtic identity longest; further east and south-east, the legacy was lost because it was probably blotted out by early Anglo-Saxon colonization. It seems most likely that Arthur was not only active within the Celtic fringe-zone just described, but also had his power base somewhere within it.

It has recently been argued that Arthur was in reality Owain Ddantgwyn, the king of Powys.[45] It is probably useful to explore the theory a little, and understand how such an improbable-sounding proposal came to be made. The elements of the theory's foundations are as follows:

1   The most powerful British kingdom at the time of Arthur was Gwynedd, so it is likely that Arthur was a member of the Gwynedd royal family, of the line of Cunedda.
2   Viroconium was the most important British city at the time of Vortigern and his successors and remained in use until 520, so it is a likely base for Arthur, who is alleged (in this scenario) to have died at Camlann in 520.
3   Medraut is a Welsh name, therefore Arthur's nephew was Welsh: Arthur too must have been Welsh.
4   Maelgwn of Gwynedd was nicknamed 'dragon of the island' by Gildas. 'The Head Dragon' or elder statesman of the Cunedda dynasty was Enniaun Girt, who was grandfather of both Maelgwn of Gwynedd and Cuneglasus of Powys. Uther Pendragon, or 'The Terrible Head Dragon', was said to be Arthur's father, therefore Arthur was Enniaun Girt's son. Phillips and Keatman were unable to find the name of Maelgwn's father, but Cuneglasus' father was Owain Ddantgwyn, therefore Arthur was Owain Ddantgwyn.

One can sympathize with anyone attempting to make a continuous story or synthesis out of such disconnected information as we have, but the weaknesses inherent in this scenario are obvious. The opening assumption, that Gwynedd was the most powerful kingdom in the fifth century, does not stand up. Certainly in the sixth century, in the reigns of King Maelgwn (reigned 517–47/51) and his son Rhun (reigned 547/51–around 580), Gwynedd was extremely powerful and dominated Celtic Britain – Maelgwn was overking – but there is no indication that Gwynedd was pre-eminent in the earlier period, before 520. The second assumption is also suspect. Although Viroconium was an important city and made an excellent centre for the kingdom of Powys until around 510, there is no particular reason to put it ahead of Carlisle, say, or Din Eidyn, or South Cadbury Castle in any urban hierarchy after that date. The third point, that Medraut is a Welsh name, is no better. Welsh obviously developed out of the Brittonic that was in general use in Celtic Britain, so the form 'Medraut' may well have been used in the sixth century far beyond the present-day frontier of Wales. Geoffrey of Monmouth in any case uses a specifically Cornish form of the word, 'Modred', and the Welsh form, 'Medraut', is exactly what we should expect in the *Welsh Annals*. The fourth point would be stronger if we knew that only the Gwynedd royal dynasty used the dragon as an emblem. It seems quite likely that, since dragons were part of Celtic mythology generally, other dynasties in Celtic Britain also used the dragon as an heraldic beast. If so, 'head dragons' might be found in kingdoms other than Gwynedd.

Norma Goodrich gives us a Scottish Arthur.[46] Her arguments are more elaborate and finely detailed, which makes them difficult to summarize fairly but, in outline, her reasoning is as follows:

1 Arthur's family tree can be reconstructed: for this Goodrich leans heavily on the work of Rachel Bromwich. Eigyr/Ygraine was Arthur's mother, and his maternal grandparents were Gwenn, the daughter of Cunedda Wledig, and Amlawdd Wledig. Both Cunedda and Amlawdd were kings of Gwynedd. This gives Arthur North Welsh blood on his mother's side.

2 Ygraine's castle was at Caerlaverock on the northern shore of the Solway Firth, not far from Dumfries where there were Roman training camps and (at least later) an abbey where the young Arthur could have been educated. Loch Ryan to the west is said in the *Welsh Annals* to be 'Arthur's Harbour'.

3 The Mount of Ambrosius alleged to be at Amesbury near Salisbury in Wiltshire was in fact Arthur's Seat above Salisbury, a suburb of Edinburgh.

While the pursuit of a pedigree for Arthur is extremely worthwhile, and the text is beautifully and persuasively written, Goodrich's arguments contain worrying leaps into assertion. Do we, for instance, really know that Amlawdd was king of Gwynedd? Very little is known of him. Why should we believe that Arthur's mother lived at Caerlaverock? No evidence connects Arthur with Dumfries. The transformation of Amesbury into Arthur's Seat is so bewildering as to defy comment. The command of sources is too imperfect for any reliance to be placed on the inferences from them. Sir Ian Richmond, the distinguished archaeologist, is described as 'the geographer Ian A. Richmond'. Sir Halford Mackinder, an equally distinguished early twentieth-century academic, this time a real geographer, is described as 'the modern historian Halford J. Mackinder'. Interesting too that by re-formatting their names Goodrich manages to turn them into surrogate Americans. And this is what she does with modern data. Ultimately, there is too much bending of cultural realities both contemporary and ancient for her case to convince.

In the nineteenth century, W. F. Skene saw Scotland as the arena of Arthur's campaigning, but there are several reasons for doubting his reasoning.[47] One problem is that much of his narrative relates to the fifth, or the later sixth, seventh and eighth centuries: little relates to the time of Arthur. Skene also deployed as evidence all the poems then ascribed to Taliesin, including *The Chair of the Sovereign*, which refers to Arthur by name and seems to associate him with Hadrian's Wall:

> From the destruction of chiefs,
> in a butchering manner,
> from the loricated Legion
> arose the Guledig,
> around the old renowned boundary.

Since Skene's time, the number of poems that can be reliably attributed to Taliesin or to the sixth century has been greatly reduced, and there seems to be no special reason to see *The Chair* as reflecting the dark age reality. Finally, a British campaign against Picts and Angles in the North could not possibly have had any effect on the progress of Saxon and Jutish colonization in the South. On a point of detail, we have no special reason to associate 'the old renowned boundary' with Hadrian's Wall. Much depends on the writer's standpoint and perspective. For those living in sixth-century Dumnonia, the most famous and important boundary would be the Wansdyke.

The majority of nineteenth- and twentieth-century seekers after the historical Arthur have come to support a focus of activity in *southern* Britain, in Cornwall, Somerset and Wales in particular. Baram Blackett and Alan Wilson argue strenuously for a power base for Arthur in South Wales, with Camelot on a hill overlooking Caerleon.[48] Their case is based on a detailed study of dark age pedigrees, but nevertheless hinges on an insistence that Arthur was Arthwyr, king of Gwent. Arthwyr was the son of Meurig (Maurice) and Onbrawst, and the grandson of Tewdrig (Theodoric). There are variants in the spellings of personal names, and it is common to find a historical figure with several names – a Brittonic name, a slightly later Welsh version of the same name, a Latinized form, maybe an English translation of the Latin form, and a corrupted high medieval form – giving perhaps five different names, in effect in different languages. Nevertheless, there is no pressing reason to equate Arthwyr with Arthur: we might expect to find a contracted Celtic form such as Arthr or Artr and a Latin form such as Arturus, not alternative Brittonic names. Spelling is given a low priority by these researchers; they write of 'Egyptian Pharoes'[49] and later mention that Adras, Arthmael, Arthfael, Arthmail, Arthwyr, Arthwys and Arthyr are all really the *same name*.[50] Obviously they are not.

Ultimately, the case rests on assertion and repetition, and on a disagreeable vein of anglophobia which distorts the authors' judgement and leads them to reject out of hand any association Arthur may have had with places outside Wales. The particular Welsh prince they focus on was in any case born too late to be Arthur: he lived a hundred years after the real Arthur.

A more sophisticated and persuasive argument for a South Welsh power base has been presented by Chris Barber and David Pykitt.[51] Once again Arthur is seen as Arthrwys, son of Meurig, king of Gwent. He inherited the small kingdom of Gwent and then, in 506, became overking by election, as described by Geoffrey. Barber and Pykitt argue that the identity of Arthur was, relatively early on, blurred and expanded by the addition of two more historical figures. One was an Arthwys, who lived a hundred years earlier and led the Northern Britons to victory against the Picts: he was a grandson of Coel Hen and was succeeded by his son Pabo Post Prydain. Further confusion arose because Arthrwys (i.e. the 'real' Arthur) had a contemporary called Arthmael, a soldier-saint born in 482 at Boverton in neighbouring Glevissig. Arthmael moved to Bodmin in Cornwall, where he married the sister of Count Gwythian, named Gwenhwyfar, or Guinevere.[52] Arthmael was in the eleventh century referred to as 'King Arthmael', indicating the level of confusion that arose. Our 'King Arthur' is, in effect, a conflation of three men, Arthwys, Arthrwys and Arthmael.

Thus far, the scenario is persuasive, but Barber and Pykitt call on the support of a 1796 *History of Monmouthshire* by David Williams and an 1803 *Cambrian Biography* by William Pughe. Both of these works assert that Arthur was the king of the Silurian Britons (= Gwent) who went on to be elected overking in 506 or 517. Nevertheless, reaching out to eighteenth- or early nineteenth-century antiquarians for scholarly support smacks of desperation.

In the end, the argument is unconvincing for the same underlying reason as before: Arthwyr son of Meurig lived a hundred years too late to be the Arthur mentioned in the annals as leading the fighting at Badon and Camlann.

The third major tradition relating to Arthur's kingdom is that it was in the West Country, more specifically in Cornwall. The *Dialogue of Arthur and the Eagle*, which was certainly written down in the twelfth century but may well be founded on older texts, is set in Cornwall and describes Arthur as 'penn kadoed Kernyw', or 'head of the battalions of Cornwall'. The same work refers to Arthur in a way that suggests he was already a well-known figure and describes him as 'strongest in valour' and 'bear of the host'.

The work of Geoffrey Ashe exemplifies the third major tradition relating to Arthur's kingdom. Ashe argues the case for a West Country power base for Arthur extremely well.[53] The evidence he calls up includes the following points:

1   Arthur first distinguished himself in the Sussex campaign, i.e. in the struggle between the British and the South Saxons. Arthur was therefore most likely a southern rather than a northern Briton.[54]
2   After the Sussex campaign, which seems to have ended in some sort of containment from the west, the Saxons next struck inland and west along the Thames valley, heading through the Vale of the White Horse towards the Wansdyke. The Badon site (at Bath) suggests a power base to the west of the Wansdyke, i.e. in Dumnonia.
3   There is more folklore and place-name evidence relating to Arthur in the West Country than in either Wales or Scotland.
4   The entire Ambrosian movement, of which Arthur's campaigns were a continuation, was shaped in Dumnonia (e.g. evidence of the Wansdyke defences).
5   The primitive Triads, the ones about Arthur's early days as a youthful adventurer, are set in Cornwall.
6   Tristan was Cornish. Medraut was a Dumnonian chief. Both were blood relations of Arthur, implying that he too was Dumnonian.
7   Camlann is on either the River Camel or the River Cam near South Cadbury.
8   The *Life of Gildas* says that when Arthur besieged Glastonbury he had all the fighting men of Devon and Cornwall under his command.
9   The title *dux bellorum* was also applied to Constantine, Arthur's immediate successor, and he was king of Dumnonia.
10 The Geraint poem suggests that a contingent in the Dumnonian army was known as 'Arthur's Men'.[55]

The first, third and seventh points may be weak and unpersuasive, but I believe the rest are valid. There is, for example, neither documentary nor even folkloric evidence that Arthur was involved in fighting the South Saxons, unless the location for the Arthurian battle on the River Glein is taken as Glynde near Lewes: really too little to provide a foundation for any hypothesis. As Ambrosius' lieutenant as well as his heir and successor, Arthur really had to have roots, contacts and a power base in the same kingdom as Ambrosius: it is hard to conceive how the transfer of authority could have worked in any other way.

So, the likeliest scenario is that Ambrosius Aurelianus was a Dumnonian king or sub-king with lands adjoining the eastern frontier, and that Arthur was also a Dumnonian king or sub-king, with lands elsewhere in Dumnonia. Dumnonia was large and broken up by a variety of physical barriers large and small, such as desolate moorlands and a strongly indented coastline punctuated by broad and deep rias. It lent itself to political fragmentation, and its divisions were governed by subordinate rulers who used the titles *regulus* or *comes*.[56] There were several autonomous tribes with their own royal kin-groups, and by 500 it is likely that any one of these might supply an overking for the whole of Dumnonia.[57]

As Arthur's kingdom tradition favours the region of North Cornwall between Bodmin Moor and the Severn Sea, between the Camel estuary and the Devon border, the region known as Tricurium in Latin and Trigg in Brittonic.[58] Within this region there is a concentration of sites with Arthurian associations. In the Celtic province as a whole, there are four regions where Arthurian traditions are linked to specific locations: the area of North Cornwall that we are about to discuss in more detail, Brittany, South Wales, and Scotland and northern England. Brittany can be discounted since there is no reason to suppose Arthur was ever active there. The Scottish and northern English region has only widely scattered associations, too widely scattered to suggest that Arthur's power base was there. South Wales has a much higher density, such that several authors have, very reasonably, proposed a South Welsh kingdom for Arthur.[59] But, overall, the greatest concentration of place-name references is certainly in and round Trigg, the area of North Cornwall between Wadebridge and Boscastle (see Figure 5.3).

First, there is the spectacularly impregnable Tintagel Island where, according to the tradition picked up by Geoffrey of Monmouth, Uther, with Merlin's help, impersonated Gorlois, made love to Ygerne and became Arthur's father: Tintagel is

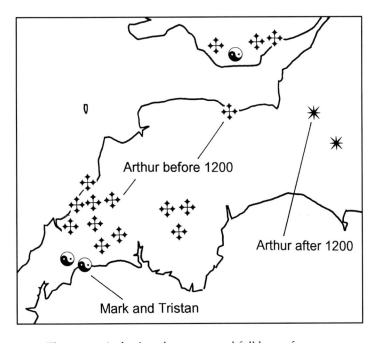

Figure 5.3 Arthurian place-name and folklore references

where Arthur's story began. Not far away in the Rocky Valley is St Nectan's Kieve (see Figure 5.4), a waterfall in a wooded ravine, where a stream drops 10 metres vertically, then pours sideways through a perfect man-sized ring of stone, then another 3 metres vertically, leaving a trail of millennia-old plunge-pools and water chutes stranded, fossilized in mid-air. Here, also according to tradition, Arthur presided on the bridge of rock above the torrent, watching his knights bathe in the water below, and make their solemn vows before setting off in search of the Grail. Here they returned to admit defeat when they failed in their quest.[60] The large capstone of a megalithic tomb near Trethevy is known as King Arthur's Quoit. Halfway between St Nectan's Kieve and Tintagel Island is Bossiney Mound, thought to be a Norman fort.[61] The feature often seen as a motte is actually a small ringwork surrounding an inner bailey. Traces of an oval outer bailey stretch 100 metres to the west of the conspicuous inner bank. Local tradition holds that the Round Table is buried under the Mound, from which it rises and becomes visible on midsummer morning.

Not far to the south is the huge Condolden Barrow, which local tradition holds to be the grave of Cador, Arthur's trusted lieutenant. It is striking that the barrow is not called Cador's Grave or Cato's Barrow. The name Condolden is of unknown antiquity, but evidently derives from the name of another dark age hero, Cynddylan, a seventh-century king of Powys who fought a reaguard action against the English and lost; he was killed in the Midlands around 658, when the English finally took Powys. It may seem at first as if there is no connection between Cynddylan and Arthurian Trigg, but Cynddylan was described in a contemporary elegy, possibly by his own bard, as one of the 'heirs of great Arthur, our strong fortress'.

Till I am in my resting place
I shall grieve for the death
Of Cynddylan, the full famed lord.

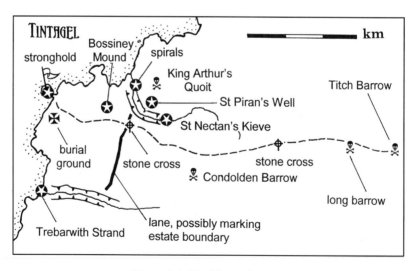

Figure 5.4 The Tintagel area

Around the time Cynddylan was killed, his ally Morfael is known to have fled to Dumnonia and taken sanctuary there.

> Cynddylan's hall. Dark is its roof
> Since the English destroyed
> Cynddylan, and Elvan of Powys.
> . . . The dykes endure. He who dug them
> Is no more.

It is possible that deep within the Dumnonian heartland, which survived as Powys fell, there was a feeling that Arthur had lived again, and been defeated again, and the Celtic taste for disaster and melancholy led to a renaming or alternative naming of the prehistoric barrow.[62]

At Slaughterbridge, near Camelford, and close to an ancient stone bridge over the River Camel, is one of the alleged sites of the Battle of Camlann. Further off to the south-west is Killibury, near Wadebridge, claimed by many as Kelliwic or Celli Wic, Arthur's favourite residence. Piran, Arthur's chaplain, lived close by on the Camel estuary. Away to the east, on Bodmin Moor, is Dozmary Pool (see Plate 5.1), the lake from which Arthur is said to have taken the sword Excalibur and to which the sword was eventually returned after his death. King Arthur's Hall, a rectangular stone setting on Bodmin Moor, may be a neolithic mortuary enclosure. In the north-eastern part of Bodmin Moor is King Arthur's Bed, which is the western end of Trewartha

Plate 5.1 Dozmary Pool

129

Tor; the hollows round it are Arthur's Troughs (for feeding his hounds). King Arthur's Stone, at the edge of Goss Moor, bears the imprint of four horseshoes, from the hoofs of Arthur's horse; this bears a family resemblance to the footprint lore from several dark age cult sites, including Tintagel itself.

A host of associations with Arthur is concentrated within this relatively small area. Tricurium therefore presents itself as a natural candidate for Arthur's territory, whether Arthur is seen as a Dumnonian sub-king with this as the entirety of his kingdom, or as king of all Dumnonia with this as his personal royal estate. Although the twelfth-century (or earlier) *Dialogue of Arthur and the Eagle* is not very specific about locations, the setting is evidently Cornish and the eagle 'roams the valley-woods of Cornwall'. Since the rare word 'glynn' is used in this context, it may be that a specific reference to the wooded valley of the River Glynn near Bodmin is intended. This would have been close to the southern border of Arthur's Tricurium.

We need at this point to take a closer look at the political geography of dark age Dumnonia, to see how Arthur and Trigg fitted into the scheme of things.

The moorlands of Dumnonia were, then as now, poor lands that never shared in the prosperity of the lowlands to the east; they never attracted much attention from the Romans, and remained untouched in the dark ages too.[63] In the fifth century there were no towns west of Exeter, so the only group that could have formed a fifth-century British dynasty was the existing tribal leadership, as in Gwent and Glamorgan across the Bristol Channel. A strong degree of continuity from the late iron age through into the post-Roman period is likely in Cornwall. The large number of stones inscribed in Latin shows that there was a British elite who recognized the status value of Latin: many aristocrats went by Latin names, though they kept their British names too. There was also a symbolic continuity in the preservation of the British tribal name: the iron age Dumnonii gave their name, intact and virtually unaltered, to the Roman and post-Roman kingdom of Dumnonia.[64] The Roman *civitas* of the Dumnonii is believed to have encompassed all of Cornwall and Devon, probably extending no further eastwards than the Somerset Levels. Dorset, the land of the Durotriges, was administered from Durnovaria (Dorchester) and Lindinis (Ilchester), though there are reasons for believing that post-Roman Dumnonia extended to include Dorset and Somerset (see Figure 5.5).

It is known that in the early sixth century Dumnonia was fragmented, that power was devolved among a number of petty kings similar to, probably identical with, the *pagorum reguli* of the sub-Roman period.[65] A kingdom was nevertheless emerging out of what had in the iron age been no more than a loose confederation of the Dumnonii.[66] That the kingdom of Dumnonia is not merely recognizable with hindsight, as a construct of the historian's imagination, but was recognized at the time is proved by a grave in Dalmatia. A woman buried at Split in 425 was described on her tombstone as *civis Dumnonia*, 'a Dumnonian citizen'.[67] Some of the Dumnonian kings probably achieved high king status over the whole region, like Maelgwn and Rhun in Wales and the North-west, and Dyfnwal and Rhydderch in Scotland. As we have seen, there were British words to describe such great kings: they were called 'Gwledic', 'Wledic', or 'Pendragon'.[68] These high kings had armed *erogatores* who toured with requisition lists, exacting tribute from their subjects in the form of food, cows, and the billeting and maintenance of the high king's army.

Figure 5.5 Dark age kingdoms and iron age confederacies, possibly founded upon still earlier bronze age chiefdoms
Source: After Burgess (1980)

The post-Roman settlement pattern as indicated by place-names was strikingly similar to that shown on the first edition Ordnance Survey map of 1813. In other words the broad outline of Cornwall's settlement pattern in Arthur's time remained unchanged until the nineteenth century. Then, as now, the higher density settlement was in areas of Grades 2 and 3 agricultural land, while less productive land (Grades 4 and 5) was empty. Trigg was quite densely and uniformly settled in the early medieval period, with a farmstead, hamlet or chapel every kilometre.[69] It is likely that the later hundreds already existed, as units of land called *keverang*, a word implying 'units for military service', so they were probably created with a view to mustering troops for defence. Within the keverang were many *trefs* or estates, each of which eventually (probably after the Arthurian period?) developed its own religious and administrative focus. Where the great seats of power were is notoriously difficult to identify. Tradition directs us to some of them; early documents to others; archaeology to others.[70]

The *Lives* of saints are invaluable in giving us short 'film-clip' views of dark age Dumnonia. Brioc (468–559) was born in Ceretigan or Coriticiana (modern Cardigan), the son of Cerpus and Eldruda. He performed various miracles, including rescuing a stag from a king in Ceretigan. He migrated with 168 companions to a port in Cornwall in about 510 and converted King Conan and his people. He later crossed the Channel to Brittany, but went back to Ceretigan to comfort his people when plague struck them in 547. The Cornish port is unnamed, but St Brioc's (now St Breock's) parish, at 30 square kilometres a very big parish and probably originally much larger, is the area south of Padstow and Wadebridge and this suggests that the north Cornish port Brioc used was on the Camel estuary. The *Lives* of St Petroc and St Samson show that the Camel estuary was certainly in use as a dark age harbour. Where Conan's kingdom was is not known; there seem to be no other references to him.

Perhaps Petroc's story throws some light on the matter. Petroc baptized the tyrant Constantine some time between 525 and 550. A 'powerful and pious inhabitant' called Kynan built an oratory in Petroc's honour. Possibly this Kynan is the same person as the King Conan earlier converted by Brioc; Kynan is in effect a different form of the same name. Kynan is not described as a king, but that may only be because he had a significantly lower status than Constantine, that Kynan/Conan was a sub-king while Constantine was a full king or perhaps, given the tradition, an overking like Arthur. The Constantinus of the early medieval British king list is given as Arthur's immediate successor as 'King of Britain'.

Kynan built his oratory at Boconion, two kilometres north of Bodmin. This may indicate that Kynan was king of the area coinciding with Brioc's parish. His headquarters may or may not have been at Bodmin: perhaps he used the fort at Dunmere Wood 2 kilometres west of Boconion or the fortlet at Cardinham.[71]

South of St Breock's parish is Castle-an-Dinas, which could have been the stronghold of a dark age king. Four kilometres further south is the church of St Dennis, which stands on the remains of Damelioc, another dark age stronghold and according to the late tradition used by Geoffrey the second castle of Duke Gorlois; within the marsh-defended circuit walls of Damelioc, which still stand, Gorlois was murdered by Uther's men while Uther made love to Ygraine at Tintagel. Nine kilometres away to the east on the far side of St Austell Moor stood Trethurgy Round, another dark age local power centre. This plough-damaged embanked enclosure consisted of a tightly organized defended complex of five houses and ancillary buildings, probably occupied as early as the late Roman period, and continuing in use until about 550. In case this should be thought from its size to be a mere farmstead, the high status of its occupants is clearly shown by their possession of imported Mediterranean pottery.[72] Eight kilometres further to the south-east from Trethurgy is the Fowey peninsula, with the iron age and dark age fortress of Castle Dore at its centre; tradition and archaeology both point to this as the residence of King Mark Cunomorus, known in the dark ages as the Villa Banhedos.

Further along the coast, at Trewithian, is the iron age hillfort called Dingerein Castle (see Figure 5.6), probably re-used in the dark ages by King Geraint, who is likely to have controlled lands westwards as far as Carrick Roads, the broad sea inlet running inland towards Truro. The *Tale of Geraint* tells of Geraint leading Dumnonian warriors into battle at Llongborth, where he fought the Saxon host alongside Arthur, as Arthur's subordinate. This is consistent with both of them being kings and Arthur acting as *dux bellorum*. Geraint was a distinguished figure, featuring in the ancient genealogies as Geraint ab Erbin, Geraint son of Erbin, son of Kynoaor, son of Tudwal.

West of Truro was another fortified residence, Goodern Round, which is mentioned, as Gudrun, in the *Life of Cynan* (who lived in Roseland on the east side

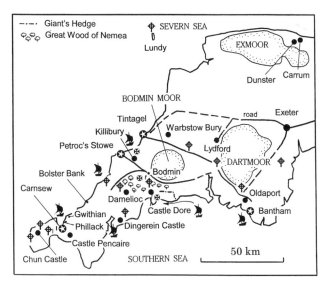

Figure 5.6 West Dumnonia

of Carrick Roads). This was the home of King Theodoric, whose power extended to the Roseland peninsula. He is mentioned as a contemporary of Idon, Gurcant, Maelgwn, Aircol, Catgucan, Tredicil and Rein: since their dates sprawl between 500 and 600, Theodoric is likely to have lived from about 500 until around 560.[73] He is more precisely located to the opening decades of the century by three independent traditions about Cynan, Petroc and Fingar, and should be seen as a younger contemporary of Arthur. Theodoric was based in Cornwall, but also active in South Wales.

Fingar of Gwinnear, son of Irish king Clyto and brother of Guiner, arrived at Hayle with 770 companions and 7 bishops. At Hayle they were attacked by King Theodoric. According to the monkish record, Theodoric was a pagan king and feared the conversion of his subjects; it is, however, more likely that he saw the approach of nearly a thousand men as more of an invasion by land-hungry Irish settlers than a Christian mission, and made an appropriately military response. Indeed, it is likely that most of these movements consisted of groups of monks accompanied by much larger groups of armed lay colonists.[74] The evidence from the wider British realm favours Irish aggression, or at the very least assertive colonization, in four widely separated provinces. The men of Leinster colonized the area of North Wales that was later to become Gwynedd; the Deisi from south-east Ireland colonized Dyfed; the Dalriadan Scots from Ulster colonized the Western Isles and part of the Scottish mainland; in Cornwall there is the widespread evidence of ogham stones bearing Irish names and some pottery that is so like Irish pottery that it can really only have been made by Irish migrants.[75] The tradition of antagonism between the Cornish and Irish seems to have been woven into the Tristan legend.

Faced with what was probably not the first onslaught from Irish colonists, King Theodoric set a watch on the coasts for the incoming horde, then descended from his fort at Phillack. Sailing separately, Guiner's party of 300 surrendered and was massacred. Two settlements close to Hayle, Gwithian and Gwinner, are associated with Fingar and Guiner. From this account, it is clear that Theodoric had subsidiary bases on the coast that he used for defence. Another was the Round Wood cliff castle 5 kilometres south-east of Goodern: positioned fairly low in the landscape and well hidden, this had a good view south down Carrick Roads. Round Wood was an iron age fort re-used in the dark ages by Theodoric and his dynasty. Welsh tradition has it that Theodoric helped Agricola of Demetia to his throne. Agricola of Demetia was referred to by Gildas as the father of Vortipor who was reigning at the time Gildas was writing mid-century, so both Theodoric and Agricola were clearly active in the early sixth century.

On the north coast the headland of St Agnes is enclosed by Bolster Bank (see Figure 5.7), a 3-kilometre defensive bank (much of it now levelled) with an outer ditch enclosing an area of 500 hectares. It is undated but may well be a dark age royal estate boundary like Giant's Hedge on the south coast. The existence of early British chapels at each end of the earthwork supports a dark age date.[76]

West of Hayle and possibly outside Theodoric's territory is the Penwith peninsula. Here, near Morvah, is the great iron age fortress of Chun Castle, which we know from the presence of imported Mediterranean pottery was a dark age power centre. This, then, was probably the principal stronghold of the dynasty that controlled Penwith. Just 2 kilometres away to the north-east is an inscribed stone with the following dedication;

RIALOBRAN – CUNOVAL – FIL
Rialobran son of Cunoval

Rialobran means 'Royal Raven,' and *Cunoval* means 'Famous Chieftain,' which tells us not just the names but the self-images of the kings of Penwith.

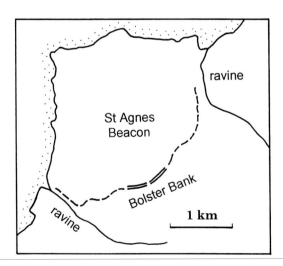

Figure 5.7 Bolster Bank, St Agnes

Four kilometres south-west of Chun Castle is another inscribed stone, the Selus Stone. The Selus in question may have been Selyf, brother of Yestin (or St Just), and son of King Geraint.

Returning to the east, Bodmin Moor made a natural no-man's-land between the north Cornish Tricurian territory of King Arthur and the south Cornish territory of King Mark. On the moor's flanks were east–west roads, one running from the Camel estuary and Killibury past the southern side of Bodmin towards Liskeard and Callington, the other running from Tintagel to Altarnun and Lewannick and from there on to Tavistock in Devon. The two routes converged on the Tamar crossing, probably at Gunnislake, and continued as a single route, marked by dark age inscribed stones, along the south-western flank of Dartmoor through Yelverton and Cornwood. This road evidently led to the major south Devon port of Bantham.

Here, on extensive sand dunes at the mouth of the South Devon Avon an important dark age emporium developed. Only two widely separated radiocarbon dates, 300 and 600, are available but they credibly suggest that Bantham operated as a thoroughgoing international port for two or three centuries. Bantham was a large and busy complex, with temporary, perhaps seasonally used shelters, middens, hollows, lots of pottery, ironwork, spindle whorls suggesting a textile industry, and bones of cattle, sheep and pigs. Probably a fishing fleet was based here too. The international dimension is indicated by sherds of Mediterranean pottery, although these could have been imported through Tintagel and distributed overland from there. Quite how ships were dealt with at Bantham is not known; possibly they were beached beam-on at high tide and unloaded onto pack animals when the tide went out, a common practice in the nineteenth century on the mudflats of the Solway Firth.[77]

Presumably there was a dark age road route along the south-eastern flank of Dartmoor, possibly coinciding with the modern A38 and connecting up with the Roman roads that converged on Exeter. Another is known to have passed from Exeter round the north flank of Dartmoor, running to the south of Crediton, through Hookway, Yeoford, Brownsland and Coxmoor to cross the River Taw near Belstone Corner.[78]

On the north-western flank of Dartmoor, about 18 km south-west of the Taw crossing, is Lydford. A single A-ware sherd may seem too little to show for the presence there of a sixth-century elite group, but that is nevertheless what it suggests, and other features of the site support the idea. Lydford consists of an area 320m by 300m enclosed by a late Saxon bank which was a replacement for an earlier rampart with timber reinforcement, not unlike the sixth-century rampart at South Cadbury. This analogy may be significant, since the size of the enclosure is similar to that of Cadbury. The natural inference is that Lydford functioned in a similar way to Cadbury.[79] Lydford's situation does not possess any very obvious strategic value in relation to any of the known aspects of the geography of Dumnonia, although it would appear to be well placed to act as a rallying point where Cornish war-bands could safely muster before riding or marching east. Maybe Lydford was a muster point for Cornish warriors while South Cadbury was a muster point for the men of Devon. Orderly musters were probably the norm for organized large-scale campaigns. There seems to be a reference to this in Taliesin's poem *The Battle of Argoed Llwyfain*, in which King 'Fflamddwyn mustered his men in four hosts: Goddau and Rheged formed their ranks, summons from Argoed to Arfynydd.'

What the role of the old Roman town of Exeter was in dark age Dumnonia is not clear, but it is likely to have been at least a local power centre, and very likely the base of another king. The post-Roman city was continuously occupied during the fifth, sixth and seventh centuries, and the qualities of the site as at least a local central place must have been appreciated by the local rulers.[80] It has been assumed, not necessarily justifiably, that only small parts of Exeter were occupied and that the dark age people who lived there were wretched, poverty-stricken squatters.[81] Pottery of Mediterranean origin was in use.[82] This may have been imported direct or through Bantham or Tintagel, but either way its presence shows that there were high-status people in Exeter. A pit was used as a quarry for the clay needed for crucibles and furnace linings and debris resulting from bronze-working filled the pit: clear evidence for dark age metal-working. In the fifth and sixth centuries the east quadrant of the city was a large cemetery,[83] the graves yielding radiocarbon dates of 420 and 490. The graves contained simple shroud-burials, without coffins and without grave-goods,[84] though this should not be taken as proof of poverty. The graves followed the same north–west to south–east alignment as the Roman basilica, which suggests that the basilica was not only still standing but possibly converted to Christian worship.[85] A Christian community is known to have lived here in the seventh century, as the contemporary *Life of St Boniface* tells us that Boniface was sent to it to be educated.[86]

Building activity continued at Exeter at least until 500. A series of well-founded rectangular rooms with drystone walls was installed between the south wall of the basilica and the boundary wall, and at the eastern end of the basilica a doorway was knocked through so as to link the new rooms into the main building. One of the most profound changes was the raising of a wall severing the street connecting the East and West Gates. Whoever ordered this evidently had power over the city as a whole, and this implies decision-making by a local ruler rather than mere squatter behaviour. There is no evidence of collapsed buildings, which shows that Exeter was continuously occupied and maintained from the time the Romans left until the occupation of the city by the Saxons in 658.[87] Even after the Saxon occupation there was a British quarter (the west quadrant of the city) until at least 928, where Bartholomew Street is today, and in the middle ages this street was still known as 'Britayne'.[88] But, however important Exeter may have been locally, it would appear not to have been ruled by one of the more powerful Dumnonian rulers in Arthur's time. The patterns of distribution of both high-status memorial stones and imported Mediterranean pottery suggest that the centres of power had shifted away from old Isca.[89] It was probably only a sub-king who ruled at Exeter.

In North Devon few sites have so far emerged as important dark age centres. In the *Life of Cernach*, who lived at the end of the fifth century, we catch sight of Dunster as a seat of power.[90] Cernach was Cornish and originally took the Latin name Carantocus: he was the son of Cereticus of Ceredigiaun (another dark age spelling of Ceretigan or Cardigan), who in turn was a son of Cunedda. Carantocus refused to succeed his father, another king, migrated to Ireland and shed his Latin name in favour of Cernach. In Ireland he was known as 'Dear Cernach' (Carus Cernachus) and he led the Irish Christians against the opposition of the magi. He returned to Cardigan, then crossed the Severn Sea and founded a religious community at Carrum, which was located on the site of Carhampton vicarage near Dunster, 'when Cato and

Arthur ruled at Din Draithou'. This clause is revealing, in confirming Arthur as a king, and in showing that more than one king could rule at a time in the West Country. Although in the *Life of Cernach* Cato is the major figure and Arthur the subsidiary ruler it is more likely that in reality it was the other way round. Cato was the local king or sub-king, most likely based at Dunster Castle. Cato's territory may have embraced the Brendon Hills and Vale of Stogumber, and possibly Exmoor and the Quantocks as well. Din Draithou or Dindraethu is listed (as Cair Draitou) in the *Welsh Annals* as one of the twenty-eight cities of Britain,[91] indicating Dunster's perceived major strategic importance in the dark ages. This assumes Din Draithou is Dunster; the context could be taken to indicate that Cato's stronghold was near Carhampton, while Arthur's was at Din Draithou, somewhere else altogether. Din Draithou could thus even be the dark age name of Tintagel, though this seems unlikely. An Irish source, Cormac's *Glossary*, mentions a West Country fort called 'Dinn Tradui', that is Dun Tredui, or Tredhui of the Three Ramparts. Charles Thomas believes the three-lobed enclosure of Dinn Tradui is Moel Trigarn in Preseli,[92] but there is an unambiguous reference in Cormac's *Glossary* to the building of Dun Tradui 'in the lands of the Cornish Britons'.[93] Dark age Dunster may well have consisted of three enclosures (see Figure 5.8). There are well-preserved small iron age hillforts on three adjacent hill tops grouped round Dunster: Bat's Castle, Gallox Hill and Grabbist Hill, with superb views across the Severn Sea. They may have been jointly occupied and refortified by a dark age sub-king.[94] Cair Draithou, certainly the same place again, features in a list of two dozen dark age British cities. The three fortlets of Din Draithou are just 2 kilometres south-west of the likely site

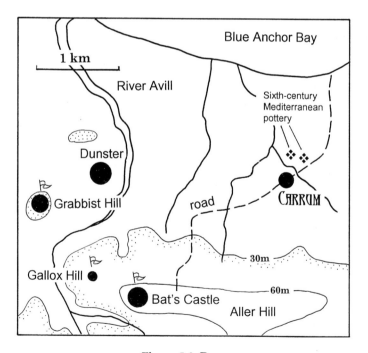

Figure 5.8 Dunster

of Cernach's dark age monastery. None of the enclosures has been excavated, so there is no evidence either way regarding their dark age occupation. Imported sixth-century Mediterranean pottery has nevertheless been found nearby, at Eastbury Farm, Carhampton, supporting the idea of a high-status settlement in the area.[95]

One significant feature of St Cernach's *Life* is that the action moves smoothly from Somerset to Cornwall, with Arthur in authority in both, an implicit reference to Arthur's kingship of Dumnonia.[96] Cato may have been the son, nephew or even younger brother of King Geraint; in genealogy X, Geraint ab Erbin has a successor 'Cado' who was also a king.[97] Both Geraint and Cato were close associates of Arthur – two of his 'knights', in fact. Geoffrey's late version of events also mentions Cato as occupying a position of great honour. Arthur summoned to his court at Caerleon a selection of leading men from the principal cities of Britain, such as Morvid earl of Gloucester and Urbgennius of Bath, and the kings of Albany, the Venedoti, the Demetae and Cornwall: 'Cador' was 'duke of Cornwall'.[98] It was Cador who reminded Arthur that a long peace softens a nation (shades of Gildas here): he stood for struggle against the foreigner and for courage.[99] Wounded, in Avalon, Arthur abdicated in favour of Cador's son, Constantine: Geoffrey makes this happen in 542. Cato/Cador/Cadw is immortalized in the Welsh Triads as one of the *Three Knights of Battle*: Cadw earl of Cornwall ranks with Lancelot Lac and Owain ab Urien Rheged.[100]

Inscribed stones (see Figure 5.9) tell us the names, usually Latinized, of quite a few noble Dumnonians of Arthur's time: Ulcagnus, Iustus, Ingenuus, Latinus, Brocognus, (Na)dottus, Dunocatus, Mescagnus, Annicus, Uailathus, Urochanus, Ranocorus, Dobunnus, Enabarrus, Sabinus, Maccodechetus, Fanonus, Rinus, Sagranus, Vitalis, Torricus, Quenataucus, Dinawus, Cumrecinus, Maucus, Nepranus, Coneuus, Principius, Audentius, Caocus, Peblig, Douithus, Docidocus, Cruarigus, Drustanus and Cunomorus.[101] One strange passage in the *Life of Carantoc* reads, 'The King ordered him [Carantoc] to receive Carrum as a perpetual possession and he afterwards built a church there. Then he [the King] sent Cato and Arthur to ask about the altar.' Although the passage is ambiguous, it implies that the writer believed that neither Cato nor Arthur was the King. While too much should not be read into it – the previous section is, after all, about a dragon – it implies some residual knowledge of a hierarchy of kings and sub-kings in dark age Dumnonia. The apparent reversal of Cato's and Arthur's roles at least may be explained quite simply by the parochial nature of the issues involved. Because the events and their ramifications were confined to the area close to Cato's stronghold, the problem was in Cato's patch and it was for Cato to deal with it; Arthur took an appropriately subordinate role.

In eastern Dumnonia, Lindinis (Ilchester), the meeting place of five Roman roads, was still functioning as an urban centre in the sixth century. The fact that it received the same high-status imported pottery that was used at Tintagel suggests it was used by the elite of Dumnonia and may well have been the seat of a king. That king's stronghold would nevertheless have been South Cadbury Castle, 10 kilometres away to the east, at least once it had been refortified.

The relationship between Glastonbury and the Tor may have been the same: a low-lying township with a well-defended royal refuge or eyrie not far away. Later tradition connects Glastonbury Tor with King Melwas,[102] and he may well have been the king of Somerset from the Quantocks to the Mendips, or even all the way to the

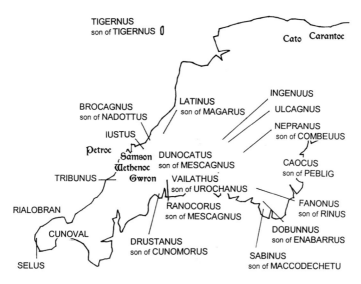

Figure 5.9 Arthur's Dumnonian contemporaries. Roman capitals = names on inscribed stones. Beaulieu lower case = documentary references.

Wansdyke 28 kilometres north-east of Glastonbury. The post-Roman city of Bath was one of the three cities the Saxons boasted of taking after the Battle of Dyrham in 577 (the others were Cirencester and Gloucester). The Saxons also boasted of killing three kings, Coinmail, Farinmail and Condidan, with the implication that each of these cities had its own king. So Bath may well have been the headquarters of a king or sub-king earlier in the sixth century, just as Geoffrey of Monmouth said.

As we saw earlier, the Amesbury area was a likely territory for Ambrosius (Elder and Younger) to occupy, with Vespasian's Camp as the likeliest focus for mustering fighting men (see Figure 5.10). This may have continued into the following generation, with Ambrosius the Younger's son and heir continuing to occupy Amesbury and Vespasian's Camp during Arthur's reign. This Ambrosian kingdom occupied the north-east corner of Dumnonia. This area may have been called Sarras,[103] and it may have become surrounded in mystique with its 'holy city of Sarras' because it was lost fairly early on to the Saxons, and therefore not much was known about its past, or because it was associated with the heroic Ambrosius, or because it had Stonehenge, a little-understood but awe-inspiring taboo place, at its centre; it was remembered that there was a sun temple in the city of Sarras.

Another Arthurian kingdom in Dorset was described as being somewhere between the Thames and the south coast and it was the kingdom of Caradoc Vreichvras ('Strong-arm') who was said to rule lands on both sides of the Channel in about 550.[104] South Dorset is the likeliest location for this otherwise unknown realm, as it was the only area on the central south coast of England that was not in Saxon hands in 550; there were Saxon colonists west of Bridport and east of St Alban's Head lay Wessex, so from Chesil Beach along to Lulworth was a British-occupied bridgehead for France, a coastline with a hinterland that could have been King Caradoc's.

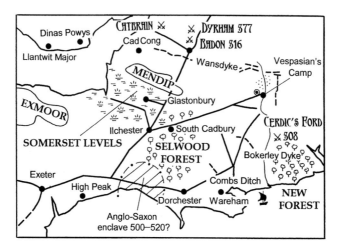

Figure 5.10 East Dumnonia. This coincides almost exactly with the diocese of Sherborne as defined in 850. The marches (stippled) near Stonehenge (dot in circle) are still heavily militarized today.

How the dark age port of Wareham fitted into the picture is not yet clear: perhaps it was the seat of yet another petty king. Wareham is confirmed as a dark age centre by the presence there of five early Christian memorial inscriptions using the *filius* form, which is considered to indicate a fifth or sixth century date. The massive defensive bank hitherto assumed to be a purely Saxon work may therefore be a development of a dark age rampart.[105]

This cursory review of the state of sixth-century Dumnonia shows a minimum of fifteen royal centres, and no doubt there were many more. If this seems like too many kings, we can compare it with the situation in modern Britain, where there are many local authorities responsible for governing counties or cities and also a central government; probably in dark age Dumnonia the situation was broadly similar, though with a much weaker central power, with many small kingdoms loosely federated under a high king. It seems that kingship was hereditary – as much is implicit in the genealogies and poems – but that high kingship, overlordship of Dumnonia as a whole, was won on military might and political status. In this way Arthur, king of Tricurium, might be high king during his reign or at least during his ascendancy, and conceivably Geraint, king of Ros-Ene, or Mark, king of whatever the Fowey area was called, might be high kings during theirs. Nomination or acclamation may have come into it as well, and there may be much in the tradition that Arthur named his successor: not his own son but Cato's son Constantine.

There were other kings in Dumnonia too. We hear of a king called Riwal ('Royal'), who apparently was known in the first half of the sixth century by his Latin name, Pompeius Regalis, so his Celtic personal name must have been Pabo. He was a relative of Geraint and Cadw, and 'chief of the British on both sides of the sea': in other words he held lands in both Dumnonia and Brittany, like Mark Cunomorus. The British who emigrated to Brittany with Riwal took the name of their homeland with them and Brittany too became known as 'Dumnonie'. Riwal is said to have had his headquarters at St Brieuc in western Dumnonie. In around 510 Riwal was allegedly helped by his younger kinsman Arthur in an armed struggle against invading Visigoths: together they repelled an invasion by sea at a place, perhaps coincidentally, called Baden, south of Vannes. King Riwal had a son called Deroch and died in 524.[106]

Some final pointers towards Arthur as not-Welsh and not-Scottish but Dumnonian come from the *Lives* of saints. The *Life of Cadoc*[107] tells us Arthur came from outside Wales; 'The most powerful king of Britain' [= Arthur] invaded south-east Wales from east of the River Wye in pursuit of Ligessauc Lauhair filius Eliman. Ligessauc Lauhair had sought refuge in south-east Wales after killing three of Arthur's warriors, when no-one [outside Wales] would shelter him for fear of Arthur. It is clear that Ligessauc Lauhair did not feel safe in what is now England (probably Dumnonia) and thought he might be safe in Wales. We also see that even if Arthur was a Dumnonian king he still had the authority, or naked power, to be able to strike at an enemy in Wales. It is rather like the US military; we expect it to be active in the USA and round its border, but occasionally see evidence of its enormous outreach and power, evidenced in one-off retaliatory strikes against installations in Libya, Sudan and Afghanistan. Most of the stories about Arthur's exploits in Wales and Scotland depict him as a violent, ruthless foreigner, coming from what is now England, and the most likely location of his power base is in the West Country. It is to the West Country and to Cornwall in particular that most of the evidence leads.

Arthur as a Christian king

Arthur was remembered in the high middle ages as a great Christian king, a pioneering, crusading king in a world still filled with paganism, magic and wizardry. In the most fully developed versions of the story, he is the king who presides over the Grail Quest, the attempt to find the cup from which Christ drank at the Last Supper, the cup that was in effect the focus of the first mass.

Some have argued that the history of Arthur and the saga of the Grail at first evolved entirely separately. The Fisher King, the Waste Land and the Sacred Vessel were images well known in old Celtic stories that were then spread in France by Breton *conteurs* before being exported to Britain. The conversion of the Sacred Vessel, a pagan horn of plenty, into a Christian chalice may have happened at the same time as the conversion of the inhabitants of Britain and Brittany to Christianity; in other words the idea of the Holy Grail may well have been born during Arthur's reign. Then, between the sixth and twelfth centuries, the stories about the Grail were powerfully combined with the stories about Arthur and his followers, some of which had already become heavily fictionalized. We need, above all, to reach back to that earlier world, before the myth-making process had begun, to the living Arthur, if we are to find the historical reality. Was there truth in the view of Arthur as a great Christian king?

Christianity did not reach Dumnonia, where Arthur was born and bred and later ruled, until 480, when Arthur was a boy. Arthur is likely therefore to have been among the first or second generation of Christians in Dumnonia. The earliest evidence of Christianity in dark age Cornwall is a number of inscribed stones at

Lewanick and Hayle, including a Chi-Rho symbol carved on a stone at Phillack. The new religion was introduced by sea, and could have come from Ireland, Wales, Gaul or the Mediterranean.[108] We know the kings of Dumnonia were receiving imports of exotic pottery from the Mediterranean: if they met the merchants or sea-captains who brought these wares they could easily have come into contact with new ideas from the Mediterranean too. On the whole, though, it was missionaries from South Wales who had a decisive influence on the introduction of Christianity and its spread through Dumnonia to Brittany; and this we know from the *Lives* of the saints written shortly afterwards.

So, there is documentary and archaeological evidence that Christianity arrived in Dumnonia, first in the extreme west, in about 480, and was spread by crusading monks during the next fifty years, during the time of Arthur. If Arthur or his parents were Christian converts, they too might have been filled with the zeal to convert others.

The support that Geoffrey of Monmouth gives to this is interesting, because it conflicts with other sources, such as the later (i.e. ninth-century onwards) *Lives* of saints, which show Arthur as perverse, lustful and anti-clerical,[109] even as an avaricious tyrant.[110] There were therefore two traditions about Arthur. One, evolving from the ninth to twelfth centuries, shows Arthur as a foil and challenge to the ever-virtuous saints: the other, parallel tradition drawn upon by Geoffrey shows him as a virtuous crusading Christian. On the whole it is likely that Geoffrey was drawing on a tradition with more ancient origins, one that originated closer to Arthur's time and was nearer the historical reality. It seems very unlikely that the early scribe who wrote the entry about Badon in the Welsh Annals would have added a reference to Arthur as a Christian hero bearing the cross of Christ unless it was true. In a description about a battle it is so incongruous, compared with the accounts of other battles, that it is likely to be true.

Nennius mentions that in one of his battles Arthur carried an image of the Virgin Mary on his shield. This also rings true. The cult of the Virgin Mary was very strong in the sixth century. The Madonna was a standard artistic image and icon (see Figure 5.11). The Emperor Justinian I (482–565), a contemporary of Arthur's, begged Mary's protection for what remained of the Roman Empire. A little later, the Byzantine emperor Heraclius (575–641) had a personal banner with Mary's image embroidered on it, and we can get a very good idea from surviving ivories what that image would have looked like. Although these are Mediterranean examples, Nennius confirms that her image was carried at the Battle of Guinnion. It would not have been an anachronism. Interestingly, Gildas mentions that Constantine, Arthur's chosen successor as king of Dumnonia, called on the Mother of God to witness an oath.

Arthur lived at a time when many well-known Christian missionaries were hard at work, especially in Ireland, South Wales, Dumnonia and Brittany. He could, for example, have met and held discourse with any of sixteen saints: Brigit, Eleutherius, Brioc, Dubricius, Illtud, Piran, Ciaran of Saigir, Wethenoc, Brendan, Kentigern, Radigundus, Remigius, Samson, Servanus, Petroc and Wronus. These and others like them covered long distances by land and sea, actively converting the people they met on the way; where possible they targeted community leaders, the chiefs, princes and kings, as the means of converting whole communities. King Arthur would have

Figure 5.11 Sixth-century ivory portraits: religious and imperial imagery contemporary with Arthur. Left: Emperor Anastasius, about 515. Centre: Virgin and Child. Right: Empress Ariadne showing robe embroidered with a diamond-framed portrait bust.

attracted itinerant saints as a lantern attracts moths, and it is likely that he saw and heard many of them preach. St Ciaran of Saigir, though coming from County Offaly in Ireland, ended his days in Dumnonia in 520. St Brioc (468–559) landed on the shores of the Camel estuary in the 520s or 530s and converted King Conan (of Bodmin?). The remarkable Irish adventurer St Brendan (486–578) sailed all the way to Iceland and Tenerife after the death of Arthur, but he is also known to have visited Gildas in Britain. Given the alleged friendship between Gildas and Arthur, it is possible that Brendan met Arthur too during that visit.

An alternative view is that a Christian gloss was added to Arthur later. It has been suggested that the 'legendary' Arthur is a composite of two or more historical figures, one being St Arthmael (born 482). Arthmael was a contemporary of Arthur, a crusading Christian and also a Dumnonian; so it may be that Arthmael's Christianity was grafted onto Arthur. Taking this idea one step further, it may be that the pervasive missionary zeal of the time was somehow grafted onto an Arthur who was, in religious terms only, a relatively bland and passive figure. As the high king at the time of the Christian conversions, Arthur naturally became identified with them.

The old pagan religion was still a major force in Britain and Ireland at the time of Arthur. In the 450s, a generation before Arthur was born, St Patrick came into conflict with the wizards of King Loegaire at Tara. It was at about the same time that Patrick wrote a letter to a King Coroticus of Ail: this was probably Ceretic of Alcluith, who was still living at the close of the fifth century when Arthur was a young man. According to Muirchu's *Life of St Patrick*, Ceretic was not only a pagan but a committed anti-Christian: Muirchu refers to the 'quite iniquitous action of a certain British king called Coroticus, an ill-starred and cruel tyrant, a great persecutor and murderer of Christians'. According to Muirchu, Ceretic was turned into a fox. Writing shortly after the death of Arthur, Gildas described the signs of pagan worship in southern Britain.

The time has come to look at the figure of Merlin, the elusive, mysterious figure who in the fully evolved versions of the Arthurian legend was nearly always at Arthur's elbow. His role is a peculiar one. He is a pagan figure, a wizard and magician, while Arthur is shown as a Christian king intent on finding a relic of Christ. The stories and images are so familiar from childhood onwards that perhaps we no longer see them as strange, but this pairing is peculiarly strange, and its very incongruity, the fact that it is *not* a stock situation, suggests that there might be an element of historical truth behind it.

We know that Merlin was a genuine historical figure. He was lifted by Geoffrey of Monmouth from a collection of old poems, riddles and triads preserved in Wales but relating to a bard called Myrddin, the Celtic form of *Martin*, who lived in the north of what is now England, near Hadrian's Wall. The aristocratic Norman-French readers for whom Geoffrey was writing would have pronounced Myrddin *Merdin*, and probably sniggered at a name so close to *merde* (= excrement), and the Latin form of Myrddin, *Merdinus*, was no better – *merda* meant 'excrement' too – so Geoffrey had no choice but to change it. He chose Merlin. The original Myrddin was the bard of King Gwenddolau, who held lands along the Wall. He fought alongside his master at the Battle of Arderydd in 573, went mad in the midst of the battle when Gwenddolau was killed and afterwards became a recluse on Hart Fell.[111] In those days every king had his own bard, who was expected to write eulogies about his master and was therefore an important shaper of the king's public image. A bard was poet laureate, cabaret entertainer, news broadcaster and PR man, all in one.

In Arthur's day, bards were known by a Latin name in keeping with the British aristocracy's association of things Roman with high status: they were called *carminators*. For instance, Gemman, who was Columba's teacher, was a *carminator* and he composed a *carmen magnificum* in honour of Finnian of Clonard (Leinster) in the 540s, so these are very much the terms that were in use in the reign of Arthur.[112] The carminators probably chanted their songs or ballads to the accompaniment of music, either on a *cruit*, a small D-shaped lyre or harp played while seated, or on a *cithara*, a more rectangular stringed instrument with a sounding board. Both of these instruments were in use in Arthur's time. When Columba died in 597 an Irish bard exclaimed, 'a cruit without a [tuning] key – a church without an abbot!'[113]

Bards were attached to the royal court and travelled with their kings wherever their peregrinations took them. They achieved what may now seem incredibly high status, on a level with the king's chief elder, in other words something close to Prime Ministerial status. They composed praise poems, occasional pieces on great victories or disastrous defeats and funeral elegies. They memorized their compositions for recitation in the feast halls. One major role of the *Bardd teulu*, the bard of the war-band, was to entertain the warriors, often with stirring tales of their own great deeds; the impression left by the surviving fragments of dark age poetry is of ceaseless warfare, feasting, drinking, boasting and general showing off. It represents at best only a partial truth, in that its purpose was to hold a mirror to the egotistical self-images of the king and his war-band.[114]

Occasionally bards confronted the warriors with truths that were uncomfortable, with the intention of provoking them or even shaming them into trying harder. In *Rheged arise*, Taliesin writes, 'Not too well did they fight around their king [Urien]: to lie would be wrong.' Although bards were technically the servants of their kings, the greatest of them were above personal loyalty. Taliesin served at least three and possibly four kings in succession, Cynan of Powys, Urien of Rheged, Gwallawg of Elmet and Owain of Rheged, and seems always to have had the greater cause of the British, the Cymry, as they called one another, at heart, even if that meant deserting white-haired Urien for the younger Gwallawg. This element of unpredictability is one distinctive trait of Merlin.

Geoffrey wrote a *Life of Merlin* which contains a mixture of old traditions about Myrddin and bits of fiction added by Geoffrey to make it more continuous. Merlin was tempted out of retirement by King Rhydderch of Clyde, but did not stay long at his court. Geoffrey quotes an extraordinary piece that purports to be a speech made by Rhydderch's wife Ganieda, whom for dramatic effect Geoffrey makes Myrddin's sister. This is the speech Ganieda is made to utter when Rhydderch dies:

Lament with me the death of Rhydderch and weep for a man such as our earth has not produced hitherto in our age so far as we know. He was a lover of peace, for he so ruled a fierce people that no violence was done to anyone by anyone else. He treated the holy priest with just moderation and permitted the highest and the lowest to be governed by law. He was generous, for he gave away much and kept scarcely anything. He was all things to all men, doing whatever was seemly; he was the flower of knights, the glory of kings, the pillar of the kingdom. Woe is me! For what you were – now so unexpectedly you have become food for worms, and your body moulders in the urn. Is this the bed prepared for you after fine silks? Is it true that your white flesh and royal limbs will be covered by a cold stone? That you will be nothing but dust and bones? So it is . . . That which excels is of brief duration, what it has does not endure; like the running stream everything that is of service passes away.

Take away the opening and closing sections, which are specific to Ganieda and may have been added by Geoffrey or his source, and this set-piece has the ring of a genuine funeral oration from the dark ages, even down to the praise for the king's just treatment of clerics and the characteristically dark age phrase 'pillar of the kingdom'. This may in substance be the funeral ode written by Rhydderch's bard at the time of his death in around 595, rather than by his widow. Rhydderch was remembered as a Christian king. Both Christian and pagan kings alike had bards. Rhydderch's contemporary Urien was the great pagan king of Rheged. After he was assassinated in 590,[115] his bard Taliesin wrote *his* funeral ode. We know the names of only a small number of the dark age bards – Myrddin, Taliesin and Aneirin – but it is fair to assume that every dark age king worthy of the name employed one. Although we have no direct evidence of him, Arthur too would have had a *carminator* in his feast hall to recite or sing of his exploits and his greatness, in part to entertain, in part to condition the king's companions and warriors to see Arthur's as the greatest cause and inspire their unswerving loyalty. He was the spin-doctor at the court of King Arthur.

Yet the Merlin of legend is more than a mere bard. He is a magus. It is often assumed that this is an invention of the high middle ages, perhaps specifically of Geoffrey, but there is plenty of evidence that sixth-century kings invariably had spiritual advisers or chaplains at their sides so that supernatural help was always on call. Mac Erca, high king of Ireland from 503 onwards, was a contemporary of Arthur's and very much an Arthur-like figure himself. He is said to have leaned heavily on the advice of a British monk.[116] Bridei, king of the pagan Picts after Arthur's death, had a chief magician called Broichan, who also functioned as a foster father and tutor to the king in true Celtic tradition:[117] the relationship between these two real, documented, truly historical figures is very similar to that described as existing between Merlin and Arthur in the fully developed medieval romances. The saints, as we saw earlier, were wayward and volatile, intensely committed to their mission, fiercely jealous and competitive and ever on the alert for the voice of God telling them to pack up and move on. This eccentric and unpredictable behaviour is very much what we see incorporated into Merlin's character, even to the disappearing and reappearing. The dark age saints were a law to themselves. We saw how King Mark tried to recruit Paul Aurelian as his personal bishop at Castle Dore, but Paul ignored the summons and went off to Brittany instead. We saw how Gildas, both historian and saint, outspokenly criticized several major kings in Wales and Dumnonia: and this virulent outspokenness seems to have been quite normal.

So Arthur's 'Merlin' may have been based on a priest-companion. One tradition has it that St Piran was Arthur's chaplain. Another possibility is that Merlin may have been based loosely on St Dubricius, the bishop credited with crowning Arthur.

Pagan kings did not usually sponsor Christian missionaries or maintain chaplains, but they did sponsor the pagan equivalents – druids, magi, sorcerers or wizards – and this brings us closer than ever to the story-book relationship between Merlin and Arthur. These wizards were required to give advice, prophesy in verse form for their masters, cast enchantments and entertain with feats of magic. The clash of cultures when Christian and pagan kings met in battle can be imagined. There were also non-military trials of strength between the missionaries and the wizards. Muirchu describes one in the *Life of St Patrick*.[118]

> The fierce heathen emperor of the barbarians reigned in Tara, the Irish capital. His name was Loegaire, son of Niall. He had wise men, wizards, soothsayers, enchanters and inventors of every black art who were also in their heathen, idolatrous way to know and foresee everything that happened. Two of them were above the rest, their names being Lothroth and Lucetmael.

They predicted that a strange, new, troublesome faith would come and overthrow kingdoms. They used a cryptic verse form for their predictions. A pagan festival is described as coinciding with Patrick's celebration of Easter. At this festival all kinds of magic feat were performed, a contest between Patrick's white magic and Lothroth's black arts developed, and during this Patrick caused one of the wizards to rise up into the air, fall headlong and brain himself on a rock. These events give a vivid impression of the sort of world into which Arthur was born some twenty years later.

During Arthur's reign, Carantoc led the Irish monks 'against the opposition of the magi' according to the *Life of Carantoc*. Carantoc, we saw earlier, was in the Dunster area founding a religious colony when Arthur and Cato were rulers in Dumnonia.[119]

After Arthur's death, in the second half of the sixth century, paganism was still rampant. St David found himself in conflict with Boia, the pagan king who lived near the place now called St David's. Boia's wife, who was also trying to seduce David's monks, invited her step-daughter Dunawd to go with her into the wood of Glyn Hodnant to collect nuts. She sat down and asked the girl to lay her head in her lap so that she could comb her hair. The girl obeyed and the stepmother cut her throat. A clear spring rose in the place where the blood flowed onto the ground. The place became known as the Martyrium of Dunawd.[120] Paganism was still a very real and living force and the struggle between the old religion and the new was a powerful one, beginning before Arthur's reign and continuing after his death.

The question remaining is whether it was a saint or a wizard who stood at King Arthur's side. Perhaps the tradition that put Merlin–Myrddin at Arthur's side incorporated elements of both into a single personality. Perhaps one of the things that made Arthur seem extraordinary in his own day was the fact that he kept a wizard even though he was a Christian. Gildas was quick to accuse kings of backsliding and inconsistency, so that possibility should be left open. There seems little doubt that Arthur was at least a nominal Christian, given the entry in the *Welsh Annals*: 'Battle of Badon, in which Arthur carried the cross of our lord Jesus Christ for three days and three nights on his shoulder'. He may nevertheless have had a wizard in his entourage.

CHAPTER SIX

CAMELOT

◆

King Arthur on Ascension Day had left Caerleon and held a most
magnificent court at Camelot with all the splendour appropriate to
the day.
(Chrétien de Troyes, *Lancelot* (1180): the earliest known
written reference to Camelot)

The medieval romances give the name Camelot to the central, most important and most romantic of Arthur's castles, and it is portrayed as a city as well as a fortress. So much did Camelot come to symbolize the new order Arthur created that its name conjures, still, a poignantly nostalgic image of otherworldly idealism, a dream of a perfect city, a perfect society. Camelot is a utopia, a castle in Never-Never Land where justice and the perfect social order prevail, a dream city where everyone has as much food and drink as they want. There is nowhere today called Camelot or anything like it, and many attempts have been made to identify its location. But did Camelot really exist, and if so where was it?

The name crops up in fifteen medieval manuscripts including the *Lancelot* and *Perceval* of Chrétien, the *Prose Lancelot* and the Glastonbury *Perlesvaus*, and in varying spellings: Camaaloit, Camaelot, Camahalot, Camahelot, Camalahot, Camaloc, Camaloth, Camellot, Camalot as well as Camelot. In spite of the changing form, the name is always instantly recognizable.

The full late medieval version of the Arthurian story given by Malory has Camelot at Winchester. This cannot be right, as Hampshire was in Saxon hands by Arthur's time, and emerged as the capital of Saxon Wessex; in fact it may be the association of Winchester with the kingship of Alfred that brought about the anachronistic connection with Arthur. Geoffrey of Monmouth describes Caerleon as Arthur's capital, or as the city where he chose to hold court after his first campaign in Gaul. Geoffrey did not use the name Camelot, though: it was Caxton several centuries later who transferred the name Camelot to it. The excavation of Roman remains at Caerleon uncovered a circular amphitheatre, causing many to wonder whether this ancient meeting place was the starting point for the stories of the Round Table.

Colchester, Cadbury and Caerlaverock

In the twentieth century, John Morris unequivocally identified Colchester as Camelot.[1] He felt that the common medieval spelling 'Camalot' showed that it was a version of a Latin place-name. He also insisted that it was the name of a large Roman town in Britain. The only town with a name remotely similar was Camulodunum, Roman Colchester. Colchester, he argued, had obvious advantages as a political headquarters in the 'reconquered' region of Britain, the area taken back from the Saxons during the Badon campaign: from there it would have been easy to supervise and intimidate the areas remaining in Anglo-Saxon hands in East Anglia and Kent. Colchester was well served by Roman roads linking it to the Celtic heartlands of the north and west. By this time London, though still in British hands, was in decline, and Colchester served as an alternative focus. I find Morris's arguments on this point entirely unconvincing, in that Colchester is on the wrong side of Britain to have been the British headquarters in the early sixth century. Although there were admittedly British territories in the east and there may even have been British military bridge-heads there, they would have been continuously vulnerable to Saxon attack. The obvious place to seek Arthur's capital is in the more secure Celtic fringe, the zone immediately to the north and west of Saxon-occupied England.

A more popular and credible identification altogether has been South Cadbury in Somerset. The huge hilltop earthworks begun in the iron age and refortified in the Arthurian period fits well with the idea of a fortress-town: within the quadruple earthworks there is room for a town as well as the palace of a great dark age king. John Selden (1584–1654) did not believe in the full-blown, exaggerated late medieval accounts of Arthur, although he believed that Arthur existed, and his scepticism makes him an interesting witness. As he himself said, he was 'not very prodigal of historical faith'. He passed on what he had heard. 'I will insert, out of the British story, what I importune you not to credit.'[2] He rightly felt that Drayton's account of Arthur's conquests of Iceland, Norway, Denmark and France was 'too hyperbolical'; the legend building had got so out of hand, had so aggrandized Arthur, that 'you can hardly guess what is true of him'. Selden commented on the *Assertion of Arthur* by John Leland (*c.* 1506–52) and accepted Leland's identification of South Cadbury as Camelot in a phrase that has become famous through repetition.

> By South Cadbury is that Camelot, a hill of a mile's compass at the top, four trenches circling it and betwixt every one of them an earthen wall. The content of it, within about 20 acres, full of ruins and relics of old buildings.

In 1532, John Leland had visited the site, observing, 'At . . . South Cadbyri standith Camallate, sumtyme a famose toun or castelle, apon a very torre or hill, wunderfully enstrengtheid of nature . . . The people can tell nothing ther but they have hard say that Arture much resortid to Camalat.'

Leslie Alcock, who excavated a substantial area of South Cadbury in 1967–70 and found archaeological proof of occupation during the dark ages, was convinced that Cadbury was a strong candidate for Camelot. The innermost bank, originally built in the iron age, had been capped with a formidable timber and masonry wall in the dark ages, at least one of the entrance gaps had been fitted with an elaborate wooden gate, and a substantial wooden hall had stood on the summit.

But was the folkloric association with Arthur invented by Leland? It seems that it was not. The Arthurian legend about the cave containing the sleeping Arthur inside the hill is probably genuinely old; a late version says that once a year a pair of normally invisible gates hidden in the hillside swing open to reveal the sleeping king. There is also a sixteenth-century reference to the summit being the site of Arthur's palace, which corroborates Leland's story. This is in the writings of the Welsh antiquary Elis Gruffudd (died 1552). He related, in Welsh, two English versions of the story, one giving the location as 'near Gloucester', the other saying Arthur 'is asleep in a cave under a hill near Glastonbury'. This has often been taken to mean Glastonbury Tor, but it need not, and as Thomas Jones suggests it may refer to South Cadbury, which is only 15 km from Glastonbury.³ Indeed, Glastonbury may only have been mentioned because of the alleged discovery there of Arthur's body in the twelfth century. It looks as if by the sixteenth century there was a genuine, locally derived tradition that Cadbury was Camelot, but that is quite late and many places had acquired Arthurian legends by then. The details of the pair of gates and the palace are curious in that they are both precise and accurate in terms of the dark age archaeology – remains of a pair of gates and a dark age palace on the summit are exactly what Alcock found – as if an oral tradition from the sixth century had been somehow kept alive across a thousand years.

By 1982, Leslie Alcock had modified his enthusiasm for a strictly Arthurian Cadbury, or at least decided to express it in more circumspect language.⁴ Cadbury was a political rather than a military centre, the seat of a king with wealth, power and manpower resources unequalled anywhere else in Britain. He based this on the enormous length of the dark age perimeter wall: most dark age royal centres were rather small, and this one was huge. The archaeological evidence nevertheless led him to the idea of a British high king, and he commented on the parallel with Vortigern: Nennius described Vortigern, an earlier high king, as building himself a grandiose fortress for himself out of timber and stone.

Alcock may be right in deducing from the huge size of South Cadbury the importance of the local chief, and in seeing the hillfort as the administrative centre for a large estate, but there is certainly another interpretation that might be drawn from the evidence. The huge enclosure was probably needed to give temporary accommodation to the Dumnonian war-bands as they gathered close to the eastern frontier ready to do battle with the Saxons. As we saw earlier, South Cadbury's position midway between the Bristol and English Channels and central within eastern Dumnonia made it an ideal location for a gathering place for Dumnonian troops. There are documentary references to roughly contemporary 'hostings' in the Irish law code. It seems there were three reasons for hosting: to repel an invading army, to guard the border of the kingdom against incursion, and to cross that border to make a pre-emptive strike against a menace.⁵

Cadbury was just far enough from the Saxon war zone to be safe, but adjacent to roads that would take Arthur's cavalry quickly to any part of southern Britain to engage the enemy. South Cadbury can be seen to occupy a key strategic position in the military defence of Celtic Britain. There may well have been a local sub-king who acted as custodian and host, and organized the provisioning, but it seems likely that it was refortified as part of a high king's regional strategy. So, even though we may not believe that Arthur actually lived at South Cadbury, he may well have 'much resorted' there, using it as a springboard for attacks on the Saxons to the east and north-east. The site was not Camelot, in the sense that Arthur's home base was elsewhere.

One location that has for some reason been overlooked as a candidate for Camelot is Exeter. As the one and only Roman city in Dumnonia, it is likely to have had some importance as a central place in the post-Roman period. At present, not enough is known of Exeter in the dark ages: the archaeology nevertheless does suggest that it was refortified in about 520. This could have been done during the Badon campaign, either in anticipation of a wholesale onslaught on the Dumnonian heartland by marauding Saxons, or as an expression of consolidation after the successful hammering of the Saxons at Badon. The scanty archaeological remains suggest that Exeter was no more than the headquarters of a sub-king, but it could nevertheless have functioned as a stronghold-city in the period of Arthur's power.

Norma Goodrich proposes Caerlaverock Castle on the north shore of the Solway Firth, leaning on R. L. Graeme Ritchie's 1952 discovery of the site.[6] She even proposes that Caerlaverock might have been known in antiquity as something like Dun Dagel, so that Caerlaverock is both Camelot and Tintagel. Goodrich's arguments are self-frustrating, in that she leans heavily on Geoffrey of Monmouth in all things except, curiously, his insistence on Cornwall and a Cornish Tintagel. Whenever he mentions a southern English location, Goodrich comments indulgently, 'Geoffrey has strayed again.'[7] There seems to be no reason at all to equate Caerlaverock Castle with Camelot – still less to equate Caerlaverock with Tintagel, the location of which is well known.

Tintagel

The re-emergence, after half a century, of Tintagel as a dark age secular centre with very high status of some peculiar kind now acquires major importance in the context of the Arthurian legends that surround the site. This issue has a particular thrust now that we are seeing the territory of Trigg or Tricurium as Arthur's home territory or personal estate.

As we saw when we reviewed the site in Chapter 3, mounting recent archaeological evidence shows that Tintagel Island was intensively occupied during the reign of Arthur. The remains there are consistent with a secular citadel defended from the sea by impressively unscaleable cliffs and from the land by a large bank and ditch. Because of its exposure to the elements it was probably visited seasonally or occasionally, and not permanently occupied, but the many small turf-walled hutments that swarmed across the centre of the Island and round its sides show that at times large numbers of exceptionally hardy people converged on it. These were probably Arthur's warriors, with Tintagel as a rallying-point for the war-bands from all over Tricurium.

There was also some speculation on the specialized use of space at Tintagel: the 'Upper Ward' crag was an obvious mainland strongpoint from which the entrance through the bank and ditch and the landward end of the neck could be supervised. The space inside the vallum but still to landward of the neck may have been reserved for stabling: it seems to me very unlikely that horses would have been taken across the narrow isthmus with its frightening drop on each side. Archaeomagnetic dating of hearths in this area shows that fires burned there in around 500. The Island end of the isthmus was the likely organizational focus of the citadel. The Iron Gate was a natural landing-place, the only one on the Island; the path leading up the slope to the nucleus, a path we still walk, was also probably well trodden in the dark ages (see Plate 6.1). The king's feast hall, which we may now think of as Arthur's hall, may have stood on the northern part of the plateau, although there is an alternative site which we will consider later.

Away to the north-west, and right on the plateau edge, is a peculiar feature that was not discussed in Chapter 3 – the Tunnel (see Plate 6.2). This seems to belong to a group of features best understood in a ritual or ceremonial context, and they may not all belong to the same period. The Tunnel is relatively short, about a metre wide at floor level and only about 10 metres long, crooked, and entirely artificial: it was cut through the living rock from the western end, using small iron tools of apparently medieval (or older) type. The floor slopes down towards the western end, which opens onto the grassy slope at the head of a steep northward-draining coombe; there is a shallow well a short distance down the slope. The tunnel is shaped like a stretched-out medieval arch, and this has led many to assume that it was made at the same time as the medieval castle in the south-east corner of the Island. The circular recesses in the floor at the western end were clearly made to hold a door frame, and the sockets at intervals along the walls must have held light horizontal beams, probably for hanging up joints of meat in a cool draught out of reach of rats. The Tunnel was therefore almost certainly utilized in the thirteenth to fifteenth centuries as a cold store for food.

The eastern end was always open. Early descriptions give it as 'a Cave, reaching once some faire way under ground'.[8] William Carnsew's poem, quoted by Carew, describes it as admitting entry but denying thoroughfare, which implies that the western end was blocked. Sir Richard Grenville in 1583 noted the medieval walled garden and 'by this walle appere the ruins of a vault'.[9] The western end as now seen was cleared in the 1930s, but the debris excavated yielded no finds that could date the feature. It is clear from Ralegh Radford's guide that he considered that the Tunnel continued further seaward 'an unknown distance'.[10]

It may be that the Tunnel was created in the thirteenth century as a meat store, though its location on the side of the Island opposite the castle, as far away from it as possible, makes that unlikely. Medieval manciples may have been indifferent to the labour involved for their scullions,[11] but it would nevertheless have been peculiar to place the meat store as far as possible from the kitchens.

The form of the Tunnel in detail may appear medieval, but its character in general is that of a distinctively Cornish antiquity, the fogou. This identification gets us little further, in that the purpose of this fundamentally iron age feature is still not fully understood. West Cornish settlements of the iron age were frequently fitted with a fogou, a short crooked tunnel descending a short distance into the earth. Some archaeologists believe they were refuges, larders or cold stores, others more recently

Plate 6.1 The Iron Gate. The dark age wharf is likely to have been at the lowest point on the rock platform (left). Beside it, to the left (off the picture) is a cave where boats might have moored.

Plate 6.2 The Tunnel

have proposed that they were shrines.[12] If the fogou was a simple shrine to the spirits of the earth, its presence on Tintagel Island acquires a special significance. It may have been made in the iron age; if made in the dark ages, it represents a self-conscious reference back to the religious practices of the past. If made in the iron age and disused in the dark ages, it may still help to explain the cultic associations the Island had acquired.

A pre-medieval date for the Tunnel is suggested by the form of its eastern end. The floor rises up and the roof simply disappears (see Plate 6.3). The Tunnel would appear to have been excavated when the general ground level was higher: a relatively long period of erosion would have been needed to take the Tunnel roof off. The southern entrance points south-eastwards on a bearing of 129°, which is the direction of the sunrise at the winter solstice. In the distance, weather permitting, Rough Tor is a skyline marker for the midwinter sunrise. This orientation may be accidental, but it suggests a kinship with a religious belief that goes right back to the bronze age and neolithic, a belief that a solar deity anually visits and impregnates an earth mother goddess.[13]

Nor is the Tunnel the only feature that suggests an ancient ritual use. On the southern edge of the plateau there is a cluster of such features. The land surface rises to a rocky knoll which seems to have been a ritual focus: it has the feeling of being a stage, a place designed for the performance of some elemental drama. It terminates southwards in a series of dramatic crags above a slope-and-wall cliff. These weathered crags are of a great age, perched as they are above a fossil hill slope that has probably changed little in 10,000 years. Carved out of the crag faces are three rectangular niches, box-shaped hollows which may be rectangular as the result of natural processes of weathering and erosion, but have every appearance of being neolithic or bronze age rock shelters or burial chambers. Rock-cut burial chambers are exceedingly rare in the British Isles, but two at least are known to exist: the Dwarfie Stane on Hoy, Orkney, and St Kevin's Bed at Glendalough in Ireland. The Dwarfie Stane's cells are 1.5m × 0.8m × 0.7m high, and the remains of the Tintagel cells are similar in scale.[14] Immediately below the centre of the 'stage' is a pair of niches side by side, separated by a holed partition slab; on the ledge connecting them is a collection of a dozen cupmarks. About 10 metres away to the west is a third chamber, known as King Arthur's Seat (see Plate 6.4). This has two and a half of its original four sides intact and a floor and roof that slope into the Island with the bedding planes of the rock. The floor carries a collection of around twenty well-made cupmarks drilled up to 15 cm into the rock, again characteristic of neolithic or bronze age religious cult activity (see Plate 6.5). Charles Thomas discovered another group close by.[15]

Although not common in Cornwall, thirty-four cupmarked stones altogether have been recorded. Collections of cupmarks in the north of England tend to be concentrated on rock outcrops that command spectacular views, just like the one at Tintagel. It has been observed in connection with rock art in Galloway that prehistoric carvings are frequently found at viewpoints, sometimes directed at coastlines and commanding significantly wider fields of view than other locations in the area.[16] It is also common for the edges of lowland, coastal territories to have relatively simple carvings. All these observations could be made equally aptly about the Tintagel cupmarks, which command spectacular panoramic coastal views. Cupmarks have

Plate 6.3 The roofless eastern end of the Tunnel

Plate 6.4 King Arthur's Seat

Plate 6.5 The cupmarks in King Arthur's Seat. Tintagel churchyard on the skyline.

been found on other stones in the area, notably inland at Camelford, where they have certainly been moved from their original location by an antiquarian collector. The three big cupmarked slabs beside the front door of Sir James Smith's School, Camelford, are said to have come from a barrow that once stood near Starapark, 8 km east of Tintagel (SX: 133863). There is what looks very much like another rock-cut niche or tomb-chamber on the mainland at Tintagel, immediately south of the Castle entrance and perched three or four metres above the path (see Plate 6.6).

The three ?bronze age tomb chambers on the Island, the fourth chamber on the mainland overlooking the approach to the Neck, together with the cupmarks associated with them indicate that the Island may have been a focus for funerary ceremonies as far back as 1500–1000 BC. A charcoal sample from the northern end of the Lower Ward, near the top of the steps, unexpectedly produced a radiocarbon date of 1000 BC.[17] It might be regarded by some archaeologists as a rogue date, perhaps contaminated in some way, and some of the pottery fragments found with it were indeed later in date. The charcoal may nevertheless be bronze age in date. The radiocarbon date is consistent with and supports the idea of bronze age activity at Tintagel. Certain elements embedded in the Arthurian tradition also have their origins in bronze age cult practice. The surrender of Excalibur to the Lady of the Lake is an obvious anachronism in both high medieval and dark age worlds, a survival of the bronze age practice of sacrificing swords in rivers and lakes.

On the bare rock surface of the knoll's summit, the 'stage', is an artificially cut hollow the shape and size of a human foot (see Plate 6.7). At the surface it measures 43 × 23 cms, the sides sloping in to a fair representation of a human foot 25 cm long:

Plate 6.6 The mainland rock shelter or tomb chamber, view south

Plate 6.7 King Arthur's Footprint on the summit platform

Plate 6.8 The Footprint

it is 9 cm deep (see Plate 6.8). My booted left foot (size 9) fits into it perfectly. This curious feature, pointed out to nineteenth-century tourists as King Arthur's Footstep or Footprint, belongs to a bronze age and iron age belief system that was not unique to Tintagel but widespread (see Figure 6.1). Similar carved footprints are known elsewhere and they are associated with oath-taking ceremonies and the bonding of chieftains to their territories. If you stand with your left foot planted in it you face the shallow saddle crossing the Island, where the war-band's bivouac tents were clustered. Turning through 180 degrees, you find yourself looking just a church-length to the east of Tintagel Church. To either side, several miles of the north Cornish coastline can be seen (see Figure 6.2).

It is easy to imagine an induction ceremony taking place here, a ceremony in which a new king planted his foot symbolically into the living rock of his dead father's kingdom, made gestures of command and uttered an oath of service to the whole of Tricurium, much of which must have seemed to be visible in the sweeping panorama. In fact the entire stretch of Trigg's coastline is visible; when standing beside the Footprint you can see from Bude in the north-east to Trevose Head in the south-west. Perhaps a specific oath was made towards Tintagel churchyard, where the bodies of his predecessors lay buried, and specifically, as often as not, the newly-buried body of the king he replaced. We can imagine his war-band standing on the lower ground among the flapping tent-skins of the bivouac (see Figure 6.3), watching awe-struck from below as the heir silhouetted against the southern sky became the new king. Pure theatre.

There may be more rock carvings awaiting discovery on the Island. On the south-west headland is a barely perceptible west–east groove, possibly an ancient wall footing. An arrow 0.5 cm deep and 20 cm long is carved into it, and it points directly towards the burial ground at Tintagel Church. A large isolated mass of quartz outcrops close by, and quartz fragments were regularly included with burials at Tintagel Churchyard until as recently as the sixteenth century, forming another link between Island and burial ground.

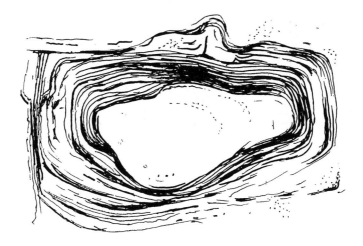

Figure 6.1 King Arthur's Footprint

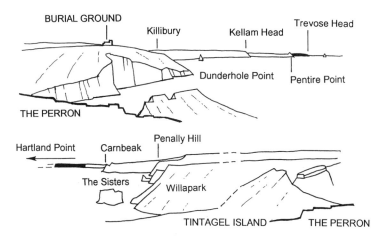

Figure 6.2 View from the Perron or Anvil Stone, Tintagel Island. The whole coastline of Trigg is visible (black = not Trigg).

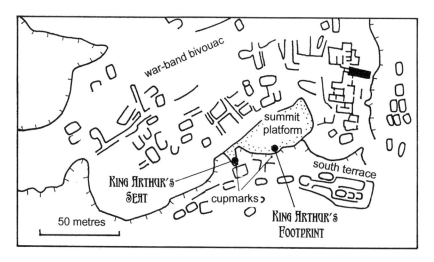

Figure 6.3 Tintagel Island: war-bond bivouac and summit platform

The Footprint belongs to the world of the non-Romanized Celts. There are places in Ireland and the Western Isles of Scotland where similar impressions of footmarks in the living rock, sometimes single, sometimes in pairs, are associated with inauguration ceremonies, with the crowning of kings. A classic example to compare with Tintagel's is the footprint carved at Dunadd. The Dunadd footprint, about 28 cm long, is at the highest point of a major centre of dark age power. Dunadd, significantly, has other rock carvings as well.[18] The symbolism of planting a foot in a prescribed mark goes back to the iron age and beyond, and can be seen as a divine marriage between the king and his kingdom.[19] Celtic literature includes allusions to this in the single golden sandal worn to mark the inauguration of a chieftain.[20] There are twin footprints beside the iron age broch of Clickhimin in Shetland.[21] These beliefs were widespread, and what we see at Tintagel is not peculiar or unique, but part of a general complex of beliefs about initiation that prevailed in the iron age; it is also in the nature of ceremonial that anachronistic acts and obsolete objects are involved, so references to iron age practices are exactly what we would expect to find at a major dark age ceremonial centre. Comparative archaeology and ethnology offer an explanation of the Footprint consistent with dark age kingship rituals.

These thoughts press other thoughts forwards. I have argued for Tintagel as a seasonal, or occasional gathering-place. Were the occasions primarily those of major induction ceremonies? If so, and if Tricurium was Arthur's kingdom as has already been argued, we are led to an inescapable conclusion: that this Footprint, this spot, must be the very place where Arthur became king.

One persistent, enduring story told about Arthur's accession to the throne is the anecdote about the sword in the stone. The fact that it is not in Geoffrey of Monmouth suggests that it may have been a French medieval invention. It does not seem to be found earlier than Robert de Boron's *Merlin* romance, although it is quite possible that Robert may, like Geoffrey, have incorporated some dark age material but from a different source. In Robert and Malory the sword is embedded in an anvil mounted on a stone, but some later writers 'improve' the story by leaving out the anvil and embedding the sword directly in the stone. Robert recognized the plucking of the sword as heavily symbolic and tried to explain it: the sword was justice, the stone was presumably Christ, and the act established Arthur's divine right to rule. Later re-tellings include the incident simply as a selection procedure for the accession or as a supernatural revelation of Arthur's kingship, rather like the dove descending on Jesus during his baptism. I do not think that it has been suggested before, that the story may be based ultimately on an inauguration ritual which actually took place at Tintagel, on the 'stage'.

In Malory's version, the sword bears an inscription, 'Whoso pulleth out this sword of this stone and anvil is rightwise king born of all England.' All the knights are allowed to try their hand. Arthur, as a mere squire, is not allowed to take part, but when he is sent to fetch his accident-prone foster-brother Kay's forgotten sword he saves himself a journey by taking the stone-sword instead. The drawing of the sword has to be repeated in the sight of the whole company of knights at Twelfth Night, Candlemas, Easter and Pentecost; finally, at Pentecost, Arthur is crowned king. Archaeological support for Tintagel as the dynastic centre for not only a king of Tricurium but a king of all Dumnonia comes from a recent analysis of the pottery; the enormous quantity of expensive imported pottery found at Tintagel marks it out as the highest-status focus in the entire West Country. This was not just one royal centre among several, but the pre-eminent Dumnonian royal centre.

King Arthur's Seat, the broken-walled rectangular chamber containing the finest collection of cupmarks, has for a roof a prow-shaped slab of rock, projecting out of the cliff top as if saluting the ancient burial place on the mainland. Seen from the east, this rock looks like an anvil (see Plate 6.9). Given that the feature was evidently a focus for cult activity, and given the peculiarities of the sword-in-the-stone story – why else is the anvil included? – it is possible that the form of this outcrop, this 'Anvil

Plate 6.9 The Anvil Stone

Stone', as we may call it, is a further clue connecting Arthur's induction ceremony with Tintagel Island. The Anvil Stone and the Footprint are just 30 metres apart. Perhaps, since there are in fact two more projecting outcrops nearby that also look like anvils, the entire summit slab was referred to as the Anvil Stone and should be equated with the perron or Stone of Honour described by Marie de France. Instead of drawing a literal sword from the stone, Arthur drew his sacred kingship from the living rock when he drew his own foot from the cavity in the Anvil Stone.

In the *Grand-Saint-Graal* of around 1200, the perron or Stone of Honour was called 'Anvil', and it was from this that the boy Arthur drew the sword prior to his general recognition as future battle-leader. The very odd circumstances relating to this incident suggest that the story contains old and unassimilated material, and it becomes easier to understand once we know that the historical original of the perron was a stone shaped like an anvil. In Marie de France the perron at Arthur's court was a marble mounting stage on which travellers to Avalon stepped. She calls it the Seat of Dread or the Seat of Honour, and on it heroes sat or were put to the test. Arthur's Camelot stood nearby. It was also a port of embarkation to Ireland.[22]

Tintagel is said in folklore to disappear at the solstices, momentarily reappearing in its ancient splendour, before once again returning to its everyday reality.[23] This beautiful image brings Tintagel closer to the Grail Castle than to Camelot. The Grail Castle of the medieval romances is surrounded by magic and mysticism. When Parzival wakes up,[24] he finds the Grail Castle unaccountably deserted, as it were reflecting Tintagel's temporary occupation; for a few days every so often the Island would be seething with excitement, noise and activity, then it would suddenly fall silent and much of the time it would have been deserted. In the *Prose Lancelot* the Grail Castle has two entrances only: one by land and one by small boat on the sea-ward side. Tintagel similarly had just two means of access: one via the neck, the other by the Iron Gate landing. The *Prose Lancelot* says it was at the Grail Castle that Merlin reigned inside the Wheel of Fire; although there is no wheel of fire at Tintagel there is Merlin's Cave deep beneath it (see Plate 6.10). The Grail Castle stands on a rocky island. Tintagel Island is the archetypal rocky island. The Grail Castle was the religious centre of Arthur's kingdom and also in some way a secret place. It may be that the highly developed versions of the Grail Castle we see in the medieval romances had their origin in dark age Tintagel, where access would certainly have been rigidly controlled and what went on there would have been for the eyes of a relatively select group of people. The steepness of the cliffs, the narrowness of the neck and the scale of the vallum ensured this. Dark age mystique about the ancient stone cups may have been woven into the fabric of the Grail legend.

'Myrddin' may have been one of the dark age names of Tintagel, apart from the surviving name Din Tagell, the Choker Fort, as 'Myrddin' means 'sea fortress', which exactly describes the site. Perhaps outside Dumnonia, as stories about Arthur and Myrddin spread, a misunderstanding developed and at some point, perhaps a century later, an equation was made with the bardic tradition. Tintagel is supposed to disappear magically at the solstices. This vanishing property is shared by Merlin. In Malory, Merlin's enemies denounce him as a 'wytche' and 'dreme-reder': 'with that

Plate 6.10 Merlin's Cave

Merlyn vanysshed aweye'. It was Merlin the magician who arranged Arthur's conception; it was *on* Myrddin, as well as *through* Myrddin, that Arthur's kingship was brought about. The 1605 Edinburgh edition of Merlin's and Thomas the Rhymer's prophecies tells us:

> Mervelous meling is wasting away,
> with a wicked woman, woe might shee be:
> for shee hath closed him in, in a Craige on Cornwel cost.

Tintagel, a crag on Cornwall's coast, encloses and incorporates Merlin.

What we see of dark age Tintagel has nothing Christian about it, everything of the ancient pagan world; everything is backward references to the beliefs and customs of Arthur's ancestors. Yet none of this is inconsistent with Arthur as a Christian convert. It was common for first generation, or even later, Christians to hang onto their pagan heritage. In every society, it is the very obsolescence of ancient custom which gives it power: inexplicably elaborate regalia, incomprehensible utterances in some antique language, and otherwise unseen hieratic gestures – all these are the essential ingredients of ceremonial activity. We should also remember the account of St Samson encountering pagan rites in Trigg in the Arthurian period.

The site, the Island, would have lent itself to rituals relating to a range of cosmic dramas. The exposures of naked rock, the sea cliffs, the foaming sea below on all sides, the five or six natural springs and shallow wells, the inexplicably overflowing well close to the hill's summit, the waterfall, the roaring tunnel – Merlin's Cave – passing right through the interior of the Island, the perilous knife-edged isthmus – all these make Tintagel Island a place where elemental forces seem to come to a focus. This may be the reason why the place became a centre for cult activity in the bronze and iron ages, and once it had become established as a cult centre with associations with the ancestors it became a place for initiation ceremonies, now remembered only in garbled form as the sword in the stone story and the ordeals of the Grail Quest.[25]

The Island Chapel (see Plate 6.11) is often seen as part of the medieval castle complex, but it actually pre-dates the thirteenth century castle and was built on the Island when no other structures were visible. Why was the chapel built on an otherwise deserted Island? The chapel as it stands was probably built at the beginning of the twelfth century and therefore marks the end of the Island's abandonment since the seventh century.[26] The granite altar stone has had a curious history,[27] since it was moved to another site on the Island, perhaps to be used as a fire-back or hearthstone during the sixteenth century fortification of the site during the Armada scare, but nevertheless represents the chapel's original altar.

The dedication to St Juliot is difficult to understand – St Julitta of Tarsus, perhaps? – in relation to Earl Richard or any royal castle and this supports the idea that the chapel was there well before 1230. The location up on the plateau, away from the castle, suggests it had nothing to do with that structure. In addition, some of the carved stones clearly belong to an earlier period than the thirteenth-century castle. The 1980s' archaeology shows that the chapel began as an unusually large dark age room, 13.5m by 5.3m externally, 11.75m by 3.7m internally (see Figure 6.4), and containing imported pottery, and Charles Thomas suggests it was probably chosen

Plate 6.11 The Island Chapel

for development into a chapel on the basis of its size and approximate west–east orientation (actually 11 degrees south of east). Two items taken across for preservation to Tintagel Church, a small granite font and a triangular slab bearing a rosette carving, indicate that the Island Chapel was built perhaps in 1100 or earlier, but on the wall-footings of an important dark age hall. Thomas suggests that the Chapel was built to serve Bossiney while Tintagel Church served Treknow,[28] but the location seems too inaccessible.

A more natural explanation is that, as at Tintagel Churchyard, tradition preserved the location of an important ancient focus. Archaeology has not yet detected any evidence of structures from the intervening centuries, but it may be that the Island was visited between the seventh and eleventh centuries and some oral tradition of the place's significance was maintained. Whether a local memory of the importance of the original building was retained cannot be known; it may be that this particular dark age building, which was significantly larger than all the other dark age buildings on the Island but one,[29] was remembered as 'special'. Was *this* Arthur's hall? If it was, it would explain why it remained a focus and why the tumbled remains of its walls were respected and rebuilt.

If this line of thought seems too speculative and insubstantial, or the proposition downright unlikely, it should be remembered that somehow a major tradition concerning dark age Cornish history was preserved for Geoffrey to write down; modern archaeology is showing that Tintagel really was a royal stronghold of the first importance in the sixth century and, though no scientifc means are available to prove the conception of Arthur, comparative ethnography shows that arcane inauguration

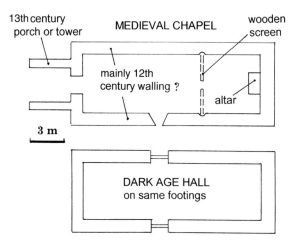

Figure 6.4 The Island Chapel, Tintagel

ceremonies are likely to have been conducted there. If Arthur's reign formally began there in a ceremony focusing on the Footprint in the Stone of Honour, in a figurative sense he *was* conceived there. At a time when the site was empty of its castle, Geoffrey of Monmouth was telling the story of a dark age dynasty founded at Tintagel. For several centuries that we know of, visitors have reacted sceptically to the local traditions about the place.

In about 1600 John Norden saw beside the Chapel the single rock-cut grave, which he was told was variable in length. Norden was openly sceptical; 'The grave will fit everye stature, as is effabuled: but experience doth not so assure me.' The lore concerning the unmeasurable tomb is often overlooked as an indicator of a Celtic cult tradition surviving at Tintagel. It appears, for instance, among the twenty 'mirabilia' listed in the *Historia Brittonum*. One of the Arthurian wonders was the unmeasurable grave of Amr:

> He was a son of the warrior Arthur, and he [Arthur] killed him [Amr] there [at a spring called Llygad Amr] and buried him. Men come to measure the tomb, and it is sometimes six feet long, sometimes nine, sometimes twelve, sometimes fifteen.

The local traditions about Tintagel have survived in the face of continuing scepticism. It is not a coincidence that an early medieval literary tradition pointed to the place as a high-status dark age political and cultural centre and twentieth-century archaeology and ethnography have confirmed that the tradition was true. Geoffrey was describing Tintagel as a dark age royal stronghold at a time, the early twelfth century, when nothing was to be seen there to support the idea: the castle was as yet unbuilt. It has been suggested that the low footings of the bivouac might have been more conspicuous in the twelfth century than in the twentieth, giving rise to the castle legend, but they cannot have been more than a few centimetres higher than they are today, and could never have looked, even to a twelfth-century layman, like the remains of a castle.

Archaeological evidence tells us that the occupation of Tintagel Island did not end straight away in the aftermath of Camlann, but continued for a couple of generations at a reduced level. It went out of use, it seems, in the seventh century. At the time Geoffrey was writing, Tintagel had been abandoned for 500 years; he was therefore presumably drawing on five centuries of local oral tradition.

Viroconium

Tintagel's claim to be Camelot appears strong, but other claims have been made. As we saw in Chapter 5, Phillips and Keatman believe that Arthur was Owain Ddantgwn, king of Powys. Owain's headquarters were at the city of Viroconium on the banks of the River Severn.[30] Therefore, if Owain was Arthur, Viroconium was Camelot. As a fortified Roman town substantially rebuilt in the Arthurian period, it seems to fulfil several of the criteria, yet Phillips and Keatman do not press the identification. Instead they emphasize that there is no positive evidence that a place with the name Camelot ever existed; that neither Geoffrey nor Wace mention it; that it does not appear in any text until the *Lancelot* of Chrétien de Troyes, and is then only mentioned once, in passing.[31] They believe Chrétien invented the name Camelot for Arthur's court in about 1180, as well as creating many of the knights, including Sir Lancelot. The graphic descriptions of the splendours of the ideal city only come later.[32]

Their argument that Arthur was King Owain of Powys is nevertheless unconvincing, so any idea of Arthur's principal stronghold or home being in the middle Severn valley falls down.

Killibury

Early Welsh traditions give Kelliwic (also spelt Kelli Wic or Celli Wig) as the name of Arthur's favourite residence, by implication his home and base. Some believe the name, which may mean 'forest grove', reinforces the magical, folkloric, unhistorical aspect of Arthur, but there is good reason to believe it was a real place in Cornwall, and therefore somewhere a real person might have lived.[33] A Welsh Triad lists *Three Tribal Thrones of the Island of Britain*, the places where Arthur held court.[34] The northern one was at Pen Rhionydd, the location of which is unknown but thought to have been near Stranraer in Galloway. The Welsh throne was at St David's, and the Cornish tribal throne was at Kelliwic. Another Triad mentions that Arthur's chief elder at Kelliwic 'in Kernow' (Cornwall) was Caradog Freichfra (or Caradoc Vreichvras). Other sources give him a kingdom of his own in south Dorset, and there is nothing incompatible in that: Geraint was a subordinate and courtier of Arthur's, yet himself a king in Dumnonia. Caradog was certainly of noble birth: he was the brother of Queen Onbrawst, wife of King Mouric. Kelliwic was thus firmly recognized as Arthur's base long before any ideas of Caerleon or Camelot were written down, not just in the Triads but also in *Culhwch and Olwen*, which mentions Arthur's court being at Kelli Wic five times. Patriotism would demand a Welsh capital for Arthur, yet the tradition preserved in Wales by Welsh copyists was that Arthur's favourite base was not in Wales but in Cornwall, and at a place called Kelliwic. Some have suggested Callington as a possible location for Kelliwic, and this was favoured among eighteenth- and nineteenth-century Cornish antiquaries, though it is not clear why as the names are not very similar.[35] There has been a consensus in the twentieth century that Killibury, near Wadebridge, was meant.

An old name for the earthwork is Kelly Rounds, which brings it even closer to Kelliwic, and the hamlet on the main road 500 metres to the north is still known as Kelly. The 1302 Assize Roll for Cornwall mentions the recent murder of a man called Thomas de Kellewik at Lanestly near Penzance, so there really was a place of that name in medieval Cornwall and, given that the mobility of people in the middle ages was greater than often credited, Kelliwic/Kellewik need not have been anywhere near Penzance. A reference in 1215 to 'Killiburgh' meant the fort at Kelly, which is not inconsistent with the use of 'Kelliwic' for the township or district. A tenth-century Anglo-Saxon charter mentions a 'Caellwic',[36] which has not been identified conclusively but is thought to have been the episcopal manor of Burniere within which there was a land holding called 'Kelly', and this almost certainly corresponds with the hamlet still called Kelly on the main road between the site now known as Burniere and Killibury.[37] There is no doubt that Kelliwic was a real place, and little doubt that it was Killibury.

Killibury Castle is a small nearly circular iron age fort on a low rounded summit 87 metres above sea level overlooking the Camel estuary (see Figure 6.5). It consists of an outer ditch 1.5 metres deep surrounding a spread bank 8 metres wide and up to 1.5 metres high. Within this is a second ditch, also with an inner bank, still 3.5 metres high in 1900, that probably had an outer revetment wall of stone blocks. The banks are unimpressive now, but they have been lowered by ploughing. Once they may have stood twice as high, with palisades on top, overlooking ditches 2 metres deep and making a secure and defensible stronghold. On the west side, where the lane still approaches, there was an outwork to protect the west gate. Even though the site is on a hill top, the ditches are water-filled in winter, like medieval castle moats.

But this Camelot must be a sad disappointment to any visitor hoping to recapture the magical atmosphere of the Arthurian legend. The earthworks of the southern half were already reduced by ploughing when Dickinson saw them at the end of the nineteenth century, then built over in the 1970s; Killibury today is dominated by a drab farmhouse and the forbidding sheds of a piggery, from which the profoundly depressing sound of crying pigs drifts ceaselessly. The farm track crossing the site connects the east and west entrances of the fort: the track is probably the original iron age high road to Killibury, connecting the hillfort with the estuary (see Figure 6.6).

As many as thirteen structural phases between 400 BC and AD 100 have been identified.[38] Charcoal in the soil from the iron age land surface inside the enclosure has been radiocarbon dated to 300–200 BC, and pieces of La Tene pottery confirm this date. The original occupation of the fort may date back several centuries further: a single sherd found entombed inside the rampart suggests that the structure may have been begun as early as the late bronze age, and charcoal deposits dated to about

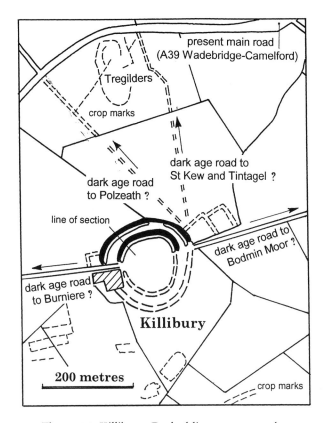

Figure 6.5 Killibury. Dashed lines = crop marks.

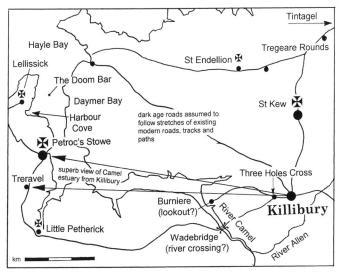

Figure 6.6 Killibury and the Camel estuary. ✠ = fifth-/sixth-century
Christian community.

1000 BC are consistent with this.[39] Like Tintagel, this site has a long pre-Arthurian ancestry.

To be associated with Arthur, Killibury must yield conclusive evidence of dark age occupation, and no evidence has yet been found to show that it was refortified in the fifth or sixth centuries.[40] On the other hand, only small areas of the banks were excavated, and they were plough-damaged. In support of a fifth- or sixth-century elite reoccupation, two fragments of high-status post-Roman pottery, pieces of amphorae imported from Athens, have been found on the site at the base of the plough-soil,[41] and that suggests that an elite group did occupy the site in the Arthurian period.

It was Dickinson, in 1900, who made the first inspired equation of Kelliwic with Killibury.[42] There is no reason to doubt that he was right, even if some of his reasoning was faulty. He was persuaded of an Arthurian connection because Tregeare Rounds lay only 6 km away to the north, a site at that time believed to be Damelioc, one of the castles of Gorlois, the husband of Ygerne, Arthur's mother. Geoffrey's Damelioc ('Dimilioc') is now seen to have been located at Domellick near St Dennis, nowhere near Killibury.

According to the Triads, some of which are genuine survivals from the sixth century, Modred attacked and took possession of Kelliwic, where he pulled Guinevere from her throne and insulted her.[43]

Geoffrey mentions that Arthur's chaplain was St Piran, who is known from other sources to have lived in a cell on the banks of the River Camel. In *Culhwch and Olwen*, which from its crudity of tone and inclusion of archaic social and legal customs must have its origins in the dark ages, it is plain that Arthur's court at Kelliwic was seen as playing a central role in the scheme of things; it was evidently the custom to seek help there from a king famed for his magnanimity. One remark in *Culhwch and Olwen* is about a marksman called Medr who could, from Kelliwic, hit a wren in Ireland. Hyperbole apart, this implies a coastal or near-coastal location on a shoreline facing Ireland. The north-west-facing coast of north Cornwall would suit the case well; in fact, one conspicuous feature of the site of Killibury is that it gives an unrestricted vista down the broad middle reach of the Camel estuary, between Treworna and Padstow, in effect pointing towards southern Ireland.

It may be this estuary view that explains the site's strategic importance. It would give plenty of warning of the approach of enemy ships, or indeed the welcome approach of allies and friendly traders. There may have been a lookout posted on Burniere, a low but prominent hill right above the estuary's east bank. A track, probably in use in the dark ages, still winds purposefully from Burniere via Tregorden and Three Holes Cross to Killibury, and may have been used by soldiers on lookout duty to gallop back to the king at Killibury with news of the identity of the new arrivals. Where the main dark age port on the Camel estuary was located is not known although it is known from archaeological finds that goods were imported by way of the estuary. It looks as if Harbour Cove, Padstow and Daymer Bay were in use as harbours,[44] and it may be that some vessels came further upstream to Trewornan or even Wadebridge. As the lowest bridging point on the River Camel, Wadebridge must also have been the head of navigation. Burniere is situated between Trewornan and Wadebridge, and could have overseen activities at both places. Possibly all four locations were in use.

Neither Killibury nor the area round it has been thoroughly explored by archaeologists, but recent aerial photography has shown that this was an unusually busy area in antiquity. There is another double-ringed enclosure less than 1 km to the south-west of Killibury, similar in shape but much smaller than Killibury. Killibury itself is at the centre of a tight cluster of crop marks showing various small rectangular and irregularly shaped enclosures which have yet to be interpreted or explored, but they seem to indicate settlement round the fort.

Immediately to the north of Killibury, just 300m away, is Tregilders, a small sub-rectangular enclosure about 75 metres across bounded by a rock-cut ditch 3 metres wide and 2 metres deep. From the finds, this may have been a farm in the sub-Roman period. Brushing past the eastern edge of the farm site was a trackway leading south to the eastern entrance of Killibury. This has traces of cart ruts 1.5 metres apart eroded up to 0.3 metres into the rock. The line of the field hedge to the north suggests that the track continued north and north-west towards the bridge at Penpont; if so the ancient road makes a very natural sweep round from the harbours on the eastern shore of the Camel estuary to Bodmin and the Fowey estuary by way of the east gate of Killibury – probably an important dark age road.[45]

Killibury was close to the important river crossing at the head of the Camel estuary (now the site of Wadebridge), and probably the focus of road routes into Tricurium from neighbouring territories to the south and south-west. From here, it seems likely that an axial road ran north–east through the kingdom towards Camelford and Launceston, skirting the northern edge of Bodmin Moor, and possibly following the course of the present A39. How this was linked to Tintagel cannot be inferred. The Roman milestones nevertheless show that there was a well-established coastal route that passed through Tintagel and this may have led on westwards to the harbours at Hayle Bay and Daymer Bay at the seaward end of the Camel estuary. The existence of Tregeare Rounds to the north of Killibury suggests that a road may have existed from the iron age onwards connecting Killibury and Tregeare Rounds via St Kew and Pendoggett. From there, the modern road route to Westdowns and Trebarwith may have been used to reach Tintagel.

At Trebarwith the road had to cross a ravine that may have marked the southern edge of the Tintagel estate, much as earth banks did elsewhere. The Rocky Valley may have marked the boundary to the north-east, with a bank possibly joining the two.[46] The Trebarwith ravine is a contender for the site of one of Arthur's battles, Tribruit, which no-one has yet convincingly located. O. G. S. Crawford identified the word *traeth* as a topographic term, meaning 'sandy shore of a river'. In Welsh, the word means more specifically 'a tract of sand lying on one side of a river'. This is very precisely what we see at the rocky mouth of the stream at Trebarwith: rocky cliffs to the south and the broad sandy beach of Trebarwith Strand to the north. The place could make sense as a location for a major battle; perhaps Arthur had to defend Tintagel against attack from the south, or an enemy temporarily occupied the prestigious site and Arthur had to retake it by storming his own defensive lines. If it seems unlikely that Arthur was ever so disadvantaged within his home territory, there is a reference to the enemy occupation of Kelliwic itself in a 'Welsh' poem written not later than the tenth century:

Cai would entreat them,
while he struck three at a time.
When Celli was lost there was fury.[47]

Tribruit too is mentioned in the poem *Pa gur?* ('What man is the porter?'). After the story of Cai's fight with Cynyn at Mynydd Eiddyn, Cai is described,

on the strands of Trywruid,
contending with Garwlwyd;
brave was his [Cai's] disposition with sword and shield.

The *Black Book of Carmarthen* also contains an account of *Taliesin and Myrddin on the Battle of Arderydd*, which carries a reference to the Arthurian battle of Tribruit:

glaring and tumultuous the slaughter;
perforated was the shield from Trywruyd.

As a youth Arthur may have been trained in the Roman cavalry tradition, and received his training not far from Killibury, at the old Roman station of Nanstallon. Nanstallon was occupied between AD 55 and 80, and no positive archaeological evidence has been found to show that it was used after the Romans left. It is nevertheless possible that the place went on functioning in the post-Roman period as a military training camp, a kind of Dumnonian Sandhurst. In the substantial open spaces between the barrack blocks and the surrounding rectangular earthworks, Fox and Ravenhill found only evidence of a lot of trampling.[48] This is exactly what we should expect if the site was used to corral horses and as a base for training cavalry. Nanstallon is 7 km south of Killibury.

The earliest known monastery in all Dumnonia was at St Kew, 3 km north of Killibury, and its proximity was surely an added attraction to a first or second generation Christian king. In Arthur's time the abbot there was Iuniavus, and it was to St Kew that St Samson came from his hermit's cave at Stackpole on the Severn, perhaps hoping to find favour with Arthur. In any event he was immediately rebuffed by Iuniavus and sent away; Samson lived for a time in a cell down by the estuary, which seems to have held an unaccountable attraction to the early saints. A king called Arthur is not mentioned in the *Life of St Samson*, only a count called Gwedian, who was presumably the holder of one of the *trefs* or estates in Trigg, a dark age lord of the manor. All we can infer from this is that Arthur played no part in the vicissitudes of Samson's career.

In the *Black Book of Carmarthen* is a poem that was written in about 950 or earlier. It is called '*Pa gur?*' and is the poem quoted above because of its reference to the temporary loss of Kelliwic: it relates an encounter between King Arthur and a castle gatekeeper, a classic 'Who goes there? Friend or foe?' routine that must have happened as an everyday event at the gates of many a fortress. The porter is a stock character, awkward, suspicious, uncooperative: even the arrival of the great king leaves him unimpressed. We can imagine this exchange happening even at the gates of Killibury itself. Arthur speaks first.

> 'What man is the gatekeeper?'
> 'Glewlwyd Great Grasp. What man asks it?'
> 'Arthur – and Cai the fair.'
> 'What band goes with you?'
> 'The best men in the world.'
> 'You will not come into my house
>   unless you vouch for them.'
> 'I shall vouch for them,
>   and you will see them . . .'

Given its relatively low altitude, Killibury commands surprisingly distant views. To the north and north-west the whole area on the east bank of the estuary can be seen, almost to the coast. To the south-west, the view extends across the estuary to the St Breock Downs. To the east, the whole of the western flank of Bodmin Moor can be seen. The whole of the southern third of the kingdom of Tricurium can be taken in, the hundred of Trigg,[49] which was probably the levy-area for one of the kingdom's three war-bands, as well as parts of the neighbouring territories to the south and south-west.[50] The value of such a view for administration, supervision and political and military control would have been great. At the same time, the site was at a moderate altitude, easily accessible on foot, cart or horseback up gentle gradients, close to a superb natural harbour, surrounded by fertile, easily cultivable farmland, and well watered with as many as sixteen springs within 2 km – an ideal peacetime location for the headquarters of a dark age king (see Figure 6.7). Small wonder that Kelliwic was Arthur's favourite residence. Killibury emerges as a very credible candidate for the base and principal residence of the dark age king of Trigg. The fortress overlooked the Camel estuary, not far from the southern corner of the kingdom whose frontier may have been marked by the River Camel. Is it possible that the place was actually called Camelot?

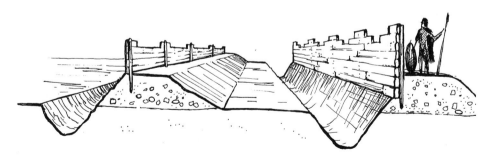

Figure 6.7 Killibury's defences (reconstructed). Although the banks and ditches look unimpressive now, they may have been more formidable during the dark age reoccupation. In this reconstruction I have put the outer (left) and inner defences close together; in reality they are 25 metres apart.

The Hammerer

The options for a historical Arthur have been progressively narrowed down. An effective commander-in-chief for the British resistance against the Saxons between 490 and 540 would have been likely to emerge from a British kingdom adjacent to and threatened by the Saxon settlers. That means Arthur must have been a king or sub-king in the Celtic fringe, a zone extending northwards from Dumnonia to Gododdin. The earliest documents we have imply that Arthur was most active in the south – South Wales, Cornwall and possibly Brittany – in common with other Welsh and Cornish kings and many of the missionaries of the period: there is a common pattern. Both tenth- to twelfth-century Welsh sources and Geoffrey of Monmouth insist that in spite of Arthur's wide outreach, with military forays far to the north, east and south, his power base was in Dumnonia.

Within Dumnonia there is a high density of Arthurian associations in the area that was the dark age petty kingdom of Trigg or Tricurium. Within Tricurium, there are two key locations with major claims to be Arthur's place of conception (whether biological or political) and Arthur's home – Tintagel and Killibury. Archaeology, geography and ethnography support the idea of Killibury as a congenial peacetime residence and trading and administrative base and Tintagel as a dynastic stronghold with a strong ceremonial, cultic element. The name 'Tintagel' may derive from 'Din Dagell', the Choker Fortress, from the narrowness of the neck that connected the Island to the mainland. Tintagel Island may have functioned in different ways at different seasons: as a secure collecting-place for slaves and other commodities ready for export, as a rallying-point for local warriors and as a place where kings were proclaimed and other promotions announced – a place of investiture, itself invested with a special mythic aura that came of arcane and anachronistic ceremonial.

Is it too fanciful to see Killibury – perhaps Killibury together with its satellite farms, hamlets and the ports along the estuary – as Camelot and Tintagel as the Grail Castle? The seeds of these ideas exist. Yet Camelot may be more elusive.

The name has often been thought to derive from another local name, such as the name of a river, and sites close to the River Camel in Somerset or the River Camel in Cornwall suggest themselves, reinforcing an identification of South Cadbury, Killibury or even Camelford as Camelot. Camel was probably quite a common name for British streams and rivers: it means 'winding'. Yet the name Camelot may, if ancient, have originated in some other way. It has been suggested that it began as Caer Malleator, 'caer' being the Welsh or British word for castle or stronghold, 'malleator' being Latin for hammerer.[51] Since both Latin and Brittonic languages were in use simultaneously by British aristocrats in the Arthurian period, a hybrid or macaronic name is possible. Camelot may therefore mean 'The Stronghold of the Hammerer', in other words 'Arthur's Stronghold'. This is not topographically specific, not geographically specific in any way.

Although late, romance-derived evidence is not the strongest evidence to call upon, there is an intriguing feature of the *Perlesvaus* romance which may point a way forward. In the *Perlesvaus* there are two castles called Camelot.

> The former Camelot stood at the head of the most savage Isle of Gales [Wales] near the sea, inclined towards the west. The only things there were the fortress

itself and the Forest and the water all around. The other Camelot sat at the entrance to the kingdom of Logres, and this was a populated area, and was the chief seat of the king's domains due to the fact that he held dominion over all the lands of that part of the country adjoining his own holdings.[52]

Dumnonia was a poor kingdom: Rome had shown conspicuously little interest in it for that reason. No doubt a king, his family and his immediate household, advisers and administrators could levy sufficient for their needs locally in the way of food, wood and other supplies, but a war-band could probably not have been sustained in this way for long. Leading a life of strenuous physical activity, often in bad weather and presumably often sleeping rough, warriors would have needed enormous quantities of food. Keeping them on the move was probably the only way to guarantee a continuous supply of food, drink and firewood. Mobility was possible because the war-band was mounted. The big, mean-tempered Destrier was not bred until the late middle ages, but the native British breeds available in the sixth century were strong, just over 13 hands high and perfectly capable of bearing a 13-stone warrior over long distances, probably averaging 60 km a day. Stirrups had not been invented, but the saddle had; the Romans introduced a strong wooden-framed, leather-covered saddle with four horns, one set at each corner to hold the rider firmly in place, rather like the leaping head on a modern lady's side-saddle. Arthur's war-band would almost certainly have used this type of saddle.[53]

The practice of itineration is one that was employed not only in the dark ages but right through the middle ages. Elizabeth I was notorious for her progresses; if she liked the hospitality and stayed for a few weeks she could – and sometimes did – ruin even a well-heeled subject. Significantly, one of the thirteen special properties in Merlin's charge was *Mwys Gwyddno*, which made the meat for one suffice for a hundred,[54] a great asset to a dark age war-band.

The motive for movement may have been fourfold. It spread the burden of maintaining the royal court and its warriors round the kingdom; it ensured the political and military control of all parts of the kingdom and a more uniform administration of justice; and in a society without newspapers, radio or television it ensured that subjects actually saw their king from time to time. Taliesin writes of Urien Rheged, 'I shout what I see as the blatant truth. I saw the one above all men, and he saw me, the beloved of his people.'[55]

The fourth motive was something subtler and mythic in nature. Arthur's knights are described in Welsh tales such as *Culhwch and Olwen* in a way that is reminiscent of the *fianna*, bands of youthful Irish outlaws who used to roam the countryside outside normal society. Their main occupations were hunting and fighting. The similarity is close enough to suggest that Arthur and his war-band may have consciously modelled themselves on the *fianna*. This meshes with the idea that at least some of the Dumnonian elites were Irish immigrants, some by way of Wales. Arthur and his followers may have consciously or unconsciously identified themselves with outcast wild men of a still earlier age.[56] A mythic reference, the absorption of this Celtic archetype, would have strengthened the war-band's sense of purpose. This process of absorbing and acting out a national archetype has been proposed for other great charismatic leaders. Hugh Schonfield believed Jesus consciously and systematically fulfilled scriptural prophecies one by one in order to be seen as,

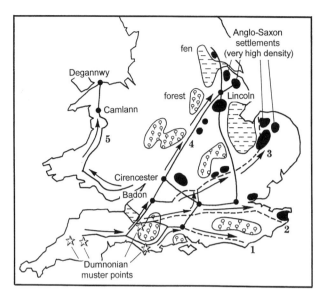

Figure 6.8 Arthur on the war-path. Roman (black line) and pre-Roman (dashed line) roads that Arthur may have used to reach his enemies. 1 = South Downs Way; 2 = Harrow Way and Pilgrims Way; 3 = Icknfield Way; 4 = Fosse Way; 5 = Sarn Helen.

actually in order to become, the Messiah.[57] Jung believed that Hitler, this time probably unconsciously, tapped and drew strength from repressed archetypes buried in the collective unconscious of the German nation by turning himself into a shamanic medium for a powerful archetype – Wotan. This enabled him not merely to pose, but actually to function as the personification of Germany.[58] It would have suited Arthur and his men to be seen as demi-gods, as irresistible forces of nature, both to frighten the enemy and to ensure the compliance and loyalty of their own communities.

So, during peacetime, Arthur probably moved around within Tricurium, possibly travelling longer circuits beyond the borders of Tricurium but within Dumnonia; during the Badon and other campaigns he moved across a huge area, grazing his war-bands like a nomadic herdsman. The idea of a movable Camelot fits this itineration model very well. It is not unlike the practice of the Christian missionaries who were Arthur's contemporaries; they too were constantly on the move and took with them small portable altars, so that anywhere they stopped to preach became a church.[59]

The mobility of Camelot explains at a stroke its elusiveness. Because it was no one place, it is not surprising that many have come to think that it was nowhere at all, a fantasy or just a name made up by Chrétien as a convenient tag for Arthur's court. Yet the name may well have been in use in the dark ages. John Morris noted the similarity between the words *Camelot* and *Camulodunum*, going so far as equating the two. Before it was a Roman garrison town, Camulodunum was the capital of the great Belgic Eastern Kingdom, and its name meant 'The Stronghold of Camulos'. Camulos was an iron age British war god, and the Trinovantes significantly dedicated their capital to the war god. Perhaps *Camelot* had a similar origin, not as a dark age name but as an iron age name for the king's military headquarters, and as mobile as a royal standard. Perhaps a name like *Camelot* – perhaps simply *Camulos* – was in use long before Arthur's time in Britain, meant little more than 'The War Base', and we only know about it because of a chance survival in one of the sources Chrétien used.

CHAPTER SEVEN

THE DEATH OF ARTHUR

A grave for March, a grave for Gwythyr,
A grave for Gwrgan of the Red Sword;
The wonder of the world, a grave for Arthur.

(*Songs of the Graves*)

Now we reach what has become the most elusive and controversial part of the Arthurian story. A veil of mystery and romantic strangeness has spread itself over the circumstances of Arthur's death.

To many commentators the story of Arthur's last battle, fought against his treacherous, black-hearted nephew Modred, his fatal wounding in single combat, his surrender of the sword Excalibur to the Lady of the Lake, and his final journey across water to Avalon and death seems the stuff of pure myth. The heavy tone of tragedy and the strong supernatural element imply that none of it is literally true. Nevertheless, some truth may lie behind it. If Arthur was a real historical figure, a war-leader, king and overking, then at some stage he must have reached the end of his career; if he lived, he must also have died, and the circumstances of his death must have been noted at the time. Only the obscure die in obscurity.

Investigating the truth behind Arthur's last weeks is made particularly difficult by the importation of religious and political themes which may or may not have been part of the mid-sixth-century history of Arthur's downfall. By the early middle ages he was already being portrayed as not just a model for manhood, but as the most perfect man since Adam. Today in Tintagel church a statue of Christ the King is on view. It was made by Faust Lang of Oberammergau and presented to the church in 1948; disconcertingly, in appearance and concept it is hard to distinguish this image of Christ from the popular image of King Arthur. Here two biographies and two myths have become dangerously interwoven!

The final phase of Arthur's story is best approached stepwise, by way of a series of separate enquiries, first concerning the last battle, then the mysterious events that are alleged to have followed it.

The last battle

Camlann was a battle that resonated through British folk memory. It was the battle that meant the end of the supremacy of Celtic Britain and the beginning of the English supremacy. Its very name became a mythic symbol of irreversible, calamitous defeat, the two sad syllables as eloquent and evocative as the final cadence of a piper's lament. In 1282, when the last native Prince of Wales was killed, it seemed natural for the poet Gruffudd ab yr Ynad Coch to see the prince's death in terms of Arthur's downfall: he described 'many a wretched cry – as at Camlann'. The two Arthurian poems that were preserved from the eighth century onwards were both songs of Arthur's defeats, one at Llongborth, the other at Camlann. It is odd that none of the victory songs that must have been composed by Arthur's bard have been preserved. Perhaps it is chance, perhaps it has more to do with an early medieval taste for the maudlin. There is an instruction in the Welsh Laws: 'When the queen wishes a song in her apartment, the bard shall sing three songs of Camlann, not loudly, that the hall be not disturbed.'[1]

We begin on solid ground. There is unimpeachable evidence of the name and date of the last battle king Arthur fought, in the *Easter Annals* for Year 93, which converts to our calendar as AD 537 or 539. Neither Gildas nor Nennius mentions the last battle specifically. Gildas simply regrets the passing of an orderly regime without dwelling on the circumstances. Nennius seems to have had access to an Arthurian battle-victory poem, which inevitably omitted all the defeats, Camlann included. The *Easter Annals* nevertheless give us a few well-defined details.

> *Gueith camlann in que arthur and medraut corruerunt, et mortalitas in britannia et in hibernia fuit.*
> The strife of Camlann in which Arthur and Medraut perished; and there was plague in Britain and in Ireland.

The passage is interesting for its use of *gueith*, a British word, instead of *bellum*, which is Latin, like the rest of the text. As we saw earlier, there are other battles in the date list that are described as *gueiths*, and this in no way impairs or detracts from the authenticity of the entry. Quite the reverse, in fact, because it implies that the memory of the battle was kept alive within the British community and implies an oral tradition reaching back to the British warriors who actually took part in the memorable battle. The entry is frustratingly brief and lacking in circumstantial detail that would help us to generate a context or background for the battle. Nevertheless, from this beginning we may explore possible locations for it. If the location can be fixed with a degree of confidence, a strategic motive may emerge; a location in the Thames valley, for instance, would imply a reckless and desperate onslaught by Arthur on the Saxon heartland, while a location in the Trossachs would imply that the Picts were threatening Clyde or Gododdin and that Arthur was trying to fulfil his role as *dux bellorum* in defending the British alliance.

The name of the battle is an obvious starting-point. Camlann may, as some have suggested, contain a reference to the River Camel. Given that a River Camel flowed through Arthur's Cornish kingdom and he may have died defending himself from a direct attack on his home territory, a location on the Cornish Camel has to be seen as a distinct possibility. Geoffrey of Monmouth put Camlann in Cornwall and, as a suspected Welshman, he had no vested interest in inventing a Cornish death for Arthur. Geoffrey's use of the Cornish form 'Modred' instead of the Welsh 'Medraut' shows that he was probably drawing on a Cornish tradition.

The (modern) tradition in Cornwall is that the Battle of Camlann took place at Slaughter Bridge a short distance north of Camelford. The bridge itself has a modern tarmac surface and modern slate and cement parapets, but the substructure appears to be ancient. Two rectangular piers built of huge blocks support enormous granite slabs, giving a megalithic appearance. The bridge may date from the dark ages or earlier. A bridge here may have had a minor strategic importance, to obviate a detour round the head of the Camel valley 4 km to the north, the road running from Tich Barrow west to Tintagel. That the bridge was regarded as a significant strategic point is certainly implied by the earthworks to the northwest. A high earthen rampart defends a square enclosure on the valleyside spur to the north-west of the bridge, and may be the remains of a dark age or iron age fortified farm. A rampart runs from it down the hillside towards the bridge, implying a functional relationship between the small fortified settlement and the bridge, and the people living in the settlement may have had the responsibility for supervising and defending the bridge. If the bridge was the focus of the battle, the fortified settlement was possibly the rallying point for Arthur's men, on the Tintagel side of the river.

The River Camel winds southwards through a wild oakwood from a prostrate inscribed stone 200 metres north of the bridge. Naturally, there has been an assumption that the stone in some way commemorated Camlann or some important figure who died in it. The stone now lies horizontal down near the water, though it must originally have been planted vertical. The pointed end, close to the west bank, is rather irregular and was hidden, planted in the ground. The dressed, squared-off part with the lettering was left visible. It can be assumed that lateral erosion by the meandering stream has unseated what was once a river-bank standing stone, causing it to fall over backwards. It nevertheless cannot be assumed that it is even close to its dark age location. In Borlase's *Antiquities of Cornwall* of 1754 we read that Lady Falmouth built 'a rough kind of hill, about 100 yards off, into spiral walks, removed this stone from a place where it served as a bridge, and, building a low piece of masonry for its support, placed it at the foot of her improvements, where it still lies in one of the natural grottoes of the hill'.[2] The stone has thus had several moves.

The stone lies in a curious triangular embayment within a rock-cut river cliff, on a slate-shingle beach that is surprisingly difficult to reach.[3] The stone may even have been raised at the spot (though not this spot) where a dark age aristocrat fell in battle.

The all-important inscription, in dark age lettering, reads:

LATINHICIACIT
FILIUSMAR–

This was optimistically developed into:

LATINUS HIC IACIT
FILIUS MERLINI ARTURUS.[4]

An alternative reading might be:

LATINI HIC IACIT
FILIUS MAGLOCUNUS REX.

Since Maelgwn succeeded to the throne of Gwynedd in about 517, he could have fought at Camlann. Maelgwn's connection with the Camlann story will be explored later, but it is sufficient to say here that modern scholarship reads the stone as:

LATINI HIC IACIT
FILIUS MAGARI.[5]
[The monument] of Latinus: here he lies, the son of Magarus.[6]

So the stone supplies no connection whatsoever with Arthur. The water meadows opposite the stone are thought to be the battlefield site; Leland certainly believed this was the place, mentioning harness and bones dug up where 'Arture fowght his last feld'.

There are nevertheless strong arguments against Slaughter Bridge as the site of Camlann. First, the inscribed stone does not mention Arthur or any of his known associates, and therefore cannot be used as evidence for Camlann. Second, the name Slaughter Bridge is clearly English, must long post-date the battle, and is more likely to refer to the battle known to have taken place in this area in 823, when Cornish Britons clashed with the Saxon forces of King Edgar.[7] The archaeological finds from the battlefield are consistent with the later date. In the end, we are left with not much more than the name of the river. At the same time, the inscription on the stone is sixth-century and commemorates a dead sixth century aristocrat, so perhaps there were two battles on the same spot in the sixth and eighth centuries.

It is not much more than a stream's name – the River Cam – that takes Camlann to South Cadbury. Geoffrey Ashe favours this location as it puts Arthur's death conveniently close to Glastonbury for his burial, but few other scholars seem to support this.[8] As we have seen, South Cadbury was not necessarily Arthur's home, and there may be reason, as we shall see later, to doubt whether Arthur was buried at Glastonbury, so the proximity of South Cadbury to Glastonbury is no help to us.

Camelford was the favoured location for Camlann until the careful and scholarly reinterpretation of the inscribed stone decisively removed Arthur from it in the latter half of the nineteenth century. Then, in the 1860s and 1870s, there was a fashion for locating Camlann and the other Arthurian battles in the north of Britain.[9] Stuart Glennie argued for Camelon in the Forth valley, on the River Carron; he knew of a Scottish tradition that Arthur fought Modred there, and that Modred was king of the Picts.[10] O. G. S. Crawford identified a site on Hadrian's Wall as Camlann; the Roman fort at Birdoswald was called Cambolanda.[11] Some say the word Camlan is Middle Welsh and derives from the British word Camboglanna. Camboglanna means 'crooked bank' while Cambolanda means 'crooked or curved enclosure'. A battle of Camlann at this location implies a conflict between Clyde and Rheged, with Arthur leading war-bands from the south perhaps in an attempt to repair a crumbling British confederacy or to suppress an open rebellion from one of the northern kings. A major battle did take place at the western end of the Wall a generation later, in 573; this, the Battle of Arderydd, was an eruption of the border conflict between the kingdoms of Rheged and Clyde.

Another candidate for the site of Camlann is Porth Cadlan, near the tip of the Lleyn Peninsula in North Wales. Chris Barber and David Pykitt chose the site for four reasons.[12] First, they noted the similarity of the place-name Cadlan to Camlann. Second, of the two known sixth-century princes named Medraut, one died in 580 and was therefore probably too old to have fought at Camlann in the 530s, while the other was the son of Cawrdaf ap Caradog Freichfras, who became a patron of Aberech in the Lleyn Peninsula. The thrust of this is that Medraut's family was powerful both at Kelliwic and in the Lleyn, creating a connection between the area and Arthur. Fourth, nearby Bardsey Island is a possible location for Avalon; it had a religious community on it and was regarded as a holy island.

Phillips and Keatman support a different Welsh location, one with a stronger claim.[13] There is a mountain side called Camlann 8 km east of Dolgellau, boldly marked on modern Ordnance Survey maps. In 1872, it was argued that several place-names in the area suggested a connection: not only Camlann, but Bron Camlan, Maes Camlan, Brithdir Coch and Pont y Cleifion. If Cornwall was out of favour and the arguments for a northern site were tenuous, there seemed no reason why a Welsh candidate should not be sought instead.[14] The site seems to have no local lore attached to it, perhaps rather surprisingly, and there is no archaeology or historiography to support it either. It has also been pointed out that the name Pont y Cleifion, 'Bridge of the Wounded', refers to a skirmish at the bridge on the Clywedog in 1644 or 1645, not to any dark age battle.[15] The general location is nevertheless credible for a conflict among neighbouring dark age kingdoms; here we are within a few kilometres of the place where the frontiers of the kingdoms of Gwynedd, Powys and Dyfed ran together, with the disputed lands of Ceretigan immediately to the south. This is border country where open attacks, guerrilla raids and ambushes must often have taken place.

The site is also at a critical point topographically, on the route into southern Gwynedd from the south, i.e. from Dyfed and Brecon, and east, i.e. from Powys. The deeply eroded glacial troughs of the Dyfi valley and its tributaries, such as the valleys of the Dugoed and Cerist, make easy low-level routes through the rugged mountain country and are today still followed by A roads, but at Camlann the route into Gwynedd encounters a feature that is commonly found at the head of a glacial valley, a trough end. The A470, following this dark age route, enters an impressive natural amphitheatre 2 kilometres in diameter and surrounded on three sides by steep rock walls rising 500 metres. There is a way out – just one – by way of a high col, the pass of Ochr-y-bwlch. In the dark ages as now, this pass was the natural route into southern Gwynedd. It was also a natural place for the warriors of Gwynedd to await and ambush their enemies, for whom it was a death-trap.

The second 'Camlann', 6 km to the south-east, is also on the Dyfi valley route north, connecting Dyfed and Gwynedd. This section of the Dyfi valley was probably the boundary between southern Gwynedd to the west and central Powys to the east. The glacial trough makes a natural corridor of north–south movement, which is now followed by the A489, and it would have been an obvious choice for any army advancing northwards from Dyfed or Brecon on the power centres of Gwynedd. This second Camlann, the Mallwyd site, is a less obvious site for an ambush than the death-trap landscape of the high pass. It is nevertheless probably significant that though Camlann as a place-name is unknown outside north-west Wales it occurs at least twice there.[16]

It is likely that medieval accounts of Arthur's campaign in Brittany are in fact misplaced, and should read as a North Welsh campaign. Stuart Piggott pointed out that the Latin name for Gwynedd, *Armonica*, would have been very easy for scribes to miscopy as *Armorica*, Brittany. If Arthur's 'Gaul' campaign was in reality against Gwynedd, Geoffrey's account of it may give clues as to the nature and purpose of Arthur's foray into Gwynedd.

Gaul was under the rule of Frollo in the name of Emperor Leo, Geoffrey tells us. Arthur attacked and ravaged Gaul, leading to Frollo's offer to fight Arthur in single combat. Frollo was killed. Then Arthur divided his forces in two, one army to go under the command of Hoel to attack Guitard, king of the Poitevins, the other under Arthur's personal command to subdue the remaining provinces. Hoel soon forced Guitard's surrender, then ravaged Gascony, forcing the submission of its leaders too. The campaign took nine years. While there is little to suggest that Arthur's activities ranged so far afield, there is plenty of evidence that his normal sphere of action covered not just Dumnonia but Wales too, especially South Wales. Mapping the cults of dark age saints, such as Dyfrig, Cadog, Illtud and Carannog, shows that there were strong social, cultural and political links across the Severn Sea. There is also a clue in *Culhwch and Olwen* in the geographical scope of the climactic boar hunt; the legendary boar Twrch Trwyth was hunted across South Wales and Cornwall before being chased off the cliffs at Land's End.

If Geoffrey's account of a Gaulish campaign is transposed more credibly to Wales, we could see Arthur's campaign as an attempt to bring to heel several Welsh kings who were resisting Arthur's overkingship, an attempt that was successful until Arthur crossed the southern border of Gwynedd and met Maelgwn's men – perhaps Maelgwn himself – in combat. If nine years (528–37) seems too long a time to spend bringing disaffected former allies into line, it must be remembered that the reason for having a *dux bellorum* in the first place was to co-ordinate resistance to the Saxon colonization along the entire eastern front. Arthur knew disunity meant defeat. Disunity and defeat in Wales would have meant a Saxon Wales and a Britain split into two widely separated and vulnerable Celtic provinces that could no longer support one another. The maintenance of a British Wales was vital to Arthur's strategy. Even so, the 'nine years' need not be taken literally: it is the magic three-times-three, a simple formula for 'a very long time'.

Remarkably, there is a third candidate for Camlann in the same area of west Wales, one which I believe has an even stronger claim than the other two (see Figure 7.1).[17] It is 6 km north of Dolgellau, in the Mawddach valley and lies on a continuation of the same dark age road route that presses northwards into Gwynedd. This route, known as Sarn Helen ('paved causeway'), was an important Roman road running from south to north through west Wales to the Conwy estuary in the north.

Contrary to popular belief, the major Roman highways remained in use in the post-Roman period, to maintain long-distance diplomatic and possibly commercial

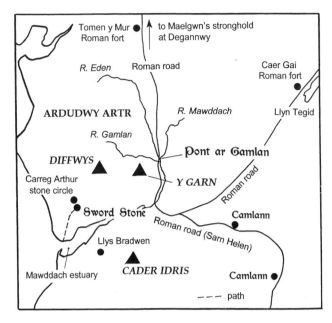

Figure 7.1 Three Camlanns near Dolgellau in Gwynedd

communication among the various Celtic communities: we know that British kings and missionaries covered long distances, and some of these journeys were probably undertaken on Roman, now post-Roman, roads. They were also used to great effect by the cavalry; it was possible to cover long distances into enemy territory, strike without warning and escape without much risk of infantry pursuit. The legacy of the Roman road system was therefore a great bonus for Arthur and his mounted war-bands, and doubtless strongly influenced his military strategy. Many of the roads seem to have fallen out of use fairly quickly once the British were conquered; it was the Anglo-Saxons who let them slide into neglect, perhaps in part because they had less use for them, perhaps they disliked them because they associated them with British cavalry attacks. There are English burials cut into the metalling of Watling Street in Warwickshire, showing that some stretches had become overgrown and unrecognizable as roadway. The Roman roads were known among the English as *herepaeths* or 'army roads', showing that they associated them with movements of war-bands, and the earliest Anglo-Saxon settlements were set discreetly back some distance from them in the hope that they would not be noticed by British war-bands as they galloped past.

Sarn Helen was an important post-Roman line of communication, joining the kingdoms of Glevissig, Dyfed and Brecon in the south with Gwynedd by way of Ceretigan,[18] and leading virtually to the gates of Castell Degannwy, the stronghold of Maelgwn, the powerful and ruthless king of Gwynedd. If Cardigan was claimed by both Dyfed and Gwynedd, fighting is likely to have broken out periodically along Sarn Helen between Llanio (Lampeter) and the site of the Roman fort at Tomen y

Mur (near Trawsfynydd). Tomen y Mur was still to be a strategic point much later, when it became the place where English armies encamped when they came to subdue North Wales.[19] In other words, the three Camlanns in west Wales are all credible locations for battles between the opposing war-bands of the Demetiae and Ordovices, the armies of Dyfed and Gwynedd, with anyone else joining in who thought they had something to gain by doing so. Borders were natural locations for battles. Taliesin writes, in *The Battle of Wensleydale*, 'I saw cross-border commotion, bringing death in its wake.'

I searched without success for a local tradition about the last battle but it seemed that the trail had gone cold. Nineteenth-century Welsh antiquaries who noticed the Camlann place-names before me commented that there was no tradition to support a west Welsh Camlann, and concluded that this must mean Arthur's last battle was after all not fought there.

There are nevertheless some traditions that seem to point to this area. Llywarch Hen, grandfather of Hywel Dda,[20] lived for a time at Caer Gai at the western end of Lake Bala: he was said to be a member of Arthur's court.[21] Camden said Caer Gai was once a castle built by Caius (Caw) 'while the Britons ascribe it to Cai, Arthur's foster-brother'.[22] Bradwen, founder of the fifteenth noble tribe of North Wales lived at Llys Bradwen, a hidden, now deserted site perched above the Mawddach estuary. Bradwen was descended from Sandde Bryd Angel, who survived Camlann thirteen generations before him.[23] In the *Black Book of Carmarthen* there is a song or *englyn* that runs, 'The grave of Osfran's son is at Camlan;/ After many a slaughter/ The grave of Bedwyr is on Tryfan Hill.' Tryfan is in Snowdonia, in Gwynedd, and this may imply that the writer of the *englyn* thought Camlann was not far away. Osfran's son has not been identified, but a twelfth-century poet mentions St Cadfan and his church at Tywyn, in the extreme south of Gwynedd and 25 km south-west of the triad of Camlann sites; the poet specifically mentions Osfran in connection with this area.[24]

The site north of Dolgellau is Ganllwyd, now a roadside village on the A470, which at this point and south to Dolgellau precisely follows the route of Sarn Helen. To the north of Ganllwyd the dark age and modern routes diverge, the A470 continuing along the Eden valley floor to Trawsfynnyd and Sarn Helen crossing the Eden immediately north of its confluence with the Mawddach, and slanting diagonally up the hillside from 75 metres to 320 metres before dropping to around 200 metres as it approaches the site of the Roman fort. A high arched stone bridge marks the site of the river crossing now, but whether there was a stone or wooden bridge there in the Arthurian period is not known. If there was a bridge, it would have been a bottle-neck for an army, a place where they would have to slow down; if there was no bridge, it would have been an even more perilous bottle-neck, as warriors tried to leap from boulder to boulder or pick their way uncertainly among the pools with their horses. Either way, the crossing was a good place for an ambush (see Plate 7.1). The bridge is known today as Pont ar Eden, but Pennant referred to it by an older name, Pont ar Gamlan.[25] Fords were classic locations for dark age battles. In *The Battle of Wensleydale* Taliesin writes, 'On the ford's brink I saw bloodstained warriors, their weapons abandoned . . . I saw men destroyed and dejected, and blood staining their clothes.' Similarly, in *Rheged arise*, 'There was a battle at the ford of Alclud.'

Plate 7.1 The scene of a dark age ambush? The confluence of the River Eden (right) and the River Mawddach (left) is the likely fording-place, close to Pont ar Gamlan

The Eden valley is particularly narrow and constricted just here, with a very narrow floor – almost a gorge. It would have been easy to predict the enemy army's route: there was little alternative but to follow the old Roman road. If forest clad the valley sides then as it does today, a war-band could be concealed until the last moment, and the ambush sprung.

The torrent running down the steep valley side from the west about 500 metres south of the river crossing is called the River Gamlan or Camlan: its peat-stained waters flow from Cwm Camlan, down the Black Falls, Rhaeadr Ddu, into Ganllwyd. In the nineteenth century a rock outcrop near the waterfall was found to carry a weathered inscription. In 1919 Eggarton Phillimore recognized the inscription as an extract from a poem by Thomas Gray;

> O thou! The Spirit 'mid these scenes abiding,
> Whate'er the name by which thy power be known.[26]

Picturesque but disappointing: it does nothing to elucidate the events of the dark ages.

This region was part of southern Gwynedd at the time of the battle, under the overall suzerainty of King Maelgwn. The area west of Ganllwyd, between the Eden–Mawddach valleys and the sea, was in the early middle ages called Ardudwy Dunoding, meaning the coastal kingdom of Dunawd, son of Cunedda. The name refers back to the pre-Arthurian king of the area and it seems the identity of the kingdom was preserved in the early medieval commote. The area east of the Eden was a separate tribal territory, the commote of Penllys. The area to the south of the lower Mawddach valley, i.e. the block south of Dolgellau which contains Cader Idris, was the cantref of Meirionydd, again a tribal territory, this time named after Cunedda's grandson Meirion, who may or may not have been its king. Another commote further to the east was Edeirnion, named after a son of Cunedda called Edern.[27] These territories were ruled by sub-kings, and any or all of them could have commissioned warriors to trap Arthur's men as they advanced north along Sarn Helen. Interestingly, the commote of Ardudwy Dunoding also became known as Ardudwy Artr, an alternative name which is very suggestive. This later became divided into two bailiwicks, Uwch Artr and Is Artr.[28]

According to later Welsh tradition, the Battle of Camlann was a massacre. The name of the battle entered the vocabulary of the medieval Welsh bards: a *cadgamlan* meant an utter rout. Very few of Arthur's men survived. One of the survivors, Tegid, fled to Lake Bala, which is in consequence also known as Llyn Tegid: this is 17 km north-east of Ganllwyd.

The topography and dark age ethnography of west Wales, together with the layout of the road system and the evidence of Gildas, point towards a possible Arthurian scenario. Gildas describes Badon as being not the last but the most decisive battle against the Saxons, and the period that followed – 'the peace' – as being spoilt by civil wars among the British. Presumably he meant intermittent disputes, skirmishes and wars between one British kingdom and another. These conflicts may have arisen for a variety of reasons: territorial claims, disputes over the control of vital resources and strategic points such as harbours, rival dynastic claims, rival claims for the high kingship. Dark has already proposed that Cardigan was disputed territory. There is also the possibility that the ruthless Maelgwn, who had already killed his uncle in order to become king of Gwynedd, was envious of Arthur's high kingship and determined to get it for himself. Whether Arthur and his men rode into Gwynedd to quell an overt rebellion and met open and anticipated hostility, or were lured there by some guile of Maelgwn's and fell unsuspecting into a trap at Ganllwyd cannot be known on the existing evidence. Two facts nevertheless are known. Maelgwn *did* gain the high kingship shortly after the battle of Camlann and Arthur's disappearance – in 546 according to one version[29] – and gained it by deception. There is also the tradition that Arthur was the victim of treachery at Camlann: perhaps the treachery was Maelgwn's, not Modred's. Perhaps Arthur was the uncle Gildas mentioned.

This leads us into a consideration of the central themes of Arthur's death, his betrayal and in effect assassination by a trusted relative. Five Welsh Triads refer to Camlann.[30] Although they are not completely consistent in the information they give,[31] together they show the strength of the tradition of the last battle as the tragic consequence of plotting, dissension at court and betrayal on the battlefield.[32] Modred came to personify that betrayal. In the fully developed medieval versions of the legend, Modred is Arthur's nephew. Geoffrey seems to have been the earliest to ascribe a specific blood relationship between the two men, making Modred the son of Arthur's sister Anna. Later writers compounded Modred's guilt by making him seduce Guinevere, which seems to be a darker poetic recapitulation of her earlier affair with Lancelot. Modred is visibly developed into a seed of destruction, like

Shakespeare's Iago: he becomes the personal destiny, the moira of Arthur. Arthur falls at Modred's hands: the ultimate tragedy of the trusting king. He goes from striding the world stage, defeating whole nations, down through civil discord with other British kings, to discord within his own family and defeat by the treachery of his own wife and nephew.

Yet there is nothing in the earliest references to Modred to suggest that he was behind Arthur's death, nor that they were on opposing sides. The fact that they both fell at Camlann does not preclude their being on the same side. Certainly Modred was an important man, or he would not have been mentioned in the *Welsh Annals* as falling with Arthur.

At least two Modreds are known from the sixth century. One was Medrawd ap Llew ap Cynvarch, the other Medrawd ap Caurdaf. The first seems unlikely to be the one we are interested in. He lived in the late sixth century and could not have died at Camlann: he also came from the north. The second was the heir to some southern dynasty though little else is known about him. A third lived at the end of the sixth and beginning of the seventh centuries: he was Moriutred, grandson of Morcant, king of Clyde from about 525.[33]

Although Geoffrey makes Modred Arthur's nephew, it is not known whether he invented this detail or derived it from some Cornish oral tradition, or copied it from Walter's ancient book. The early Welsh tradition treats Medraut differently, making him and Arthur feuding near-equals.[34] The early bardic references to Medraut favour him and confirm the suspicion that in reality Modred/Medraut and Arthur were on the same side at Camlann.[35] The fact that both fell proves nothing to the contrary: a great many of Arthur's allies and companions fell at Camlann.

Given the north-west Welsh location, it is more likely that Arthur and his allies were ambushed by Ordovician warriors acting on Maelgwn's orders. In other words, in historical terms, Maelgwn was Modred. I discovered after developing my thesis to this point that Sir John Rhys independently came to the same conclusion over a hundred years ago;[36] he concluded that Maelgwn was Arthur's nephew, and that his role in betraying Arthur and usurping his throne led to Gildas calling him 'dragon of the island' (i.e. Pendragon). It also explains why Maelgwn and his successors were referred to not as *gwledigs* but as kings. Rhys *may* be going too far in making Maelgwn Arthur's nephew: we know too little of Arthur's family connections to say that. Maelgwn nevertheless survived Camlann in terms of dates: he died some ten or twenty years later and is known to have become high king, perhaps as Arthur's immediate successor. From this point of view, he could easily have been the victor at Camlann. A tradition of treachery is now firmly attached to Modred's name, thanks to the work of medieval writers, but it is possible that it was Maelgwn who was the arch-traitor, ambushing Arthur's host at the Pont ar Gamlan on the River Eden.

The distribution of Arthurian place-names is consistent with a betrayal by Gwynedd: there are significantly fewer places with Arthur's name attached to them in Gwynedd than elsewhere in the Celtic fringe,[37] which suggests either an antipathy to Arthur or an expunging of his memory by a ruthless supplanter. If Maelgwn was guilty of the killing, and of bringing the Arthurian peace to an end, Gildas's extraordinary hatred and condemnation of Maelgwn's many-sided wickedness would be understandable. Arthur was behind the golden years of (relative) stability and justice between Badon and Camlann, and those years came to an end with Arthur's final defeat. Gildas specifically mentions that Maelgwn removed and killed many tyrants (i.e. kings, not necessarily tyrants in the modern sense), that Maelgwn was 'last in my list but first in evil', and that Maelgwn 'cruelly despatched the king your uncle'. Perhaps the king referred to was not the king of Gwynedd, as one might at first suppose, but the high king, Arthur. Here, in any event, is the uncle-slaying regicide motif, the motif that would later be attributed (by Geoffrey – and possibly mistakenly) to Modred.

Arthur's disappearance

What happened to Arthur after the Battle of Camlann is surrounded by uncertainty. The *Welsh Annals* show that both Arthur and Modred fell in the battle, which strongly implies that they both died. There are nevertheless various traditions, of unknown age and origin, that Arthur was carried from the battlefield mortally wounded and either died elsewhere or simply disappeared. One explanation is that locally, in Wales, the truth of the matter was known – that Arthur had died on or near the battlefield – and this tradition was preserved and passed on through Welsh families, like the details about the few who survived the battle. Meanwhile, people in Cornwall and perhaps Brittany too had less detailed information about what had happened to the king; all they knew was that he had not returned. In the days and weeks following Camlann all kinds of misinformation and rumour may have circulated.

Geoffrey of Monmouth was aware of the uncertainties. In his version of Arthur's disappearance he describes Arthur as 'mortally wounded' (*letaliter vulneratus*) on the battlefield, yet moved to Avalon 'to have his wounds healed' (*ad sananda vulnera sua in insulam Avallonis evectus*). J.E. Lloyd argues that Geoffrey was deliberately ambiguous about Arthur's death because he had on his desk two different versions of the king's fate, one originating in Wales and giving Arthur as killed in battle, the other from Cornish or Breton sources and giving Arthur as surviving the battle and being transported elsewhere to recover or die.[38] This is persuasive and goes a long way towards explaining the post-Camlann confusion. Even Padel, who does not believe in the historicity of Arthur, acknowledges that the two different traditions are preserved in Geoffrey and that they must both pre-date Geoffrey.[39] This would certainly be in line with the view that is now emerging, of Geoffrey of Monmouth as a rather better historian than has generally been believed.

If Arthur died in the battle or was so seriously wounded that he died close to the battlefield, where was he buried? Great play was later made of the absence of 'a grave for Arthur'. The sixth- or seventh-century poem *Songs of the Graves* gives the locations of the graves of many dark age heroes, for instance:

The grave of Owain ap Urien in a secluded part of the world,
under the grass at Llan Morvad;
In Aberech, that of Rhydderch Hael. (Stanza 13)
The wonder of the world, a grave for Arthur. (Stanza 44)

The missing grave became a major part of the mystique surrounding the vanished king. If Arthur was the great overking, chief of the kings of Britain and *dux bellorum*, we might expect to see an impressive monument of some kind raised on his grave, or at any rate for its location to have been remembered. But there is nothing. On the other hand, where is the grave of Aelle, first Saxon bretwalda? Where is Vortigern's mausoleum?

There is a tradition that Arthur was buried secretly. The *Life of St Illtud* (Section 22) credits Illtud with being the priest who conducted Arthur's secret funeral. If it was done in secret, probably only those who were actually present – perhaps only ten people altogether – ever knew where the king was buried, and as likely as not those ten took the secret with them to their own separate graves. One question naturally arises. Why should those close to Arthur have wished to bury him in secret? Obviously the king's death was disastrous to the British cause. If he had succeeded only recently in re-cementing the loyalty of the kings of southern and central Wales to a common cause, the news of his death could have precipitated immediate fragmentation, laying Wales open to attack from the east; alternatively, and equally dangerously, it could have exposed Powys and the southern kingdoms to attack from Gwynedd first, rendering them powerless to resist Saxon incursion from the east. The continuing expansionism of Gwynedd a century or two later seems to show that this was an ever-present danger. If news of his death reached the Saxons, who had been held at bay by his power for twenty years, they would have pushed westwards with confidence and ease. If news of his death spread widely among the Britons they would have become demoralized and given in under the renewed Saxon onslaught. In every way and for every reason it was important to conceal the death of Arthur, and those close to him may have hoped to hide the catastrophic truth long enough for a successor to be found and for him to establish his position as overking before too many people realized what had happened.

It was probably in this way that doubt arose about the king's fate. What was intended as a short-term delay in releasing the news – perhaps a month or two at most is all that was envisaged by the king's lieutenants – became a key part of the Arthurian legend.

It may be that it was an alternative fate that was concealed, but for the same reason. If Arthur was not killed at Camlann but so badly wounded that he was clearly going to be unfit to fight or even ride for a long time, he would have been forced to retire. It was relatively common for dark age kings to retire when they were physically incapable of fighting through age or infirmity; they withdrew from public life completely by entering monasteries. Several examples are known from the period. In around 580 Tewdrig or Theodoric king of Glevissig (Glamorgan) abdicated in favour of his son Meurig and retired to a religious house at Tintern. He made the mistake of coming out of retirement in about 584, when his son met the Saxons in battle nearby; Tewdrig was mortally wounded in the battle. Pabo Pillar of Britain, king of the Pennines, similarly abdicated in favour of his sons and went to live in seclusion in a remote monastery in Gwynedd, far from his own kingdom; he later died and was buried there, in the church at Llanbabo in Anglesey.[40] A link between the Pennine kingdom and Gwynedd is suggested by another example. In the church at Llanaelhaearn on the Lleyn is a fifth- or sixth-century memorial stone inscribed with the words:

ALIORTVS ELMETIACO HIC IACET
Aliortus, a man from Elmet, lies here.[41]

There are hints in the medieval genealogies that a much earlier Dumnonian king, Coel Godhebog, also retired a long way from home: he died and was buried in York in 300.[42]

Did Arthur, now aged 62 and badly wounded,[43] decide to abdicate and retire immediately after Camlann? *The Legend of St Goeznovius*, a Breton saint, exists in a fourteenth-century copy, but the original story may well have been told in the seventh century. *The Legend* includes some information which is corroborated by other sources, such as the migration of British saints to Brittany in the fifth and sixth centuries and the introduction of Saxon auxiliaries by Vortigern. It also perhaps overstates Arthur's achievement, in boasting that the Saxons were largely cleared from Britain by 'the great Arthur, king of the Britons'. In a telling phrase, *The Legend* tells how Arthur's career ended when he 'was summoned from human activity'. This is equivocal, in that it does not quite say that Arthur died, although most readers would infer that meaning; the expression might equally be taken to mean that Arthur withdrew from secular affairs to lead a purely religious life.[44]

If Arthur's reign ended at Camlann but he lived on in retirement, it could explain the discrepancy between the date of 537 (or 539) given in the *Welsh Annals* for Arthur's fall at Camlann and the date of 542 given by Geoffrey of Monmouth. Did Geoffrey perhaps have access to a tradition of Arthur living on for another five years after the battle, and was Geoffrey's 542 not the date of the battle but of the death?

Avalon

If Arthur retreated, wounded, from the final battle he must have been taken to a place of safety, and that place of safety must have been well outside Gwynedd, beyond Maelgwn's dangerously long reach. The later traditions hold that he was taken to Avalon, a place with otherworldly, holy associations, a place that no-one has successfully located on a map. Geoffrey of Monmouth mentions Avalon twice, first as the place where Arthur's sword was forged, second as the refuge to which Arthur was taken to have his battle-wounds tended. In the *Life of Merlin*, Geoffrey has the bard Taliesin relate how he accompanied Arthur to Avalon in a boat piloted by Barinthus, a semi-legendary figure who is sometimes portrayed as a Celtic Charon, ferrying the dead to the otherworld. In Avalon, Taliesin relates, Arthur was received by Morgan, the chief of nine sister-enchantresses who lived there. Morgan looked at Arthur's wounds and offered to heal him if he promised to stay in Avalon for a very long time.

Avalon becomes a mystical island across the sea, a place somehow apart from normal geography, and we may suspect that Celtic beliefs about the afterlife have been woven into the story. This is confirmed from other sources. The first-century Roman writer Pomponius Mela described nine priestesses living on the Isle of Sein off the Brittany coast. The stories of the sleeping Arthur entombed in a cave or on an island were similarly shaped by pre-Arthurian Celtic beliefs. In AD 82 a Roman official called Demetrius visited Britain and noted one of the few myths of the British ever to be recorded objectively in plain, straight terms. His report was transmitted by Plutarch and told of an exiled god lying asleep in a cave on an island, a warm place in the general direction of the sunset. Probably both cave and island stories about Arthur's end date back to pre-Arthurian beliefs, or those beliefs added a mythic resonance to the actual events of Arthur's last months.

The idea that Arthur did not die but will one day return may seem to remove Arthur entirely from history and the consideration of historians, placing him firmly in the world of myth and mysticism. Yet he is but one of many great charismatic leaders, many of them kings, who were believed to have lived on after their 'official' deaths. The last Saxon king of England, Harold Godwinsson, officially died at the Battle of Hastings close to the site of the high altar of Battle Abbey, and his remains were buried on the same spot. The Bayeux Tapestry is unambiguous – *Harold interfectus est* – but even in 1066 doubts were circulated about the official story. The Norman chronicler William of Poitiers reported that the Conqueror contemptuously ordered Harold's body to be buried on the seashore. Further uncertainties arose because the king's body was mutilated beyond recognition, so even a burial in Battle Abbey might have been that of another battle victim. By the thirteenth century, an Icelandic story was told of Harold being found alive on the battlefield by two peasants who were looting corpses the night after the battle. They took Harold home with them. It was suggested that he should rally the English once more, but Harold knew that many would have sworn fealty to William and he did not want to compromise them. He would retire to a hermitage at Canterbury. Three years later, when Harold died, William was told and he saw that Harold was given a royal burial. Gerald of Wales, writing in 1191, also affirmed that the Saxons clung to the belief that Harold was alive; as a hermit, deeply scarred and blinded in the left eye, he lived for a long time in a cell at Chester, where he was visited by Henry I. A *Life of Harold* written in around 1216 says Harold died at Chester after living for a long time abroad.

The Norwegian king Olaf Tryggvason was defeated in the sea-battle of Svold in 999. Wearing a scarlet cloak, he leapt from his ship, the *Long Serpent*, and drowned himself. The survival version of the story, that under water he had swum under enemy ships and been taken away by a friendly cutter, later going on a pilgrimage to the Holy Land, was concocted immediately after his death; it was referred to by his friend Hallfredar the Troublesome, who did not believe it. According to *The Longer Saga of Olaf Tryggvason*, Edward the Confessor, whose father Ethelred had also been a friend of Olaf's, did believe the story, and read it to his court every year on Easter Day. Eventually, Edward announced that news had come that Olaf had died, thirty-six years after his official death.

There are numerous later examples, most but not all of them kings; the Grand Duchess Anastasia, Richard II, Alexander I of Russia, Sebastian of Portugal and Holger Danske, who lies sleeping beneath Kronborg Castle until the hour of Denmark's greatest danger. Regardless of the mystification surrounding their deaths, all these people definitely existed as real flesh and blood. There is no question that they were real, living people. The fact that there is a long-lived legend that Arthur survived death and lies in a perpetual sleep inside a hill somewhere does not mean that he is really a Celtic god in disguise and never lived as a human being.

Many subscribe to the view that Glastonbury was Avalon, and this view is now so rooted in popular tradition that it is hard to conceive of alternatives. Yet Glastonbury was not mentioned by Geoffrey, writing in 1136, and the view that Glastonbury was Avalon seems to post-date the 'discovery' of Arthur's tomb at the abbey. If Arthur was buried at Glastonbury, then Glastonbury had to be Avalon, and following the discovery the Glastonbury monks were able to claim Glastonbury as Avalon. Caradoc of Llancarfan's *Life of Gildas*, written in about 1140, was the first text to link Arthur with Glastonbury.[45] Melwas of the Summer Region carried off Guinevere, then Arthur brought all the warriors of Devon and Cornwall to Glastonbury to get her back. Caradoc explains that the word 'Glastonbury' derives from 'Island of Glass', which gives the place an otherworldly sound. Somerset, the Summer Region, also implies an otherworldly setting, paving the way for a connection later on in the century between Glastonbury and Arthur's otherworldly destination.[46]

The positive linking of Glastonbury with Avalon came late in the reign of Henry II. According to the contemporary account written by Gerald of Wales, when the king was travelling through Wales he was told by a bard that Arthur was buried at Glastonbury: the king passed the information on to the abbot. A fire caused extensive damage to the abbey in May 1184 and large sums of money were desperately needed to fund the rebuilding. It was, significantly, after the first bout of fund-raising and building was completed in 1190 and the abbey still needed large sums to complete the task,[47] that the abbot ordered the excavation in the old burial ground to the south of the Lady Chapel.[48] The place where the monks were to dig was very precisely indicated by the alleged Welsh bard, between two 'pyramids'. William of Malmesbury described two great stone crosses in the churchyard, one standing four stages, the other five stages high: they were probably inscribed funerary obelisks. The monks dug a hole and found a stone slab seven feet below the surface. Under it they found a lead cross (see Figure 7.2) bearing the inscription HIC IACET SEPULTUS INCLITUS REX ARTURIUS IN INSULA AVALONIA: 'Here lies buried the renowned king Arthur in the Isle of Avalon.'

There was still no sign of the burial itself, so they went on digging. Sixteen feet below the surface they came upon a slightly tilted coffin made out of a massive hollowed oak tree trunk. The bones inside were large, the shin bone being three finger widths longer than the shin of the tallest monk present at the exhumation. The skull bore the marks of 'ten or more' heavy blows, all healed except one and that, near the left ear, was evidently the death blow. The lighter bones of a woman were also found, complete with strands of fair hair, but they disintegrated into dust when one of the monks touched them; Guinevere's name was – suspiciously helpfully – scratched into the coffin to show whose bones they were.

It is not clear how much of this Glastonbury legend is true. There are certainly cases of the graves of famous people being faked. George Steevens, a Shakespeare commentator in the eighteenth century, faked a 'tomb of Guinivere' and also a marble tomb of Harthacanute which almost persuaded the antiquaries of the day.[49] The discovery of Arthur's grave and the tourist draw it inevitably became were suspiciously well-timed in relation to the abbey's fund-raising programme. The circumstantial details about Arthur's bones are quite convincing, apart from the measurement given of the distance between the eyes. In his eagerness to impress us with the giganticness

Figure 7.2 The Glastonbury lead cross, as shown in Camden's *Britannia*

of Arthur, the chronicler has given an absurd measurement across the bridge of the nose, the width of a man's palm. The normal distance between the eyes is 3 or 4 cm: 10 cm is impossible. As Dickinson said, 'Doubts gather round the grave.'[50]

Even so, the lead cross certainly existed. Leland saw it at the abbey in the early sixteenth century; Camden saw it in the early seventeenth; it is known to have been in the possession of Chancellor Hughes of Wells in the eighteenth century, after which it disappeared. It is said that the cross was found again in the mud of an old lake-bed at Forty Hall, Enfield by a metal-detectionist called Derek Mahoney; Enfield Council prosecuted him in 1982 for retaining the cross, which was found on their land. Mr Mahoney refused to give it up and was jailed for contempt of court. The judge ordered his release on 21 March 1983, when it had become clear Mr Mahoney was prepared to stay in prison for ever rather than give up the cross. Suspicions that the cross was a fake were aroused when it was revealed that Mr Mahoney had been employed as a mould-maker by Lesney Toys, yet it would be strange for even the most determined hoaxer to endure a nine-month prison sentence to support a fake with a relatively low commercial value. It is more likely that Mr Mahoney genuinely believed in the cross's authenticity, and it is possible to explain how the object came to be at the Forty Hall site. It is known that in the eighteenth century Forty Hall was the home of Richard Gough, who in 1789 brought out an English translation of Camden's *Britannia*. Perhaps the Mahoney cross was a copy made for Gough in the eighteenth century, as the British Museum suggested. Perhaps Gough's interest in the cross was aroused by seeing Camden's illustration of it and he was able to acquire the real cross from Mr Hughes. Where the Mahoney cross is now is not known; one version of its fate is that it was thrown into a reservoir, where it may still lie, awaiting a third discovery.[51]

The style of lettering shown in Camden's drawing is earlier than twelfth century, but not as old as sixth century: the Ns, for instance, are distinctively written as Hs. This may indicate a bungled attempt to fake an antique, or a grave genuinely believed to have been Arthur's in the tenth century and labelled in good faith at that time. Dunstan walled and raised the level of the graveyard in about 950, to make 'a fair meadow, where the bodies of the saints could rest undisturbed by those who passed by': this explains why the burial was so deep and why the stone slab and lead cross were seven feet down. Spreading a two-metre layer of soil over the ancient graves was obviously going to conceal them, and it may be that the ones that were considered the most important were systematically tagged immediately before the ground level was raised.

The hollow tree trunk is a problem, as it represents a very ancient style of burial now known to have been used occasionally in the sixth and seventh centuries in the Celtic west and it is unlikely that the Glastonbury monks would have known enough archaeology to have faked it; it was not, for instance, like the other early Christian burials on the site. The pre-Christian nature of the tree-trunk burial suggests that it was not a dark age Christian king but a pagan king instead – perhaps Arthur's enemy Melwas or, as others have suggested, the much earlier Arviragus, a British king who perished in about AD 61 and who may have died in the massacre by the Romans at South Cadbury.[52]

The finding of Arthur's grave was good propaganda for the Plantagenets as it suggested they were heirs to a glamorous inheritance as well as proving that the hoped-for Rescuer of the British, the sleeping Arthur, was well and truly dead. In 1168, a subversive curiosity in verse had been written by Etienne de Rouen, a monk at the abbey of Bec, called *Draco Normannicus*, 'The Norman Standard'. This was in effect a challenge to Henry II's supremacy. It opened with a letter ostensibly from Roland of Dinan to Arthur, pleading for help against Henry II. Although apparently residing at the ends of the earth, Arthur answered by addressing Henry II directly, recalling his own early victories over the Saxons and his withdrawal to Avalon. Arthur was gathering his troops in the woods of Cornwall – the French saw Cornwall as Arthur's home territory – and warned Henry to leave the Bretons alone. Though long-dead, Arthur was paraded as a living threat to the living king. Henry II was represented as being entertained by all this, undertaking to hold Brittany as Arthur's vassal. It was dangerous to have challenged Henry in this way – only two years later, he was to have his archbishop of Canterbury Thomas Becket murdered – but he responded stylishly, with proof that the warrior-king he was threatened with was no more than a box of old bones.

The finding of Arthur's grave was also good for Glastonbury, in that it raised the abbey's profile on the pilgrimage map. These facts should make us deeply suspicious. The 'discovery' of Arthur was too well-timed, too convenient financially and politically, to be true. It was certainly exploited by Richard I; in March 1191, the year after the exhumation, he presented Tancred of Sicily with Excalibur, apparently also found in the Glastonbury grave.

The monks at twelfth-century Glastonbury were re-inventing the past on a grand scale. At the same time that the grave of Arthur was discovered, another chapter in the abbey's history was being invented. Joseph of Arimathea, who offered his own tomb for the burial of Jesus, journeyed to Cornwall and then Somerset to found the first Christian church in Western Europe, a simple wattle building on the site of the Glastonbury Lady Chapel. Founded in about AD 60, this was far and away the oldest and therefore holiest Christian centre in the West. The story is found in the earliest surviving copy of *De Antiquitate Glastoniensis Ecclesiae* (The Early History of Glastonbury Church) by William of Malmesbury. William visited Glastonbury in 1129–39 and while there wrote the *De Antiquitate*, using all the available documents at the abbey back to its foundation in the eighth century. Unfortunately no copy from the 1140s has survived, and it is quite possible that the earliest copy we have, dating from 1247, had its opening chapter on Joseph of Arimathea added later to fall in line with the late twelfth-century Glastonbury promotional campaign; William was writing his *Gesta Regum Anglorum* ('Deeds of the Kings of England') at the same time as the *De Antiquitate* and he naturally copied the Glastonbury sections into the *Gesta*. There is no reference to Joseph in the *Gesta*, which strongly suggests there was no section on Joseph in the original *De Antiquitate* either. The Joseph story was therefore almost certainly invented and added between 1140 and 1247 to inflate Glastonbury's reputation.

William of Malmesbury provides us with good evidence that Glastonbury's past was being deliberately manipulated, glamorized and falsified in the late twelfth century. If the Joseph connection was a cynical invention, so too was the Arthur connection.[53] It must also be significant that William does not mention any link between Arthur and Glastonbury in either of the two books he wrote while at the abbey. If there had been a Glastonbury tradition that Arthur was buried there he would surely have mentioned it. In fact he insists in the *Gesta* that there was no grave: 'the tomb of Arthur is nowhere to be seen, wherefore the ancient songs fable that he is yet to come'.

In spite of these historiographical problems, the identification of Glastonbury with Avalon was made and, like many another news story, it has been accepted as fact. The rationalization of Glastonbury as Avalon is exemplified in the carefully and persuasively argued work of Geoffrey Ashe. The *Life of St Collen* is cited to show that Glastonbury was identified as Annwn, a marshalling-place for the souls of the newly-dead, in the dark ages. St Collen, a Welsh dark age saint, made his cell on the lower slopes of the Tor. One day he overheard two peasants outside his cell discussing Gwyn, king of the Fairies and Lord of Annwn, and went out to tell them they should not stand in awe of the fairies, who were really no more than demons. The peasants were scandalized and said Collen would now have to meet Gwyn. Shortly after this Collen was visited three times by Gwyn's messenger and he reluctantly climbed to the Tor's summit where he entered a magical world with a beautiful castle in which King Gwyn sat enthroned on a golden chair. Collen wisely refused the food the fairies offered and scattered the holy water he had taken with him: Gwyn and his castle vanished, leaving the saint standing alone on the windy hilltop. This story clearly identifies Glastonbury Tor as a moongate, a point of access to the otherworld, and identifies it with the Celtic Avalon, the realm of Gwyn or Avallach, the Lord of the Dead.

The 'Isle' of Avalon might at first sight seem inappropriate, but Glastonbury was in the Roman and post-Roman periods a near-island, surrounded in summer by fen and in winter by shallow sheets of water. The Somerset Levels have been artificially drained only in the last few centuries, and it is easy to imagine the extensive flats of the Somerset Levels as a shallow sea inlet gradually converting to saltmarsh and fen. Glastonbury in the dark ages would have been extremely isolated, virtually unreachable from north, west and south, and accessible only by way of a narrow neck of land on the eastern side, where it was defended by a short earthen bank, Ponter's Ball. Glastonbury was therefore all but an island. Glastonbury was, at least in the twelfth century and later, identified with another magical place, the Glass island, Ynys Witrin, because of the form of the name *Glas*-tonbury. This was taken up by Chrétien, who actually placed the Glass Island in the domain of Melwas.

The arguments are nevertheless inconclusive, as Chrétien may simply have accepted and followed the 'propaganda' emanating from Glastonbury. Even the *Life of St Collen* is poor as uncorroborated evidence: the copy that survives is a late copy and the location could easily have been shifted to Glastonbury in order to fit in with late twelfth-century notions of political correctness. Ashe praises Gerald of Wales for being the first to speak of Glastonbury as Avalon: 'The voice that breaks the silence belongs to Giraldus Cambrensis.'[54] But Gerald was writing in the 1190s,[55] *after* the discovery of the oak coffin in the old burial ground, which he reports. Even the equation of Glas-tonbury with the Glass Island is weakly founded. Ashe himself admits that the name is likely to be derived from the name of the Saxon tribe who colonized the site in the seventh century and called it 'burh of the Glaestings': *Glaestingaburg* is an early documented form of the place-name.

'Island of Glass' in Brittonic was *Ynys Witrin*, and this exotic ancient name was apparently woven into the Glastonbury legend in the twelfth century. William of Malmesbury quotes a charter of 601 from the Glastonbury archives in which the unnamed king of Dumnonia granted to the old church (*vetusta ecclesia*) at Glastonbury the estate known as Yneswitrin, on the petition of Abbot Worgret. If this document was authentic it would prove that the old church attributed to Joseph of Arimathea was at least as old as the sixth century. Although Ralegh Radford was ready to believe in the charter's authenticity, many other scholars are not.[56] By the twelfth century the Glastonbury monks had a vested interest in producing evidence of the antiquity of their abbey, and in fabricating documents that supported the association with Joseph of Arimathea and Arthur: the ancient charter did both.

So, the post-1200 rationalization of Glastonbury as a Celtic Avalon is not well founded. Whether the excavation of the old burial ground really turned up a dark age royal grave or not must remain an open question. Ralegh Radford's re-examination of the site in 1962–3 was nevertheless very revealing, in showing that there was some truth in the story. To the south of the Lady Chapel, he found a pit one metre in diameter, the right size to have held one of the great stone crosses described by William of Malmesbury. To the south of the stone socket he found traces of the footings of an ancient mausoleum that had been demolished apparently at Dunstan's orders just before the land level was raised: this was evidently the site of another high-status burial. Between the two he found that a large pit had been opened up in the 1180s or 1190s and immediately backfilled. Radford was sure about the date because there were masons' chippings of the Doulting stone[57] used only in the building of the Lady Chapel, and that is known to have been built between 1184–9; so the pit is almost certainly the 'grave of Arthur' that was opened in 1190.[58] The description of the oak coffin suggests that an early pagan royal burial was found; the depth of the burial and the lead cross suggest that it was remembered as a special royal burial in the eighth or ninth centuries, at which time it was believed – though possibly wrongly – to be that of Arthur.

There is no inconsistency in believing that Arthur died on a battlefield in north-west Wales and was buried at Glastonbury. That would have been possible. There has been a tendency to assume that a West Country location for Avalon has to go with a West Country location for Camlann, at Slaughter Bridge or South Cadbury, but there is no reason why the two sites should not have been widely separated geographically.[59] The corpses of important people were frequently transported long distances in the dark ages. St Samson died in Brittany, having been unwilling to go there in the first place, and requested that his body should be returned to Llantwit for burial.[60] An extreme example is St Docco, who died in Jerusalem and was brought back, right across Europe, to Congresbury in Somerset for burial.[61] Locating Camlann in Gwynedd does nothing at all to help us to locate Avalon.

If Arthur was not taken to Glastonbury to die and be buried, where was he taken? If Glastonbury is not Avalon, is there a place with a stronger claim?

Chris Barber and David Pykitt make a case for Bardsey Island off the south-western tip of the Lleyn Peninsula.[62] This leans principally on the idea that Camlann was fought on the mainland nearby, at Porth Cadlan; since we have already rejected Porth Cadlan as Camlann, the case for Bardsey as (a nearby) Avalon is a weak one. A second argument introduces the old Welsh tradition that the Fortunate Isles, the source of the Elixir of Life, where Celtic heroes went after death, lay 'beyond Cardigan Bay, the Annwn of the old sun, in the direction of Ireland'.[63] The location of Bardsey does fit this description. Third, Bardsey was a religious focus in the dark ages, described later as 'the Iona of Wales': specifically, it was the place St Cadfan chose for the location of his monastery at the time of Arthur. Fourth, islands generally were associated with the otherworld.

I find none of these arguments really compelling, although it is certainly true that Bardsey acquired a special mystique by the high middle ages, when it was known as 'the resting-place of twenty thousand saints', and the tradition was preserved in the *Lives* of Welsh saints so that many people wanted to be buried on Bardsey, so as to be 'sure of Heaven'.[64] This tells us something important: that the choice of a retirement home would have been a matter of great significance to dark age aristocrats; those who were rich and powerful enough would have chosen the places of greatest sanctity.

The Isle of Man has been proposed by Graham Phillips and Martin Keatman.[65] They suggest that Geoffrey of Monmouth could have based his Avalon on the Annwn of Celtic legend, but point out that he does include other elements, like longevity and self-sowing vines, clearly originating from classical stories about the Fortunate Isles. The nine holy women come from the Celtic past, and Morgan comes from Morrigan, a Celtic goddess: the name 'Avalon' too is Celtic in form. An ancient Irish poem cycle has the sea-god Manannan ruling over a magic island that is 'rich in apples', *ablach*.

Geoffrey specifically refers to Avalon as 'Insula Pomorum', the Isle of Apples, in his *Life of Merlin*. The Isle of Man takes its name from Manannan.

The problem with all of this is that in the Welsh tradition, a tradition that is nearer to home, Annwn is actually identified as Ireland.[66] In the middle ages Scilly was identified as the dwelling of Queen Morgan. In Scotland, Iona was referred to as the Isle of Dreams, a phrase later applied to Avalon in medieval romances. It begins to look as if Annwn or Avalon was not always precisely located in people's minds, and seems to have shifted through time. One common thread, though, is that it is always isolated and separated from the normal course of the action, removed from the secular world in general, *by water*. Can it be narrowed down any more than that as a destination for the dying Arthur?

The most promising candidate by far for Avalon is Whithorn in Galloway, on the northern shore of the Irish Sea (see Figure 7.3). Today Whithorn is a small town, neither an island nor on an island, on a peninsula with water to the west, south and east and the Southern Uplands of Scotland to the north. The peninsula, known as the Machars, is a glaciated lowland, with smooth spreads of soft fertile till pierced by outcrops of jagged greywacke. It is a benign landscape, with much about it to remind one of South Wales or Cornwall. Here and there shrublands of bracken and hawthorn break up the undulating pasture, and ravines running down to the coast enfold dense dark woods of sycamore and beech.

In the lee of Burrow Head, the southern tip of the peninsula, is the tiny sleeve-like harbour of the Isle of Whithorn (see Figure 7.4). This is where St Ninian landed in 397; it was the focus of trade and travel in the dark ages, connecting Whithorn with all the British lands bordering the Irish Sea. The eastern side of the harbour is separated from the open sea by an island 400 metres long, of which the southern third was turned into a tiny British fortress to defend the harbour mouth against pirates or invaders.

Some 5 km north-west of the harbour, St Ninian founded a priory on the site of an existing Christian settlement: it had the reputation in Arthur's time of being the very earliest Christian community on the Scottish mainland. The Welsh Triads list Three Perpetual Choirs, religious houses where services were chanted or sung continuously.

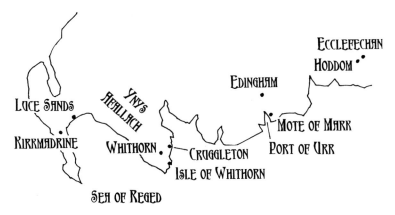

Figure 7.3 Dark age Galloway

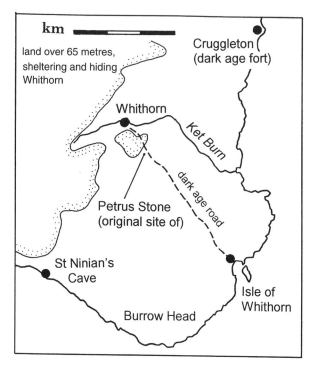

Figure 7.4 Whithorn

One was Cor Emrys at Caer Caradoc, which corresponds to Mynydd-y-Gaer, and it was founded round about the time of Arthur's birth. The second was Bangor of Illtyd Farchog at Caerworgorn, which is now known as Llantwit Major: that monastery was founded some thirty years earlier. The third, and holiest of the three, was the Cor of Bangor Wydryn at Ynys Afallach. This corresponds to Whithorn. The group of names in the Triad includes the word 'Wydryn', which became anglicized in the seventh century into the Old English 'Hwitern' and later the modern English 'Whithorn', and could also have been an alternative form of 'Witrin', meaning 'glass.' So *Ynys Wydryn* (or the Isle of Whithorn), and not Glastonbury, was the legendary Glass Island. The location is clearly given as Ynys Afallach, the Isle of Afallach or Avalon, identifying Whithorn as both Witrin and Avalon.

Whether the 'isle' in each case refers to a literal island or to an area more or less cut off from the rest of the world by water is unclear. The word 'ynys' was sometimes used to describe an open cleared area on a peninsula – either of these older connotations of the word 'ynys' would apply to the Machars of Galloway. It has recently been suggested that the words for 'island' in Anglo-Saxon, Brittonic and Scandinavian – words such as *ynys* and *holm* – underwent a semantic shift in the dark ages, and came to mean monastic retreats, whether they were located on islands or not: the religious communities were in effect spiritually islanded from the rest of the world.[67] It is a little like the twentieth-century borrowing of the word 'oasis', which we apply more often in a figurative than in a literal sense; people often refer to a park, a church or a garden as an oasis of peace and quiet in relation to the rest of their urban environment, and the qualifying phrases that make clear that a figurative sense is meant are often left out. Many dark age religious refuge communities were literally on islands – Puffin Island and St Tudwal's Island in Wales, St Agnes in Scilly, Ardwall Island in Scotland, Scelig Michael in Ireland – so the island idea may have become indissolubly connected with remote religious communities.[68] Following the semantic line of thought further, it also seems to me more likely that *Ynys Wydryn* originally meant not 'Island of Glass', which makes little sense, but 'Island of Protection': *wydrin* in Old Welsh means 'protection'.[69] That would reinforce the idea of the religious community as a sanctuary, a place of refuge.

Though it was the oldest and holiest, Whithorn was not the only dark age monastery in Galloway. There were at least three others, each of them, like Whithorn, hidden safely away in an obscure inland site but not too far from a coastal landing place that provided easy access from the Irish Sea. The religious community of Kirkmadrine, which was possibly then called Rhionydd, Ptolemy's Rerigonium or 'very royal place', was on the Mull of Kintyre a short distance inland from Luce Sands, a known dark age landing place. The next headland to the east, the Machars, is where Wydryn was located, a short distance inland from the Isle of Whithorn, a perfect miniature dark age harbour. Possibly the fortress at Cruggleton was the royal stronghold for the southern Machars. Further east again, the monastery of Edingham was a short distance inland from a natural harbour overlooked by the dark age fortress called the Mote of Mark.[70]

The long and complex history of Whithorn, illuminated by an admirable and remarkably thorough recent excavation programme, began with its founding by St Ninian. In 397 St Ninian took the already well-used road from the harbour to the priory site five kilometres inland, where he built a small stone church. The site was a low oval knoll 150 metres from east to west and 75 metres from north to south, and rising about 5 metres above the Ket Burn which supplied it with water. The church Ninian built, probably towards the western end of the low summit ridge became known as the Candida Casa, the White House. Bede refers to it by this name, and it has often been assumed, perhaps rightly, that this was because it contrasted with the dark wattle and daub huts of the local people. There is, however, another possibility. Camden suggested that Whithorn was the place referred to in the second century AD by Ptolemy as Loukophibia, meaning 'The Shining Place'. The root 'leuco' means bright, shining or white in Brittonic. The Ravenna Cosmography similarly referred to Whithorn as Lucotion, which may be another variant of a lost Brittonic name.[71] If that is so, and 'Candida Casa' could easily be translated by the same phrase, the name could be significantly earlier than Ninian and incorporate a reference to the place as some sort of centre of British trade and power during the Roman occupation.

It may even have been a religious centre in the sub-Roman period and before; there is a high density of prehistoric rock carvings (at least thirty) on the southern half of the Whithorn peninsula as well as the remains of a stone circle.[72] Christian missionaries were often drawn to pagan sanctuaries which they then set about converting.[73] A standing stone evidently stood on the Whithorn site, near Ninian's church, and it was pulled over and buried during the fifth century, presumably once the Christian missionaries felt they were fully in control of the site. It is also interesting that in the immediately post-Arthurian phase at Whithorn there seems to have been a temporary reversion to something looking rather like pagan cult practices, with the building of ritual stone settings and circular arrangements of posts in the pagan neolithic and bronze age traditions – even if they were made to celebrate the Christian word.

The question of the original significance of the name Candida Casa probably cannot be resolved now, but it is certainly true that in the fifth and sixth centuries a stone building stood on the low hill at Whithorn, and that it was coated with white limewash. A scatter of limewashed plaster fragments found in 1986–91 across the Arthurian layers shows that such a building had indeed stood on the upslope side of the dwellings.[74] It is thought that Ninian was buried in a small separate mausoleum immediately to the west of the church. He may have been aware of the propaganda value of the place-name, and deliberately whitewashed his church so that it was not only plainly visible across the undulating lowland but would itself become known as 'The Shining Place'.

Like many another early missionary, Ninian felt the need to withdraw from society sometimes to pray, and there is no reason to doubt the tradition that he used 'St Ninian's Cave' on the still-deserted coast 4 kilometres away to the south-west as his oratory when he found the bustle of Whithorn too distracting. I found the cave and the whole stretch of coastline much as they were in Ninian's time, empty and silent but for the sounds of sea and wind, even at the height of the tourist season – an oasis, in fact – and in Arthur's day they would already have become part of the legendary fabric of the Whithorn landscape.

The first monasterium, dating from around 450–75 but not firmly dated, had its focus on the summit of the low hill. To the west was the little limewashed church and the founder's tomb. To the east, more or less on the crown of the hill, was a stone memorial pillar, the Latinus Stone. A roughly circular ditched boundary was thrown round the hill top, marking a sacred precinct or 'termon' about 75 metres across. A stream, the River Ket, meandered round the west, north and east sides. An approach road curved up the southern slope between modest rectangular huts, each 6 or 8 metres long with a central hearth. Later, around 500, a second, alternative or additional, road ran up from the south-west, with Huts 6 and 7 to the west and Hut 1 to the east. Hut 1 was not aligned along either of these roads; instead, its back ran close to the precinct boundary. It lay due south of the hilltop, facing the warmth of the midday sun. It seems to have been a favoured dwelling in other ways, as we shall discover.

Several significant changes occurred in about the year 550 (see Figure 7.5).[75] Huts 6 and 7 were taken down and replaced by Hut 9. Hut 5 was also demolished. Hut 1 was taken down and on its site a shrine was set up consisting of wattle fences laid out in two concentric circles 4 metres and 7.5 metres in diameter, as if to commemorate the site of a house that was particularly special. Fitted radially exactly between the two circles was an unusual grave, the first in the area and of a design that was unique at Whithorn, though not unlike the earliest cist (or slab-lined) graves at Tintagel, which date from around 500. The excavators call it 'the special grave'. Its site coincided with the eastern corner of the interior of Hut 1.

Fences ran southwest from the outer circle to create an enclosed graveyard 19 metres by 7.5 metres with an entrance on the west side onto the road (see Figure 7.6).

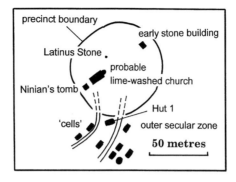

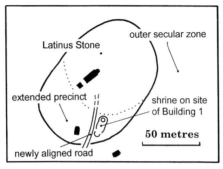

Figure 7.5 Whithorn: above, in about 530; below, in about 550

Everyone who passed along the road to the church would have walked along the side of this unusual graveyard, which housed just three more burials and one or two large ceremonial posts or masts. The sacred precinct was enlarged at this time, specifically to encompass the site of the special house and the new cemetery enclosure with its shrine and four graves.

'The wonder of the world'

These developments on the southern slope of the hill at Whithorn happened around the year 550. Later, more of the humble wattle dwellings or monks' cells were cleared away and successive circular shrines were created on the other side of the road slanting up towards Ninian's church. One would become the focus for the first Northumbrian (Anglian) church at Whithorn in about 650. At least one of the early shrine pillars was preserved inside it and, in spite of many changes, it was respected and left in position until about 830: it is not known what happened to it afterwards. The first burial, in the special grave, became the focus of a burial ground which eventually came to cover the whole site. It is likely that this special burial was the grave of a special person, perhaps a bishop, chief or king: and it looks as if all the other alterations, including the enlargement of the sacred precinct, were associated with and precipitated by the burial of that special person.

This happened at the time of Arthur's death.

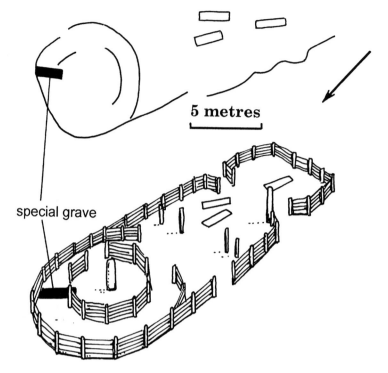

5 metres

special grave

Figure 7.6 The special grave enclosure: above, plan; below, perspective view

At this point it is necessary to make an imaginative leap, with all the attendant risks, and launch a new hypothesis. Was the shrine designed to commemorate the site of Arthur's cell? Was the odd, asymmetric placing of the special grave designed to mark the position of a particular location within the monk's cell – perhaps the exact location of his deathbed? Do the position and orientation of these structures show not only where but how he died, huddled unobtrusively in the eastern corner of his hut, all vestige of kingship and earthly glory gone? The hypothesis can only be tentatively floated. No 'Arturus rex' or 'Artognou' inscription survives to prove or support it.

This grave was special in its location, but also in the unique way in which it was sealed with a large slab of local greywacke. When I first read about the special grave I wondered if the excavators had stumbled unwittingly on the long-lost grave of Arthur;[76] though remarkable, it would not have been impossible. But the more detailed report published after a long delay five years later made me doubt it. Peter Hill now believes that the special grave – Hill's own phrase – was designed to receive successive burials. The walls of the 2-metre-long pit were lined with stones and the slab covering the cavity was flush with the ground. There were signs that at least four people had been buried successively in the same grave, two of them youths, though little more than their teeth survived. This was profoundly disappointing, and seemed to prove that the grave could not possibly be Arthur's. The hypothesis was foundering.

Also within the wicker-walled enclosure were three other lintelled graves, numbered 4, 5 and 6 by the excavators. Since all four graves must date from about the same time, the creation of the small graveyard, it was possible that 4, 5 or 6 might be Arthur's grave instead. They were lined with timber and had planks for lintels.[77] Unfortunately, the skeletal remains in them were too negligible for Hill to report on them. The humble finds of 'grave-goods' – an iron finger ring, a nail, pebbles – do not suggest the burial of a king, or even an ex-king. This impasse made me turn back to review all the other evidence about the site and I was driven to consider once more the possibility that the special grave might after all be the king's. Clearly it is not the founder's tomb, as it was made 150 years too late and we know that Ninian would have been buried either in or very close to the church, but it was made for someone very special, and it looks from the flurry of activity and change that accompanied the burial that the death was seen as a significant event.

The earliest graves that are so far known at Whithorn were lined and covered with planks or slabs. Some were covered with white quartz fragments. Like the standing stones and the post circles, these are part of a much older ritual tradition: the association of white stone with funerary monuments seems to reach right back to the white long barrows made in the English chalklands in the fourth millennium BC.[78] Some graves had a boulder near the head of the grave, some a small pillar planted directly above the corpse's head: most were not marked at all. None of the graves so far found had stones with carved inscriptions or decoration. There is nothing to say who any of these people were, and unfortunately most of the human remains had completely decayed away.[79] Later British (as opposed to Northumbrian) graves, from around 600 onwards, contained massive split tree trunk coffins, laboriously hollowed out to make a space for the bodies. It was, curiously and possibly coincidentally, exactly this sort of burial that was found at Glastonbury and claimed as Arthur's, but at Whithorn at any rate it seems to be a little too late to have been Arthur's.[80]

Peter Hill says in a carefully worded description that the stone-lined, slab-covered special grave was apparently designed to receive several successive burials.[81] The fact that its cover slab was at ground level, readily accessible, shows that the four people entombed there were only intended to be there temporarily. They needed to draw virtue out of the magical circular shrine, whatever power it contained, before they were taken away to be buried elsewhere. Interestingly, this two-phase burial recalls a much earlier burial practice dating from the neolithic, when it was the norm over much of Britain. It was not just the circular settings of posts that referred back to the bronze age and beyond.[82] Perhaps these were monks and novices who for some reason were deemed to have died in a state of sin, and this preliminary treatment helped to redeem their souls. It is nevertheless a puzzle that the partial remains of four people were left in the pit, not removed for careful reburial somewhere else. If the grave was designed to house successive burials, there should still be the remains of only one person at most in the grave at the close of its period of use.

Perhaps the remains of the two men and two youths were left in this way because they mark the end of a distinctive practice that was properly observed at first, in 550, but treated in a far more casual and desultory way, say, fifty years later. That implies that the four corpses of which we see traces were not the first but the last in a series of burials.

The first occupant of the special grave could therefore have been Arthur. The Whithorn monks may have buried him in an easily accessible grave because they expected a ship to come from the south to take him home for a worthier burial elsewhere, probably in Dumnonia, perhaps at Tintagel.[83] Whether that happened there is no way of knowing, but if the body of Arthur was at some stage taken out for reburial somewhere else, the empty grave of Arthur would have been there, in itself to become a wonder of Britain, and available for secondary use, to supply the 'virtue' some Christian corpses were deemed to need.

What claim can Hut 1 have to be Arthur's cell? Humble though it and the other cells appear to be by other standards, Hut 1 was oriented with care, backing onto the sacred precinct's boundary, and facing the midday sun on the warmest slope, a favoured spot. It was not built along a street but stood between two roads, which like the precinct boundary at the back may have given it a little more privacy. More significant, more telling still, is the fact that it was surrounded by a scatter of high-status imported Mediterranean pottery and broken drinking glasses. The debris was spread around the site of Hut 1 and along the roadway that passed between Huts 1 and 6. Some of it was African red slipware from Carthage, found at only seven sites and only in any quantity at Tintagel and Dinas Powys, and between 525 and 550, in other words dating only from the time of Arthur's high kingship, defeat and retirement. Given the distribution pattern, it is likely that this material was imported from Tintagel; Whithorn is the only northern British site to have had Phocaean red slipware. The scatter of debris in this Whithorn street yields the 'furthest-north' example of Biv ware; the rest of the sites are all in Wales and Cornwall, including South Cadbury and Tintagel. The Bv ware fragments are known from only five sites altogether, and the largest quantities have been found, once again, at Tintagel.[84]

The so-called D ware was a rare import from France. Ten British sites are known to have imported it, including Dinas Powys, Dunadd and the Mote of Mark: usually fortified high-status centres with royal associations.[85] The scatter of fragments near Hut 1 at Whithorn included D ware; Whithorn was a monastery, but perhaps the presence there of D ware hints at the peculiar circumstances I am envisaging in my hypothesis: a monastery sheltering a retired and renowned high king, who lived in Hut 1.

The remains of imported pottery and glass at Whithorn tell us that the place held high status in Arthur's time. Table 7.1 shows how Whithorn compares with other prestige sites of the same period.[86]

The Latinus Stone supplies yet another Dumnonian connection. At the crest of the hill a memorial stone was erected by a man called Latinus in about 450. When first recorded it had a distinctive Constantinian chi–rho symbol carved above the inscription, a chi–rho drawn as a six-armed cross, or asterisk, with the curving limb of the rho meeting the centre. The significance of this has not been fully appreciated before, but this particular symbol was inscribed on stones in Dumnonia, but nowhere north of Dumnonia apart from two isolated examples in Roman forts at Maryport and Catterick.[87] The chi–rho cut in about 450 and the pottery arriving in about 540–50 provide evidence of a long-continuing cultural dialogue between the religious community at Whithorn and the ruling elites of Dumnonia.

We know from a reference in a single Irish document that Whithorn was the mysterious Rosnat, a place of great sanctity that some observers have despaired of

Table 7.1 Imported pottery and glass at high-status dark age sites

	Imported pottery		Glass
	A-ware	*B-ware*	
Tintagel	36+	1495+	?
Cadbury-Congresbury	173	547	48
Whithorn	*9*	*211*	*421*
Dinas Powys	86	170	256
South Cadbury	12	131	29
High Peak	–	84	–
Longbury Bank	13+	65	63
Trethurgy	5	47	?

locating. Rosnat or the Magnum Monasterium was founded about a hundred years after St Ninian's initial colony, and it was this place of special sanctity that stood near the Galloway coast in Arthur's time. It was special because it was believed to be the oldest Christian community in Scotland, because it was one of only three perpetual choirs in Britain, and because it was a great seat of learning. The single Irish reference telling us that Rosnat and Whithorn were one and the same also tells us that Irish monks were sent there for training. Princes and princesses from all over Britain, from every Celtic kingdom – British, Irish and Pictish – were sent there to be educated in the fifth and early sixth centuries. Whithorn was both a holy place and the dark age equivalent of a great co-educational public school.

Excavations at Whithorn in the 1980s and 1990s have revealed an astonishing amount of detail about the complex sequence of events spanning the period from Ninian to the Reformation and beyond.[88] In the Arthurian period a road perhaps 4 metres wide passed up the south-facing slope towards Ninian's church between the humblest of dwellings made of sticks and wattles, some of them round, some roughly rectangular, although sharp corners were impossible with this method of construction.[89] The houses were between 4 and 9 metres across, each with its own central hearth. They may have been smeared with mud to make them windproof and were probably thatched; some seem to have had stone pavements round them. What Ninian's church looked like is not known, since its footings have been destroyed by repeated rebuilding on the crest of the hill, but it may have followed the form common in the late Roman period: a lofty rectangular hall with a thatched pitched roof, perhaps 10 metres long, with a semi-circular apse at the eastern end. Though neither large nor ostentatious, a building of this kind raised on a hill 64 metres high would have been a striking and dramatic feature of the subdued Machars landscape.

A second road ascended the hill from the west, again passing informally between tiny round-cornered wattle huts, some as small as 3 metres across, heading for

Ninian's white church. The road was once again of the simplest kind. The topsoil and subsoil were worn away by the passage of foot traffic, carts and horses and the out-cropping bedrock was broken and trampled down into a fairly smooth gravelly surface. It may have led westwards to the Ket Burn, the source of the monastery's water supply: it would have made sense to collect on the upstream side of the settlement where there was a better chance of its being clean.[90]

It was in around 650 that the old British settlement at Whithorn was engulfed by the expanding Anglian kingdom of Northumbria, which by then stretched all the way from the Humber to the Forth. A great wooden church was raised, incorporating the two early shrines raised after Arthur's death. It was burnt down, possibly during a Viking raid, in the 840s. A new church was built on the same site. Then, in the twelfth century, the Northumbrian church site was abandoned; instead the summit of the hill 40 metres away was redeveloped by Fergus, king of Galloway, as a cathedral with an adjoining priory. Only the shell of the nave and a few other fragments of masonry remain of this later structure, and inevitably this large-scale building work will have destroyed almost every trace of any dark age structures on the hilltop. It was once thought possible that a rectangular building protruding from the eastern end of the medieval priory site represents the Candida Casa but this is now believed to be an early chapel of perhaps tenth- or eleventh-century date.[91]

If Whithorn is the place of safety to which Arthur was brought after Camlann, we need to ask, of all the monasteries in Britain, why was he brought to this one?

If Arthur was wounded rather than killed at Camlann, and many of his men were killed, his surviving lieutenants would have needed to make all speed to get him out of the area. Had he fallen into the hands of Maelgwn, he would have been killed at once. He had to flee Gwynedd, and the quickest escape route was by sea, by way of the Mawddach estuary. It was there that at last I found one piece of local folklore to support a west Welsh Camlann and Arthur's escape by way of Barmouth. In 1850, a story was in circulation about a stone on a hillside overlooking the Mawddach estuary.[92] The stone, at Sylfaen Farm opposite Llys Bradwen, bore two carvings of a sword that were produced magically when Arthur threw his sword at it. I searched for the stone initially at Cerrig Arthur, the ruined stone circle just above Sylfaen (see Plate 7.2), thinking it was likely that the stone selected for this special treatment must already have been conspicuous, but none of the circle stones or any others nearby were marked in any way. Eventually I found the Sword Stone 400 m down the slope, lying in a field full of boulders, presumably collected during field clearance. The Sword Stone is about 1.8 m long by 0.5 m across, thicker at the southern end and tapering to the north (see Plate 7.3). It looks as if at some stage it could have been planted upright on its thicker end as a marker or memorial stone, and may not be in its original position. The natural joints in the rock have been a focus for weathering and this has produced two thin straight parallel lines about 5 centimetres apart etched on both sides of the stone, the pair on the west-facing side terminating abruptly in a projecting and slightly sinuous edge: this looks like a hilted broad-bladed sword.

The significance of the Sylfaen Sword Stone lies in the fact that Arthur only disposed of Excalibur – in Malory it was Bedivere who eventually threw it into the lake – when he was close to death. Arthur threw his sword away after Camlann, when he was relinquishing his earthly roles. This fits exactly with the scenario proposed

Plate 7.2 Cerrig Arthur, a stone circle at Sylfaen

Plate 7.3 The Sword Stone at Sylfaen

here: that Arthur was wounded at Camlann and was then taken from the battlefield to board ship at Aberamffra harbour at the seaward end of the estuary. The Sword Stone story tells us that people living in the Mawddach valley, especially Bradwen and his ancestors, who lived opposite Sylfaen and had their own tradition of Camlann, may also have believed that this is what happened.

We have then to explain why the king was taken north to Whithorn rather than south to Padstow, which might seem the more natural course. The explanation is probably twofold. First, the losses of men sustained in the battle were so great that Arthur could not have recovered the situation: after so total a defeat his career was manifestly over. Second, he was over 60 and badly injured; he was incapable of fighting again for the foreseeable future, if ever, and therefore not capable of continuing as king. These decisions may have been made by Arthur himself or, if he was insensible, by his lieutenants as he was carried on a litter or carriage the short distance south to board ship for Whithorn. The decision to sail to Whithorn was in itself a decision to resign the military command, to retire from public life, to withdraw to a life of obscurity, to abdicate. There were strong reasons for choosing Whithorn; it was far removed from the arena of conflict; it also had special religious associations and resonances; it was a place of special sanctity and great learning; it may even have been the place where Arthur was educated as a boy, if, like many other young princes of his day, he was sent far away to school; it was also far removed from the kingdom he had ruled, which gave his successor a freer hand. There is another possible reason: that Maucennus, the prior of Whithorn, was already known to the Dumnonian elite. Charles Thomas points out that the north Cornish patronal saint Mauchan or Mawgan was none other than Maucennus, although without pursuing the point's significance.[93] The dedications indicate that in all likelihood Maucennus was a visitor, and a significant visitor at that, to north Cornwall. Given that Trigg, Arthur's kingdom, was in north Cornwall, it is likely that Arthur knew Maucennus. This gives us a tangible and specific link between Arthur and Whithorn: he very likely knew the man in charge there.

In *The Spoils of Annwn*, the bard describes how 'thither [to Avalon] after the battle of Camlann we took the wounded Arthur, guided by Barinthus to whom the waters and the stars of heaven were well known'. Geoffrey of Monmouth mentions Barinthus in his *Life of Merlin*, and makes him less of an earthly pilot, more of a Celtic Charon, an otherworldly ferryman who guides both Merlin and Taliesin to Avalon with the wounded Arthur. Barinthus, 'the Navigator', acquired a reputation in bardic literature for being an accomplished sailor who could navigate by the stars. The stories of the Brendan voyages also feature Barinthus, as St Barrind, and he was in effect Brendan's captain.[94] It may be significant that St Brendan was a younger contemporary of Arthur's, so it would have been quite possible for an accomplished navigator and sea-captain used to sailing the waters round Ireland to have been employed by both Arthur in the aftermath of Camlann in the late 530s and Brendan ten years later in the 540s and 550s. Arthur may have commissioned an Irish flotilla to stand by in the Mawddach estuary to rescue his men from enemy territory if the fighting went against them. Men like Barinthus would have been indispensable in undertakings like these. It seems probable that Barinthus was a real, flesh-and-blood seafarer, navigator and pilot.

Barinthus took Arthur west (the traditional direction of Avalon) to round the Lleyn Peninsula, north along the west coast of Holy Island and Anglesey, the home territory of his enemy Maelgwn, then north through the centre of the Irish Sea. Reaching the Isle of Man, Barinthus probably followed the more sheltered east coast of the island to the Point of Ayre, then navigated through open water due north, crossing the *Merin Rheged*, the British name for the Solway Firth,[95] finally reaching the little fortified harbour of Whithorn after a journey of some 300 kilometres. From there Arthur was carried along the short road that still, as a field path, leads over low undulating terrain to the Magnum Monasterium, the Great Monastery of Rosnat.[96]

We can imagine the mixed feelings of the Whithorn monks when they saw Arthur alive but wounded: the excitement they must have felt at seeing the high king whom, until now, they had probably only heard about in songs and stories chanted to the accompaniment of the plangent cithara, mixed with sadness at the sight of the great warrior stricken and brought low. There was nothing sadder than an ex-king beginning an exile. He would have been formally welcomed by the abbot, at that time either Maucennus or Mugentius, possibly also by the local sub-king, a shadowy figure who may have been called Mermin.[97] After what were probably low-key and perfunctory greetings, Arthur would have been taken in to have his wounds tended. Whether he died shortly after arrival or recovered from his battle wounds is not known, but even if he recovered he remained out of sight, thereafter leading a life of religious seclusion. As mentioned earlier, Geoffrey gives 542 as the date of Arthur's death. In the *Brut of England* Arthur is said to have died in Avalon in 546.[98] Chapter 88 of the *Brut* concludes with some dates that have important implications;

> *Arthure was born to Auyoun pe xxij zere of his regne. After pe Incarnacions of oure lorde Ihesu Crist v.C and xlvi zere.*
> Arthur was carried to Avalon in the twenty-second year of his reign. After the Incarnation of our lord Jesus Christ, 546 years.

If we take his 'reign' to mean his reign as overking, it is likely that that was inaugurated in or around the year of Badon, 516. A reign of twenty-two years would take us to 538, very close to the 537 or 539 given for the battle of Camlann in the *Welsh Annals*. The second sentence in the *Brut* extract may be ambiguous simply because its compiler assumed that Arthur died at or immediately after Camlann. Nevertheless, the discrepancy between, on the one hand, the date of 538 implied for Camlann and the formal end of Arthur's reign and, on the other hand, the date of 546 for his death in Avalon *in the same text* can now be explained. It is possible that Arthur made a recovery and lived on in retirement for five or even nine years, just like several other dark age British kings. It is also possible that by the time he died and was buried in the graveyard at Whithorn he had, as far as the people of Wales and Dumnonia were concerned, already long before entered the worlds of history, fable and myth.

If Arthur was spirited away to Whithorn in this fashion, it is not surprising that in Cornwall and Brittany there was bewilderment about his disappearance. When would he return? It is easy to see how this circumstance could turn Arthur into a Christ-like figure. He was already seen as a saviour, rescuing the British from the Saxons. He was

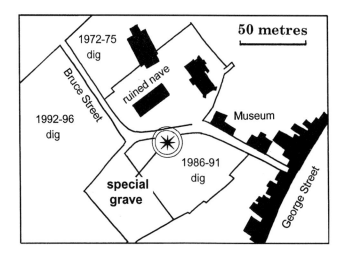

Figure 7.7 Special grave: location

betrayed on the battlefield by someone who ought to have been a loyal ally, a Judas Iscariot; the uncertainties surrounding his death and the prospect of his second coming completed this cycle of ideas. Arthur nevertheless did die, and it is possible that his grave is somewhere among the large number of graves at Whithorn. I have outlined the arguments in favour of the initial 'special grave' being a temporary resting place for Arthur. For those, like me, who want to see the exact spot, its site is 7 metres to the south of the mid-point of the section of Bruce Street that runs along the south side of the ruined church (see Figure 7.7); it was covered in the eighteenth century by a west wing extension to the manse, which has also now disappeared. Even if this was Arthur's initial grave, it was not his final resting-place, which remains to be discovered.

If we have difficulty in identifying Arthur's grave, we may already have his funeral ode. '*Marwnad Uthyr Pendragon*' ('The Funeral Ode to the Wonderful Pendragon')[99] has for long been seen as either a medieval fake or the funeral ode written for Arthur's father Uther.[100] Given that '*uter*' can be an adjective meaning 'terrible' or 'wonderful' and that '*pendragon*' may be a Celtic synonym for *dux bellorum* or high king, the dedication is more open-ended. If it really is an ode for the wonderful high king, it could as easily have been for Arthur as for his father. On top of that, Arthur is actually named in line 14.

The longing and lamentation of the multitude
Are unceasing throughout the host.   2
They earnestly yearn for the joyful prize of blue enamel.
There your stone with your name became a riddle.   4
They also wish for their Prince.
All around appears the rule of order at the head of the feast.   6
They seek to dress the head of the feast with black.
They unendingly shed blood among the war-bands,   8

Longing for you to defend them and give them succour.
At the vanishing of Caesar's kinsman   10
They will shout in blood and anger.
The sword that was in the van in taming the brothers of Caw of the Wall.   12
They crave with longing for a portion of your cause
And for refuge in the manliness of Arthur.   14
They long for your coming in a hundred fortresses.
A hundred manors long for your assurances.   16
They long for you in a hundred schools.
A hundred chieftains long for your coming: 18
The great and mighty sword that supported them.
They look for your best judgements of merit,   20
The restoration of principalities.
Your sayings are remembered, soothing the aggressive,   22
Not without faith or the yelling of your offspring.
The eloquence of the bards is not great enough: 24
Toiling for weeks with the eagerness of beavers,
With the names of men and war-bands to compare you.   26
With determination to spread the jewel of your order through the four
   quarters of mankind,
Climbing to Heaven with hunger for you.   28
Above the eagles, above the fear of disorder,
I am the one who is with the great Warrior.   30
I am the bard, the bagpiper. I am with the Creator;
Seventy musicians create the great rhapsody of the first power . . .

The Leader of Heaven has left the nation without a roof.   40

The ode is full of reflections of various aspects of Arthur's life and death. Line 15 gives us the idea of itineration in poetic form: the king had been accustomed to travel regularly from fortress to fortress, and now his visitations were missed. In line 4 we see that Arthur's gravestone has already become an enigma; this may be because the ode was written by a bard in Cornwall who had no knowledge of Arthur's grave at Whithorn. A gravestone would not in any event be raised immediately, and that may suggest that the ode was not composed in the first few days after the king's death. The design of the special grave reflects uncertainty at Whithorn about the final arrangements for a grave and, as a temporary structure, it was probably not inscribed in any way. Line 8 confirms what Gildas tells us, that the civil war among the Celtic war-bands went on, possibly flaring up after the king's death. Lines 9, 14 and 40 show that Arthur was seen as the defender of his people and that without him they were left dangerously unprotected. Line 10 gives us Arthur as 'Caesar's kinsman'. Like Ambrosius before him, he was seen as the inheritor of the imperial mantle, the conservator of the best Roman values. It also tells us that Arthur vanished.

'The joyful prize of blue enamel' in line 3 shows that objects decorated with enamel were very expensive objects conferring high status on their owners. Enamelled objects were made and prized by the Anglo-Saxons – they buried them with their kings, as we know from the Sutton Hoo ship burial, but they were also made earlier, by Britons in both Ireland and Scotland. The 'English' enamelling of the later sixth century was distinctive in style and the technique may have been local, learnt from the indigenous Britons, so the reference to enamel in the poem could be consistent with a mid-sixth century date.[101] In the second half of the sixth century, Taliesin wrote of 'Urien's retinue, all iron-grey, enamel-blue'.[102] Almost exactly the same line crops up in another poem, The *Spoils of Taliesin*, where the retinue is once again 'all iron-grey, enamel-blue'. Taliesin associated the king's war-band with the grey of steel armour and weaponry and the blue of enamel, which was presumably used to pick out decorative detail. Probably only the war-bands of kings were allowed to wear enamel.

Later, the sword would come to symbolize Arthur's kingship, yet already in lines 11 and 19 of this early poem Arthur is personified by his sword. In several lines we hear of the general and unceasing longing for Arthur; this insatiable yearning for the king and his lost glory is again a feature that we might have supposed grew into the legend much later, and yet it seems to have been there from the very beginning. Lines 14–15 are more startling still, in that they confirm that the combination of Arthur's disappearance and the great love and need felt for him led to an expectation that he would one day return. This feeling is relatively common when a family member goes missing: those closest to the missing person are unable to accept the loss as final, and part of them at any rate continues to wait for ever for the loved one to return.

Line 12 offers what seems to be an opportunity to date the subject of the poem. Whoever was being honoured was a contemporary of the brothers of Caw of the Wall. Who was Caw of the Wall? In the *Life of St Cadoc*, there is a figure known as Caw and he lived in southern Scotland, not far to the north of Hadrian's Wall. Gildas is reported, in the ninth-century *Life of Gildas*, to be the son of 'Caunus', a name that was probably a misreading or mis-hearing of Cauus, the Latin form of Caw, who had four sons besides Gildas. Although the brothers of Caw of the Wall are not named, one of his sons is mentioned in the *Dream of Rhonabwy*; Arthur is described as sitting between bishop Bedwin and Gwarthegydd, son of Caw. Gwarthegydd and Gildas were younger contemporaries of Arthur, so Caw and his brothers were older contemporaries. Consistent with this is the story in *Culhwch and Olwen* in which Arthur kills the chief boar with the help of Caw of Prydain.[103] Caw became a great hero in Welsh tradition, and it is clear from all this that Caw of the Wall could easily have been a contemporary of Arthur.

Another reference to Caw transports him to Gwynedd, into the very area where Arthur rode into the fatal trap at Camlann. A stone inscription from Llanfor, near Caer Gai, reads 'Cavo[s] Seniargii [filius]', 'Caw, son of Seniargius'. Another inscription from Caer Gai itself gives us the sixth-century name of the old Roman fortlet: 'Hic iacet Salvianus Burgo Cavi, filius Cupetiani'. In the time of Arthur, Caer Gai was actually named after Caw – 'Caw's Fort' – and Salvianus seems to have succeeded Caw as its lord. A nephew rather than a brother of Salvianus, Barrectus, held the Roman fort on Sarn Helen, Tomen-y-Mur. The family of this Caw evidently held key positions in the area of southern Gwynedd where Arthur was ambushed. It is not possible to tell on which side the sons or legatees of Caw fought; possibly they conspired to betray Arthur in revenge for 'taming the brothers of Caw'.

The detail and the cumulative effect of the poem leave no doubt that this was the Dumnonian response to the loss of Arthur. The fears implicit in it were real and justified. After Camlann, the British cause gradually disintegrated. Gildas confirms that the victor of Badon maintained order for a generation, but then power passed into the hands of regional war-lords whose violence overrode law and convention and corrupted the church. He points to an alarming phase of disorder, corruption and civil discord. In surviving fragments of letters, he says, 'cursed is he who removes the boundary stones, particularly those of his neighbour', and 'when the ship is holed, let him who can, swim'.[104]

The overall political geography of Britain changed after Camlann. Gildas discloses the beginning of a well-recognized process, the removal of central authority followed by a slide into disunity and disorder. Britain, Celtic Britain, became divided into three sub-Britains: North Britain (the Pennines and southern Scotland), Wales and the West Country. That fragmentation was accompanied by further fragmentation within those regions. The kingdom of Rheged, ruled by Cynfach in Arthur's time, split into two around 540, to form North and South Rheged, corresponding to Cumbria and Lancashire. The kingdom of York, ruled by Gurgust in Arthur's time, was partitioned into three kingdoms; York, ruled by Eliffer, The Wall, ruled by Keidyaw, and The Pennines, ruled by Pabo Post Prydain. The Wall was further split into three among Keidyaw's sons, Gwendoleu and his two brothers. The Pennines too were divided on Pabo's retirement between his sons Dunawt (Donatus), who ruled in the north, and Sawyl Benasgell (Samuel), who ruled the kingdom of Elmet in the south Pennines.

These smaller units had probably seen an earlier history as tribal territories, and what we seem to be seeing during the iron age, sub-Roman and post-Roman periods is a cyclical process of aggregation and disaggregation, centralization and decentralization, integration and devolution. Elmet was the southernmost of a chain of Brigantian territories that emerged or re-emerged after the Romans left: this was probably a return to much older, perhaps middle iron age, small territories.[105]

This splintering process weakened the Celtic fringe, and made it easier for the Saxon colonization to resume. The creeping encroachment started again. From around 550 in both Wessex and Northumbria the English advance was under way.[106] The more the Saxons encroached from the east, the more widely separated and confined the Celtic communities became. After the Battle of Dyrham in 577, the Saxons advanced steadily although still slowly. By 580 Gloucestershire had fallen and Somerset was encroached upon. Eastern Dumnonia, now Dorset, was still British, still not taken. It was partly defended by large tracts of unattractive heathland in the New Forest and east Dorset and partly defended by Bokerley Dyke,[107] which blocked the chalk downland route into Dorset. The Dyke was refurbished, probably at Ambrosius' or Arthur's orders, and the Roman road blocked off to make a major line of defence against the Saxons. Coastal attack was unappealing as the Dorset coastline was so varied that detailed local knowledge was needed to ensure a safe landfall.

When Bokerley Dyke fell in around 600 the British fell back 20 km to another line of defence, Combs Ditch, through which the Saxons appear not to have broken until about 650.[108] It was not until 658 that the West Saxons under Cenwalh invaded and took Somerset, 120 years after Camlann (see Figure 7.8). By 620, out of what is now

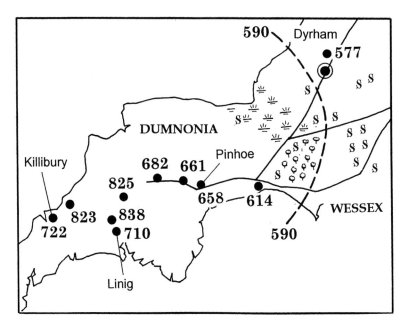

Figure 7.8 The final conquest of Dumnonia by the Saxons. Dashed line = approximate eastern frontier of Dumnonia in 590. Note key role of Roman road system, which was still in use. Date = documented battle. S = find of early Saxon material, pagan period, 577–610.
Source: After Hoskins 1960b; Blair 1977

England, only Cumbria and the South-West were still British.[109] In the north, what is now Scotland also came under attack, and Edinburgh fell to the Saxons in 638.[110]

The more immediate consequences of Arthur's retirement are easier to see. He named Constantine son of Cato, said to be a kinsman, as his successor.[111] Whether Arthur intended Constantine to be high king as well cannot be known. Probably he did: he cannot have wished to be succeeded by Maelgwn.

The rise to pre-eminence of Maelgwn is nevertheless what followed. Indeed, if Maelgwn was the foe who betrayed and defeated Arthur at Camlann, his rise was already under way, and we can see in his rise his ambition, the clearest motive for betraying and destroying Arthur. Maelgwn was seen by later generations as a 'king of Britain', on the evidence of the king lists, and from that point of view he was Arthur's successor. His military might was feared and he was remembered in northern poems as a great commander; he fought several battles against the northern Angles; his heirs prolonged his power; his son Bridei created the strongest kingdom in the north when he accepted the invitation to become king of Pictland; his son Rhun was able to march a great cavalcade of warriors unopposed through northern Britain. Like Cunedda before him, Maelgwn was accorded the British title 'Gwledic'.[112] The overkingship passed from Dumnonia, where it had been held by perhaps two Ambrosiuses, then Uther and Arthur, to Gwynedd. It was not just Arthur's kingship that was ended, but the supremacy of Dumnonia, just as the supremacy of Powys under Vortigern had earlier given way to that of Dumnonia.[113]

Maelgwn's appointment to the office of high king is described in the Welsh Laws, where it is understandably seen as applying only to Wales: perhaps it did. The Welsh aristocracy held 'an inquiry to see who should be supreme king. The place appointed was on Traeth Maelgwn at Aber Dyfi, and there came the men of Gwynedd, the men of Powys, the men of South Wales, of Reinwg, of Morgannwg and Sessllwg.' After a strange ceremony involving a floating chair and what sounds like more deception on Maelgwn's part, 'Maelgwn became supreme King with Aberffraw for his principal court and the Jarll Mathraval and the Jarll Dinevwr and the Jarll Caer Llion subject to him.' The folklore describes Maelgwn as gaining the high kingship by a trick, the creation of a waxed swan's feather throne on which he floated in the sea at the mouth of the River Dyfi, the sandbank still known as Traeth Maelgwn.[114]

How far things deteriorated in Dumnonia after Arthur's abdication is not clear. According to one later tradition,[115] the aged King Mark exploited the power vacuum when he heard that Lancelot (not an historical figure) was dead. Mark ventured forth, invading 'Logres' and destroying Joyous Gard, Lancelot's castle; he also destroyed Lancelot's tomb, Camelot and the Round Table. This may be a long way from the literal truth, but it may reflect the general picture; in the absence of a strong king of Dumnonia, sub-kings like Mark were no longer held in check and took the opportunity to settle old scores. It is easy to believe that Mark did go on a spree, wrecking cherished strongholds like Killibury and – metaphorically – destroying the Arthurian vision symbolized by Camelot. Gildas had nothing encouraging to say about Arthur's successor to the Dumnonian throne, Constantine. He accused Constantine of both sacrilege and cruel murder in dressing as an abbot, entering a church and killing two royal princes and their tutors at prayer. He also accused Constantine of parricide, which implies that he killed his father Cato.[116]

The late medieval chivalry we now associate with King Arthur and his knights was probably not the norm for behaviour in the dark ages. There is a temptation to write off the Knights of the Round Table as a complete fiction, a romantic fantasy invented by medieval troubadours, but as we saw earlier there was a practical need for that sort of male bonding when the chiefs and sub-kings from different kingdoms brought together their war-bands under the overking's command. If the war-band's overriding loyalty was to its king, the overking needed to be able to depend on the loyalty of his brother kings. Perhaps the Round Table was a partial remembrance of Arthur's relationship with the other British kings – or with the officers within his own war-band. The Geraint poem is nearly contemporary with Arthur, and speaks of 'Arthur's Men', so an heroic elite group was recognized as existing at the time. As for their names, apart from Geraint and Cador, we shall not find them in the developed medieval romance accounts.

A separate, Celtic, tradition may nevertheless have preserved their names. *Some of King Arthur's Wonderful Men* is a tenth-century document, clearly based on earlier documents that probably reach back to a dark age oral tradition.[117] The men described are larger-than-life saga heroes, some with magical abilities. Of Morfran son of Tegid it was said that no man set his weapon against him at Camlann because he was so ugly people thought him a devil. Sandde Angel-Face survived Camlann because he was so beautiful people thought him an angel. There were Sugu, son of Sugnedudd, Gwefl, son of Gwastad, Uchdryd Cross-Beard, Clust, son of Clustfeinad, Gwiawn

Cat's-Eye, Hir Erwm, Hir Atrwm, Huarwar, son of Halwn, Sol and Gwaddn Osol, Gilla Stag-Leg, Gwallgoig and the three sons of Erim, Henbeddestr, Henwas the Winged and Scilti the Light-Footed. There were Medr, son of Medredydd, who could shoot a wren at Esgeir Oerfel in Ireland from Celli Wig in Cornwall; Gwaddu of the Bonfire, whose shoes gave off sparks; Osla of the Big Knife, who could bridge a river with his magic knife; Drem son of Dremidydd, who could see Scotland from Celli Wig; Teithi the Old, whose father Gwynhan had lost his kingdom to the sea; Cynyr of the Beautiful Beard, who was thought to be Cei's father. Finally, there was Cachamwri, who was Arthur's servant.

The twenty-four names are authentic Brittonic names. They may or may not be the names of Arthur's companions. Two of the men in the list are described as being able to perform extraordinary feats at Celli Wig, which reinforces the idea of Kelly (Killibury) as Arthur's principal base. It was said to be one of the Three Excessive Plagues of Cornwall and Devon when Huarwar ate his fill. This reinforces two earlier ideas: that Arthur's kingdom comprised Cornwall and Devon (with Somerset and Dorset as well), and that such a company of men was difficult to keep adequately supplied with food. Here we catch sight of the followers and companions of Arthur, Arthur's Wonderful Men, with their huge appetites supplying one of the driving motives for itineration, war and adventure in distant parts.

Arthur himself was seen by the British, even after his abdication and disappearance, as the ultimate Rescuer, the prototype and still the stereotype of the knight in shining armour who could be relied upon to come to the aid of a community in distress. His overkingship of part of Britain only ran parallel with the overkingship of MacErca, the high king of the whole of Ireland, yet people were not in later centuries to look back wistfully to MacErca as a model. MacErca's career came to an end just one premonitory year before Arthur's final defeat at Camlann; he was drowned in wine at Cleitech by a woman called Sin.[118] In some ways, MacErca might appear to make a more significant figure than Arthur, dominating the whole island of Ireland in a way that Arthur can never have dominated the whole island of Britain.

Yet it was Arthur who was to become the model for kingship. In part it must be conceded that this was the result of a conscious effort to hold up something British to compete with the Charlemagne model that was so admired on the European mainland. Or indeed to compete with Clovis, the king of the Franks who was Arthur's contemporary, and who has over the centuries held an equivalent place in French hearts; he was adopted by the extreme right as a symbol of ultra-nationalism, and in 1996 Pope John Paul II travelled to Rheims to celebrate the 1500th anniversary of Clovis's baptism and yet, as with Arthur, relatively little is known for certain about him.

In spite of the propagandizing of Arthur – we saw the local effects of this at Glastonbury – there is still a real Arthur behind the heavily mythologized later image.

It is worth pausing to ask whether you, reading this book, really want the real Arthur, the historical Arthur. The press response to the 1998 discovery of the Arthnou Stone at Tintagel was cautious, even nervous. Dr Geoffrey Wainwright, speaking for English Heritage, affirmed that while the King Arthur of high medieval legend did not exist, the dark age warlord Arthur who fought and won battles in the sixth century did: he was an historical reality. A leader in *The Times* suggested that

Arthur is ultimately not the exclusive preserve of archaeologists; he is an important national archetype well fitted for endless embroidery and re-presentation and should, by implication, be available as a vehicle for unbridled fantasy. The *Sunday Times* voiced similar feelings; 'What a tragedy if we lost the cornucopia of Arthurian legend to a welter of data, facts and historical truth, all started off by an 8in by 14in piece of slate that was used as part of a drain.' *The Guardian* took a similar line. 'Legends like that of King Arthur often have greater power to influence us than real events . . . Maybe the myth and the man shouldn't come too close together. Sometimes truth needs to be kept at a distance – so memories can live on.' The *Daily Telegraph* decided to use heavy irony to mock the whole idea of examining the Arthurian story by rational method, urging English Heritage to return to the site without delay and predicting the imminent discovery of a stone with a curious sword-sized aperture, a round table, a sword in the bed of a dried-up mere and the Holy Grail. 'This is no time for dry as dust historical reservations. Dig, dig, dig, Dr Wainwright.'[119]

If the British press speaks with the voice of the people, then the people would rather dream their dreams than know the reality of the past. But the reservations are, I suspect and hope, a response to an unfortunate debunking trend dating from the last few decades. Reacting to the Victorian hagiographical tradition, biographers have increasingly seen it as their duty to expose, harry, denounce and belittle their subjects. With that background, a 'biography of Arthur', for which this book might be considered a sketch, might well be anticipated with trepidation. Tread softly, Yeats pleaded, for you tread on my dreams. Revisionism rules. The past has become a stamping ground for polemicists determined to project their own social and political agendas onto the lives and careers of the dead, who are doubly unfortunate in being unable to protest at the misrepresentation.

No wonder people fear what they may read concerning the matter of Arthur. His legacy as a national archetype has been one of astonishing potency, a magnificent icon of what leadership and nationhood might have been and might one day be. No wonder people fear he will emerge from behind the glittering golden legend as a minor Celtic warrior chieftain who actually achieved rather little. Yet the truth is worth hearing and seems to me no less marvellous than the legend. 'For herein may be seen', just as Malory wrote of his own version of Arthur's story, 'noble chivalry, courtesy, humanity, friendliness, hardiness, love, cowardice, murder, hate, virtue and sin.'

Geoffrey of Monmouth's vision of The King has been excessively vilified, and the picture emerging from a close inspection of the archaeological evidence and all the documents is that he has been treated unfairly. He did add fictional passages and details of his own inventing, but rather more of what he wrote is true than has hitherto been realized. The Cornish scholar John Trevisa (1342–1402) annotated the *Polychronicon*, a universal history written by Ranulph Higden in 1387. Higden in places followed William of Malmesbury in being sceptical of Geoffrey's stories about Arthur. Trevisa wrote:

> Here William telleth a maggle tale without evidence; and Ranulph's reasons, that he moveth against Arthur, should move no clerk that can know an argument, for it followeth not . . . Though Geoffrey speak of Arthur's deeds,

that other writers speak of darkly, or make of no mind, that disproveth not Geoffrey's story . . . and in the third book, chapter 9, [Higden] sayeth himself that it is no wonder though William of Malmesbury were deceived, for he had not the British book. It may well be that Arthur is oft overpraised, but so be many other. Sooth saws be never the worse though mad men tell maggle tales – and some mad men will mean that Arthur shall come again, and be afterward king here of Britain, but that is a full maggle tale, and so be many other that be told of him and others.[120]

It may seem as if we have made little progress if this 'millennial' review of the early sources and dark age sites has simply led to the same general conclusion that Sharon Turner reached in the late eighteenth century. The differences are crucial, though. One difference lies in the development of scholarship. Modern analytical techniques have been applied to the documents and more information has been squeezed out of them. Another difference is that over the last 200 years archaeology has turned up substantial quantities of new hard evidence – think of South Cadbury and Tintagel alone – evidence supporting the idea of Arthur and the sort of dark age society, economy and polity that would generate and sustain such a leader. Archaeology provides him with an entirely credible cultural setting. If, after the addition of all this new material and new analysis and interpretation, Arthur *still* appears to have existed, then the assertion that he existed has far more potency than it did before.

To turn the arguments on their head for a moment, we could ignore all the positive evidence in favour of an historical Arthur, forget him altogether, forget his name, even, and we would discover when we looked at the course of events in the fifth and sixth centuries that there was an Arthur-shaped gap between 500 and 540. There was a time when the progress of Saxon colonization in Britain not only slowed but halted, a time when the Saxons were held back by some Churchillian figure rallying, inspiring and masterminding the British resistance to the invaders. As we saw when we assembled all the evidence for the history of Britain from 420 through to 590, it is very clear where an historical Arthur – for whom there is documentary evidence – fits into it.

When the excavators of Pompeii discovered strange irregular cavities in the solidified deposits of the pyroclastic flow of AD 79, they poured plaster into them, removed the ash and other debris and found that the hardened plaster had taken the form of human beings who had been overwhelmed in 79. Our journey through dark age British history reveals something akin to this. It creates a mould round the dead figure of a great Celtic resistance leader, and this negative image can in its turn tell us something about the dimensions, muscularity and bearing of the king, what his funeral oration called 'the manliness of Arthur'.

When we compare what was happening in France it is perhaps even clearer that this figure existed. The Frankish conquest of Gaul under Clovis, the conquest that laid the foundations of the renamed kingdom of France, was far faster and smoother than the Saxon conquest of Britain. Clovis was master of nearly all of Gaul by 510. In Britain, the rally led by Ambrosius and then Arthur prevented this sort of blanket conquest from happening. For some decades the idea of a Saxon bretwaldaship went into abeyance and the Anglo-Saxon 'realm' remained splintered. Badon, Arthur's triumph, effectively atomized the Anglo-Saxon province.

Geoffrey Ashe has persuasively argued that the delay in the Anglo-Saxon colonization led to the decelerated evolution of a national monarchy in Britain, even in England, with feudal lords (the descendants of former kings and sub-kings) only partially surrendering their power to central control, and then only reluctantly and conditionally.[121] The contrast in France was very great. Clovis created a single absolute monarchy, perhaps prematurely, and it had to be repeatedly asserted as successive nobles tried to usurp the Crown's powers. The strength of the Celtic resistance to Anglo-Saxon incursion in Britain may thus have made a crucial difference in shaping a different kind of future, preparing the way for the evolution of a constitutional monarchy with circumscribed powers. Perhaps by decisively shaping the sixth century in Britain, Arthur shaped the succeeding centuries too, and in this very potent way became the Once and Future King.

THE KINGS OF POWYS

—◆—

It is possible to assemble a pedigree for the dark age kings of Powys with a fair degree of internal consistency. I have used, in chronological order, Pedigrees XXII, XXVI, XXXI and XXX from the Old Welsh genealogies. Elisse is known to have reigned between 700 and 750, and may therefore have been born around 680. Allowing 25 years per generation gives us an approximate birth date for each of the preceding kings, and gives a notional birth date of 480 for Cynan. This was the 'Cuneglasus' Gildas wrote of in around 540, when Cynan could still have been alive, aged about 60.

Pedigree XXII	Selemiaun b. 305
	Catell b. 330
	Cattegir b. 355
	Pascent b. 380
	Maucant b. 405
Pedigree XXVI	Cyngen b. 430
	Brocmail b. 455
	Cynan b. 480, the king of Powys described by Gildas
	Eliud b. 505
	Eli b. 530
	Guilauc b. 555
Pedigree XXXI	Elisse b. 580
	Brochmail b. 605
	Cadell b. 630
Pedigree XXX	Cyngen ab Cadell b. 655 = Sannan
	Elisse b. 680

Sannan, wife of Cyngen ab Cadell (who set up the Eliseg Pillar), was descended from Noe ab Arthur or Nougoy map Arthur. The Arthur from whom she claimed descent was not Arthur of Dumnonia, but a lesser, later prince of Demetia. Regrettably, there are no equivalent full genealogies for Dumnonia.

THE KINGS OF DEMETIA

———— •◆• ————

It is possible to assemble a pedigree for the kings of Demetia in the same way, using Pedigrees II, X and XII, but with less confidence, as there are more inconsistencies among the various versions. The initial third of this list is extremely suspect: Roman emperors are claimed as ancestors and some of the other names look like later inventions to fill gaps. Presumably the king Arthur in this list was named after the Dumnonian king. Aircol and Vortipor were our Arthur's contemporaries, to judge from Gildas' references, and Petr must have named his son Arthur just twenty or thirty years after Camlann.

Constantius = Helen
Constantine the Great
Constans
Pinc miffer
Stater
Eliud
Ebiud
Protecoz
Protec
Maxim Guletic
Dimet
Nimet
Cloitguin
Clotri
Triphun ('The Tribune')
Aircol
Guoztepir or *Gordebar* or *Vortipor* ('The Protector')
Cincar or Kyngar
Petr or Peder
Arthur
Nougoy or Nennue
Cloten or Eleothen
Cathen

Catgocaun or Gogaon
Regin
Teudof or Teudos
Margetiut
Tancoyfit merc Ouein
Himeyt
Loumarc
Ouein

THE ARTHNOU STONE
FROM TINTAGEL

———— ◆ • ————

On 4 July 1998, a team of archaeologists from Glasgow University led by Professor Christopher Morris discovered a broken slate plaque 35cm by 20cm, bearing a sixth-century inscription. It was found on a terrace on the upper east slope of Tintagel Island within a stratified, undisturbed sixth-century debris layer. The smooth flat surface of the stone was inscribed with a knife point with the words, 'PATER COLIAVIFICIT ARTOGNOV'. A cross hovers above the end of the word 'pater'. Charles Thomas, spacing the inscription as 'PATER COLI AVI FECIT ARTOGNOV', offers as a likely translation: 'Artognou, father of a descendant of Coll, has had this [building] made'. Artognou was probably pronounced Arthnou, and the tone and content of the inscription indicate that Arthnou was an educated nobleman.

The Morris team was re-excavating round Radford's site C, the Middle Terrace on which a neatly restored building consisting of three contiguous rooms can be seen. Immediately to the south of the southern end of the Radford building is a wall stub that is probably the northern end of another building, as yet unexplored, which may have been 4 or 5 metres wide and 10 or 15 metres long. The Arthnou slate may have been a wall plaque on this unexplored early sixth-century building: it bears part of an even earlier inscription (the letters – VAXE–) and was broken on all sides before being recycled as a drain cover in the middle or later sixth century. If funds can be raised, the Morris team wants to excavate the southern building, which may survive intact and undisturbed under the scree. The drain passed through the narrow gap between the older southern building and the newer northern building, first serving the southern and then rebuilt on a different orientation to serve the northern building.

Geoffrey Wainwright, speaking for English Heritage, described the discovery as the find of a lifetime and saw it as evidence for the historical existence of Arthur. There are two main areas of uncertainty. One is the authenticity of the inscription, and the possibility of a student hoax is a very real one. A 28-year-old shop worker from Plymouth, Andy Gillies, claims he wrote the Tintagel inscription with a pair of compasses while on a school trip in 1980, copying the letters from a book he had on King Arthur. While a forgery is possible, Mr Gillies' claim is unconvincing, partly because he would have composed this clever and subtle fake at the tender age of ten, using authentic sixth-century lettering, an unusual Latin formula and a previously unseen form of Arthur's name – if indeed it is Arthur's name. Christopher Morris dismisses Mr Gillies' claim because the slate was found beneath undisturbed layers of earth deposited in the sixth century. Suspicion that a hoax might have been perpetrated by one of Professor Morris's own archaeology students recedes when we learn that the stone was discovered by the project officer and supervisor, Kevin Brady.

The second area of uncertainty concerns the identity of Arthnou. The name Coll may suggest an Irish colonist, or at least an Irish–Welsh ancestry. On the other hand, 'Arthnou' is recorded in Brittany in 882 and may well have been a Brittonic name in general use in Brittany, Dumnonia and Wales. There were in addition several dark age princes with names that began with 'Art' or 'Arth', so this man may not be the dark age king we seek after all. On the other hand, as we have seen from the rest of the evidence, this is the right kingdom, the right royal stronghold, the right time and the right social class for Arthur.

The discovery of the 'Arthnou Stone' has had the benefit of concentrating people's attention on the central issue, which is that the accumulating evidence points to Tintagel as a very high-status royal stronghold, from which a dynasty of literate princes ruled at least part and possibly all of Dumnonia in the sixth century.[1]

NOTES

<hr>
—•—
<hr>

CHAPTER 1 'WHO THIS ARTHUR WAS'

1 For example, Padel 1994, who takes an even more extreme position, arguing that the Arthur references in the Annals are later fake entries.
2 'DRT' Anon 1876, for instance, sees the early, pre-medieval Arthur as the Sun, centre of the universe, source of light and life. He was the son of the blue heavens (ab Uthir), married to the bright waving light Guinevere (Gwen Chwyfio), and defeated by his nephew Modred (Bawd-rhudd), the fiery redness of the sunset; the round table is the zodiac, etc. Padel 1994 stands back from the detail of this interpretation, but nevertheless sees the primary, or original, Arthur as mythic and the historical fleshing-out as a later addition; this he calls the 'historicizing' of Arthur.
3 Dickinson 1900, p. 3. The Rillaton cup passed into the royal collection at Osborne later in the nineteenth century, then it disappeared. It was found after George V's death that he had been using it as a toothmug; presumably he took it from Osborne.
4 Rowse 1943; McLynn 1996, p. 392.
5 Clark 1859.
6 Hartshorne 1848, p. 222.
7 John Lydgate (1370–1451) *Fall of Princes*.
8 Jackson 1949.
9 Ashe 1968; Alcock 1971.
10 Rahtz 1993.
11 Higham 1994, p. 211.
12 Padel 1994.
13 Padel 1994, pp. 23, 94.
14 Padel 1994, p. 19.
15 Padel 1994, p. 24 admits in any case that he cannot put a date to this 'historicizing' process.
16 Padel 1994, p. 31.
17 Laing and Laing 1979a, pp. 127–31.
18 The most recent and powerful advocate of this view is Oliver Padel 1994.

CHAPTER 2 THE DOCUMENTS

1 Morris 1995b (AS Vol. 3).
2 Dark age Dumnonia included present-day Cornwall, Devon, Dorset and parts of Somerset

and Wiltshire. The dark age kingdom of Powys included the modern Welsh county, i.e. east mid-Wales, and the border country.

3 Germanus had Lupus bishop of Troyes, a man about ten years his junior, at his side during the action.

4 Morris 1993, p. 62. In this chapter and elsewhere, I use the word 'Saxon' in a very loose way, to refer to Germanic immigrants whether Angles, Saxons or Jutes. I apologize if that offends purists but the British, who are the focus in this book, seem to have made no distinction. The 'Saxons' for their part lumped all the indigenous people together as 'Welsh'.

5 Certainly, the focus of detail on Vortigern strongly suggests that Germanus had direct dealings with his court.

6 Morris 1995b (AS Vol. 3).

7 Morris 1993, p. 346.

8 Alcock 1971, pp. 240–1.

9 Thomas 1971, p. 111.

10 Compare 'Uncle Joe' Stalin and 'Papa Doc' Duvalier.

11 Radford 1983.

12 Thomas 1971; Davis 1982.

13 Morris 1993, p. 143.

14 Morris 1993, p. 145.

15 Bassett 1989.

16 Though at this early period it may be more appropriate to attribute twenty-five years.

17 Alcock 1971, p. 43.

18 Jesus College MS Pedigrees.

19 Alcock 1971, pp. 125–7.

20 Barber and Pykitt 1993, p. 203. In the genealogies quoted, I have italicized the names of people who are likely to have been alive at the same time as Arthur, taking his putative lifespan as 475–537.

21 Morris 1995d (AS Vol. 5), p. 17, No. II.

22 Morris 1995d, (AS Vol. 5).

23 Dumnonia (pronounced 'Doom-*no*-nia') was the dark age kingdom that comprised Cornwall, Devon, Dorset and part of Somerset.

24 Penarth Manuscript No. 27, part II.

25 Harleian MS 3859, folios 174–98.

26 Alcock 1971, p. 35.

27 Jackson 1963.

28 Chadwick 1976, pp. 112–16.

29 Chadwick 1976, p. 118.

30 Alcock 1971, p. 48.

31 Although it is possible that he meant something else.

32 For example, Jones 1964.

33 Perversely, some extend the 'false entry' argument to entries, like the Camlann entry, which are 'deceptively typical in form': these too are deemed suspect! See, for instance, Thomas Charles-Edwards 1991, p. 28. This style of argument obviously leads nowhere.

34 Helmut Nickel in Lacy 1986, pp. 12–13.

35 Chadwick 1976, pp. 110–12.

36 Vaughan 1884, based on Harley 4181, etc.

37 Dickinson 1900, p. 13.

38 Chadwick 1976, p. 104.

39 Dickinson 1900, pp. 14–15.

40 Chadwick 1976, pp. 105–8.
41 Padel 1994, pp. 13–14. The line is line 1241 in *Canu Aneirin*; the warrior's name was Gwawrddur.
42 Garmonsway 1953, pp. xxxi–xxxiv.
43 Bede, Book XVI.
44 Burkitt and Burkitt 1990.
45 Ashe 1968, p. 63.
46 Miller 1979, p. 116.
47 Dickinson 1900, p. 20.
48 Dickinson 1900, p. 19.
49 Jackson 1963.
50 Oman 1924, p. 212.
51 See Alcock 1995, p. 149.
52 Gildas, *The Ruin of Britain*, section 26.
53 Thompson 1979.
54 Williams 1899.
55 Thompson 1979.
56 Dark 1994 gives arguments in favour of a Dorset vantage point for Gildas.
57 Roberts in Bromwich *et al.* 1991, p. 98.
58 For example, Alcock 1971, p. 249: 'the remains are unequivocally those of a Celtic monastery'.
59 Piggott 1941; Ashe 1981, pp. 301–3.
60 That is, not used for inhumation burials except for two or three special cases widely separated in time, like the archer buried in the ditch in 2200 BC.
61 The disastrous fire at Glastonbury Abbey in 1184, for instance, is known to have been responsible for the loss of many manuscripts.
62 Jenkins 1990, p. 63; Ellis 1993, p. 67.
63 Dickinson 1900, p. vii.
64 Chadwick, in Jackson 1963, p. 6.
65 Roberts 1991, pp. 82–3.
66 Dickinson 1900, p. 49 rightly and neatly describes Geoffrey as 'a writer who sometimes finds the corroboration which he always needs'.
67 Geoffrey 1966, p. 175.
68 Geoffrey 1966, p. 18: Lewis Thorpe's Introduction.
69 Castleden 1993, pp. 112–22.
70 *De Miraculis S. Mariae Laudunensis*, quoted by Tatlock 1933.
71 Probably a confusion of several names – Dumnonia, Devon, Exeter – according to Pearce 1978.
72 Chambers 1927, p. 184; Tatlock 1933. Even Padel 1994 accepts that the story of the Laon canons confirms that belief in Arthur's immortality was strong in the Bodmin area in 1113, well before Geoffrey of Monmouth wrote his book. Padel also concedes that such beliefs could not have developed overnight.
73 Tatlock 1933.
74 Thorpe 1966, p. 19.
75 Barber and Pykitt 1993, p. 42, though other modern scholars argue that the form 'x – mab – y' elsewhere in the same text clearly means 'x, son of y', so there is a *prima facie* case for seeing Uther as Arthur's father. The argument is unresolved.

CHAPTER 3 THE ARCHAEOLOGY

1 See Chapter 4 for discussion of the location of Badon.
2 Arnold 1984.
3 Thomas 1963.
4 Fowler and Thomas 1962.
5 Smith 1987.
6 Rose and Preston-James 1995.
7 For example, Arnold 1984, pp. 37–40.
8 1984, p. 161.
9 Cleary 1995, p. 12.
10 Anon 1985.
11 Tatton-Brown and Macpherson-Grant 1985.
12 Anon 1992a.
13 Quinnell 1986.
14 Thomas 1964.
15 Dark 1992.
16 Laing and Laing 1993, p. 97.
17 Alcock 1971, p. 267.
18 Curle 1914.
19 Anon 1992b.
20 Henderson 1967, pp. 46–7.
21 Bullock in Meldrum 1971, pp. 37–49.
22 McCarthy *et al.* 1990.
23 Dark 1994.
24 Burgess 1980.
25 Alcock 1971, p. 214.
26 Alcock 1971, p. 199.
27 Alcock 1971, p. 206.
28 Anon 1912, p. 150.
29 Alcock 1971, pp. 358–9.
30 Alcock 1971, p. 215.
31 Alcock 1971, pp. 358–9.
32 Compare Phillips and Keatman 1992, p. 109.
33 Alcock 1971, p. 318.
34 In this respect, South Cadbury emerged as significantly different in being a very large dark age enclosure: Alcock 1971, p. 348.
35 Phillips and Keatman 1992, p. 139; Barker 1981.
36 Phillips and Keatman 1992, p. 141; Barker 1981; Barker 1990.
37 Dark's stage 2 to stage 3; Dark 1994, pp. 23–4.
38 Dark 1994, p. 165.
39 Garrod and Heighway 1984.
40 1976, pp. 167–8.
41 McWhirr 1976, p. 42.
42 Atkin 1992.
43 Savile 1984, p. 229.
44 Interestingly, though, Bath's name was not conserved. The Saxons renamed the city Acemannesceater, which only changed back to Bath in 676. Dobson 1931, p. 163.
45 Leech 1981, p. 17.
46 Reece and Catling 1975, p. 9.

47 McWhirr 1976, p. 15.

48 Dobson 1931, p. 161 actually states, 'When the Roman legions left Britain, they left a sinking ship.'

49 McWhirr 1976, p. 16.

50 McWhirr 1976, p. 17; Gerrard 1994, pp. 87–8.

51 Preston-Jones and Rose 1986.

52 Dark 1994, p. 199.

53 Alcock 1972, p. 172.

54 Aston and Burrow 1982.

55 Alcock 1995, p. 40 says Cadbury 11 must have been raised by the immediate forerunner of the kings criticized by Gildas, but Constantine's immediate predecessor was Arthur, and elsewhere Alcock argues that it was Ambrosius who refurbished Cadbury; in reality, the dating evidence is not precise enough to allow us to choose between Ambrosius and Arthur as the organizer of the refortification.

56 Alcock 1995.

57 Alcock 1972, p. 176.

58 Alcock 1972, pp. 176–7.

59 Fox and Ravenhill 1972.

60 Data from Alcock 1995.

61 1995, p. 180.

62 Arnold 1984.

63 Alcock 1995.

64 Aston and Burrow 1982.

65 Aston and Burrow 1982.

66 Arnold 1984.

67 Carr 1989. The Mound was destroyed in 1972 prior to the industrial development of the site.

68 Ashe 1968, pp. 114–18.

69 Ashe 1968, p. 121.

70 Thomas 1993, p. 84.

71 The granite waymark is now in a Trethevy market garden; the slate slab is on view in the south transept of Tintagel church.

72 Thomas 1993, pp. 82–3.

73 Thomas 1993, p. 61: no pottery has been found from the intervening centuries.

74 Dickinson 1900, pp. 51–66.

75 Thomas 1989, pp. 49–60, 61–6. Hardy was an architect by profession, so it is surprising that this drawing is so poor.

76 Geoffrey 1966, pp. 182–3.

77 The 'narrow isthmus' reference may more naturally be related to the knife-edged ridge that used to connect the Island to the mainland, and which has since collapsed into the sea. If so, the reference cannot be used as any kind of evidence of date for the vallum.

78 Thomas 1989, p. 55.

79 Thomas 1989, p. 56.

80 Harry and Morris 1994.

81 Thomas 1993, p. 69.

82 Thomas 1993.

83 Aston and Burrow 1982.

84 Thomas 1993, pp. 69–71.

85 Thomas 1957.

86 Thomas 1993, p. 85.

87 Thomas 1993, pp. 87–92.

88 Thomas 1993, pp. 70–1.

89 Thomas 1993, p. 90.

90 The name Iron Gate may be a mistranslation from Cornish. 'Iron' is 'horn' in Cornish. The original name of the site is likely to have been Porth Hawn, or 'Haven Landing Place': see Thomas 1993, p. 43.

91 Round houses: e.g. the 4m diameter huts at Gwithian, dating to the sixth–eighth centuries, each with a hearth, Preston-Jones and Rose 1986.

92 Of the Tunnel and the Island's summit, the crag overlooking the southern cliffs, with Arthur's Footprint and Cups and saucers, there will be more discussion in Chapter 6. For a fuller discussion of the so-called 'Arthur Stone', see Appendix C.

93 Thomas 1993, p. 102.

94 Nowakowski and Thomas 1992.

95 Thomas 1993, p. 105.

96 It has also been suggested that henbane seed may have been taken to the cemetery to be smoked to induce hallucinations. See Nowakowski and Thomas 1992, p. 8.

97 Thomas 1993, pp. 109–10.

98 Thomas 1988, p. 89.

99 Thomas 1964.

100 Alcock 1995, p. 152.

101 Radford and Swanton 1975, pp. 25–8.

102 Quinnell and Harris 1985.

103 Rahtz 1971.

104 This is suggested by Quinnell and Harris (1985).

105 Dyer 1973, pp. 37–8.

106 See Chapter 6.

CHAPTER 4 ARTHUR'S BRITAIN

1 Diodorus Siculus V. 21.

2 Jackson 1963, p. 11.

3 Cleary 1995, p. 22.

4 Morris 1993, p. 441.

5 Alcock 1971, p. 325.

6 Laing and Laing 1979a.

7 Alcock 1971, p. 272.

8 Morris 1993, pp. 458, 486; Alcock 1971, p. 324.

9 Morris 1993, p. 486.

10 Jackson 1963.

11 Hood 1978, pp. 55–9.

12 Chadwick 1976, p. 67.

13 Sutherland 1994, p. 50.

14 Sutherland 1994, pp. 220–1. The stone is from Meigle monastery.

15 Taliesin *Gwallwag is other.*

16 Morris 1993, pp. 162, 450.

17 See Higham 1986.

18 Morris 1993, pp. 76, 137, 211–12.

19 Morris 1995b (AS Vol. 3), p. 172.

20 Ellis 1993, p. 31.

21 Morris 1995b (AS Vol. 3), p. 79.

22 Morris 1993, pp. 75–80.

23 In the *Tale of Emrys*, in Nennius XLIV. See Winterbottom 1978.

24 Ellis 1993, p. 39.

25 Morris 1995b (AS Vol. 3), p. 155.

26 'Argoed Calchvynydd rhwng Trenn ag Afon Tain' in a Welsh list of the principal territories of Britain is translated as 'the Land of Limestone Hills between the Trent and the River Thames'. Davis (1982) argues that this is the Chilterns, but the Cotswold region suits the description just as well, and the dark age name of this latter area, the former territory of the Dobunni, is not otherwise known. Davis' case for the Chilterns as a British enclave is founded on a lack of evidence of Anglo-Saxon occupation; there seems to be no positive evidence for British occupation in the sixth century.

27 Myres 1986, pp. 212–13.

28 Ashe in Lacy 1986, p. 5.

29 In *Cartularium Saxonicum* ed. w. de G. Birch No. 553.

30 Dark 1994, pp. 134–5.

31 Ellis 1993, p. 40.

32 Morris 1993 thinks 475 was the beginning of Arthur's military career, but this is really too early from him to have fought at Camlann in 537. Although there must be continuing uncertainty about the exact date of Arthur's birth, it is pragmatic for the clear development of the thesis I am advancing to work from a specific putative date; it should always be remembered that this is only a 'best-fit' estimate, not a fact.

33 Myres 1986, p. 137.

34 Morris 1995b (AS Vol. 3), p. 154.

35 Morris 1993, p. 356.

36 The name Merchiaun seems to be a British form of 'Marcianus', the name of the Roman emperor who ruled 450–7; *two* British kings were born in around 450 and named after the emperor; see Chadwick 1976.

37 Morris 1995b (AS Vol. 3), pp. 80–1.

38 Morris 1995b (AS Vol. 3).

39 Morris 1993, p. 361.

40 Morris 1995b (AS Vol. 3), p. 122.

41 Morris 1993, p. 366.

42 This supports the idea that Mark ruled lands in Cornwall and Brittany, and possibly the Channel Islands too.

43 Thomas 1993, p. 102.

44 That Lundy was on the dark age map is shown by the presence on the island of fifth- or sixth-century inscribed memorial stones: Chadwick 1976, pp. 40–1. Lundy may have been an island retreat for religious fanatics or a refuge for travellers making the dangerous crossing of the Severn Sea.

45 Morris 1995c (AS Vol. 4), pp. 91–2 mentions 'St Martha's' church, Guildford which is a rare survival of 'Martyrium' in the English lowlands, at a place that appears to be an ancient pre-Christian cult site; no other church in England is dedicated to St Martha, which strongly suggests that that was not the original intention. The strange conical hill on which the church stands was actually known as Martyr Hill in the middle ages.

46 Morris 1995e (AS Vol. 6), p. 77.

47 Morris 1993, pp. 104–6.

48 Morris 1995e (AS Vol. 6), p. 77.

49 Jesus College genealogy.

50 Sims-Williams 1991, p. 47.

51 Blackett and Wilson 1986, p. 90.

52 Ellis 1993, p. 47.

53 Myres 1986, p. 147.

54 Myres 1986, pp. 148–9.

55 Morris 1993, pp. 112–13.

56 Padel 1994, p. 17. Cotton Vitellius A.vi in the British Library. The copy was fire-damaged in 1731 but is still legible.

57 David Dumville, another Arthur sceptic, differs from Padel in conceding that 'Ambrosius had ceased to lead or rule before Mount Badon' (Dumville in Lapidge and Dumville 1984, pp. 75–8). Padel's insistence on Ambrosius commanding at Badon would appear to be rooted in a determination to undermine the authority of the Arthurian battle list.

58 Some believe Ambrosius was killed at Badon and that the command passed over to Arthur during the battle, but it seems far more likely that, as tradition has it, Ambrosius had been dead for several years.

59 Myres 1986, pp. 158–60.

60 Burkitt and Burkitt 1990.

61 Burkitt and Burkitt 1990. *A Fool's Bolt soon shott at Stonage* probably by Robert Gay is a whimsical and sarcastic piece, but its several references equating Bath and Badon suggests that the identification was felt to have been established at the time of writing, almost certainly the 1660s; see Legg 1986.

62 Major and Burrow 1926.

63 Williams 1899.

64 Morris 1993, pp. 136, 286–91. Morris cites the historian Procopius and the distribution of place-names as his evidence.

65 Myres 1986, p. 154.

66 Chadwick 1976, p. 68.

67 Phillips and Keatman 1992, p. 62.

68 Lloyd 1872.

69 Morris 1980 p. 62.

70 Williams 1899.

71 Morris 1993, p. 225.

72 Taylor 1970.

73 Morris 1993, p. 226.

74 Davis 1982.

75 Myres 1986, p. 169.

76 Wacher 1974, p. 314.

77 Myres 1986, p. 168.

78 Ellis 1993, p. 84.

79 Source: Llandaff and Llancarfan texts and Welsh genealogies; this episode is very well documented. See Morris 1993, p. 228.

80 Myres 1986, p. 169.

81 Ellis 1993, p. 84.

82 Morris 1993, p. 229.

83 Morris 1993, pp. 123–4.

84 Morris 1993, p. 215.

85 Chadwick 1976, p. 68.

86 Morris 1993, p. 124.

87 Chadwick 1976, pp. 89–90.

88 Rhun lived on until 586, when he was succeeded by his son Beli, who in turn died in 599, to be succeeded by his son Iago who was assassinated by Cadafael Wyllt in 603; see Lloyd 1872.

89 Tigernach Annals: 'Flight of the Scottishmen before Bruide son of Maelchon, king of the Picts'. *Irish Annals*: '559, Expedition by the son of Maelchon'. See Chadwick 1976.
90 Morris 1993, p. 217.
91 Morris 1993, p. 217.
92 Lloyd 1872.
93 Gruffydd 1994.
94 Bernicia had been the British kingdom of Byrnaich in the fifth century. Anglian colonization under Ossa began about 500; Gruffydd 1994.
95 Triad 84.
96 Chadwick 1976.
97 Tolstoy 1985, pp. 82–7.
98 Copy of Domesday Book fly leaf: Tolstoy 1985, p. 67.
99 Chadwick 1976, pp. 82–3.
100 Anon. 'DRT' 1876.
101 Morris 1980 (AS Vol. 8), p. 63, quoting *Historia Brittonum: Kings of the Bernicians*; Chadwick 1976, p. 102.
102 Morris 1993, p. 232.

CHAPTER 5 THE MAN, THE KING AND THE KINGDOM

1 In this I part company from John Morris, who puts Badon at 495 and Camlann at 515 (Morris 1993, p. 513). Further confusion is created by the Breton *Chronicle of Mont St Michel*, which records that Arthur was king of Britain in 421, which is obviously far too early.
2 Alcock 1971, p. 359.
3 Ashe 1957, p. 74.
4 Morris 1980 (AS Vol. 8), p. 56, *De Arturo*.
5 Rhys 1891.
6 Chadwick 1976, p. 66.
7 Chadwick 1976.
8 Lee 1876.
9 Anon 1851.
10 Geoffrey 1966, p. 189.
11 Morris 1995e (AS Vol. 6), p. 169.
12 Alcock 1971, p. 101.
13 Gibson, in Arnold and Gibson 1995, p. 276.
14 Alcock 1995.
15 Chadwick 1976, p. 88.
16 Nennius.
17 Padel 1994, p. 7.
18 The tradition that Arthur was educated as a small boy by Merlin is paralleled by the foundation-history of Brycheiniog, in which King Brychan was brought up between the ages of 4 and 11 by a sage. There are several parallels between the lives of these two kings, and they suggest to me that both were conforming to a norm for dark age kingship.
19 Every king needed the loyalty of his war-band. Taliesin said of Gwallawg, king of Elmet, 'Your retinue loves you, ferocious man.'
20 Morris 1995c (AS Vol. 3), pp. 80–1.
21 The Welsh romance *Geraint and Enid* is no help in telling us about the historical Geraint. It was written in the thirteenth century and was plagiarized from Chrétien's *Erec et Enide*, with the hero renamed after a well-known Dumnonian king.

22 Probably in the same spirit of bitter sarcasm in which the Duke and Duchess of Windsor referred to the Queen, behind her back of course, as 'Shirley Temple' (Bradford 1996).

23 Compare modern Cornish *cun* = dogs; *glas* = pale.

24 *Life of St Arthmael.*

25 Taliesin, *To Cynan Garwyn.*

26 The name Theodoric was in use elsewhere too; Ida, king of the Bernicians, called one of his twelve sons Theodoric: see Nennius, *Northern History*, Morris 1980 (AS Vol. 8).

27 Morris 1993, pp. 130–2.

28 Jesus College list LI.

29 Lacy 1986, pp. 25–7.

30 Wakeman 1850, p. 208.

31 Jesus College LI.

32 That is, the laws of the Jarlls Dirlevwr, Mathravall and Caer Llion.

33 Dark 1992.

34 Oman 1924, p. 212.

35 Blair 1977, p. 30.

36 Padel 1994, p. 24.

37 Oman 1924, p. 211.

38 Bromwich *et al.* 1991, p. 5.

39 Although Tigernach gives the date of Arthur's death as 596: see Rees 1898.

40 *Irish Annals.*

41 Jesus College III.

42 Ffoulkes 1850, quoting Ritson's *History of King Arthur*, p. 77.

43 Ashe 1957, p. 83. This Constantine Goreu is the same man as the Constantine Arthur named as his successor.

44 Ashe 1957, p. 84.

45 Phillips and Keatman 1992.

46 Goodrich 1986.

47 Bryce 1988.

48 Blackett and Wilson 1986.

49 Blackett and Wilson 1986, p. 68.

50 Blackett and Wilson 1986, p. 176.

51 Barber and Pykitt 1993.

52 Pieced together from *Lives* of St Arthmael, Paul Aurelian and Samson.

53 For example, Ashe 1957.

54 Ashe 1957, p. 79. Ashe argues that it was Arthur who contained the South Saxons in East Sussex, that the colonization of Hampshire was the Saxon response to this blocking manoeuvre, and that it was in this campaign that Arthur first distinguished himself. While this is an intriguing piece of hypothetical strategy – and biography – I know of no reliable source or even indirect evidence that has Arthur fighting (specifically) in Sussex.

55 Ashe 1957, pp. 92–3.

56 Thomas 1994, p. 212.

57 Thomas 1994, p. 214.

58 'Trigg' was first recorded in the seventh century *Life of St Samson*. In King Alfred's will, the area is called 'Tricorshire'.

59 Dickinson 1900, p. 6.

60 Folktale reported in Snell 1926; see Seddon 1990.

61 Rose 1992.

62 Dickinson 1900, p. 36: he gives the nineteenth-century name of the barrow as Cadon. The

Cynddylan elegy is in the Llywarch Hen collection, but was probably written by Cynddylan's bard (Morris 1993, pp. 241–2).

63 Morris 1993, p. 429.

64 Dark 1994, p. 92.

65 Morris 1993, p. 225. The existence of petty kings in the sixth century is borne out by a line in Taliesin's *The Conciliation of Urien*: 'I will not go to the half-kings of the north.'

66 Fox and Ravenhill 1968.

67 Fox 1973.

68 Morris 1993, p. 220. Cunedda, Ambrosius, Arthur, Maelgwn, Rhun, Urien, Dyfnwal and Rhydderch were all referred to as 'gwledics'.

69 Preston-Jones and Rose 1986.

70 Preston-Jones and Rose 1986, p. 137.

71 Dickinson 1900, pp. 74–7, though Dickinson can surely not be correct in identifying Cardinham as Ceretigan, which is Cardigan. In size and form, the site may have been the fortified residence of a sixth-century chief.

72 Miles and Miles 1973.

73 Morris 1995b (AS Vol. 3), p. 168.

74 Morris 1995e (AS Vol. 6), p. 131.

75 Thomas 1957.

76 Johnson 1980.

77 Alcock 1995, pp. 144–5.

78 Salvatore and Knight 1991.

79 Alcock 1995, pp. 145–6.

80 Griffiths 1972, p. 4.

81 Hoskins 1960, pp. 11–12.

82 Griffiths and Bidwell 1973, p. 17.

83 Griffiths 1972; Cooper 1990.

84 Bidwell 1980.

85 Cooper 1990, p. 24.

86 Cooper 1990, p. 24.

87 Griffiths and Bidwell 1973, p. 17; Hoskins 1960, pp. 11–12.

88 Hoskins 1960, pp. 11–12.

89 Fox 1973.

90 *The Life of Cernach* or Carantoc is in the British Library: Cotton MSS Vespasian A.XIV.

91 Morris 1980 (AS Vol. 8).

92 Thomas 1994, pp. 45, 57–80.

93 Doble 1932.

94 Dixon 1980; Dunning 1988, pp. 122–3, arrived at the same conclusion.

95 Harl. 3859: see Chadwick 1976; Mercer 1998.

96 Padel 1994 mentions this, apparently unconscious of the support it gives to the idea of Arthur as king of Dumnonia.

97 *Anglo-Saxon Chronicle*.

98 Geoffrey 1966, p. 203.

99 Geoffrey 1966, pp. 207–8.

100 Anon 1846.

101 Thomas 1994, pp. 257–80.

102 *The Life of Gildas* has Gildas going to Glastonbury in 566, at which time Melwas was still alive.

103 See Darrah 1981 for the argument.

104 Morris 1993, pp. 210–11.

105 Alcock 1995, p. 146.
106 Morris 1993, p. 251.
107 Morris 1995b (AS Vol. 3).
108 Preston-Jones and Rose 1986.
109 For example, *Life of Cadoc*, written about 1090.
110 For example, *Life of Padarn*, written as late as 1120.
111 Tolstoy 1985, p. 82.
112 Morris 1995b (AS Vol. 3).
113 Sutherland 1994, p. 212.
114 Chadwick 1976, pp. 70–1.
115 Morris 1993, pp. 234–5, 417.
116 Morris 1993, p. 167.
117 Sutherland 1994, p. 50.
118 Morris 1995d (AS Vol. 5), pp. 122–39.
119 Morris 1995b (AS Vol. 3).
120 Jones 1954, *The Holy Wells of Wales*, p. 41; see Darrah 1994.

CHAPTER 6 CAMELOT

1 Morris 1993, p. 138.
2 Selden's *Illustrations*.
3 Jones 1966.
4 Perhaps for the benefit of academic colleagues when the fashion had shifted towards scepticism: that pressure is always there.
5 Laing and Laing 1993, p. 59.
6 Goodrich 1986, p. 35.
7 Goodrich 1986, e.g. p. 42.
8 For example, Carew 1602.
9 Thomas 1989, p. 43.
10 Radford 1935a, p. 26.
11 See Thomas 1993, p. 47.
12 Cooke 1994.
13 Castleden 1983, pp. 98–100, 107–8.
14 Castleden 1992, p. 303.
15 Hartgroves 1987.
16 Bradley *et al.* 1993.
17 HAR-8273; see Thomas 1989, p. 27.
18 Thomas 1989, p. 41.
19 Thomas 1989, p. 98.
20 McCana 1970, see Thomas 1989, p. 41.
21 Laing and Laing 1993, p. 97.
22 Goodrich 1986, p. 235.
23 Underwood 1983, pp. 85–6. I have been at Tintagel on the winter solstice, more than once, and regret that I saw nothing out of the ordinary.
24 As told in Wolfram von Eschenbach.
25 This is not to say that I support the Seddon–Steiner approach which relies on an acceptance of Tintagel as a religious cult centre through intuition.
26 With the exception of a flurry of activity during the Armada invasion scare in the 1580s.
27 This is traced in detail in Thomas 1989, pp. 31–6.

28 Thomas 1993, p. 113.
29 The exception is the post-built structure on the northern part of the plateau, which may after all be a much later barn.
30 Phillips and Keatman 1992.
31 Phillips and Keatman 1992, p. 13.
32 Phillips and Keatman 1992, pp. 5, 15.
33 Padel 1994, p. 13.
34 Lacy 1986, p. 314.
35 The earliest known documented support for Callington as Kelliwic is Hals 1735, Vol. 1, p. 168.
36 Preston-Jones and Rose 1986.
37 Padel, in Bromwich *et al.* 1991, p. 236.
38 Quinnell 1986.
39 Miles 1977. There are two bronze age radiocarbon dates: 1050 and 950 BC.
40 Miles 1977.
41 Miles 1977; Preston-Jones and Rose 1986.
42 Dickinson 1900, pp. 70–4.
43 Dickinson 1900.
44 See Chapter 4. The itineraries of the early Christian missionaries show how important the Camel estuary was as a port in the fifth and sixth centuries.
45 Trudgian 1977.
46 There is a lane which may follow the dark age boundary running from Halgabron to Trewarmett with a stone and earth bank on each side.
47 *Pa gur?* ll. 31–3.
48 Fox and Ravenhill 1968; 1970.
49 That is, the old hundred of Trigg, which is probably the original British name of the area; the other two divisions of Tricurium or 'Triggshire' were Lesnewth and Stratton.
50 To the south-west was a kingdom corresponding to the later hundred of Pydar; to the south, the Bodmin area, was a kingdom corresponding to the later hundred of Powder; to the south-east was Wivelshire.
51 Goodrich 1986, pp. 155, 275.
52 *Perlesvaus* 10, vv. 7280–7. Goodrich 1986, p. 146 is wrong to equate either of these with Carlisle, or to place either in the north of Britain.
53 Hollick 1997.
54 Anon 'DRT' 1876.
55 *Spoils of Taliesin.*
56 Padel 1994, pp. 13, 20–1.
57 Hugh Schonfield outlines his hypothesis in *The Passover Plot.*
58 Jung 1964. Jung and his wife visited Arthurian sites in the West Country, including Tintagel, in the summer of 1939: see McLynn 1996, p. 415.
59 Fragments of St Cuthbert's portable altar, a 5-inch square oak panel, still survive and are on display in Durham. The only other surviving ancient portable altar is made of stone and was dredged up from the seabed near Wick: it is 4 inches square. Thomas 1971, p. 193.

CHAPTER 7 THE DEATH OF ARTHUR

1 *The Chief of Song*, Gwent Code, quoted in Morris 1995b (AS Vol. 3).
2 See Anon 1896, pp. 149–50.

3 No wonder Tennyson fell into the river when trying to reach the stone with Palgrave during their visit to the Tintagel area in August 1847. Palgrave's diary records:

> Near the little town [of Camelford] on the edge of the river, is shown a large block of stone upon which legend places Arthur, hiding or meditating, after his last fatal battle. It lay below the bank; and in his eagerness to reach it and sit down, Arthur's poet slipped right into the stream, and returned laughing to Camelford.

4 Geoffrey 1966, p. 235, note.
5 From Rhys 1875 onwards. It was the Revd W. Iago who deciphered the badly worn letters using rubbings.
6 Dickinson 1900, pp. 31–2, gives *Magarii*, but *Magari* is now thought more likely.
7 Later chroniclers record a battle in 823 at a place called 'Gavelford', which may be Camelford.
8 Ashe 1957, p. 98.
9 Skene and his supporters: see Anon 'Tydecho' 1872.
10 Dickinson 1900, p. 38.
11 Crawford 1931; Crawford 1935.
12 Barber and Pykitt 1993.
13 Phillips and Keatman 1992, pp. 159, 161.
14 Anon 'H' 1872.
15 Anon 'Tydecho' 1872.
16 Curiously, more than one correspondent to *Archaeologia Cambrensis* in the 1870s drew attention to these Welsh sites, but none of them argued the implications through to a conclusion.
17 John Stuart Glennie, see Anon 'H' 1872, drew attention to the River Camlan flowing into the Eden here, though he still persisted in supporting Skene in a Scottish location for the battle, on the River Carron near Falkirk.
18 Which according to Dark was disputed territory.
19 Vaughan 1850, p. 203.
20 Harley MS 3859, dating from around 960.
21 Hughes 1885; but Llywarch lived too late to be at Arthur's court.
22 Hughes 1885.
23 Anon 1876.
24 Sims-Williams, in Bromwich *et al.* 1991, pp. 50–1.
25 Pennant 1883.
26 Anon 1874, p. 168.
27 Bowen 1967.
28 Vaughan 1850, p. 202.
29 See Lloyd 1872.
30 Triads Nos 51, 53, 54, 59, 84.
31 In this respect, the mystery of the death of Arthur is similar to that of Urien's death: in the *Historia Brittonum* account Urien is the victim of treachery prompted by jealousy, whereas in Taliesin's poem the king dies a hero at the end of a successful campaign in Byrnaich, apparently though not explicitly in battle, with no mention of treachery. See Chadwick 1976, p. 104.
32 Roberts, in Bromwich *et al.* 1991, p. 81.
33 Morris 1993, p. 140 mentions that this Modred had a son apparently living in Suffolk, which seems very odd for a British prince in 537. Moriutred is listed in Genealogy XXV.
34 Lacy 1986, p. 77.

35 Morris 1993, p. 140.

36 Rhys 1891.

37 Ffoulkes 1850, p. 182.

38 Lloyd 1941–44.

39 Padel 1994.

40 Blackett and Wilson 1986, p. 175.

41 Gruffydd 1994.

42 Lee 1876.

43 This follows my 'most likely' scenario of Arthur's birth in 475, which would have made him 41 at the time of Badon and senior enough to be overking at that time, while not too old to be able to fight at Camlann in 537.

44 Ashe, in Lacy 1986, p. 246.

45 According to JPC in Lacy 1986, p. 83.

46 JPC in Lacy 1986, p. 83.

47 The Great Church was not completed until Christmas 1213.

48 The exhumation was recorded by a contemporary chronicler, Ralph of Coggeshall; by Giraldus Cambrensis who visited the site shortly afterwards and interviewed those involved; and by Adam of Domerham, who wrote the history of the abbey in about 1291 and presumably drew on Glastonbury archive material.

49 Boon 1987.

50 Dickinson 1900, p. 45.

51 Boon 1987. It is not clear what became of Mr Mahoney either. According to one account there was an incident at Enfield Council Offices in which Mr Mahoney brandished a home-made gun, afterwards returning home where he committed suicide. A note was left mentioning that the lead cross had been moved from its earlier hiding place. I do not know how true this account (from Street 1998) is.

52 Barber and Pykitt 1993, p. 159. Lovegrove 1997.

53 Boon 1987.

54 Ashe 1957, pp. 19–20, 93.

55 *De Principis Instructiones*, 1193–9.

56 See Woods 1995.

57 The stone was from Doulting near Shepton Mallet, not Doulton as Alcock 1971, p. 75 says.

58 Alcock 1971, p. 75.

59 Ashe 1957, p. 98 implies that a Camlann site at South Cadbury supports Glastonbury as Avalon.

60 Radford 1983, quoting *Life of St Illtud*.

61 Morris 1995b (AS Vol. 3).

62 Barber and Pykitt 1993.

63 Barber and Pykitt 1993, p. 137.

64 Chadwick 1976, p. 41.

65 Phillips and Keatman 1992.

66 Represented for instance in *Culhwch and Olwen*.

67 Smith 1996.

68 Chadwick 1976.

69 Gruffydd 1994.

70 Hill 1997, pp. 11–14.

71 *Encyclopaedia Britannica* entry on Whithorn.

72 Morris 1979.

73 See Castleden 1996, pp. 86–92, 190–3.

74 Hill and Pollock 1992, p. 4.

75 Hill 1997, p. 28.
76 Hill and Pollock 1992, p. 8.
77 Hill 1997, pp. 87–8.
78 Castleden 1992, pp. 43, 349–50, 369. Some of the early Christian graves in Tintagel churchyard also had pieces of quartz included, suggesting a similar reach back to ancient religious beliefs at Tintagel.
79 Hill and Pollock 1992, p. 8.
80 The later seventh- and eighth-century graves of Northumbrian aristocrats in the royal mausoleum at Whithorn were of a different type again; they were burials in iron bound chests.
81 Hill 1997, p. 96.
82 Castleden 1987, pp. 184–6; Castleden 1992, pp. 39, 49, 61, 138–9, 159, 167, 184, 241, 283, 318, 321.
83 It seems unlikely to me that Arthur's body was returned to Tintagel or anywhere else in Dumnonia, or the mystery surrounding his disappearance and death would surely have been dispelled; there would have been no mystery surrounding the whereabouts of the grave either.
84 Hill 1997, pp. 315–16.
85 Hill 1997, p. 319.
86 From Alcock 1995, p. 41.
87 Hill 1997, p. 614.
88 Several publications, principally Hill 1997.
89 Pollock 1995, p. 2.
90 Pollock 1995, pp. 2–3.
91 Thomas 1971, pp. 26–7 believed the foundations to belong to the seventh century, but following the excavations of the 1980s and 1990s this now seems very unlikely.
92 Pennant 1883.
93 Thomas 1971, pp. 26–7.
94 *Navigationes Sancti Brendani.*
95 Chadwick 1976, p. 81; the phrase 'beyond the Sea of Rheged' is used by Taliesin. *Merin Iodeo* was the Firth of Forth.
96 The sea route to the north was probably in regular use, as it was particularly difficult to travel north through Rheged, which was forested in some places, swampy in others, and crossed by many westward-flowing rivers; the Irish Sea route was probably in common use between Wales and northern locations such as Carlisle and Whithorn.
97 Chadwick 1976, p. 86, mentions Mermin Mawr as one of the kings occurring in the genealogies who are difficult to account for: Chadwick thought Mermin was probably a king in Galloway.
98 Blackett and Wilson 1986, p. 28.
99 Published in *Myvyrnian Archaiology*, 1801.
100 Blackett and Wilson 1986, p. 162.
101 Wilson 1992, p. 114.
102 *'What if Urien were dead?'*
103 Chadwick 1976, pp. 90–1.
104 Gildas: Letters 6 and 10 in Winterbottom 1978 (AS Vol. 7).
105 Gruffydd 1994.
106 Davis 1982.
107 The Dyke was probably built in about 367, a year of severe Saxon raids all over southern Britain.
108 Taylor 1970, pp. 42–4.

109 Davis 1982.

110 Davis 1982. I am here still using 'Saxons' in the loose sense, to include all interlopers of Germanic origin.

111 According to Geoffrey, and there is no reason to doubt this, since from other dark age sources we can identify Geoffrey's 'Cador, Duke of Cornwall' as Cato son of Geraint – both of them co-rulers in Arthur's Dumnonia. Both were kings, both were loyal, trusted lieutenants in the field: Cato's son would have been likely to have had all the right credentials, in Arthur's eyes, to be his successor as king of Dumnonia.

112 Morris 1995b (AS Vol. 3).

113 The king list enshrined in Jesus College Pedigree LI implies the following sequence for our period: Vortigern the Elder (Powys), Vortigern the Younger (Powys), Ambrosius (Dumnonia), Uther (?Dumnonia), Arthur (Dumnonia), Constantine (Dumnonia), Aurelius Conanus (?Calchvynydd), Ivor (?), Maelgwn (Gwynedd). Geoffrey of Monmouth follows this king list fairly closely, succeeding Maelgwn with Keredic, then Gormund, under whose rule the thin semblance of British nationhood was ended.

114 Blackett and Wilson 1986, pp. 97–8.

115 In *Palamedes*, a thirteenth-century romance.

116 Winterbottom 1978 (AS Vol. 7), pp. 28–9.

117 Penguin *Celtic Miscellany* pp. 202–4.

118 Morris 1995a (AS Vol. 2).

119 Bruxelles 1998; Anon 1998a; Roberts 1998; Anon 1998c; Anon 1998b.

120 Fowler 1971, quoting John Trevisa's notes to Higden's *Polychronica* V 337–9.

121 Ashe 1968, pp. 183–6.

APPENDIX C

1 Kennedy 1998; Bruxelles 1998; Spratt 1998.

BIBLIOGRAPHY

———— ·◆· ————

The full list of the published versions of the original dark age and medieval sources is too long to include here. Those readers who wish to pursue them can refer to John Morris's *The Age of Arthur* (1993), pp. 522–39.

Adkins, L. and Adkins, R. (1992) *A Field Guide to Somerset Archaeology*. Dovecote Press.
Alcock, L. (1968) Wales in the Arthurian age, in G. Ashe (ed.) *The Quest for Arthur's Britain*, London: Pall Mall Press, pp. 79–96.
—— (1971) *Arthur's Britain*. London: Penguin Books.
—— (1972) '*By South Cadbury is that Camelot . . .*' London: Thames and Hudson.
—— (1988) The activities of potentates in Celtic Britain, AD 500–800: a positivist approach, in S.T. Driscoll and M.R. Nieke (eds) *Power and politics in Early Medieval Britain and Ireland*. Edinburgh: Edinburgh University Press.
—— (1995) *Cadbury Castle, Somerset*. Cardiff: University of Wales Press.
Anglo-Saxon Chronicle, see Garmonsway (1953).
Anon. (1851) untitled correspondence. *Arch. Cambrensis* 2, 65.
—— (I. O. W.) (1852) Seal of Hawys Gadarn. *Arch. Cambrensis* 3, 71.
—— (T. S.) (1853) Letter. *Arch. Cambrensis* 4, 74–6.
—— (E. H.) (1872a) Arthurian localities in the principality and the Marches. *Arch. Cambrensis Fourth Series* 3, 269.
—— (H.) (1872b) The site of the battle of Camlan. *Arch. Cambrensis Fourth Series* 3, 71–2.
—— (Tydecho) (1872c) Site of the battle of Camlan. *Arch Cambrensis Fourth Series* 3, 266–7.
—— (1876a) The tribe of Ednowain Bendew. *Arch. Cambrensis Fourth Series* 7, 197–206.
—— (DRT) (1876b) On the myths and legends of Wales. *Arch. Cambrensis Fourth Series* 7, 247–58.
—— (DRT) (1885) The Roman station of Caergai. *Arch. Cambrensis Fifth Series* 2, 196–205.
—— (1896) Worthyvale, early Christian inscribed stone. *Arch. Cambrensis Fifth Series* 13, 149–50.
—— (1905) *Report on the preliminary exploration on Little Down Field, Lansdown, June 1905.* Bath.
—— (1908) The Roman station of Caergai. *Collections Historical and Archaeological relating to Montgomeryshire* 68, 196–205.
—— (1912) Report of 65th Annual Meeting, Cambrian Archaeological Association. *Arch. Cambrensis Sixth Series* 12, 109–51.
—— (1985) Dorchester. *Current Archaeology* 97, 38–42.
—— (1992a) Dark Earth and the end of Roman Lincoln. *Current Archaeology* 129, 364–7.

—— (1992b) Edinburgh Castle. *Current Archaeology* 131, 460–5.

—— (1998a) The Once and Future King. *The Times*. 7 August.

—— (1998b) Arthur was here. *Daily Telegraph*, 7 August.

—— (1998c) Arthur's slate: is he better as fact or fiction? *The Guardian*, 7 August.

—— (1998d) Tintagel. *Current Archaeology* 159, 84–8.

Arnold, B. and Gibson, D. (1995) *Celtic Chiefdom, Celtic State*. Cambridge: Cambridge University Press.

Arnold, C.J. (1984) *Roman Britain to Saxon England*. London and Sydney: Croom Helm.

Ashe, G. (1957) *King Arthur's Avalon*. London: William Collins.

—— (ed.) (1968) *The Quest for Arthur's Britain*. London: Pall Mall Press.

—— (1981) A certain very ancient book. *Speculum* 56, 301–23.

Aston, M. and Burrow, I. (eds) (1982) *The Archaeology of Somerset*. Taunton: Somerset County Council.

Atkin, M. (1992) Gloucester. *Transactions of the Bristol and Gloucestershire Archaeological Society* 110, 218–19.

Barber, C. and Pykitt, D. (1993) *Journey to Avalon: The Final Discovery of King Arthur*. Abergavenny: Blorenge Books.

Baring-Gould, S. and Fisher, J. (1913) *The Lives of the British Saints*. London: Hon. Society of Cymmrodorion.

Barker, P. (1981) *Wroxeter Roman city excavations, 1960–1980*.

—— (1990) *From Roman 'Viroconium' to Medieval Wroxeter*. Worcester: West Mercian Archaeological Consultants.

Bartholomew, P. (1982) Fifth century facts. *Britannia* 13, 261–70.

—— (1984) Fourth century Saxons. *Britannia* 15, 169–85.

Bassett, S. (ed.) (1989) *The Origins of Anglo-Saxon Kingdoms*, Leicester: Leicester University Press.

Batey, C., Sharpe, A. and Thorpe, C. (1993) Tintagel Castle: archaeological investigation of the Steps area 1989 and 1990. *Cornish Archaeology* 32, 47–66.

Bede, see Colgrave and Mynors (1969).

Begg, E. and Rich, D. (1991) *On the Trail of Merlin*. London: Aquarian Press.

Bidwell, P.T. (1980) *Roman Exeter: Fortress and Town*. Exeter: Exeter City Council.

Blackett, B. and Wilson, A. (1986) *Artorius Rex Discovered*. Cardiff: King Arthur Research.

Blair, P.H. (1977) *An Introduction to Anglo-Saxon England*. Cambridge: Cambridge University Press.

Born, G.C. (1987) Camden and the Britannia. *Arch. Cambrensis* 136, 1–19.

Bowen, E.G. (1954) *The Settlements of the Celtic Saints in Wales*. Cardiff: University of Wales Press.

—— (1967) The dark ages, in E.G. Bowen and G.A. Gresham, (eds) *History of Merioneth*, Dolgellau: Merioneth Historical and Record Society, pp. 264–79.

Bradford, S. (1996) *Elizabeth: A Biography of Her Majesty the Queen*. London: Heinemann.

Bradley, R., Harding, J. and Mathews, M. (1993) The siting of prehistoric rock art in Galloway, south-west Scotland. *Proceedings of the Prehistoric Society* 59, 269–83.

Brahmer, M. (ed.) (1966) *Studies in Language and Literature in Honour of Margaret Schlauch*. Warsaw.

Broadhurst, P. (1992) *Tintagel and the Arthurian Myths*. Launceston: Pendragon Press.

Bromwich, R., Jarman, A.O.H. and Roberts, B.F. (eds) (1991) *The Arthur of the Welsh*. Cardiff: University of Wales Press.

Brooks, D.A. (1983–4) Gildas's De Excidio. *Studia Celtica* 18/19, 1–10.

Bruxelles, S. de (1998) Old slate brings King Arthur back to life. *The Times*, 7 August.

Burgess, C. (1980) *The Age of Stonehenge*. London: Dent.

Burkitt, T. and Burkitt, A. (1990) The frontier zone and the siege of Mount Badon: a review of the evidence for their location. *Somerset Archaeology and Natural History* 134, 81–93.

Burley, D. (1994) As a prescription to rule. *Antiquity* 68, 504–17.

Burrow, I. (1981) *Hillfort and Hilltop Settlement in Somerset in the First to Eighth Centuries AD*. BAR British Series 91.

Campbell, J., John, E. and Wormald, P. (1982) *The Anglo-Saxons*. Oxford: Phaidon.

Canner, A.C. (1982) *The Parish of Tintagel: Some Historical Notes*. Tintagel.

Carew, R. (1602) *The Survey of Cornwall*. London: John Jaggard.

Carr, J. (1989) Excavations on the Mound, Glastonbury, Somerset, 1971. *Proceedings of the Somerset Archaeological and Natural History Society* 129, 37–62.

Castleden, R. (1983) *The Wilmington Giant: The Quest for a Lost Myth*. Wellingborough: Turnstone Press.

—— (1987) *The Stonehenge People*. London and New York: Routledge.

—— (1992) *Neolithic Britain: New Stone Age Sites of England, Scotland and Wales*. London and New York: Routledge.

—— (1993) *The Making of Stonehenge*. London and New York: Routledge.

—— (1996) *The Cerne Giant*. Wincanton: Dorset Publishing Company.

Chadwick, N. (1976) *The British Heroic Age*. Cardiff: University of Wales Press.

Chambers, E. K. (1927) *Arthur of Britain*. Cambridge: Cambridge University Press.

Charles-Edwards, T. (1991) The Arthur of History, in R. Bromwich *et al*. (eds) *The Arthur of the Welsh*. Cardiff: University of Wales Press.

Chrétien de Troyes (1991) *Arthurian Romances*. London: Penguin Books.

Christie, P. (1986) Cornwall in the Bronze Age. *Cornish Archaeology* 25, 81–110.

—— (1988) A barrow cemetery on Davidstow moor, Cornwall: wartime excavations by C.K. Crift Andrew. *Cornish Archaeology* 27, 27–169.

Clark, G. (1859) The earls, earldom and castle of Pembroke. *Arch. Cambrensis* 5, 188–202.

Cleary, S.E. (1995) Changing constraints on the landscape, AD 400–600, in D. Hooke and S. Burnell (eds) *Landscape and Settlement in Britain AD 400–1066*. pp. 11–26.

Colgrave, B. and Mynors. R. (trans.) (1969) *Bede's Historia Ecclesiastica Gentis Anglorum*. Oxford: Oxford University Press.

Collingwood, R.G. and Myres, J.N.L. (1932) *Roman Britain*. Oxford: Oxford University Press.

Collingwood, R.G. and Wright, R.P. (1965) *The Roman Inscriptions of Britain: I. Inscriptions on Stone*. Oxford: Oxford University Press.

Cooke, I. M. (1994) *Mother and Son: The Cornish fogou*. Penzance: Men-an-Tol Studio.

Cooper, N.H. (1990) *The Exeter Area*. Exeter: Royal Archaeological Institute.

Copley, G.J. (1954) *The Conquest of Wessex in the Sixth Century*. London: Phoenix House.

Crawford, O.G.S. (1931) King Arthur's last battle. *Antiquity* 5, 236–9.

—— (1935) Arthur and his battles. *Antiquity* 9, 277–91.

Cummins, W.A. (1992) *King Arthur's Place in Prehistory*. Stroud: Alan Sutton.

Cunliffe, B. (1971) *Roman Bath Discovered*. London and New York: Routledge.

Curle, A.O. (1923) *The Treasure of Traprain*. Glasgow.

Dark, K.R. (1985) The plan and interpretation of Tintagel. *Cambridge Medieval Celtic Studies* 9, 1–17.

—— (1992) A sub-Roman re-defence of Hadrian's Wall. *Britannia* 23, 111–20.

—— (1994) *Civitas to Kingdom: British Political Continuity 300–800*. Leicester: Leicester University Press.

Darrah, J. (1981) *The Real Camelot: Paganism and the Arthurian Romances*. London: Thames and Hudson.

—— (1994) *Paganism in Arthurian Romance*. Woodbridge: Boydell Press.

Davies, J. (1884) The Celtic element in the dialects of the counties adjoining Lancashire. *Arch. Cambrensis Fifth Series* 1, 1–31.

Davis, K.R. (1982) *Britons and Saxons: The Chiltern Region 400–700*. Chichester: Phillimore.

Davis, W. (1982) *Wales in the Early Middle Ages*. Leicester: Leicester University Press.

Denholm-Young, N. (1947) *Richard of Cornwall*. Oxford: Blackwell.

Dickinson, W.H. (1900) *King Arthur in Cornwall*. London: Longmans, Green and Co.

Dixon, J. (1980) *Parish Surveys in Somerset: 3, Carhampton*. Taunton: Somerset Archaeological and Natural History Society.

Dixon-Kennedy, M. (1995) *Arthurian Myth and Legend*. London: Blandford.

Doble, G.H. (1927) *Saint Docco and Saint Kew*. Truro: Netherton and Worth.

—— (1932) *Saint Carantoc. A Cornish Saint*. Long Compton: The King's Stone Press.

—— (1938) *Saint Petrock*. Long Compton: The King's Stone Press.

Dobson, D. (1931) *The Archaeology of Somerset*. London: Methuen.

Dumville, D.N. (1984) The chronology of De Excidio Britanniae, Book 1, in M. Lapidge and D.N. Dumville (eds) *Gildas: New Approaches*. Woodbridge: Boydell, pp. 61–84.

Dunning, R. (1988) *Arthur, The King in the West*. London: Grange Books.

Dyer, J. (1973) *Southern England: an Archaeological Guide*. London: Faber.

Elliott-Binns, R. V. (1955) *Medieval Cornwall*. London: Methuen.

Ellis, P.B. (1993) *Celt and Saxon: The Struggle for Britain AD 410–937*. London: Constable.

Evison, V.I. (1965) *The Fifth Century Invasions South of the Thames*. London: Athlone Press.

Ffoulkes, W. (1850) Castra Clwydiana. *Arch. Cambrensis* 1, 174–87.

Ford, J. (1997) Birth, life, death: a look at some of the traditional Arthurian sites. *Pendragon* 26, 3, 23–6.

Fowler, D.C. (1971) John Trevisa: scholar and translator. *Transactions of the Bristol and Gloucester Archaeological Society* 89, 99–108.

Fowler, P.J. and Thomas, A.C. (1962) Arable fields of the pre-Norman period at Gwithian. *Cornish Archaeology* 1, 61–84.

Fowles, J. and Legg, R. (1980) *John Aubrey's Monumenta Britannica*. Wincanton: Dorset Publishing Company.

Fox, A. (1973) *Exeter in Roman times*. Exeter: University of Exeter.

Fox, A. and Fox, C. (1958) Wansdyke reconsidered. *Arch. Journal* 115, 1–48.

Fox, A. and Ravenhill, W. (1968) Excavation of the Roman fort at Tregear, Nanstallon: Third Interim Report. *Cornish Archaeology* 7, 40–2.

—— (1970) Excavation of the Roman fort at Tregear, Nanstallon; Fourth Interim Report. *Cornish Archaeology* 9, 99–101.

—— (1972) The Roman fort at Nanstallon, Cornwall. *Britannia* 3, 56–111.

Gantz, J. (trans.) (1976) *The Mabinogion*. London: Penguin Books.

Garmonsway, G.N. (1953) *The Anglo-Saxon Chronicle*. London: J.M. Dent.

Garrod, A. and Heighway, C. (1984) *Garrod's Gloucester*. Gloucester: Western Archaeological Trust.

Geest, A. van der (1997) Tintagel. *Pendragon* 26 (3), 5–9.

Geoffrey of Monmouth (1966) *The History of the Kings of Britain*. trans. L. Thorpe, London: Penguin Books.

Gildas, see Winterbottom (1978).

Godwin, M. (1994) *The Holy Grail: Its Origins, Secrets and Meaning Revealed*. London: Bloomsbury.

Goodrich, N. (1986) *King Arthur*. New York: Harper and Row.

Griffith, F.M. (1986) Salvage observations of the dark age site at Bantham Ham, Thurlestone, in 1982. *Proceedings of the Devon Archaeological Society* 44, 39–57.

Griffiths, M. (1972) *Cathedral Close Excavations, Exeter*. Exeter: Exeter City Library.

Griffiths, M. and Bidwell, P. (1973) *Cathedral Close excavations*. Exeter: Exeter Museums and Art Gallery.

Griffiths, W. (1956) The hill-fort on Conway Mountain, Caernarvonshire. *Arch. Cambrensis* 105, 49–80.

Gruffydd, R. (1994) In search of Elmet. *Studia Celtica* 28, 63–79.

Hals, W. (1735) *A Complete Parochial History of the County of Cornwall*. Truro: Joseph Polsue.

Hamilton, J. (1968) *Excavations at Clickhimin, Shetland*. Edinburgh: HMSO.

Harden, D.B. (1956) *Dark-Age Britain*. London: Methuen.

Harry, R. and Morris, C. (1994) *Tintagel Castle: Excavations 1994*. University of Glasgow and English Heritage.

—— (1997) Excavations on the lower terrace, Site C, Tintagel Island 1990–94. *Antiquaries Journal* 77, 1–143.

Hartgroves, S. (1987) The cup-marked stones of Stithians Reservoir. *Cornish Archaeology* 26, 69–84.

Hartgroves, S. and Walker, R. (1988) Excavations in the Lower Ward, Tintagel Castle, 1986. *Cornish Studies* 16, 9–30.

Hartshorne, C. (1848) The councils and parliaments of Shrewsbury. *Arch. Cambrensis* 3, 213–24.

Henderson, I. (1967) *The Picts*. London: Thames and Hudson.

Higham, N.J. (1986) *The Northern Counties to AD 1000*. London: Longman.

—— (1991) Old light on the Dark Age landscape: the description of Britain in the De Excidio. *Journal of Historical Geography*, 17, 4, 63–72.

—— (1994) *The English Conquest: Gildas and Britain in the Fifth Century*. Manchester: Manchester University Press.

Hill, P. (1997) *Whithorn and St Ninian: The Excavation of a Monastic Town 1984–91*. Stroud: Sutton Publishing.

Hill, P. and Pollock, D. (1992) *The Whithorn Dig*. Whithorn: Whithorn Board of Management.

Hinton, D.A. (1990) *Archaeology, Economy and Society: England from the Fifth to the Fifteeenth Century*. London: Seaby.

Hollick, H. (1997) Arthur and the careful historian. *Pendragon* 26, 4, 4–6.

Hood, A. (1978) *St Patrick*. Chichester: Phillimore.

Hooke, D. and Burnell, S. (eds) (1995) *Landscape and Settlement in Britain AD 400–1066*.

Hopkins, A. (1993) *Chronicles of King Arthur*. London: Collins and Brown.

Hoskins, W.G. (1960a) *Two Thousand Years in Exeter*. Exeter: James Townsend and Sons.

Hoskins, W.G. (1960b) *The Westward Expansion of Wessex*. Leicester: Leicester University Press.

Howe, N. (1989) *Migration and Mythmaking in Anglo-Saxon England*. New Haven and London: Yale University Press.

Hughes, W. (1885) Llanuwehllyn. *Arch. Cambrensis Fifth Series* 2, 183–91.

Iorwerth, G. ap (1997) The forgotten Badon. *Pendragon* 26, 3, 20–3.

Jackson, K. (1949) Arthur's battle of Bregouin. *Antiquity* 23, 48–9.

—— (1959) The Arthur of history, in *Arthurian Literature in the Middle Ages*. Oxford: Clarendon Press.

—— (1963) *Celt and Saxon*. Cambridge: Cambridge University Press.

Jenkins, E. (1990) *The Mystery of King Arthur*. London: Michael O'Mara.

Jenner, H. (1914) Some possible Arthurian place-names in West Penwith. *Journal of the Royal Institution of Cornwall* 19, 46–89.

Johnson, N. (1980) The Bolster Bank, St Agnes – a survey. *Cornish Archaeology* 19, 77–88.

Johnson, N. and Rose, P. (1994) *Bodmin Moor: An Archaeological Survey*. London: English Heritage.

Jones, A.H.M. (1964) *The Later Roman Empire, 284–602*. Oxford: Blackwell.

Jones, F. (1954) *The Holy Wells of Wales*. Cardiff: University of Wales Press.

Jones, L.W. (1911) *King Arthur in History and Legend*. Cambridge: Cambridge University Press.

Jones, T. (1964) The early evolution of the legend of King Arthur. *Nottingham Medieval Studies* 8, 5.

—— (1966) A sixteenth century version of the Arthurian cave legend, in M. Brahmer (ed.) *Studies in Language and Literature in Honour of Margaret Schlauch*, Warsaw. pp. 175–85.

Jope, E. and Threlfall, R. (1954) A late dark ages site at Gunwalloe. *Proceedings of West Cornwall Field Club (New Series)* 2, 136–40.

Jung, C.G. (1964) Wotan, in *Civilization in Transition, Collected Works*, Vol. 10. London: Routledge, pp. 179–93.

Kennedy, M. (1998) Do these markings mean that the legend of King Arthur is now fact? *The Guardian*, 7 August.

Lacy, N. (ed.) (1986) *The Arthurian Encyclopedia*. Woodbridge: Boydell Press.

Laing, L. and Laing, J. (1979a) *Celtic Britain*. London: Routledge.

—— (1979b) *A Guide to the Dark Age Remains in Britain*. London: Constable.

—— (1993) *The Picts and the Scots*. Stroud: Alan Sutton.

Lapidge, M. and Dumville, D. N. (eds) (1984) *Gildas: new approaches*. Woodbridge: Boydell.

Lee, M.H. (1876) Maelor Saesneg. *Arch. Cambrensis* 7, 287–99.

Leech, R. (1981) *Historic Towns in Gloucestershire*. Committee for Rescue Archaeology in Avon, Gloucestershire and Somerset.

Legg, R. (1986) *Stonehenge Antiquaries*. Milborne Port: Dorset Publishing Company.

Lloyd, C. (1872) History of the lordship of Maelor Gymraeg. *Arch. Cambrensis Fourth Series* 3, 277–96.

Lloyd, J.E. (1941–44) The Death of Arthur. *Bulletin of the Board of Celtic Studies*, 11, 158–60.

Loomis, C.G. (1933) King Arthur and the saints. *Speculum* 8, 478–82.

Loomis, R. S. (1926) *Celtic Myth and Arthurian Romance*. Columbia University Press.

—— (1933) The Irish origin of the grail legend. *Speculum* 8, 415–31.

Lovegrove, C. (1996) A trusty shield. *Pendragon* 26/1, 17–22.

—— (1997) Arthur's Cross? *Pendragon* 26(4), 17–19.

McCana, P. (1970) *Celtic Mythology*. London: Hamlyn.

McCarthy, M. *et al.* (1989) Carlisle. *Current Archaeology* 116, 298–302.

McCrone, P. (1995) Carhampton, Eastbury Farm. *Proceedings of the Somerset Archaeological and Natural History Society* 138, 177.

McLynn, F. (1996) *Carl Gustav Jung*. London: Bantam Press.

McWhirr, A. (ed.) (1976) *Studies in the Archaeology and History of Cirencester*. London: BAR 30.

—— (19) *Roman Gloucestershire*. Stroud: Alan Sutton.

Major, A. and Burrow, E. (1926) *The Mystery of Wansdyke*. Cheltenham: E.J. Burrow.

Malory, Sir T. (1969) *Le Morte d'Arthur. Caxton's Text*. Harmondsworth: Penguin.

Marples, M. (undated) *Sarn Helen: A Roman Road in Wales*. Newtown: Welsh Outlook Press.

Matarasso, P.M. (trans.) (1969) *The Quest of the Holy Grail*. London: Penguin Books.

Mercer, B. (1998) Arthurian Carhampton. *Pendragon* 27, 1, 4–5.

Miles, H. (1977) Excavations at Killibury hillfort, Egloshayle 1975–6. *Cornish Archaeology* 16, 89–121.

Miles, H. and Miles, T. (1973) Excavations at Trethurgy, St Austell: Interim Report. *Cornish Archaeology* 12, 25–30.

Miller, M. (1979) *The Saints of Gwynedd*. Woodbridge: Boydell Press.

Mitchell, F. (1886) Notes on the history of Monmouthshire. *Arch. Cambrensis Fifth Series* 3, 1–27.

Morris, J. (1980) *Arthurian Sources Vol. 8: Nennius: British History and the Welsh Annals.* Chichester: Phillimore.

—— (1993) *The Age of Arthur: A History of the British Isles from 350 to 650.* London: Weidenfeld and Nicolson.

—— (1995a) *Arthurian Sources Vol. 2: Annals and Charters.* Chichester: Phillimore.

—— (1995b) *Arthurian Sources Vol. 3: Persons: Ecclesiastics and Laypeople.* Chichester: Phillimore.

—— (1995c) *Arthurian Sources Vol. 4: Places and Peoples, and Saxon Archaeology.* Chichester: Phillimore.

—— (1995d) *Arthurian Sources Vol. 5: Genealogies and Texts,* Chichester: Phillimore.

—— (1995e) *Arthurian Sources Vol. 6: Studies in Dark-Age History.* Chichester: Phillimore.

Morris, R. (1979) *The Prehistoric Rock Art of Galloway and the Isle of Man,* London: Blandford Press.

Myres, J.N.L. (1986) *The English Settlements.* Oxford: Oxford University Press.

Nennius, see Morris (1980).

Nowakowski, J.A. and Thomas, C. (1992) *Grave News from Tintagel: and Account of a Second Season of Archaeological Excavation at Tintagel Churchyard, Cornwall, 1991.* Exeter: Cornwall Archaeological Unit and Institute of Cornish Studies.

Oman, C. (1924) *A History of England before the Norman Conquest.* London: Methuen.

Owen, W. (1803) *A Dictionary of the Welsh language.* London: E. Williams.

Padel, O. J. (1981) The Cornish Background of the Tristan Stories. *Cambridge Medieval Celtic Studies* 1, 53–81.

—— (1984) Geoffrey of Monmouth and Cornwall. *Cambridge Medieval Celtic Studies* 8, 1–28.

—— (1988) Tintagel in the twelfth and thirteenth centuries. *Cornish Studies* 16, 61–6.

—— (1994) The nature of Arthur. *Cambrian Medieval Celtic Studies* 27, 1–31.

Pearce, S.M. (1978) *The Kingdom of Dumnonia: Studies in History and Tradition in South-West Britain.* Padstow: Lodenek Press.

Pennant, T. (1883) *Tours in Wales.* Caernarvon: Thomas Humphreys.

Pennar, M. (1988) *Taliesin Poems: New Translations.* Lampeter: Llanerch Enterprises.

—— (1991) *Peredur: An Arthurian Romance from the Mabinogion.* Lampeter: Llanerch Enterprises.

Phillips, G. and Keatman, M. (1992) *King Arthur: The True Story.* London: Century Random House.

Pierce, S.M. (1978) *The Kingdom of Dumnonia: Studies in History and Tradition in Southwest Britain.* Padstow: Lodenek Press.

Piggott, S. (1941) The sources of Geoffrey of Monmouth. *Antiquity* 15, 269–86.

Pollard, S.H.M. (1967) Radiocarbon dating neolithic and dark age settlements on High Peak, Sidmouth, Devon. *Devon Archaeological Society* 25, 41.

Pollock, D. (1995) *Whithorn 6: Interim Report on the 1993 Excavations at Whithorn Priory.* Whithorn: Whithorn Trust.

Preston-Jones, A. (1987) King Arthur's cups and saucers. *Cornish Archaeology* 26, 83.

—— (1992) Decoding Cornish churchyards, in *The Early Church in Wales and the West.* *Oxbow Monograph* 16, 105–24.

Preston-Jones, A. and Rose, P. (1986) Medieval Cornwall. *Cornish Archaeology* 25, 135–85.

Quinnell, H. (1986) Cornwall during the iron age and Roman period. *Cornish Archaeology* 25, 111–34.

Quinnell, H. and Harris, D. (1985) Castle Dore: the chronology reconsidered. *Cornish Archaeology* 24, 123–40.

Radford, C.A.R. (1935a) *Tintagel Castle, Cornwall.* London: HMSO.

—— (1935b) Tintagel: the castle and Celtic monastery – interim report. *Antiquaries Journal* 15, 401–19.

—— (1939) *Tintagel Castle, Cornwall.* London: HMSO.

—— (1968) Romance and reality in Cornwall, in G. Ashe (ed.) *The Quest for Arthur's Britain.* London: Pall Mall Press, pp. 59–78.

—— (1969) An early Christian inscription at East Ogwell. *Devon Archaeological Society* 27, 79–81.

—— (1983) Two datable cross shafts at Llantwit Major. *Arch. Cambrensis* 132, 107–15.

Radford, C.A.R. and Swanton, M.J. (1975) *Arthurian Sites in the West.* Exeter: University of Exeter.

Rahtz, P. (1968) Glastonbury Tor, in G. Ashe (ed.) *The Quest for Arthur's Britain.* London: Pall Mall Press. pp. 97–110.

—— (1971) Castle Dore – a reappraisal of the post-Roman structures. *Cornish Archaeology* 10, 49–54.

—— (1993) review of Thomas, C. (1993) Tintagel: Arthur and Archaeology. *Cornish Archaeology* 32, 178–80.

Ratcliffe, J. and Parkes, C. (1989) Lost and found on Chapel Down: idol speculation. *Cornish Archaeology* 28, 259.

Ravenhill, W. (1970) The form and pattern of post-Roman settlement in Devon. *Proceedings of the Devon Archaeological Society* 28, 83–94.

Rawlings, M. and Fitzpatrick, A. (1996) Prehistoric sites and a Romano-British settlement at Butterfield Down, Amesbury. *Wiltshire Archaeological and Natural History Magazine* 89, 1–43.

Reece, R. and Catling, C. (1975) *Cirencester: The Development and Buildings of a Cotswold Town.* London: BAR 12.

Rees, J. (1898) The Norse element in Celtic myth. *Arch. Cambrensis Fifth Series* 15, 312–44.

Rhys, J. (1875) On some of our inscribed stones. *Arch. Cambrensis Fourth Series* 6, 359–71.

—— (1891) *Studies in the Arthurian Legend.* Oxford: Clarendon Press.

Richmond, I. (1946) The four coloniae of Roman Britain. *Archaeological Journal* 103, 57–84.

Ritson, J. (1825) *The Life of King Arthur from Ancient Historians and Authentic Documents.* London: William Nicol.

Roberts, A. (1998) Hail King Arthur, and farewell. *Sunday Times*, 9 August.

Roberts, B.F. (1991) Culhwch ac Olwen, the Triads, Saints' Lives, in R. Bromwich, A. Jarman, and B. Roberts (eds) *The Arthur of the Welsh.* Cardiff: University of Wales Press, pp. 73–95.

Robinson, J.A. (1921) *On the Antiquities of Glastonbury.* Somerset Historical Essays. British Academy and Oxford University Press.

Rose, P. (1992) Bossiney Castle. *Cornish Archaeology* 31, 138–42.

—— (1994) The medieval garden at Tintagel. *Cornish Archaeology* 33, 170–82.

Rose, P. and Preston-Jones, A. (1995) Changes in the Cornish countryside AD 400–1100, in D. Hooke and S. Burnell (eds) *Landscape and Settlement in Britain AD 400–1066.* pp. 51–68.

Rowse, A.L. (1943) *The Spirit of English History.* London: Cape.

Saville, A. (1984) *Archaeology in Gloucestershire.* Cheltenham: Cheltenham Art Gallery and Museum.

Seddon, R. (1990) *The Mystery of Arthur at Tintagel.* London: Rudolf Steiner Press.

Sims-Williams, P. (1991) The Early Welsh Arthurian poems, in R. Bromwich *et al.* (eds) *The Arthur of the Welsh.* Cardiff: University of Wales Press.

Skene, W.F. (1988) *Arthur and the Britons in Wales and Scotland*. Lampeter: Llanerch Enterprises.

Smith, C. (1987) Excavations at the Ty Maur hut-circles, Holyhead, Anglesey. *Arch. Cambrensis* 136, 20–38.

Smith, G. (1996) Recovering the lost religious place-names of England. *At the Edge*, 3, 12–19.

Snell, F.J. (1926) *King Arthur's Country*. London.

Spratt, J. (1998) Arthur Stone found at Tintagel Castle. *Cornish Guardian*, 13 August.

Steer, K.A. (1958) Arthur's O'on: a lost shrine of Roman Britain. *Archaeological Journal* 115, 99–110.

Street, C. (1998) untitled letter. *Pendragon* 27, 1, 32.

Sutherland, E. (1994) *In Search of the Picts*. London: Constable.

Taliesin, see Pennar (1988).

Tatlock, J.S.P. (1933) The English journey of the Laon canons. *Speculum* 8, 454–65.

Tatton-Brown, T. and Macpherson-Grant, N. (1985) *Current Archaeology* 98, 89–93.

Taylor, C. (1970) *Dorset*. London: Hodder and Stoughton.

Thomas, A.C. (1963) Unpublished material from Cornish museums: 2) Gunwalloe pottery, Helston Museum. *Cornish Archaeology* 2, 60–75.

Thomas, C. (1957) Cornwall in the dark ages. *Proceedings of the West Cornwall Field Club (New Series)* 2, 2, 59–72.

—— (1964) Settlement-history in early Cornwall. 1: the antiquity of the hundreds. *Cornish Archaeology* 3, 70–9.

—— (1971) *The Early Christian Archaeology of Northern Britain*. Oxford: Oxford University Press.

—— (1988) The context of Tintagel: a new model for the diffusion of post-Roman Mediterranean imports. *Cornish Archaeology* 27, 7–25.

—— (1989) Minor sites at Tintagel Island. *Cornish Studies* 16, 31–43.

—— (1993) *Tintagel: Arthur and Archaeology*. London: Batsford.

—— (1994) *And Shall These Mute Stones Speak? Post-Roman inscriptions in Western Britain*. Cardiff: University of Wales Press.

Thomas, C. and Fowler, P.J. (1985) Tintagel: a new survey of the Island. *Annual Review 1984–85, Royal Commission on the Historical Monuments of England*, 16–22.

Thompson, E.A. (1979) Gildas and the History of Britain. *Britannia*, 10, 203–26.

Thorpe, C. (1988) Incised pictorial slates from Tintagel. *Cornish Studies* 16, 69–78.

Thorpe, L. (1966) Introduction to *The History of the Kings of Britain* by Geoffrey of Monmouth. London: Penguin Books, pp. 9–30.

Todd, J. H. (1848) *The Irish Version of the Historia Brittonum of Nennius*. Dublin: Irish Archaeological Society.

Tolstoy, N. (1985) *The Quest for Merlin*. London: Hamish Hamilton.

Trudgian, P. (1976) Cup-marked stones from a barrow at Starapark near Camelford. *Cornish Archaeology* 15, 49.

—— (1977) Excavation at Tregilders, St Kew, 1975–6. *Cornish Archaeology* 16, 122–8.

—— (1987) Excavation of a burial ground at St Endellion, Cornwall. *Cornish Archaeology* 26, 145–52.

Underwood, P. (1983) *Ghosts in Cornwall*. St Teath: Bossiney Books.

Vaughan, H. (1884) Oswestry, ancient and modern, and its local families. *Arch. Cambrensis Fifth Series* 1, 193–224.

Vaughan, R. (1850) Merionethshire. *Arch. Cambrensis* 1, 200–5.

Wacher, J.S. (1974) *The Towns of Roman Britain*. Berkeley, CA: University of California Press.

Wakeman, T. (1848) Caerleon. *Arch. Cambrensis* 3, 228–344.

—— (1850) The stone of St Cadvan. *Arch. Cambrensis* 1, 205–12.

Webster, G. and Barker, P. (1991) *Wroxeter Roman City*. London: English Heritage.

Westwood, J. (1986) *Albion: A Guide to Legendary Britain*. London: Book Club Associates.

Williams, H. (1899) *Gildas: The Ruin of Britain*. London: David Nutt.

Wilson, D. (1992) *Anglo-Saxon Paganism*. London: Routledge.

Winterbottom, M. (1978) *Arthurian Sources Vol. 7: Gildas: The Ruin of Britain and Other Works*. Chichester: Phillimore.

Wright, T. (1861) Caernarvonshire antiquities. *Arch. Cambrensis Third Series* 7, 140–55.

Woods, H. (1995) Excavations at Glastonbury Abbey 1987–1993. *Proceedings of the Somerset Archaeological and Natural History Society* 138, 7–73.

INDEX